Counselling Ethics
Casebook 2000

Consent - Gabby

Counselling Ethics Casebook 2000

by William E. Schulz

Canadian Counselling Association

Canadian Counselling Association
700-116 Albert Street
Ottawa, Canada K1P 5G3

ISBN 0-9697966-1-7

Printed in Canada

To

The Year 2000 Presidents of the Canadian
Counselling Association:

Karen Wright, the past president, who asked me to
write this casebook, and whose understanding and
sensitive leadership has been an inspiration to me;

Renée Piché, the current president, whose warmth
and energy is always encouraging; and to

Glenn Sheppard, the present-elect, who not only
understands and writes about counselling ethics,
but, more importantly, personifies what ethics
in counselling are all about.

CONTENTS

CONTENTS *continued*

ACKNOWLEDGEMENTS

I very much value the excellent co-operation I received from everyone who contributed to this casebook. First, and foremost, my thanks are extended to counsellor-educators, graduate students and Manitoba practitioners, who helped provide counselling cases that exemplify positive and negative counsellor behaviour.

I am especially appreciative of the contributions of counsellor-educators and others who readily agreed to write essays related to the six major sections of our CCA *Code of Ethics*. Thank you Margaret Schneider, Walt Pawlovich, John Sumarah, Ron Lehr, Linda Wheeldon, Jo-Anne Sargent, Ed Drodge, Glenn Sheppard, Thomas Kerr, Beth Haverkamp, Jaye Wald, John Stewart, Renate Schulz, Paul Madak, Sandra MacDonald, Kathleen A. Irvine, Max Uhlemann and John Gawthrope. Thank you as well to the Counsellor Educators' Chapter of CCA for their financial contribution.

Finally, a very big thank you to Alice Turman, Liz Bachmann and Dallas Ballance for their work in producing the final version of this casebook.

Essay Contributors

A. Professional Responsibility

Margaret S. Schneider is an associate professor in the Department of Adult Education, Community Development and Counselling Psychology at the University of Toronto. She regularly teaches an ethics course to graduate students in the counselling psychology program. Her research interests include: psychosocial aspects of sexual orientation and transgender issues, gender issues, community psychology and community mental health, and sexual health education.

Walt Pawlovich is a professor in counsellor education at the University of Saskatchewan. Walt is a former president of CCA.

B. Counselling Relationships

John Sumarah is a counsellor-educator at Acadia University in Nova Scotia.

Ron Lehr is a counsellor-educator at Acadia University in Nova Scotia. Ron is the Nova Scotia director for CCA.

Linda Wheeldon is a counsellor-educator at Acadia University.

These counsellor-educators have experience in school, universities, private practice and community agencies. Their research and publications demonstrate interest in ethics, school counselling, therapeutic alliance and human services. Their article on confidentiality is a collaborative effort.

Jo-Anne Sargent is a doctoral student in educational psychology at the University of Victoria in British Columbia. She is a member of the ethics committee of the Canadian Association for Music Therapy, and is co-author of the association's code of ethics. Ms. Sargent is a sessional instructor in the counselling program at the University of Victoria, and also has a private counselling practice. Previous research activities include an assessment of the privacy protection standards of registered psychologists of British Columbia. She is also interested in conflict resolution and violence prevention programming in schools. Ms. Sargent plans to become registered as a psychologist, and to continue writing and consulting in the area of ethics.

Ed W. Drodge is an assistant professor of education, Faculty of Education, University of Ottawa. He has been a secondary school teacher, guidance counsellor, and health-counselling practitioner. His research activities include counselling-program evaluation, chaos and complexity theory in counselling, and ethical/legal issues in counselling and counsellor training

Glenn W. Sheppard is a former professor, counsellor-educator and department head, in the Faculty of Education, Memorial University of Newfoundland (1973-1996). He now works as a sessional lecturer, and maintains a private practice in St. John's, Newfoundland. Dr. Sheppard was director of the Canadian Guidance and Counselling Association for four years, and is currently on the Board of Governors of the Canadian Career Development Foundation. He was co-chair of the CCA committee that developed the new Code of Ethics, and is now chair of CCA Standing Committee on Ethics, chair of the CCA Committee on Standards of Practice, and is president-elect of CCA.

C. Consulting and Private Practice

Thomas Kerr is a doctoral student in educational psychology at the University of Victoria in British Columbia. He also works as a counsellor and the co-ordinator of Practice Standards and Research at the Dr. Peter AIDS Foundation, Vancouver, B.C. In addition to his work as counsellor, Mr. Kerr is an accredited music therapist, and is the ethics chair for the Canadian Association for Music Therapy. He also co-authored the *Canadian Association for Music Therapy's Code of Ethics.* Mr. Kerr's research activities include investigation of emotional-change processes in counselling, and rehabilitation for persons with HIV/AIDS. Recently, he has also worked for Health Canada and the Canadian AIDS Society, developing training curriculum for health care professionals.

Jo-Anne Sargent
See "B. Counselling Relationships."

D. Evaluation and Assessment

Beth E. Haverkamp is associate professor of counselling psychology at the University of British Columbia in Vancouver, where she is involved in research and teaching in the area of ethics and assessment.

Jaye Wald is a doctoral student in counselling psychology at the University of British Columbia in Vancouver. She has completed coursework in vocational, psychoeducational and personality assessment.

John Stewart is a professor in the Faculty of Education at the University of New Brunswick in Fredericton. He holds undergraduate degrees from Acadia University and graduate degrees from the University of New Brunswick and the University of Toronto. Prior to coming to UNB, he worked as a secondary school teacher and school counsellor in Prince Edward Island. His research interests include the application of psychological theory to issues in vocational development and decision making, and school counselling.

E. Research and Publication

Renate Schulz is an associate professor in the Faculty of Education, University of Manitoba in Winnipeg. She has consulted, presented, and published on the topic of practitioner research.

Paul R. Madak graduated from the University of Manitoba and is currently a professor and chair of education at the University of Northern British Columbia in Prince George. His areas of interest are research methodology, program evaluation, sexual abuse prevention, school dropouts, middle school education.

Sandra L. MacDonald is a graduate of the University of Manitoba in Winnipeg. Sandra has lived in British Columbia since 1994, has worked as a school psychologist, private consultant/counsellor-practitioner, and is a sessional instructor at the University of Northern British Columbia in Prince George.

F. Counsellor Education, Training and Supervision

Beth E. Haverkamp
See "D. Evaluation and Assessment"

Kathleen A. Irvine is a doctoral student in counselling psychology at the University of British Columbia in Vancouver; her doctoral research is focussed on ethics and religion in counselling.

Max R. Uhlemann is a professor in the Department of Educational Psychology and Leadership Studies at the University of Victoria in British Columbia. He is co-ordinator of the counselling program at the university and editor for the Canadian Journal of Counselling. He is a member of the ethics committee for the Canadian Counselling Association. His research interests include stress and vicarious traumatic stress experienced by counsellors, counsellor-skill acquisition, expectations in counsellor assessment, and ethics education. His practice interests include stress, trauma, grief, loss, and ethics and legal education of practitioners.

John C. Gawthrop is a registered clinical counsellor with over twenty years experience in the field and has been involved in ethics training and consulting for 10 years. He is deputy registrar of the British Columbia Association of Clinical Counsellors (BCACC) and for three years served as chair of that organization's ethics and standards committee. As a certified regulatory investigator, he investigates ethics complaints against counsellors and is well-versed in the regulatory process and its impact on his peers. Mr. Gawthrop's masters thesis evaluated the efficacy of formal ethics teaching and earned the CGCA's biennial Masters Thesis Award in 1991. He teaches a course on professional ethics at Camosun College in Victoria, B.C. and works part-time for the Ministry of Social Development and Economic Security in the area of freedom of information and protection of privacy.

Chapter One

---❖---

Professional
Counselling Ethics

---❖---

A real value in examining ethical dilemmas is that, in the process of going through the steps of ethical decision making, counsellors can promote their own professional growth.

INTRODUCTION

Counsellors are considered to be a professional group because they are educated in special knowledge and skills to perform a unique service, counselling. Members of a professional group are typically expected to perform their services as described by their professional association, and are responsible for assessing and upgrading their profession. Counsellors also have a code of ethics to help them clarify major ethical issues.

Codes of ethics offer directives to counsellors rather than absolute answers. There are many issues that cannot be handled completely in any code of ethics, and at times there are clear conflicts among the articles in the code, counsellor values, and institution or employer practices. Counselling casebooks have been developed to help provide some clarification of counselling issues and dilemmas.

Counselling casebooks are relatively new in Canada. The first casebook was published by the Canadian Counselling Association (CCA) in 1994. The general intent of casebooks on counselling ethics is to help educate counsellors, counsellor-educators and counselling researchers. The specific objectives of this second edition of the casebook are:

1. To promote discussion of ethical issues in the professional practice of counselling, on the counselling relationship, on testing and research, on consultation and private practice, and on counsellor preparation standards;

2. To demonstrate the willingness of our professional counselling association to regulate itself and to provide a process for self-regulation;

3. To protect our counselling association by setting standards of practice through case examples of both ethical and unethical behaviour in counselling;

4. To provide material that will assist the CCA Ethics Committee in dealing with complaints of ethical violations in a variety of situations;

5. To be a guide to counsellors in their everyday conduct and in the resolution of ethical dilemmas;

6. To help define and facilitate counsellors' relationships with employers and supervisors;

7. To provide examples that will help clarify each of the 70 ethical articles in the CCA *Code of Ethics*;

8. To clarify major issues such as confidentiality, dual relationships and training through informed essays on these and other topics.

For both experienced and new counsellors, this casebook should further counsellors' knowledge of counselling ethics; knowledge that will help when they are faced with ethical conflicts.

Following this introductory chapter, this casebook is divided into six additional chapters, each one dealing with one of the six sections of the CCA *Code of Ethics*. Beginning with Chapter Two, specific cases are presented, designed to illustrate, clarify and analyse each of the 70 ethical articles in the CCA *Code of Ethics*. In Chapter Two, two ethical cases and two unethical cases are presented for each of the 10 articles of Section A. This section deals with the general issues of the professional behaviour of counsellors. Following these cases, a brief commentary is presented, as well as a number of questions designed to stimulate further discussion of the specific ethical article under review.

It should be noted at this time that the cases presented vary both in style and length, reflecting the fact that many people contributed cases for this casebook. Every attempt has been made to reflect a variety of work settings for counsellors. Some cases have been altered to reflect more accurately the article under discussion. All names used in the cases are fictitious. Also, cases have been labelled "+" and "-" to designate whether the case reflects positive behaviour or negative behaviour in accordance with the ethical article. No attempt has been made to specify the seriousness of any behaviour presented in the cases. As a result, some cases will exemplify very serious unethical behaviour while others will simply illustrate ignorance or questionable behaviour on the part of the counsellor. After the cases for Section A have been discussed, two essays dealing with Section A of the CCA *Code of Ethics* are presented.

Chapter Three of this casebook consists of cases related to Section B of the CCA *Code of Ethics*: namely "Counselling Relationships." The articles in this section deal with important issues related to confidentiality, record-keeping, informed consent and many others. As was the case in the previous chapter, each of the 18 articles in this section are clarified by presenting two cases that reflect positive behaviour on the part of the counsellor, and two cases that demonstrate negative behaviour. Some commentary on the article and cases is presented. As well, five discussion questions are presented for each article, with the intention of furthering discussion of ethics and ethical guidelines. Four counsellor-educators have prepared essays for this section on counselling relationships.

The last four chapters are organized in the same way, with case presentations, commentary, questions and essays. Chapter Four deals with Section C of the CCA *Code of Ethics*, "Consulting and Private Practice."

In Chapter Five, Section D of the CCA *Code of Ethics* is presented; namely, articles

exemplifying ethical behaviour in "Evaluation and Assessment." The last two chapters deal with "Research and Publication" and "Counsellor Education, Training, and Supervision."

Background to Counselling Ethics

The CCA is a relatively new association, having its beginnings in 1965 as the Canadian Guidance and Counselling Association (CGCA). The first ethical guidelines for the CGCA were printed in 1981, and contained four sections (General, Counsellor-Counsellee Relationships, Measurement and Evaluation, and Research and Publication), with a total of 46 guidelines. The American Counseling Association (ACA), formerly the American Personnel and Guidance Association, had given the CGCA permission to adapt many of their ethical articles. This influence of the ACA has continued to the present time. (See Appendix for a copy of the ACA ethical articles.)

In 1987, William Schulz, Manitoba director of CCA, was asked to revise the Canadian counselling ethical articles resulting in *Guidelines for Ethical Behaviour* (1989). The ethical articles were divided into five sections: general; counselling relationships; testing, research and publication; consulting and private practice; and counsellor preparation with a total of 63 ethical articles. The CCA decided that to help educate their membership about counselling ethics, a casebook was needed that would provide examples of ethical and unethical behaviour as well as essays on key ethical issues such as boundary violations, confidentiality, and counsellor preparation.

In 1993, Schulz agreed to write an ethics casebook resulting in the *Counselling Ethics Casebook* (1994). Many counsellors contributed case studies for the book and counsellor-educators from across Canada contributed a total of 10 essays dealing with ethical issues.

In 1998, the CCA decided to update their 1989 *Code of Ethics*, and William Schulz and

Glenn Sheppard, two CCA directors who had been very involved in counselling and ethics, were asked to co-chair an ethics committee to revise the CCA *Code of Ethics*. In May 1999, the CCA approved the new *Code of Ethics*. This present code has six major sections:

a) professional responsibility,
b) counselling relationships,
c) consulting and private practice,
d) evaluation and assessment,
e) research and publication, and
f) counsellor education, training and supervision,

with a total of 70 articles. The CCA realized that a casebook should be published as soon as possible after the ethical code was revised, and the gathering of cases for this book began while the CCA *Code of Ethics* was being revised.

Dealing With Ethical Complaints

Members of the CCA are expected to know and adhere to the CCA *Code of Ethics*, and the CCA Ethics Committee is responsible for dealing with violations of ethical behaviour.

It is difficult to assess the actual number of ethical violations in Canada, but there is some American evidence as to the types of complaints being made. A study by Neukrug, Healy and Herlihy (1992) showed that of 749 complaints examined, 27 per cent were made for misrepresentation of credentials, 20 per cent for having sex with a client, 12 per cent for inappropriate fees, 7 per cent for dual relationships, 7 per cent for failure to provide informed consent, 5 per cent for breaking confidentiality, 4 per cent for not reporting abuse, and 2 per cent each for improper group facilitation and not informing authorities of potential harmful acts. The other 15 per cent consisted of a wide variety of "other" ethical violations.

In 1991, *Procedures for Processing Complaints of Ethical Violations* was adopted by the CCA. These procedures show the responsibilities of the Ethics Committee, the complainant and the person who is the subject of the complaint.

The Ethics Committee

The role of the CCA Ethics Committee is to assist in the arbitration and conciliation of conflicts among members of the CCA. The Committee is also responsible for:

1. Educating the membership as to the CCA Ethical Articles;

2. Periodically reviewing the CCA Ethical Articles and the *Procedures for Processing Complaints of Ethical Violations*;

3. Processing complaints of ethical violations; and

4. Receiving and processing questions.

The CCA Ethics Committee consists of four (4) members (including the chairperson) of the CCA membership. Two (2) members are appointed annually for a two (2)-year term by the president. Appointments must be confirmed by the CCA Board of Directors.

The chairperson of the four (4)-member committee is appointed by the president subject to confirmation of the Board of Directors. The chairperson has the responsibility of:

1. Receiving from the CCA headquarters complaints about and from CCA members;

2. Notifying the complainant and the accused of receipt of the case;

3. Notifying the members of the CCA Ethics Committee of the case within two (2) weeks after it is received;

4. Presiding over the meetings of the CCA Ethics Committee;

5. Preparing and sending communications on the recommendations and decisions of the CCA Ethics Committee.

Procedures for Submitting Complaints

The CCA Ethics Committee will act only on those cases where the accused is a member of the CCA. The Committee will not act on anonymous complaints. All correspondence, records and activities of the CCA Ethics Committee will remain confidential.

The procedures for submission of complaints to the CCA Ethics Committee are as follows:

1. If feasible, the complainant should discuss with utmost confidentiality the nature of the complaint with a colleague to see if she or he views the situation as an ethical violation.

2. Whenever feasible, the complainant is to approach the accused directly to discuss and resolve the complaint.

3. In cases where a resolution is not forthcoming at the personal level, the complainant shall prepare a formal written statement of the complaint, stating the details of the alleged violation and shall submit it to the CCA Ethics Committee.

4. Written statements must include a statement indicating the section or sections of the CCA *Code of Ethics* that are allegedly being violated as well as the date(s) of the alleged violation. The written statement shall also contain the accused member's full name and address.

5. All complaints shall be mailed to:

   The Ethics Chairperson
   Canadian Counselling Association
   700-116 Albert Street
   OTTAWA, Ontario K1P 5G3

   The envelope must be marked "Confidential."

Procedures for Processing Complaints

The procedures for processing complaints are as follows:

1. Within two (2) weeks after a written complaint is received at the CCA headquar-

ters, the case is sent to the chairperson of the CCA Ethics Committee. CCA staff verification of membership for the accused shall be included among the documents sent to the Ethics Committee chairperson.

2. Within two (2) weeks of receipt of the written statement of the alleged violation of ethical practices, the chairperson of the CCA Ethics Committee shall:

   a) acknowledge receipt of the complaint,

   b) direct a letter to the complainant acknowledging receipt of the complaint, informing the complainant that the case will be investigated by the Committee, and outlining the procedures to be followed in the investigation,

   c) direct a letter to the accused member informing the member of accusations lodged against her or him, asking for a response and requesting that relevant information be submitted to the chairperson within thirty (30) days,

   d) direct a letter to members of the CCA Ethics Committee notifying them of the case and presenting them with an action plan for investigation.

3. The CCA Ethics Committee will review the case and make a recommendation for disposition and/or resolution of the case within 200 days following its receipt.

Disposition and/or Resolution Options

After reviewing the information submitted by the accused, the CCA Ethics Committee shall have the power:

1. To dismiss the charges, find that no violation has occurred, and dismiss the complaint;

2. To find that the practice(s) in which the member engages is(are) the subject of the complaint and is(are) unethical, notify the accused of this determination, and request the member to voluntarily cease and de-

sist the practice(s) without imposition of further sanctions;

3. To find the practice(s) in which the member engages, that is(are) the subject of the complaint, is(are) unethical, notify the accused of this determination, and impose sanctions. These sanctions include:

    a) issuing a reprimand with recommendations for corrective action, subject to review of the CCA Ethics Committee,

    b) withdrawing membership in the CCA for a specified period of time,

    c) placing the member on probation for a specified period of time, subject to review by the Committee,

    d) expelling the member from the CCA permanently.

4. At the conclusion of the deliberations of the CCA Ethics Committee, the chairperson shall notify the accused and the complainant of the Committee's decision in writing. All of the written evidence and a summary of the decision of the Committee shall be forwarded to the CCA headquarters.

Appeal Procedures

Appeals will be heard only in such cases wherein the appellant presents evidence that the sanction imposed by the CCA Ethics Committee has been arbitrary or capricious or that proper procedures have not been followed. The complainant and the accused shall be informed of the appeal procedure by the chairperson of the CCA Ethics Committee. The following procedures shall govern appeals:

1. A three (3) member review committee is established, composed of the president, president-elect and past president of CCA.

2. The appeal, with supporting documentation, must be made in writing within 60 days to the president of the CCA and indicate the basis upon which it is made.

3. The review committee shall review all materials considered by the CCA Ethics Committee.

4. Within 60 days the review committee shall submit a written statement regarding the decision of the CCA Ethics Committee from the following alternative:

    a) support the decision of the CCA Ethics Committee,

    b) reverse the decision of the CCA Ethics Committee.

5. The parties to the appeal shall be advised of the action in writing.

Procedures for Submitting and Interpreting Questions of Ethical Conduct

1. Whenever possible, the questioner is first advised to consult other colleagues seeking interpretation of questions.

2. If a national-level resolution is deemed appropriate, the questioner shall prepare a written statement, detailing the conduct in question. Statements should include the section or sections of the CCA *Code of Ethics* to be interpreted relative to the conduct in question. Questions are mailed to CCA Headquarters to be forwarded to the Ethics Committee chairperson.

3. The Ethics Committee chairperson shall direct a letter to the questioner acknowledging receipt of the question, informing the member that the question will be interpreted by the CCA Ethics Committee, and outlining the procedures to be involved in the interpretation.

4. The CCA Ethics Committee will review and interpret the question and, if requested by the questioner, make recommendations for conduct.

ethics - moral
legal - enforceable in courts

Ethical Principles

Kitchen (1986) believes that "ethics involves making decisions of a moral nature about people and their interaction in society" (p. 306). She presented the following five moral principles as being crucial in ethical decision making:

- autonomy: individual freedom of choice and action
- non-maleficence: not causing harm to others
- beneficence: contributing to the welfare of the client
- justice: treating equals equally and unequals unequally
- fidelity: loyalty, faithfulness and honouring commitments.

These principles were set out to stimulate counsellors to analyse and evaluate critically any ethical dilemmas they faced.

The expectations for ethical conduct, as expressed in the CCA *Code of Ethics*, are based on the following fundamental principles:

a) respect for the dignity of persons,
b) not willfully harming others,
c) integrity in relationships,
d) responsible caring,
e) responsibility to society, and
f) respect for self-determination.

a) Respect for the Dignity of Persons

Counsellors respect the individuality of clients. They respect the right of clients to have values, opinions, interests and attitudes that are different from those of their counsellors. Counsellors need not approve of clients' values, but the way in which counsellors deal with differences in values is all-important. Counsellors need not hide their values, nor should they promote their values; rather, counsellors should respect the dignity of their clients and allow them to examine freely, differences they may have with counsellors and others.

b) Not Willfully Harming Others

This principle extols counsellors to avoid doing any harm. This means that counsellors recognize the boundaries of their competencies and the limitations of their expertise. Inherent in this principle is the need for ongoing education for counsellors. This principle also implies that counsellors have cultural awareness and sensitivity, knowing that some diagnostic and counselling procedures may be harmful to specific cultural or ethnic groups.

c) Integrity in Relationships

Integrity in relationships refers to providing all people with fair and equal treatment. No exceptions to good counselling services are made because of the economic status of clients, clients' cultural background, age, religion, gender or lifestyle.

d) Responsible Caring

Caring for clients, especially children, in a responsible way is another important value or principle. This ethical principle can result in many dilemmas for counsellors. On the one hand, counsellors know that their primary obligations are to help their clients, but counsellors also have responsibilities to parents, society and their employer.

e) Responsibility to Society

Counsellors need to be constantly aware of their professional responsibility to society and the community in which they live. This responsibility is necessary not only in their day-to-day counselling, but in their advertising, presentations, research and publications. This responsibility to society could include consulting with social agencies, advocating initiatives to promote wellness, and reaching out to special needs clients and minority groups.

f) Respect for Self-Determination

This principle refers to clients' right to choose their own direction. Clients need to have the right of autonomy. Autonomy, then, deals with the value that counsellors put on their clients' freedom of choice and freedom of action.

The Process of Ethical Decision Making

One of the key characteristics of any profession is the existence of a professional code of ethics. Codes are intended to educate the members of the counselling profession, and to provide for professional accountability and improved practice in ethical decision-making.

Counsellors will face moral, ethical and legal dilemmas in counselling. Some of the articles from the ethical standards of either the national or provincial professional counselling organizations are bound to come into conflict. Very frequently the ethical dilemmas will arise from cases that may put the client or others in danger, and the articles on confidentiality. How can counsellors resolve these ethical questions?

Capuzzi and Gross (1999) have set forth a number of suggestions intended to help counsellors faced with ethical dilemmas:

- Review the code of ethics of your professional organization. Review other codes of ethics if necessary.

- If more information is needed, review this Casebook or other counselling ethics casebooks such as the American Counseling Association's Ethical Standards Casebook (Herlihy & Corey, 1996).

- Talk with colleagues and ask them for assistance.

- If the dilemma has legal implications, review the legal statutes that have implications for counselling.

- Talk with members of the legal profession.

- If the situation stems from differences between organizational and professional requirements, review the organization's policies and procedures. If questions arise, check with your supervisor to gain appropriate clarification.

- If the situation stems from questions of professional competence or personal issues that may affect counselling, review the situation with a colleague or supervisor. Based on the results of the review, either continue with the client or make an appropriate referral.

Other authors have produced models and procedures for examining ethical dilemmas. Following the examination of three such models, I will put forward an integrated approach based on the three models and combined with the six ethical principles in the CCA *Code of Ethics.*

The Rest Model

The first model to be outlined briefly is the four-step model for ethical decision-making by James Rest (1979). Rest is concerned with the judgments people make regarding important but conflicting issues. He emphasizes the need to balance the interests of all individuals involved in the ethical issue.

In *step one*, counsellors recognize that an ethical dilemma exists. Counsellors who are familiar with counselling codes of ethics, their responsibility to clients, and their need to be fair both to society and themselves, will recognize situations where confidentiality, danger to clients or others, client attraction and many other ethical problems come into conflict. In this step, then, the counsellor is aware of the ethical problem.

Step two in Rest's model consists of counsellors carefully examining the consequences of various courses of action. Typically, the courses of action are based on some ranking by counsellors of important principles such as the following:

- Veracity – telling the truth
- Privacy – respecting other people and their propert
- Autonomy – respecting people's rights to determine their fates
- Promise keeping – keeping promises
- Parentalism – safeguarding the rights of those who cannot do so themselves
- Self-improvement – improving ourselves
- Non-maleficence – doing no willful harm to others
- Equality – generally treating everyone equally
- Sanctity of life – believing all living things are intrinsically valuable.

Rest makes no attempt to provide any ranking of these principles, and therefore, counsellors need to carefully examine their values and the possible outcomes before weighting the principles to guide them in making an ethical decision.

In *step three*, the counsellor's skills and attitudes become particularly important. During this important step, counsellors develop a plan of action whereby they attempt to resolve the ethical dilemma.

Step four in the Rest process involves putting the plan of action into motion. That is, counsellors do what they have planned. Acting ethically may come at a price: a loss of friendship, disappointment from clients or even the loss of a job. This final step, carrying out the ethical decision, is vital.

In using the four-step Rest Model, Biggs and Blocher (1987) have indicated that counsellors will need to ask themselves a series of questions as they work through the process:

1. How does the counsellor's behaviour effect others? To what extent?

2. Which of the nine principles apply in this ethical situation? Which are the most important principles?

3. Which are the positive values that should be maximized? What negatives should be avoided?

4. What alternative courses of action are possible? What are the consequences of each action to the counsellor? To the client? To others?

5. How do these consequences compare in terms of the overriding principle in this situation?

6. What plan of action can be developed to implement the principles and values?

7. How can the counsellor act on these principles? What prices may the counsellor have to pay? How will the counsellor's actions reflect on the counselling profession and on the counsellor's future practice?

The Canadian Psychological Association Model

In the *Canadian Code of Ethics for Psychologists* (1991) ethical principles and standards are articulated for psychologists. In spite of the fact that counsellors' roles and functions are different than psychologists, these ethical principles and articles for decision making are well worth considering.

Four ethical principles are presented and psychologists are implored to consider all principles in ethical decision making. Unlike other ethical decision-making models, the four principles have been ranked according to the weight each principle should be given when the principles are in conflict. The rank order of principles is as follows:

1. *Principle I: Respect for the Dignity of Persons.* This principle, with its emphasis on moral rights, generally should be given the highest weight, except in circumstances in which there is a clear and imminent danger to the physical safety of any individual.

2. *Principle II: Responsible Caring.* This principle generally should be given the second highest weight. Responsible caring re-

quires competence and should be carried out only in ways that respect the dignity of persons.

3. *Principle III: Integrity in Relationships.* This principle generally should be given the third highest weight. Psychologists are expected to demonstrate the highest integrity in all of their relationships. However, in rare circumstances, values such as openness and straightforwardness may need to be subordinated to the values contained in the Principles of Respect for the Dignity of Persons and Responsible Caring.

4. *Principle IV: Responsibility to Society.* This principle generally should be given the lowest weight of the four principles when it conflicts with one or more of them. Although it is necessary and important to consider responsibility to society in every ethical decision, adherence to this principle must be subject to and guided by Respect for the Dignity of Persons, Responsible Caring, and Integrity in Relationships. When individual welfare appears to conflict with benefits to society, it is often possible to find ways of working for the benefit of society, which do not violate respect and responsible caring for individuals. However, if this is not possible, then greater weight must be given to individual welfare.

The Canadian Psychological Association (1991) suggests the following steps to ethical decision making:

a) Identification of ethically relevant issues and practices;

b) Development of alternative courses of action;

c) Analysis of likely short-term, ongoing, and long-term risks and benefits of each course of action on the individual(s)/ group(s) involved or likely to be affected (e.g. client, client's family or employees, employing institution, stu-

dents, research participants, colleagues, the discipline, society, self);

d) Choice of course of action after conscientious application of existing principles, values and standards;

e) Action, with a commitment to assume responsibility for the consequences of the action;

f) Evaluation of the results of the course of action;

g) Assumption of responsibility for consequences of action, including correction of negative consequences, if any, or re-engaging in the decision-making process if the ethical issue is not resolved.

The American Counseling Association Model

In 1985, the ACA provided funding for a series of video cassettes dealing with ethical issues. In the video, *Confidentiality: The Professional's Dilemma,* Holly Stadler provides the listener with her views on ethical behaviour and she outlines an ethical decision-making model. Her model consisted of the following four steps:

1. The counsellor identifies competing moral principles (non-maleficence, beneficence, autonomy and justice).

2. The counsellor implements a moral reasoning strategy. There are four sub-steps to this process:

   a) Securing additional information concerning the ethical dilemma;

   b) Examining special circumstances surrounding a particular case;

   c) Ranking the moral principles;

   d) Consulting with colleagues for comments and additional ideas.

3. Counsellors prepare for action. To do this a typical problem-solving approach is suggested:

a) Identification of hoped-for outcomes, (e.g. protect the client or protect confidentiality);

b) Listing of possible actions;

c) Evaluation of the actions on the client or related others, and on society;

d) Identification of any competing non-moral values, (e.g. financial or religious considerations);

e) Choosing a specific course of action;

f) Testing that choice in terms of universality, publicity and justice.

4. In the final step, counsellors put into action their ethical decision. If the decision is difficult, counsellors may need to engage in some ego-strengthening activities such as making a contract with a colleague to carry out the action, or to visualize the completed task with the results being favourable. Next, concrete steps should be laid out on how to complete the task. The action is taken, and finally, the action is evaluated.

Two additional publications by the ACA have enhanced Stadler's earlier work; namely, *A Practitioner's Guide to Ethical Decision-Making* (Forester-Miller & Davis, 1995) and ACA *Ethical Standards Casebook* (Herlihy & Corey, 1996).

The ACA ethical decision-making model has been expanded to a seven-step model.

1. Identify the problem.
   Gather as much information as possible. Is it a legal, professional, or clinical problem?

2. Apply the ACA *Code of Ethics*.
   If there is an applicable article or several articles or standards, following the course of action suggested may alleviate the problem.

3. Determine the nature and dimensions of the dilemma.

a) Consider the moral principles of autonomy, non-maleficence, beneficence, justice, and fidelity;

b) Review relevant professional literature;

c) Consult with professional colleagues;

d) Contact your professional organizations.

4. Generate potential courses of action.

5. Consider the potential consequences of all options and determine a course of action.

6. Evaluate the selected course of action.

7. Implement the course of action.

The Canadian Counselling Association Integrative Model

If an examination of models of ethical decision-making is to be truly useful, it is important that each counsellor examine various models of decision-making, and then attempt to use a model that makes the most sense, or integrate ideas from several models. Following is my attempt to integrate the three models outlined and to develop them into an integrative model that seemed reasonable for me. Mainly, two features have been changed or added to the models already outlined: first, different words were used for principles such as non-maleficence, beneficence and fidelity; secondly, a feeling/emotional dimension was added to the largely cognitive/rational decision-making steps of the three aforementioned models.

The CCA model (as previously summarized in the CCA *Code of Ethics*) would consist of six steps:

1. The key ethical issues of a particular situation are identified.

2. The CCA *Code of Ethics* is examined to see if the ethical issue is dealt with. If there are appropriate articles (e.g. on confidentiality or informed consent), following the articles may be sufficient to resolve the ethical dilemma. If the ethical problem is

more complex, the following further steps will be needed.

3. The third step consists of examining the moral and ethical principles that are important in the situation. The principles in the three models could be condensed to include an examination of the following six principles:

    a) Respect for the dignity of persons
    b) Not willfully harming others
    c) Integrity in relationships ✓
    d) Responsible caring ✓
    e) Responsibility to society ✓
    f) Respect for self-determination. ✓

4. This step consists of choosing the most important principles and relevant ethical articles and beginning to implement some possible action by:

    a) Generating alternatives and examining the risks and benefits of each alternative;
    b) Securing additional information and/or consulting with colleagues;
    c) Examining the probable outcomes of various courses of action.

5. Until this point, this decision-making process has concentrated on fairly cognitive, rational steps, so the fifth step should include involving feelings and emotions in the decision-making. Time permitting, counsellors should use emotional decision techniques such as the following:

    a) Quest - a solitary walk in the woods or park where your emotions are allowed to interact with the ethical dilemma being faced;
    b) Incubation - "sleep on it,"
    c) Time projection - projecting the ethical situation into the future and thinking about the various fantasized scenarios.

6. The final step consists of taking some action. Counsellors should follow a concrete action plan, evaluate the plan, and be prepared to correct any negative consequences that might occur from the action taken.

A brief example will help to show how these six steps might work in actual practice. Questions are presented to help counsellors consider each of the steps in this six-step, integrated approach. A high school counsellor has seen a seventeen-year-old, Grade 11 student, John, on numerous occasions. Initially, these counsellor visits came as a result of teacher referrals. Teachers found that John was a "nuisance in the classroom." Over the months a good relationship developed between the counsellor and John, and frequently John just dropped in to chat. On one such occasion, John talked about his part-time job at a hardware store and how he made quite a bit of extra money "lifting" the occasional article from the store and selling it. When the counsellor got more of the details, he was convinced that considerable theft was involved. He didn't know what to do, since he had assured John on more than one occasion that "Things said in my office will never leave this office."

① *What are the key ethical issues in this situation?*
The counsellor had promised confidentiality, yet the student's actions were illegal. In the long run, the thefts would probably be discovered and John would be in serious trouble.

② *What ethical articles are relevant to this case?*
The ethical articles relating to confidentiality provide for a respect for privacy, unless there is danger to the client or to others. The ethical articles also state that the counsellor's primary responsibility is to help the client. Furthermore, the counsellor needs to inform the client of the exceptions to confidentiality before the counselling begins.

(3) *What ethical principles are of major importance in this situation?*

Six principles were identified earlier, and the following principles are important in John's situation: integrity in relationships, responsible caring, not willfully harming others, responsibility to society, and respect for self-determination. (Schulz, 1994).

(4) *What are the most important principles and what are the risks and benefits if these principles are acted upon?*

The counsellor examined each one of the principles and considered what would happen if he reported the theft, what would likely happen if he kept quiet and continued to work with John, and how could he best help John. Without identifying John, the counsellor discussed the situation with another counsellor, and was told that "to cover yourself you'd better tell the principal." The counsellor felt at this time that "responsible caring" and "responsibility to society" were of greatest importance. Before acting, the counsellor asked himself a fourth question:

(5) *Will I feel the same way about this situation if I think about it a little longer?*

The counsellor decided to "sleep on it" and the following day he took specific steps to deal with this ethical dilemma.

What plan of action will be most helpful in this situation?

The counsellor made an appointment with John and informed him that he would have to break confidentiality, since he felt that he just would not be acting responsibly if he allowed the stealing to continue. He tried to convince John that in the long run he might actually be helping him as well. John was given several options by the counsellor regarding the reporting of the theft himself, by the counsellor, or with the two of them seeing the appropriate authorities together.

Some counsellors like to develop a decision-making chart to help them with their ethical dilemmas. John's case could be presented as follows:

Options for Action	Benefits	Risks	Probable Outcomes
Option 1 Avoid the issue	May be the easiest	The problem is not resolved.	Counsellor could lose his job
Option 2 Keep counselling John and encourage him to make restitution.	I can keep using my professional judgment as to what is best for John.	John comes for counselling but does not provide restitution.	Things might work out, but what about the owner of the hardware store.
Option 3 After telling John, report the activities to the appropriate authorities.	In the long run help John to act more responsibly.	Lose John as a client. Possibly, other clients.	Initially, John would be angry, but would see that the stealing had to stop.

A Short Inventory of Counselling Ethics

To show that there is seldom one absolutely correct response to ethical situations, and to have you think about the CCA *Code of Ethics,* the following short inventory is included. These 18 inventory items correspond to the 18 ethical articles in the main section of the Code; namely, Section B, "Counselling Relationships."

For each of the 18 items, identify the response or responses that best reflect your views, or add your own response if none of the responses appeals to you.

1. The counsellor's primary responsibility is:

   a) to promote the values of the community/society,

   b) to respect the client and promote the welfare of the client,

   c) to avoid ethical and legal violations,

   d) _____ .

2. The most important exception to confidentiality is:

   a) when a child is in need of protection,

   b) when legal requirements demand that confidential material be revealed,

   c) when the client threatens suicide,

   d) _____ .

3. When a client threatens another person, the counsellor:

   a) must phone the police,

   b) must warn the person threatened,

   c) must tell his/her supervisor/director,

   d) _____ .

4. Informed consent for clients means that the clients:

   a) expect complete confidentiality,

   b) can refuse the counsellor's suggestions,

   c) will understand what the counselling will be all about,

   d) _____ .

5. Informed consent for counselling young children should:

   a) be given by parents or guardians,

   b) be given by the children themselves,

   c) not be necessary,

   d) _____ .

6. Regarding the keeping of records of counselling interviews, counsellors:

   a) must keep all records for seven years,

   b) have no legal or ethical obligation to keep records,

   c) keep records so they can better help their clients,

   d) _____ .

7. With respect to access to counselling records, the client:

   a) owns the content of the records,

   b) can release the records to others,

   c) can prevent his/her parents from seeing the records if he/she is under 18 years of age,

   d) _____ .

8. Dual relationships can exist when a counsellor:

   a) is both a teacher and counsellor,

   b) teaches and supervises a student counsellor,

   c) is both a group facilitator and a teacher evaluating a group member's performance,

   d) _____ .

9. Counsellors should not discriminate based on differences of:
   a) culture,
   b) sexual orientation,
   c) age,
   d) _____ .

10. When consulting with other professionals, counsellors:
   a) must keep the name of their client confidential,
   b) must get consent from the client to consult with others,
   c) can reveal the client's name, if necessary,
   d) _____ .

11. Counsellors should be very cautious about relationships with former clients, relationships such as:
   a) business,
   b) friendship,
   c) financial,
   d) _____ .

12. Sexual intimacy with clients:
   a) is illegal,
   b) is acceptable once the client/counsellor relationship ends,
   c) is always unethical,
   d) _____ .

13. When counsellors provide counselling to two or more persons (e.g. parents and children):
   a) all persons in the counselling become clients and have the same rights,
   b) the counsellor needs to clarify the nature of the relationship with each person,
   c) only the person who initiated the counselling is the client,
   d) _____ .

14. If counsellors learn that their client is seeing another counsellor, they need to:
   a) clear this with the other counsellor,
   b) discontinue the counselling,
   c) discuss the issues related to having multiple helpers,
   d) _____ .

15. In group counselling, the group leader has the responsibility:
   a) of providing physical and psychological safety for all group members,
   b) of screening group members,
   c) of providing follow-up after the group terminates,
   d) _____ .

16. When counsellors use computers as part of the counselling service, counsellors ensure:
   a) that the client fully understands the computer application,
   b) that follow-up to the computer application is provided,
   c) that the computer application is appropriate,
   d) _____ .

17. If counsellors determine that they cannot be helpful to a client, they:
   a) should refer the client,
   b) should terminate the counselling,
   c) should discuss the situation with the client,
   d) _____ .

18. Counsellors end counselling sessions when:
   a) the client isn't paying her/his fees,
   b) the counselling services are no longer needed,
   c) the counsellor feels no progress is being made,
   d) _____ .

References

Biggs, D., & Blocher, D. (1987). *Foundations of ethical counselling.* New York: Springer Publishing Company.

Canadian Counselling Association. (1999). *Code of Ethics.* Ottawa: Author.

Canadian Psychological Association. (1986). *A Canadian code of ethics for psychologists.* Ottawa: Canadian Psychological Association.

Canadian Guidance and Counselling Association. (1989). *Guidelines for ethical behaviour.* Ottawa: Author.

Capuzzi, D., & Gross, D. (1999). *Counseling and psychology* (2nd ed.). Upper Saddle River, N.J.: Merrill.

Forester-Miller, H., & Davis, T.E. (1995). *A practitioner's guide to ethical decision making.* Alexandria, VA: American Counseling Association.

Herlihy, B., & Corey, G. (1996). *ACA ethical standards casebook* (5th ed.). Alexandria, VA: American Counseling Association.

Neukrug, E., Healy, M., & Herlihy, B. (1992). Ethical practices of licensed professional counselors. An updated survey of state licensing boards. *Counsellor Education and Supervision,* 32, 130-141.

Pettifor, L. (1991). *How well does the Canadian Code of Ethics serve community psychologists?* Psynopsis, Winter 11-12.

Rest, J. (1979). *Development in judging moral issues.* Minneapolis: University of Minnesota Press.

Rest, J. (1984). *Research on moral development: implications for training psychologists.* The Counselling Psychologist, 12, 19-30.

Schulz, W. (1994). *Counselling ethics casebook.* Ottawa: Canadian Guidance and Counselling Association.

Schulz, W. (1995a). *Ethics for career development professionals.* Alberta Regional Consultation for Career Development, Building Tomorrow Today. (April 25-27, 1995). Consultation Proceedings (31-35).

Schulz, W. (1995b). Interview. In Canadian Association of Rehabilitation Professionals, British Columbia Society. *Rehab Review,* XVI, (3), Fall, 1995.

Stadler, H. (1985). *Confidentiality: The professionals' dilemma.* AACD Video Cassette Series. Alexandria, VA: AACD Foundation.

Chapter Two

---------- ❖ ----------

Professional
Responsibility

---------- ❖ ----------

Counselling is a professional occupation,
and one of the unique roles of a profession
is that members exercise independent judgment, make decisions and provide help.

Ethical Articles on Professional Responsibility

A1 **General Responsibility**
Counsellors maintain high standards of professional competence and ethical behaviour, and recognize the need for continuing education and personal care in order to meet this responsibility.

A2 **Respect for Rights**
Counsellors participate in only those practices which are respectful of the legal, civic, and moral rights of others, and act to safeguard the dignity and rights of their clients, students, and research participants.

❖

A3 **Boundaries of Competence**
Counsellors limit their counselling services and practices to those which are within their professional competence by virtue of their education and professional experience, and consistent with any requirements for provincial and national credentials. They refer to other professionals when the counselling needs of clients exceed their level of competence.

A4 **Supervision and Consultation**
Counsellors take reasonable steps to obtain supervision and/or consultation with respect to their counselling practices and, particularly, with respect to doubts or uncertainties which may arise during their professional work.

A5 **Representation of Professional Qualifications**
Counsellors claim or imply only those professional qualifications which they possess, and are responsible for correcting any known misrepresentation of their qualifications by others.

A6 Responsibility to Counsellors and Other Professionals

Counsellors understand that ethical behaviour among themselves and with other professionals is expected at all times.

A7 Unethical Behaviour by Other Counsellors

Counsellors have an obligation, when they have serious doubts as to the ethical behaviour of another counsellor, to seek an informal resolution with the counsellor, when feasible and appropriate. When an informal resolution is not appropriate or feasible, or is unsuccessful, counsellors report their concerns to the CCA Ethics Committee.

A8 Sexual Harassment

Counsellors do not condone or engage in sexual harassment, which is defined as deliberate or repeated verbal or written comments, gestures, or physical contacts of a sexual nature.

A9 Sensitivity to Diversity

Counsellors strive to understand and respect the diversity of their clients, including differences related to age, ethnicity, culture, gender, disability, religion, sexual orientation, and socio-economic status.

A10 Extension of Ethical Responsibilities

Counselling services and products provided by counsellors through classroom instruction, public lectures, demonstrations, publications, radio and television programs, computer technology and other media must meet the appropriate ethical standards of this *Code of Ethics*.

❖ ❖ ❖ ❖ ❖ ❖ ❖ ❖ ❖ ❖ ❖ ❖

Case Studies in Professional Responsibility

A1 **GENERAL RESPONSIBILITY**
Counsellors maintain high standards of professional competence and ethical behaviour, and recognize the need for continuing education and personal care in order to meet this responsibility.

Improving Professional Practices (+)

An experienced elementary-school counsellor, upon arriving in a new school in a different school division, realized that many of the children in her school had problems that were a result of poor parenting. Also, due to the high number of immigrant families in this counsellor's school, she attributed some of the children's problems to their families' unfamiliarity with Canadian customs.

The counsellor spent the remainder of the year with these children researching their needs, their parents' needs and the differences in these families' cultures in comparison to Canadian ways. She worked to improve her skills in cultural diversity in order that she could better serve her students.

After much research and consultation with other counsellors, she felt better qualified to facilitate evening parenting workshops for the community. Four such workshops were run throughout the school year, dealing with topics such as discipline and family-life education. All were highly regarded by parents, staff and administration.

Counsellor Networking (+)

A counsellor in a small, rural school division organized counsellor peer group meetings so that she could meet with her colleagues on a regular basis. This group periodically joined forces with a group of counsellors from two neighbouring school divisions so that they could invite speakers from a major urban centre. The speakers kept them informed about urban counselling issues, new research and upcoming professional-development opportunities. Other speakers and workshops helped them upgrade their skills. In their own divisional meetings they were able to consult with their colleagues about their clients while still maintaining confidentiality.

Ensuring Children Receive Guidance From a Competent Counsellor (-)

An urban school division had more teachers returning from leaves than they had positions available for the 1998/99 school year. An extremely competent and highly regarded Grade 2 teacher in the division returned from a two-year leave-of-absence. She was given a few alternatives after she had notified the superintendent of her desire to return. Yet, being primary, the only position she felt remotely capable of accepting was a guidance position in a kindergarten through grade 8 school. The school division did require that guidance counsellors be trained. The school with the opening was one of the toughest in the division. The previous counsellor had quit as a result of the stress he experienced from the job, and internal advertising had resulted in no other interest from qualified staff. The superintendent awarded the primary teacher the position in spite of her having no training in counselling.

Professional Development Missing (-)

A school counsellor got his master's degree in counselling in the late 1970s. Over the next 20 years he took no additional course work in counselling, seldom went to counselling in-services, and never attended a national counselling conference.

COMMENTS AND QUESTIONS

The first ethical article on the need for high standards of professional competence from counsellors raises a number of questions. Who determines a counsellor's competence? Should competence be determined by the counsellor or should it perhaps be other members? Should a client determine a counsellor's competence since it is the counsellee who can truly speak of the counsellor's effectiveness?

Counsellors are professionals. Therefore, members of professional organizations and clients assume that counsellors are capable of determining their own competence. Professionals must be treated as professionals. They must be trusted to make sound judgments, to know their limitations and to know when consultation, re-training and/or additional education is necessary.

Still, counsellors are human and humans are known to make mistakes and can be misunderstood. Thus, to protect counsellors and their clients the following two criteria are recommended before the public can enter into a counselling relationship:

a) *Professional Disclosure* - Prior to beginning a counselling situation, the client would be informed of the counsellor's qualifications, services offered, therapeutic process, nature of confidentiality, administrative procedures and finally, the client's own rights and responsibilities.

b) *Written Contract* - After discussing the terms and coming to a mutual agreement of the upcoming counselling situation, the counsellor and the client should enter into a formal contract so that there will never be future questions of what was expected or promised by either partner in counselling.

1. How do counsellors recognize their own competence and how do they set limitations for themselves?

2. Degrees, licensing and/or certification do not ensure competence of psychologists, social workers or counsellors, so what can clients do to ensure they are receiving the best counselling available to them?

3. Is it ethically wrong to hire a teacher who is not certified as a trained counsellor for a school counselling position?

4. What are some things that counsellors could do to improve present professional practices?

5. What are some things counsellor can do with regards to their own personal care?

A2 RESPECT FOR RIGHTS
Counsellors participate in only those practice which are respectful of the legal, civic, and moral rights of others, and act to safeguard the dignity and rights of their clients, students, and research participants.

Suicide Threat (+)

Jane Sutherland has been engaged in counselling a client for two years as part of court-mandated treatment. Jane schedules a brief appointment at 4:00 p.m. and expects to be home with her family by 5:00. During this scheduled appointment, Jane is diverted by the comment, "I don't know if I'll make it to September." Jane asks for clarification of the emotions behind the statement and determines that the client is depressed and has been contemplating suicide all week, having given hints to staff of a residential treatment centre where he has been staying for the last two months. The client has several plausible and available methods to meet his intentions. No intensive or extensive intervention has been done to that point by the facility staff. Jane Sutherland continues with a suicide check and is unable to move the client toward committing to living another day. She tells the client that she has no choice but to escort him to the hospital for follow-up. Jane notifies agency staff of the predicament and transports him to the hospital where a series of interviews occur and suicidal ideation diminishes. Jane remains as a support for the client during the hospital intake/treatment period.

Theft Disclosure (+)

A client discloses to his counsellor that he has stolen something from his employer. This disclosure occurs well after qualitative gains have been made in counselling. The counsellor is torn by his commitment to the client and confidentiality, and the legalities of knowing about an illicit activity. The counsellor works

for an agency funded by the Justice Department. The agency guidelines to counsellors indicate that all known or potential criminal activity is to be reported. The counsellor encourages the client to turn himself over to authorities and indicates that he will accompany him to the police, acting as a support.

Gathering Court Data (-)

A counsellor is instructed to compile a report for the court regarding a subject charged and having pleaded guilty to sexually assaulting an 11-year-old girl. As part of the report, a victim impact statement is to be included. The counsellor will be required to obtain information regarding the psychological and physical damage to the victim. This agency has guidelines regarding the interviewing of any victim who may be further traumatized by having to reiterate already available information. The counsellor contacts the victim directly to arrange an interview. The interview takes place at the counsellor's office, where a series of questions are asked. Examples of these questions include:

- What emotional impact has this assault had on you?
- What physical impact has this assault had on you?
- Why did you allow the assault to occur?
- What attempts did you make to stop the assault?
- Why did you wait so long to report the assault?
- Are you sure about the assault occurring?

During the course of the interview the victim becomes overwhelmed by the focus of the questions, but the counsellor continues with the battery of questions slated for the agenda.

Inadequate Information (-)

A counsellor is employed at an agency that provides pregnancy information services to adolescents. The agency is of the opinion that clients have the right to be advised of all available resources in the community and be referred to these if they so choose. A female adolescent comes to the counsellor and requests information on different options regarding her pregnancy. The counsellor, who is anti-abortion, fails to provide the client with information on abortion, but provides information related to adoption and keeping her expected baby.

COMMENTS AND QUESTIONS

This ethical article provides a clear understanding that the professional member must demonstrate "responsible" behaviour to the client as well as to the institution or agency within which the counsellor is working. At all times the counsellor must be respectful of the rights of others. Despite this crucial and well-meaning mandate, it would be rare to find a counsellor who has not been challenged at some level where he or she would be required to reflect on this ethical article and seek a creative response to remain ethical.

Counsellors will invariably find conflict in responsibility to clients or the institution they serve. This may arise when an employer or institution requests a specific level of service for its clients that is not commensurate with professional standards and therefore represents a breach of responsibility. The question remains as to who is ultimately responsible: the employer who is underfunded to provide the actual number of staff or services to meet the needs of the client population, or the counsellor who gives in to the supervisor's advice to provide limited service to the majority of clients. It is likely that in many cases the supervisor and counsellor follow the same code of ethics, or at least, a similar series of ethical instructions. It would be easy to say that the supervisor should cut down the number of cases the agency is willing to handle. This may be appropriate for private agencies, however, government agencies may not

have this option. They are expected to provide the service despite the lack of staff or resources.

Clients have many legal and moral rights. Counsellors need to respect these rights. One way of showing respect is for counsellors to have clear "informed consent" statements that spell out conditions of confidentiality, counsellor competencies and typical counsellor techniques and strategies.

1. List some counsellor practices where the legal, moral or civil rights of others could be jeopardized.

2. In the second case presented, what would you have done as a counsellor if the client was not willing to go to the authorities and admit his theft?

3. In the third case, what should the counsellor have done as a respectful measure in his treatment of the victim?

4. Is it realistic, with large client caseloads, to expect the counsellor to provide full services to all clients? What would you do if you were a counsellor in an agency that received too many clients?

5. What type of orientation should counsellors receive in regards to the ethic of "safeguarding the rights of their clients"?

A3 BOUNDARIES OF COMPETENCE
Counsellors limit their counselling services and practices to those which are within their professional competency by virtue of their education and professional experience, and consistent with any requirements for provincial and national credentials. They refer to other professionals when the counselling needs of clients exceed their level of competence.

Referral (+)
A beginning counsellor is speaking with a student about the student's recently declining grades. In the course of the discussion, they get into reasons why the student's school work is down and in a moment of disclosure the student admits to abuse in the home. The counsellor immediately recognizes that this is beyond the scope of his abilities and he notifies the proper authorities and refers the student to qualified counselling facilities specifically geared for dealing with abuse cases such as this.

Career Counsellor (+)
A graduate student from a department of educational psychology in a Canadian university decides to begin her own private counselling service. In spite of the fact that many clients ask to see her for marriage counselling, she refuses all these clients, pointing out that her own training and practicum experiences were mainly in employment and career counselling.

Avoiding Teacher Layoffs (-)
A school division has had a declining student population for the past three years. The school superintendent makes the decision that 15 teachers will have "to be terminated." At the same time, this division makes the decision to have a school counsellor in each of their 18 elementary schools. Teachers, both with and without counsellor training,

apply for the counselling positions. The counselling jobs are offered to several trained counsellors, but 12 of the new elementary school counselling positions are offered to teachers in the division with no counsellor training. All 12 teachers accept the counselling positions for which they have no training.

No Training in Marriage Counselling (-)
An employment counsellor with eight-years experience decides to begin private counselling on a part-time basis. Her first clients are a couple who wish to receive marriage counselling. The counsellor happily accepts these clients for counselling even though she has had no training in marriage counselling.

COMMENTS AND QUESTIONS
This ethical article clearly dictates that counsellors need to evaluate their abilities and level of experience. When situations arise that are beyond the training or experience of a counsellor, it is unethical to proceed blindly into counselling. As Section B, Article 10 indicates, consultation with other professionals about such situations is both ethical and recommended. Furthermore, counsellors should consider even casual discussions with colleagues an important means to determine others' experience and expertise and then should not hesitate to tap into these resources whenever the need arises. This article suggests that counsellors provide only those services for which they are qualified. A natural extension of this article is that counsellors maintain active enrolment in professional groups (determine areas of expertise among colleagues, and services available), and participate regularly in professional development activities.

Lastly, the article clearly states that counsellors accept only those positions for which they are professionally qualified. This means that teachers should not become school counsellors if they have not received counsellor training.

1. How do counsellors determine their "boundaries of competence"?

2. What should be the training of a "professionally qualified" counsellor?

3. How can counselling organizations stop the practice of school divisions giving teachers (with no counsellor training) positions in counselling?

4. Is it better to offer "non-expert counselling" than no counselling at all, especially when someone is working in a remote area where referral services are limited or non-existent?

5. Should counsellors accept positions in private practice knowing that they will see clients with difficulties in areas where they have little or no expertise?

A4 SUPERVISION AND CONSULTATION
Counsellors take reasonable steps to obtain supervision and/or consultation with respect to their counselling practices and, particularly, with respect to doubts or uncertainties which may arise during their professional work.

Improving Counselling (+)

The director of a large private counselling service meets with all her counsellors twice a year to discuss their counselling practice. The director and counsellors discuss feedback forms from clients and counselling tapes of interview sessions. There is a great deal of back-and-forth discussion of the counselling and the climate during the sessions is open and congenial. Both the director and the counsellor have opportunities to contribute to the final report, which is placed in the counsellor's file.

Counselling Supervision (+)

Counsellors and therapists in one Canadian city decided to organize a small professional organization whereby they could readily discuss counselling issues as well as receive feedback on their counselling. Guest speakers were invited to talk about current issues. The most valuable feature of this professional organization for many was the opportunity for each counsellor to present her or his counselling tape for discussion with two other counsellors. These groups of three met four times a year to listen to each other's counselling tapes and to discuss counselling cases.

Little Professional Development (-)

In one school division where there had been severe cutbacks, resulting in fewer counsellors for many schools, the director of counselling for the division suggested that counsellors might wish to use "brief counselling," hoping to limit the total amount of time that counsellors would need to help their clients.

The brief counselling in-service for counsellors consisted only of three weekend workshops. The director made no attempt to follow-up or evaluate the brief counselling provided by the counsellors.

Personal Problems (-)

Janice P., a counsellor, is experiencing a great deal of personal distress, including losing her mother and going through a bitter divorce. She realizes that she is just going through the motions with her clients and is not being at all helpful. She is unable to concentrate on her clients' problems since her own are so severe. When things get too overwhelming, she phones in sick. She is afraid she might lose her counselling position if she lets others know about all her personal problems.

COMMENTS AND QUESTIONS

One of the key elements of successful counselling is the trust that clients have in counsellors. This trust will be greatly enhanced when counsellors are competent practitioners. It is not possible to be competent in all areas of counselling. Counsellors who are extremely competent when they work with potential suicide clients may or may not be competent when working with young children. Other counsellors may be very effective when counselling the elderly, but not know how to work with adolescents in a junior high school. Counsellors must practice within the bounds of their competence and must be very willing to seek supervision and consultation with other professionals if they have "doubts or uncertainties" about their work with specific clients. When counsellors are learning new specialty areas in counselling (for example, brief counselling, career counselling, or crisis counselling), they need to take education or training under supervision to ensure the future competence of their work.

It is ethical counselling practice to consult with other counselling professionals when counsellors have doubts about what to do with a client. As Article B10, "Consulting With Other Professionals," states in the next section: "Counsellors may consult with other professionally competent persons about the client."

1. How would you determine competence for counsellors in specific areas such as schools, careers, crisis or pastoral counselling?

2. If you were the director or superintendent of counselling for a large school division, would you mandate that all counsellors be involved in a certain number of hours of professional development annually? Would you specify the type of professional development?

3. How should supervision be provided for counsellors in established counselling positions?

4. What should counsellors do when their personal concerns appear to be interfering with their counselling?

5. List some "doubts and uncertainties" that may arise in your particular type of counselling?

A5 REPRESENTATION OF PROFESSIONAL QUALIFICATIONS

Counsellors claim or imply only those professional qualifications which they possess, and are responsible for correcting any known misrepresentation of their qualifications by others.

No Master's Degree (+)

A private counselling agency hired a person with a master's degree in Social Work. He claimed to have attended a particular university in England. During the time he was employed in the agency, he became the assistant to the director and was expected to become director. In anticipation of his taking this position, his credentials were checked. For some reason this had not been done when he was first hired. He had never attended the university and did not have a degree at all. He was fired from his position and a procedure was instituted so that all prospective employees had their credentials confirmed before they were offered a position.

Needed Referral (+)

Gail Bruce had counselled her client for 12 sessions with limited progress. During this time she was able to build a good rapport with her client and she felt this rapport was the strongest part of the counselling. Gail Bruce believed that the client needed treatment that was beyond the scope of her training. Although the client was given an information and consent form before counselling began, Ms. Bruce did not believe the client fully understood her qualifications. She felt she had two choices: to continue to treat her client to the limits stated on her consent form, or to refer the client to another counsellor who was known to be successful in using the treatment procedures needed by the client. Gail Bruce felt she was ethically bound to do what was best for her client and referred the client to her associate.

Cultural Differences (-)

An Aboriginal child was referred to Bob Smith for consultation. Though he had never worked with Aboriginals before, Bob was confident in his ability to help Nancy work through her problems. He learned that Nancy had lived with her family on a reserve her entire life and had recently moved to the city to live with her grandmother. He also learned of the importance of culture in Nancy's life. After 15 sessions, Bob Smith was at a loss as to what to do. He was not making any progress with Nancy using techniques he had been successful with in the past. His success in the past had been with white, middle-class clients. He found it difficult to establish a relationship with Nancy due to his limited knowledge of her culture. He consulted with his associates, but they did not feel confident to counsel Nancy. They encouraged him to remain in the relationship as he had a good success rate with his therapeutic process in the past. Pushing his doubts aside, Bob did as the associates suggested. He continued to be unsuccessful with Nancy and was later informed she was returning to her home reserve. Bob Smith was relieved to discover he would not be counselling Nancy again; but at the same time he felt he should have sought help in working with Nancy or referred her to someone with experience in working with clients other than "white, middle class."

Continuing Education (-)

Fred Campbell was licensed in 1965 during a time when there were many advancements being made in counselling. He often attended workshops and lectures to keep up-to-date on any developments in his field. During his career, Dr. Campbell was often asked to present at various workshops due to the success of his work and research. When he was approached to join a private practice in 1980, he did so due to his failing health. Over the years Fred Campbell continued with his private practice, but he failed to keep abreast of any new developments in counselling. He felt he had devoted enough of his life to theories and wanted to end his career applying those theories to clients. While discussing a recent development presented at a workshop, Fred's associates were surprised to discover he knew nothing about this information. The associates encouraged him to update his knowledge and skills, but he declined. Fred insisted he had sufficient counselling knowledge to treat his clients. The associates did not force the issue and Fred Campbell continued to remain on the counselling institute's information form; a form that informed clients that all counsellors were continuing their education in counselling.

COMMENTS AND QUESTIONS

As professional counsellors become more popular and powerful in people's lives, there is a greater need for guidelines to protect both counsellor and client. Upon meeting a new client, counsellors should be responsible for providing an information form that is mutually beneficial. The consent forms would contain all pertinent information about counsellors and their practices. It would be the counsellor's responsibility to clearly define and explain all information on the document to client satisfaction. Ideally, a professional counselling association would certify all counsellors and verify the information on the consent form to protect both the client and counsellor.

Some questions that could be considered when examining the ethics involved in professional qualifications are:

1. Should it be necessary to continue training after certification to maintain qualifications?

2. Is it realistic to list specific requirements that need to be met every two to five years in order to continue practising?

3. What rights, beyond terminating counselling, does a client have if he or she discovers that the counsellor's stated or implied qualifications are inaccurate?

4. What questions should a client ask upon entering a counselling relationship?

5. If you have seen a counsellor, did she or he have an informed consent form?

A6 RESPONSIBILITY TO COUNSELLORS AND OTHER PROFESSIONALS
Counsellors understand that ethical behaviour among themselves and with other professionals is expected at all times.

Reporting Objective Data (+)

A composite high school in the city core of a large metropolitan found that it had been experiencing increasing demands from government agencies for reports on specific cases. While some of these demands were internal, most came from outside the school system, as changing social conditions involved students in custody cases and with juvenile courts and child welfare agencies. The counselling department head recognized this growing trend early in its development and engaged the counsellors in establishing protocols to ensure that reports would consist only of factual, objective data. Advice from the CCA was sought, counsellors attended in-services in observational skills, and a record-keeping system was devised that would aid counsellors in discerning between the various degrees of objectivity, from scientific data to impressionistic comments. A protocol was established, ensuring that the more impressionistic observations were excluded from reports.

Ethical Behaviour Among Counsellors (+)

Six counsellors in private practice had decided to open one larger counselling centre. They appointed a director for their new centre. One of the first things the director did was distribute the CCA *Code of Ethics* to all the counsellors and then together with them worked out a confidentiality policy, fee structure and informed consent forms. The director then discussed ways in which their policies would be put into practice.

Beyond Counselling (-)

A counsellor in private practice is asked by parents of a 12-year-old boy to counsel him relating to severe behaviour problems that are causing him trouble both at school and in the community. The counsellor develops a liking for the boy and begins to see him outside of the counselling sessions, taking him to movies, etc. This practice continues as the counsellor finds that he enjoys spending time with the boy and the child seems to be responding well to the attention. The parents are also pleased with the arrangement as it provides some respite from the tensions in their home. The relationship continues to grow until the boy is spending weekends at the home of the counsellor, a single man.

Limited Responsibility to Counsellors (-)

The director of a counselling clinic, Evelyn Sundin, has responsibility for the many volunteer counsellors who answer the telephone crisis-line. She does provide the crisis counselling volunteers with some initial workshops, but since she has found that most of the volunteers are experienced counsellors, she sees no need to have more extensive training, nor to provide ongoing supervision to the "telephone" crisis counsellors.

COMMENTS AND QUESTIONS

Counsellors are professionals who are ethically obliged to act in the best interests of the client. Because of the nature of the counselling relationship, counsellors are in a position of power, while the clients are in a very vulnerable position. If counselling is to be an effective activity, the public must be able to trust that a counsellor will avoid situations where there is a conflict between the best interests of the client and those of the counsellor. The individual counsellor must consider how his or her actions reflect upon the profession as a whole. The trust of the public can be lost over the unethical, unprofessional or irresponsible behaviour of one member of the profession.

Counsellors should endeavour to become aware of their own needs and how these could interfere with the counselling relationship. This does not imply that counsellors must be without personal problems or areas that they need to deal with, but that counsellors should be aware of these issues and not bring them into the counselling relationship. Counsellors have responsibilities to themselves and their clients to seek help in dealing with problems that could interfere with their functioning within a counselling relationship, and to consult with colleagues or supervisors in cases where they are unsure about the extent to which their own needs are interfering with their ability to be effective in the counselling relationship. If counsellors become aware that they are using the counselling relationship to meet their own needs rather than the needs of the client, counsellors have a responsibility to refer clients to another counsellor and to terminate the relationship.

Counsellors are also ethically required to work with other counsellors in a professional manner. Speaking negatively about a colleague, not consulting with more experienced counsellors, and not working with other counsellors to obtain supervision and additional professional development, are all questionable ethical practices.

1. What are some personal needs you or others might have that could interfere with your being an effective counsellor?

2. What political considerations might occur that would pressure the counsellor to tell less than "the truth, the whole truth, and nothing but the truth" in reporting counselling results to other professionals?

3. What biases, institutional and personal, might come into play to limit the counsellor's ability to work effectively with other counsellors?

4. Should counsellors deliberately keep somewhat distant from clients to avoid any possibility of too much intimacy in the counselling relationship?

5. What responsibilities do you have to other non-counselling professionals whom you work with?

A7 UNETHICAL BEHAVIOUR BY OTHER COUNSELLORS

Counsellors have an obligation when they have serious doubts as to the ethical behaviour of another counsellor to seek an informal resolution with the counsellor, when feasible and appropriate. When an informal resolution is not appropriate or feasible, or is unsuccessful, counsellors report their concerns to the CCA Ethics Committee.

Reporting of Abuse (+)

After an appointment with a school counsellor, a 15-year-old male student sought an interview with another counsellor who discovered during the conversation, through student disclosure and physical evidence, that the student had been physically abused by his guardian the previous evening. The student volunteered further information that indicated that he was no longer permitted to enter his home and that no action had been taken by the school counsellor to secure his safety and well-being. Following guidelines for legal responsibilities and school division protocol, the teacher contacted Child and Family Services to report suspected abuse, informed the principal of this action, then sought out the school counsellor to advise him of the actions that had been taken. Once approached on the issue of abuse, the counsellor and teacher discussed the school policy regarding ethical responsibilities and the importance of reporting information to proper authorities.

Mentorship Program (+)

A high school principal acknowledged that some of the new counsellors he had recently hired were having difficulty integrating the ethical articles set forth by the CCA, the school's policies and procedures, and the provincial laws. In order to address this issue, he implemented a mentorship program where-

by experienced counsellors were paired with novice counsellors. The ultimate goal of the program was to promote and encourage ethical behaviour within the classroom and within the school. Through modelling, supervision and consultation, the experienced and exemplary counsellors guided the novice counsellors to resolve ethical dilemmas as they occurred naturally.

Conduct of an Associate (-)

During a routine counselling session prior to graduation, a distraught Grade 12 student confided to her counsellor that one of her teachers had abruptly ended an intimate relationship with her. She indicated that her life was "falling apart" and she didn't know what she was going to do after graduation. The student requested that no action be taken since she would be graduating in two weeks and she did not want to harm anyone's reputation. The counsellor consoled the student, and the request by the student for no further action was granted.

Dating a Student (-)

A teacher is secretly dating one of his Grade 12 students. The school counsellor, who happens to be one of the teacher's good friends, sees them out together once and dismisses it. As the school year continues, the counsellor sees them together on numerous other occasions. The counsellor realizes the teacher-student relationship of dating is inappropriate. However, he chooses to remain silent and ignore the matter for fear of jeopardizing the teacher's job and losing a good friend.

COMMENTS AND QUESTIONS

This ethical article is a mandate to guide counsellors in their everyday conduct and in the resolution of ethical dilemmas. It assists in the evaluation of questionable behaviour by colleagues. The basic principles underlying this article are the respect for the dignity and integrity of persons, responsible caring in counselling relationships, and responsibility to society.

Doubts should be raised as to the ethical or non-ethical behaviour of professional associates, both members of CCA, and non-members, in the following situations:

a) where the welfare of a student is at risk,

b) where the reputation of a school could be compromised, and

c) where confidence in the counselling profession could be diminished.

Questions to consider, in reference to this ethical article and the cases presented, include:

1. This ethical article refers to counsellor obligations when other counsellors are not acting ethically. Do the same articles apply to colleagues such as teachers? What would you do in the third case entitled "Conduct of an Associate"?

2. What are some common feelings and/or thoughts experienced when a counsellor has serious doubts about the ethical behaviour of a colleague?

3. Has the CCA set up steps to follow when unethical behaviour is suspected? If so, what is the process?

4. What is the protocol for reporting known unethical behaviour of a colleague?

5. What are the likely short-term, ongoing, and long-term risks and benefits (i.e. consequences) of each course of action (e.g. reporting, not reporting) on the individual(s)/group(s) involved or likely to be affected (e.g. student, school, colleague, profession, society, self)?

A8 SEXUAL HARASSMENT

Counsellors do not condone or engage in sexual harassment, which is defined as deliberate or repeated verbal or written comments, gestures, or physical contacts of a sexual nature.

Not Condoning (+)

At a junior high school, the guidance counsellor has had a number of female students coming to see him regarding a certain science teacher on staff. This staff member has always taken a great interest in promoting science among girls and encouraging them to become actively involved in their own science education. To this end, he has set up a special science club for the girls in his classes, and has made participating in the club a requirement for extra marks. He has club meetings after school and has each of the girls in the club working on a project. Recently, he has suggested that some of the girls see him on an individual basis for extra help with their projects. He has given the girls various reasons; for example, one girl was told she had exceptional abilities and he wanted to help her develop these talents. Another was told she was not going to pass science unless she came for extra help. All of the girls report that in these individual meetings, Mr. X becomes overly friendly, sitting very close to the students, sometimes touching their arms or putting an arm around their shoulders. The girls are feeling very uncomfortable about this, but nothing overtly improper in nature has occurred. The guidance counsellor decides to have a talk with Mr. X to inform him of the concerns of the female students, and to let him know that his behaviour could be construed as sexual harassment. The counsellor suggests to Mr. X that he should probably cease insisting on having private meetings with female students after school hours, and if a student requires help, he should have the meeting in a more public forum, such as the office or library, rather than in his classroom. The counsellor also informs Mr. X that she will continue to check in with the students in question, to ensure they are feeling more comfortable in Mr. X's science classes. Privately, she makes a notation of the date and nature of the conversation, as well as plans to check with the students periodically to ensure that there are no further incidents. She decides that should she have any more complaints, she will make a report to her department head and the administration.

Education (+)

The guidance counsellor at a certain high school has become increasingly concerned about the issue of sexual harassment, and knows that while many staff members are aware of the issue, most are not knowledgeable about the type of behaviours that could be construed as sexual harassment. He decides to approach the administration of the school about holding a workshop at the upcoming school in-service. He plans to invite speakers to explain to staff members what types of actions or comments constitute sexual harassment, how to respond to student concerns regarding the behaviour of fellow students or teachers, and how to handle situations in which they (teachers) feel they are the victims of harassment, by both students or other people with whom they may come in contact. His rationale for suggesting the in-service presentation is that once teachers have clear guidelines for proper behaviour, they will be less likely to find themselves in a compromising position, and hopefully, they will pass their new knowledge on to their students, who in turn will become more aware of behaviours that may make others uncomfortable.

Condoning (-)

In a junior high school, the physical education teacher, who also happens to be the guidance counsellor, notices a problem developing in one of the co-educational gym classes. One of the students, a boy named Justin, has been harassing some of the more physically mature girls during the 10-minute run at the start of every class. He began by staring overtly at their chests as they ran by him, and has now progressed to making suggestive comments. The girls are clearly uncomfortable with the attention, and have become increasingly resistant to doing the run. The gym teacher feels that Justin is just being a typical adolescent boy, preoccupied with his sexuality, and this will pass in time. On the other hand, he feels the girls are over-reacting to a situation that they will have to get used to anyway, since "boys will be boys," and he lets the girls know that he will impose penalties if they refuse to participate in the 10-minute run at the beginning of the class.

Student Discomfort (-)

The guidance counsellor in a high school has been asked to teach the new "Life Skills" course to all Grade 10 students. The course includes a unit on human sexuality, and is designed to be taught in co-educational classes. The counsellor believes students get the most out of classes if they are made to feel as though they are active participants, and follows this philosophy in teaching the human sexuality component of the course. He begins the unit by having each student fill out an explicit questionnaire on his/her sexual maturation, asking such questions as when the girls first started menstruation, and when the boys first noticed they were maturing sexually. He then uses the results to compare students to one another in a discussion of how maturation occurs at different times for different members of the class. Even when he notices some of the students becoming embarrassed at having such personal details revealed to the class, he persists in making reference to the questionnaire results at various times during the ensuing weeks. He continues to make sexual comments about specific students in spite of the fact that students are openly uncomfortable with his sexual descriptions.

COMMENTS AND QUESTIONS

Harassment has been defined as disturbing or troubling another person by persistent, repeated attacks. This article is clear; members do not condone or engage in sexual harassment. Members of a professional counselling association are expected to do something about colleagues involved in sexual harassment. This action may consist of confronting a colleague on her or his sexual harassment, and it may mean reporting continued harassment to appropriate authorities.

1. What is your definition of sexual harassment? Give some specific examples.

2. What resources or assistance is available for members who must deal with sexual harassment?

3. What are some of the risks involved in reporting a case of sexual harassment? What are the benefits?

4. If a colleague appears to be sexually harassing another person, would you confront the individual or would you report the individual? Comment.

5. What is the counsellor's responsibility if he or she senses sexual attraction on the part of the client?

A9 SENSITIVITY TO DIVERSITY
Counsellors strive to understand and respect the diversity of their clients, including differences related to age, ethnicity, culture, gender, disability, religion, sexual orientation and socio-economic status.

Counselling Services (+)

At a divisional meeting of administrators and school counsellors, the counsellors submitted to the administration that their schools must make every attempt to provide students with as many options as possible. The submission included recommendations regarding the equitable hiring of qualified male and female counsellors, providing each student the opportunity to seek counsel from someone they felt comfortable approaching, regardless of their gender. It was also suggested that the division expand the current facilities to allow for the increase in personnel and the appropriate confidential space required by each counsellor.

Sexual Stereotyping (+)

During a Grade 8 team meeting, teachers, administrators and counsellors examined the results of the eighth grade on the Canadian Tests of Basic Skills. Comments were made about many of the female students' low scores in Mathematics. One male teacher said these results were not unexpected and that "girls never do as well as boys in mathematics" since they don't understand mathematics. Several teachers agreed. The counsellor felt this was unfair to the girls and talked to the group about their attitudes towards females and mathematics.

Stereotypical Jobs (-)

When considering post-secondary education, a graduating female student made an appointment with the guidance office to discuss the options available to her. She was referred to the female counsellor. While waiting in her office, the student noted that most of the literature that the counsellor had displayed was in the areas of education, nursing, and secretarial studies, all of which could be labelled as traditional female employment. When she posed the question about alternative career choices in other fields, the counsellor responded with skepticism about non-traditional jobs for females and stated that she was not familiar with the requirements for fields such as engineering or medicine, nor would she advocate the pursuit in such a career for any young woman.

Discriminatory Counselling (-)

During a rash of break-and-entry crimes in a small town, local authorities suggested that the high school provide guidance and counselling for the student body to discuss the problem as well as outline the possible outcomes of such behaviours. The school agreed and the counsellor proceeded to organize group counselling sessions for the Aboriginal students within the student population. The session was announced over the school's public address system as being mandatory for all Aboriginal students, but no provisions were made for counselling other students because it was assumed that they would probably not be involved in the break-and-entry crimes.

COMMENTS AND QUESTIONS

With the global community gradually becoming a reality, the importance of multiculturalism in counselling is increasingly important. The Canadian Charter of Rights and Freedoms does not allow for discrimination and guards the rights of all Canadians. Racial and sexual stereotypes and discrimination must not be allowed. Counsellors can not be "culturally encapsulated" and rely on stereotypes when working with culturally diverse clients.

1. What efforts are being made in your counselling centre to promote non-traditional work for women and men?

2. Is it the responsibility of counsellors to educate others regarding sexual and racial stereotyping?

3. What are the more subtle forms of racial and sexual stereotyping that counsellors must guard against?

4. Should re-education or education of counsellors on multicultural issues be mandatory?

5. Is the provision of specific ethnic or cultural counsellors for specific ethnic or cultural groups a form of discrimination?

A10 EXTENSION OF ETHICAL RESPONSIBILITIES

Counselling services and products provided by counsellors through classroom instruction, public lectures, demonstrations, publications, radio and television programs, computer technology and other media must meet the appropriate ethical standards of this *Code of Ethics*.

Boundaries of Competence (+)

A school counsellor is a guest on a radio program and receives a call from a listener asking advice about her troubled marriage. The counsellor has very little experience in marriage counselling and explains that he is not qualified to comment, but refers the caller to an appropriate agency for information and help.

Professional Qualifications (+)

A family counsellor was prepared to speak at a public lecture. The counsellor was introduced by the lecture co-ordinator, who gave a short personal history of the counsellor and listed the counsellor's qualifications and experience. The counsellor realized that her educational qualifications had been incorrectly stated and corrected the error for the audience before starting her lecture.

Post-Secondary Career and Educational Information (-)

The post-secondary career and educational information in one high school was provided by the counselling department. This information was placed on display and was available for viewing by the entire school body. Unfortunately, the information available only applied to a small percentage of students, those wishing to attend university. The information did not apply to vocational training or job training for those students not aspiring to university. Also, the counselling offered about this information was only avail-able to those meeting requirements for university.

Psychodrama (-)

A counsellor-educator has been invited to demonstrate several new psychodrama techniques in front of a large audience. She asks for volunteers on whom to demonstrate the techniques. The demonstration begins without any arrangements having been made regarding confidentiality, audience involvement or follow-up.

COMMENTS AND QUESTIONS

Counsellors must make every attempt to insure that media materials:

a) are appropriate for the reading level and maturity of the audience,

b) are accurate, unbiased, and gender and culture fair,

c) are distributed with appropriate explanations, and

d) are giving a fair representation of all sides of an issue.

1. What range of materials should be available in a high school, junior high school, and elementary school counselling office regarding sensitive life issues, future education options, and future job opportunities?

2. How can educators and counsellors increase the availability of media materials that are more culturally aware?

3. What factors would you need to consider when using media materials to discuss a cultural issue?

4. What precautions should be taken to make sure that all media materials meet ethical standards?

5. What are some of the possible ethical concerns regarding counselling and the internet?

❖ ❖ ❖ ❖ ❖ ❖ ❖ ❖ ❖ ❖

Essays on Professional Responsibility

Ethics and the Professional Responsibilities of Counsellors

Margaret S. Schneider

We are taught from an early age how to make ethical decisions. We learn this in a variety of ways: through explicit instruction in the home, at school, or through religious doctrine; by observing ethical role models; by noting the repercussions when others make unethical decisions and; by experiencing the consequences of our own decisions. In other words, long before we become engaged in our professional work as counsellors we have been well-versed in how to make decisions concerning ethical matters. Why then do counsellors need a code of ethics?

Counselling shares a number of inherent characteristics with all professions. Counsellors, a) provide a service to individuals and society; b) have specialized knowledge and skills that develop during a long process of education, practice, and continuing education; c) constitute a community that determines entry requirements, training, socialization of new members, and regulates and monitors practices; d) are accountable to their own professional community and to society at large, and; e) have a code of ethics (Sinclair, Simon, & Pettifor, 1996).

By virtue of these special characteristics, professionals are expected to be trustworthy, competent and to cause no harm. Ironically it is precisely because of counsellors' specialized knowledge and status as well as the nature of the counsellor/client relationship, that they have the potential to harm, as well as to assist their clients. While the life-long process of ethical decision making affords a solid foundation for counsellors, the unique quality of the counsellor/client relationship requires special standards and sensitivities.

Boundary issues provide a useful illustration. The nature of the counselling relationship draws the client and practitioner together into what may sometimes feel, to either or both, like a friendship or, in extreme cases, a love relationship. Counsellors who leave these feelings unexamined or decide to act upon them risk harming the client. Yet, our early development as ethical decision makers does not usually provide us with the awareness and the analytical tools that are necessary to recognize these types of boundary issues and to make consistently ethical choices when they arise. To do this requires a special awareness. It is not coincidental that the CCA *Code of Ethics* deals with boundary violations in three separate articles (A8, B8, B12).

In short, as professionals, counsellors must have unique mechanisms that ensure the protection of the people with whom they work because of the distinctive nature of the profession. Those mechanisms are founded on a system of principles which delineate right and wrong acts and activities, that is, a code of ethics (Keith-Spiegel & Koocher, 1985). Codes of ethics provide a guide to ethical behaviour. They sensitize and alert professionals to ethical issues and dilemmas (Keith-Spiegel & Koocher, 1985). They "clarify the rights and responsibilities of mental health professionals; provide standards of conduct, common values, attitudes, and principles for using the knowledge and skills of the profession. ...Codes of ethics are ...essentially a social contract" (Larsen & Rave, 1995, p.1).

Code of Ethics in Context

A code of ethics is one of several methods by which professionals are regulated. The other sources of regulation include statutory and case law, standards of practice and guidelines, and peer influence. It is the obligation of professionals to be aware of these and to understand how they relate to ethical practice.

Statutory Laws

There are a number of federal laws in Canada as well as provincial laws (that vary from province to province) that have a potential impact on counselling practice. In some instances the law and the ethical principles are parallel. For example, there are both laws and ethical principles (A8) prohibiting sexual harassment. In other cases the law is an elaboration of principles that are found in the CCA *Code of Ethics.* For example, confidentiality, an ethical imperative for practitioners, is addressed in various pieces of legislation; for example, in the Young Offenders Act (1985), which is federal, and in sections of provincial legislation related to education, mental health, child welfare, and social services. Although the specifics vary depending upon the wording of the legislation (and can vary from province to province) these laws regulate, among other things, the instances in which personal information about a client can be divulged, where records should be kept, and who has access to a client's records. Laws pertaining to the duty to report cases of child abuse and neglect, even if it means breaching confidentiality, are particularly significant.

In other instances, the law establishes somewhat arbitrary rules that affect counselling practice. The legal age of consent is a prime example. Whether the age of consent for a teenager should be 12, 14, 16 or 18 is not an ethical issue per se. The ethical issue is to ensure that consent is meaningful; that is, voluntary and informed. In addition to behaving ethically, however, it is also incumbent upon the counsellor to uphold the law (A2). This poses problems when the law is contradictory.

For example, in Ontario, the age at which teenagers may seek treatment, mental health services or counselling without the knowledge or permission of their parents varies depending upon the setting and the legislation which governs the setting — be it the Children's Aid Society, a mental health centre, or a school system. Professionals who work in multidisciplinary teams, or who work in multiple settings may find themselves confused or in conflict with colleagues as to whether an adolescent's parents must be informed if the child seeks assistance. Again, the ethical issue here is not age, per se. The ethical issue is that the counsellor has a professional responsibility to obtain informed consent from clients in addition to respecting the law (A2). The ethical challenge for the counsellor in this situation is the obligation to resolve the confusion or conflict in a way that a) protects clients b) is respectful of colleagues, and c) upholds the law.

Case Law

Case law is a body of precedents that arise from civil lawsuits. The most notable example in the area of counselling is *Tarasoff v. Regents of the University of California (1976)*. This case established the principle that a counsellor has the duty to warn third parties about dangers posed by clients even when it means breaching confidentiality. Following *Tarasoff*, codes of ethics for helping professionals routinely began to include a duty to warn (B3).

Tarasoff is a good example of the way in which case law can assist in reducing ethical dilemmas. Prior to the establishment of the duty to warn, practitioners who feared that their client might harm someone, could find themselves in a no-win situation. *Tarasoff* set the precedent, which would allow them to warn the party in danger. However, the decision was not universally welcomed (Keith-Spiegel & Koocher, 1985). Some believed that it legitimized breaches of confidentiality, while others have noted the difficulty in assessing dangerousness (Josefowitz, 1997). Furthermore, the impact of *Tarasoff* in Canadian courts has not yet been tested (Josefowitz, 1997).

Thus, rather than giving closure to the issue, *Tarasoff* created a ripple effect. On the one hand it serves to protect the public, while on the other hand necessitates being prepared to assess dangerousness if the need should arise, and adding caveats when confidentiality is discussed with clients. The far-reaching impact of *Tarasoff* illustrates the way in which case law effects ethical practice and also, the way in which various aspects of ethical practice are inter-related.

Guidelines and Standards of Practice

These types of documents serve to operationalize certain ethical principles. For example, Article A9 directs counsellors to strive for sensitivity to diversity. Yet, those counsellors who are unfamiliar with the implications of differences related to age, ethnicity, disability, and so on may need some guidance as to what this might entail. Practitioners can seek formal training in these areas, but might also turn to published guidelines which sensitize service providers to particular issues. Examples of these include the American Psychological Association's *Guidelines for Psychotherapy With Lesbian, Gay and Bisexual Clients* (APA, 2000) and its *Guidelines for Providers of Psychological Services to Ethnic, Linguistic and Culturally Diverse Populations* (APA, 1990). These types of guidelines describe the ideal to which practitioners should aspire.

Professional organizations often develop standards that prescribe appropriate service delivery. They cover topics such as advertising of services, fee schedules, adequate storage of records, appropriate use of fax machines and e-mail to transmit confidential information, and so on. On one level, these activities comprise the nuts and bolts of operating a counselling practice; however, they also have the potential to involve ethical issues. For example, fee schedules may seem like a straight-forward issue and it usually is, especially when clients have adequate financial resources. What about clients who cannot afford counselling, but who have a marketable skill. Is it appropriate to barter with these clients? Alternately, would it be all right to let clients run up a bill until they are able to pay for the counsellor's services? While these alternatives may seem generous and benevolent at first glance, they have the potential to create resentment between the client and counsellor, thereby undermining the therapeutic relationship and doing harm to the client.

Guidelines and standards regulate specific activities by prescribing as well as setting limitations upon specific behaviours, and by modelling ideal practices. They assist counsellors in maintaining a high standard of professional competence (A1), respecting the rights of others (A2) and avoiding conflicts that might undermine the integrity of the counsellor/client relationship (B1). Guidelines and standards not only protect the client, but also enhance the credibility of the profession as a whole.

Peer Influence

In addition to a variety of influences that are codified in print, professionals also rely on each other for guidance. Colleagues can provide consultation on an ad hoc basis when ethical dilemmas arise. Some counsellors, particularly those in private practice, form peer supervision groups in which they regularly review tricky cases together. In addition, the standards of practice within a professional community constitute a baseline or frame of reference for determining whether a particular procedure is ethical or not (Crowhurst & Dobson, 1993). Professional peers provide an important touchstone in keeping each other aware of ethical issues.

Balancing Professional Obligations

Ideally, the various influences on the ethical obligations of a professional are consistent and even enhance each other. This is not always the case, however. Situations do arise in which an action may be unethical but legal, or vice versa (Cottone & Tarvydas, 1998). For example, violating professional guidelines for advertising services is unethi-

cal but rarely illegal. Withholding a client's confidential records when they are subpoenaed may be ethical but definitely illegal.

Some existing professional codes of ethics prioritize practitioners' responsibilities when they are faced with a choice between upholding an ethical imperative as opposed to upholding the law. Other codes either leave the decision to the practitioners' judgement or are simply silent on the issue (Cottone & Tarvydas, 1998). Furthermore, there may be times when the ethical codes, themselves, seem to contradict each other. For example, a practitioner might begin counselling with a client whose issues seem well within the counsellor's professional competence; but as counselling progresses, issues may arise that are well beyond the counsellor's expertise. Should the counsellor jeopardize the client's well-being by severing an established positive relationship in order to avoid practicing in an unfamiliar area, or should the counsellor maintain the integrity of the relationship by continuing to work with the client in spite of a lack of expertise?

There are relatively satisfactory solutions to these types of dilemmas, although they require some thought and may not be immediately obvious. The point here is that even when practitioners abide scrupulously by their code of ethics there is no guarantee that they will be able to avoid dilemmas that have the potential to adversely affect themselves or their client.

Most ethical codes represent a balance between prescriptions and aspirations (Sinclair, 1996); that is, they not only outline activities that are clearly mandatory or clearly prohibited, but also propose goals toward which to strive. The aspirational nature of ethics codes recognize that it may not be possible to adhere completely to all principles all the time, because of human limitations, because of individual differences in the interpretation of the principles, and because of possible conflicts between principles.

The CCA *Code of Ethics* strikes such a balance. While some articles clearly prescribe specific behaviour (for example, A8: "Counsellors do not condone or engage in sexual harassment...") there are others that outline goals to which counsellors are urged to aspire (for example, A9: "Counsellors strive to understand and respect the diversity of their clients...").

Summary

Practitioners must maintain an awareness of the various influences on their practice at any given time, keep up with the changes in law, standards and codes, and establish an ongoing system of support and dialogue among colleagues. Viewing ethical decision making as an ongoing process ensures that the practitioner will be prepared to make difficult decisions in a timely and responsible way.

Whom Do Codes of Ethics Protect?

First and foremost, codes of ethics address the protection of the client, but they also serve to protect the welfare of other professionals, employers, employees, students, supervisors and employing agencies (Keith-Spiegel & Koocher, 1985). Each of these groups benefit when counsellors behave ethically and each can be harmed when counsellors behave unethically.

Why do clients, in particular, need the special protection of a code of ethics? Why are the laws, which protect consumers from an unscrupulous salesperson, insufficient to protect clients who use the services of a counsellor? The need is a function of the power differential that often characterizes the client/counsellor relationship. That power differential arises from two aspects of the client/ counsellor relationship. First, most clients do not have the specialized skill and training to evaluate whether or not the counsellor is competent and behaving in the clients' best interests. Second, clients often seek counselling at a time when they are troubled, confused, depressed, and, in short, vulnerable. Thus, they may be particularly unable to

evaluate the counsellor's performance, or confront the counsellor if they have doubts. Codes of ethics ameliorate the power differential by articulating the rights of the client and the responsibilities of the practitioner (Larsen & Rave, 1995). Similarly, they also serve to relieve the power differential between counsellors and their students and/or employees.

There are other individuals, aside from the client, who depend upon the counsellors' fair and competent performance. The reputations of colleagues, employers, and supervisors can be jeopardized when a counsellor behaves unethically. In some cases these people may be held morally responsible and legally liable if the counsellor's unethical behaviour leads to harm. In addition, the credibility of the entire profession is undermined when individual members are found to behave unethically. On a larger scale, codes of ethics protect the general public who are not clients per se, but make use of a counsellor's expertise through classroom instruction, public lectures, the media including publications, radio and television programs, and the Internet. Article A10 recognizes this protection.

Lastly, codes of ethics serve to protect counsellors themselves. Codes alert professionals to ethical issues, highlight particularly problematic areas, and provide a benchmark for determining whether or not a professional is behaving ethically. In an increasingly litigious society, helping professionals are increasing concerned about how to avoid complaints and law suits (Sinclair, Simon & Pettifor, 1996). Being able to demonstrate that one's practice is consistent with a clearly articulated code of ethics is an important safeguard (Crowhurst & Dobson, 1993).

When Ethical Dilemmas Arise

Maintaining an ethical counselling practice is routine much of the time. Competent counsellors are aware of their rights and obligations and the rights of their clients, and incorporate this knowledge into their usual practice. But in spite of the best of intentions ethical dilemmas do arise. What constitutes a dilemma?

First, not all situations in which ethical codes are breached are dilemmas. They may simply be the result of malice, greed, expediency, or self-serving motives. There is no dilemma when counsellors make sexual advances toward a client, administer unnecessary psychometric tests in order to significantly increase the fee for service, or take work that is outside their area of expertise because they need the business. These are clear instances of misconduct.

In contrast, a dilemma is a situation in which, "[a]ny combination of one's values, ethical codes, the law, one's personal or professional loyalties, clinical knowledge or personal feelings ...come into conflict in a particular situation" (Hill, Glaser, & Harden, 1995, p. 18). It is "a problem for which no course of action seems satisfactory....the dilemma exists because there are good, but contradictory ethical reasons to take conflicting and incompatible courses of action" (Kitchener, 1984, p. 43). A dilemma may also arise when a code of ethics does not clearly address a particular conflict (Hill, Glaser & Harden, 1995).

The case entitled "Theft Disclosure" is a good example of a dilemma. Here the counsellor is caught between his commitment to maintaining confidentiality and his responsibility to his agency that demands he report any criminal activity. In this case the dilemma is resolved when the client agrees to turn himself in. But what if he hadn't? How might the counsellor have reconciled two competing imperatives in a satisfactory manner?

Dilemmas occur for a variety of reasons. On the one hand, there are instances when there are no relevant articles and/or laws directly governing the situation; on the other hand, however, sometimes the relevant codes, laws, articles, etc. contradict each other. Dilemmas may also arise if the magnitude of the problem is underestimated or consequences are unforeseen or unanticipated due to inexperience or lack of knowledge. Some situations are simply unpredictable or unavoidable (Keith-Spiegel & Koocher, 1985).

Practitioners' responses to dilemmas will also vary depending upon individual biases, attitudes, beliefs, experiences, definitions of and commitments to professional obligations and responsibilities, and the degree to which the situation is perceived to be serious (Keith-Spiegel & Koocher, 1985). There are no easy answers to dilemmas, and people who, in good faith, follow all the appropriate procedures in attempting to arrive at a reasonable solution, may still disagree as to how to resolve the dilemma satisfactorily. That is not to say, however, that counsellors are absolved once they have used due process to arrive at a solution. Counsellors must take responsibility for the outcome of ethical dilemmas that arise in their practice.

The best strategy for dealing with dilemmas is to avoid them in the first place. Practitioners who are familiar with the code of ethics, standards of professional conduct, the relevant laws as well as the policies and procedures within their workplace, are well on their way to avoiding dilemmas by anticipating them (Evans, 1997). For example, a clear statement to all clients about the limits of confidentiality as part of a practitioner's informed consent procedure would have done much to avert the dilemma described in "Theft Disclosure." When dilemmas are unavoidable, extensive consultation with colleagues is one of the best ways to arrive at a resolution.

Planning Ahead

Maintaining an ethical counselling practice is an ongoing process that takes place in the context of a complex system of regulatory mechanisms. Therefore, ethical practice requires planning ahead. It means anticipating ethical issues and putting procedures in place to avoid them, or to deal with them if and when they occur. DePauw (1986) suggests that counsellors view their practice chronologically, in order to identify specific issues that might arise at specific stages of service delivery.

The stages that DePauw (1986) identifies include: (a) *initiation phase issues* such as advertising and assuring adequacy of skills; (b) *ongoing counselling issues* such as confidentiality, consultation and record keeping; c) *crisis concerns* such as threats to self and others, and; d) *termination issues*. This systematic approach can be used to identify potential problems that are common to all counselling practices, as well as those which might be unique to a particular type of practice. For example, counsellors who work with terminally ill people face end-of-life issues, which pose unusual ethical challenges.

A thorough knowledge of the code of ethics is only one element in practicing ethically. Maintaining an ethical practice is an organic process that requires planning, anticipating difficulties, keeping current with new developments, and having a support system of colleagues in place for ongoing consultation. This is the best way to ensure protection of clients, colleagues, the public, and oneself.

References

American Psychological Association (1990). *APA guidelines for providers of psychological services to ethnic, linguistic and culturally diverse populations* [On-line]. Available: http://www.apa.org/pi/oema/guide.html.

American Psychological Association (2000). *Guidelines for psychotherapy with lesbian, gay and bisexual clients.* [On-line]. Available: http://www.apa.org/pi/lgbc/guidelines.html.

Cottone, R.R. & Tarvydas, V.M. (1998). *Ethical and professional issues in counselling.* Columbus, Ohio: Merrill.

Crowhurst, B. & Dobson, K. (1993). Informed consent: Legal issues and applications to clinical practice. *Canadian Psychology, 34*(3), 329-346.

DePauw, M.E. (1986). Avoiding ethical violations: A timeline perspective for individual counseling. *Journal of Counseling and Development, 64*(5), 303-305.

Evans, D.R. (1997). Law, standards, and ethics in the practice of psychology. In D.R. Evans (Ed.), *The law, standards of practice, and ethics in the practice of psychology.* Toronto: Emond Montgomery.

Hill, M., Glaser, K., & Harden, J. (1995). A feminist model for ethical decision making. In E.J. Rave & C.C. Larsen (Eds.) *Ethical decision making in therapy: Feminist perspectives.* New York: Guilford.

Josefowitz, N. (1997). Confidentiality. In D.R. Evans (Ed.), *The law, standards of practice, and ethics in the practice of psychology.* Toronto: Emond Montgomery.

Keith-Speigel, P., & Koocher, G.P. (1985). *Ethics in psychology: Professional standards and cases.* Toronto: McGraw-Hill.

Kitchener, K.S. (1984). Intuition, critical evaluation and ethical principles: The foundation for ethical decisions in counseling psychology. *Counselling Psychologist, 12* 43-55.

Larsen, C.C., & Rave, E.J. (1995). Context of feminist therapy ethics. In E.J. Rave & C.C. Larsen (Eds.) *Ethical decision making in therapy: Feminist perspectives.* New York: Guilford.

Sinclair, C. (1996). A comparison of codes of professional conduct and ethics. In L.J. Bass, et al. (Eds), *Professional conduct and discipline in psychology.* Washington: American Psychological Association.

Sinclair, C., Simon, N.P., & Pettifor, J.L. (1996). The history of ethical codes and licensure. In L.J. Bass, et al. (Eds), *Professional conduct and discipline in psychology.* Washington: American Psychological Association.

Establishing and Maintaining Competence: An Ethical Responsibility

Walt Pawlovich

Competence and the Rights of the Client

Professional competence has been defined as the provision of quality services through the application of professional knowledge, skills and abilities (Overholser & Fine, 1990). Incompetence occurs when professionals continue to provide services that they are not fully capable of performing (Keith-Spiegel & Koocher, 1985). Failure to recognize one's fallibilities and limitations as a professional and as a person are also elements of incompetence (Van Hoose & Kottler, 1977). Therefore, as a basic ethical principle, competence involves the expectation for therapists to recognize their own personal and professional limitations. Ethical counsellors should not employ diagnostic or treatment procedures that are beyond the scope of their training, nor should they accept clients whose personal functioning is seriously impaired, unless they are qualified to work with those clients.

The duty to be competent and maintain competence is absolute because clients have a right to receive services of consistently high quality, and to have that service provided by an individual who is competent (Rosenbaum, 1982). Incompetent counsellors have actually harmed their individual or group clients, largely because of the trust given to them as "experts" (Thompson, 1990). The duty to be competent entails the duty to respect the rights of individual clients and in part to understand what constitutes morally legitimate decisions (Carroll, Schneider & Wesley, 1985).

Elements of Competence

In order to establish competence, it is first necessary to recognize and understand what is required in all areas of counselling, in order to ensure professional competence to the fullest extent. Competence should be established not only in the domains of skill and knowledge acquisition, but in areas involving professional and personal judgment. Norman (1985) proposed a categorization scheme describing five domains of professional activities deemed essential to competent performance: knowledge and understanding, clinical skills, technical skills, problem solving and clinical judgment, and personal attributes.

Counsellors are expected to attain and maintain adequate levels of knowledge regarding the scientific basis of the services they provide (Overholser & Fine, 1990). It is essential not only to attain adequate knowledge, but to maintain it over time. Therefore, it is important that counsellors know, understand, and use the published literature that pertains to a particular diagnosis and its treatment (Sheldon-Wildgen, 1982). Professional knowledge also includes the ability to recognize the limitations of one's knowledge and expertise. Thus, it is vital for counsellors to recognize and limit their practice to areas for which they have sufficient expertise to perform in a competent manner. It is also the responsibility of the therapist, in collaboration with the client, to evaluate the progress that has been made, and if deemed inadequate, to change modalities or terminate therapy and refer the client elsewhere (Keith-Spiegel & Koocher, 1985).

Counsellors and therapists also need to have general clinical skills and the basic interviewing skills necessary to assess and treat clients. In psychotherapy and counselling, adequate levels of empathy, warmth, and genuineness are often considered important for positive therapeutic outcomes regardless of theoretical orientation. Other relevant skills include composure and sensitivity, the ability to communicate with a variety of clients, and the ability to maintain an appropriate professional relationship with clients (Overholser & Fine, 1990).

The technical skills necessary for competence include the ability to use special procedures or techniques in the clinical setting. This may involve special assessment procedures or treatment techniques specific to a particular treatment orientation. Specialized techniques require specialized training in the theory and application of such interventions. Competent counsellors have the ability to determine what techniques are most appropriate for the client's particular problem (Carroll et al., 1985). This involves being able to understand what counts as improvement and to change behaviour in light of this understanding.

Competence also pertains to problem solving and clinical judgment, which refers both to the ability to apply knowledge and clinical skills to assess or treat a particular client, and the ability to make reasonable judgments in resolving the dilemmas that arise in therapy (Carroll et al., 1985). Responding well to different situations requires knowledge of relevant legal and ethical guidelines, training in how to manage them, and judgment regarding effective ways to respond.

The interpersonal attributes of the professional are essential to his or her competence. Professional demeanour, including one's appearance and attire as well as a calm and confident manner, plays an important role in therapy. As well, personality characteristics, social skills, and emotional problems may affect the ability to function in a professional capacity. The manner in which individuals take care of themselves, and the lifestyles they maintain, directly influence not only their personal happiness but their productivity as well (Thoreson, Miller & Krauskopf, 1989). Recent concern over the incidence of impaired practitioners has suggested

that personal and emotional problems may interfere with effective professional functioning. Although it is not a sign of incompetence for professionals to suffer emotional problems, it is considered incompetence if they continue to provide services when unable to function adequately (Overholser & Fine, 1990).

Does Licensing Ensure Competence?

A commonly accepted requirement of competence emphasizes the training of counsellors or therapists. However, it must first be specified as to what counts as relevant training. Although typically assumed otherwise, academic degrees, credentials, and courses or workshops completed are not necessarily good indicators of competence (Bervan & Scofield, 1987). Professionals who point to degrees and certificates as "proof" of their competence may only be deluding themselves. Licence and certification are not necessarily useful as criteria of competence. Licences mainly assure the public that the licencees have completed minimum educational programs, have had a certain number of hours of supervised training, and have gone through some type of evaluation and screening (Corey, 1991). Licences imply that their holders have had a certain level of professional training, but they do not assure the public that practitioners can effectively and competently do what their licences permit them to do (Corey, Corey, & Callanan, 1979). Most licences are generic in nature; they usually do not specify the types of clients or problems the licencee is competent to work with, nor do they specify the techniques that a practitioner is competent to use. A licence permits the professional to provide a wide range of services, yet it is the professional's responsibility to determine which services he or she is actually competent to provide.

Alternative Methods to Establish and Maintain Competence

Counsellor competence could and should be maintained through both an external and internal frame of reference. Licensing is an external frame of reference necessary to ensure that the professional has met the required minimum standards of the profession. From an external perspective, it is important for counsellors to realize that processes such as reviewing, evaluating, examining, and screening, will continue to be handled by external forces such as licensing boards and professional groups (Gross & Robinson, 1987).

Counselling education programs are also needed as an external verification of competence. In order to provide adequate training and supervision to establish competence, counselling programs need to incorporate both academic and experiential phases, and provide appropriate supervision for the sake of both the client's welfare and the intern's professional growth. The problem of incompetence can be reduced if graduate training programs promote an interest in learning and an emphasis on professional development as a lifelong process (Corey, 1991).

From an internal perspective, it is the counsellor's responsibility as a professional to gain the skills and knowledge basic to the profession, as well as maintain the personal and professional ethics necessary to work within the boundaries of his or her competence. This can be done through continuing education, professional disclosure and consultation and referrals.

It is important for the professional to realize that pre-doctoral training is not sufficient to guarantee a high level of competence in professional areas of functioning (Corey, Corey & Callanan, 1979). Even the best present education and training will become obsolete within a relatively short period of time unless counsellors make a very determined effort to expand their professional base of knowledge and techniques. Therefore,

continuing education is needed to prevent the obsolescence of a professional's knowledge (Jensen, 1979). It is essential for keeping up to date with new knowledge in professional specialties. Counsellors have an ethical responsibility to engage in continuing education in order to maintain high levels of competence, and consequently, counsellors who fail to keep informed about new developments in both theory and research can be vulnerable on both ethical and legal grounds.

Another internal frame of reference for competence works as an alternative to the present licensing practices. This involves requiring practitioners to fully disclose information about themselves and their practice. Professional disclosure should ideally contain the following: informing prospective clients about one's qualifications, describing the counselling services offered with an explanation of the therapeutic process, describing the rights and responsibilities of clients, clarifying the nature of confidentiality and the release of information, and outlining the administrative procedures relating to time and money (Lovett & Lovett, 1988). The rationale is that clients must have this information to make intelligent decisions about the use of practitioners' services. It is the responsibility of the therapist to provide clients at the outset of treatment with specific information regarding training, status and competency.

Professional disclosure has benefits for both clients and practitioners. It provides a basic assessment of how well services are being provided, as well as setting up a structure by which consumers can protect themselves, implying an informed or informable public. Self-report on the part of professionals reflects honesty and may be the only criterion available from the consumer's or client's point of view (Gross, 1977).

Counsellors not only have the responsibility to accurately express their qualifications and competencies, but to be aware of and make clients aware of, their professional limitations. It is not an infrequent situation for therapists to find themselves operating out of their area of expertise. Counsellors, who become aware of their lack of competence in a particular case, have the responsibility to seek consultation with colleagues or a supervisor (Corey, 1991). Competent counsellors are also aware of the available resources and are prepared to make referrals when they do not feel competent or prepared to help (Van Hoose & Kottler, 1977). Counsellors should continually assess competence through conferring with colleagues to share perceptions of what is occurring with their clients, themselves, and between them and their clients (Corey, 1991). At times it can be appropriate to work as a "team," and seek out a group of colleagues whose judgment is trusted and regularly present difficult cases to this "team."

Competence as an Ethical Responsibility

Counsellors must become aware of the boundaries of competence, and seek qualified supervision or refer clients when they recognize that they have reached their limit. They must also become familiar with community resources so they can make appropriate referrals (Corey, 1991). This ethical ideal of competence reflects the expectation that professionals in the counselling field must possess an ability to evaluate honestly and objectively their own skills, and make reasonable, responsible decisions of both a professional and a moral nature. As counsellors, it is important to be able to recognize and accept the position they are in regarding the well-being of those whom their actions may affect (Carroll et al., 1985).

Competence ultimately involves a willingness to continually question whether counsellors are doing their work as well as they might, and search for ways of becoming more effective as therapists (Corey, Corey & Callanan, 1979). In order to do this, it is es-

sential to have an understanding of the importance of the elements of competence in all areas of counselling including skills, knowledge, judgment abilities, and interpersonal attributes. The continual maintenance of competence will consist of external references, such as training and licensing, but more importantly, will require the counsellor to participate in continuing education, professional disclosure, and seek consultation and make referrals when necessary.

The ultimate duty of the counsellor is to protect and benefit clients. The establishment of all elements of competence and the maintenance of competence through both external and internal sources will ensure that this duty is fulfilled for the client in the counselling experience.

References

Bervan, N. & Scofield, M. (1987). Ethical responsibility in establishing and maintaining professional competence. *Journal of Applied Rehabilitation Counseling, 18*, 41-44.

Carroll, M., Schneider, H., & Wesley, G. (1985). *Ethics in the practice of psychology*. New Jersey: Prentice-Hall.

Corey, G. (1991). *Theory and practice of counseling and psychotherapy*. Pacific Grove: Brooks/Cole Publishing Company.

Corey, G., Corey, M., & Callanan, P. (1979). *Professional and ethical issues in counseling and psychotherapy*. Monteray: Brooks/Cole Publishing Company.

Gross, S. (1977). Professional disclosure: An alternative to licensing. *Personnel and Guidance Journal, 55*, 586-588.

Gross, D., & Robinson, S. (1987). Ethics in Counseling: A Multiple Role Perspective. *TACD Journal, 15*, 5-15.

Jensen, R. (1979). Competent professional service in psychology: The real issue behind continuing education. *Professional Psychology, 10*, 381-389.

Keith-Spiegel, P., & Koocher, G. (1985). *Ethics in psychology: Professional standards and cases*. New York: Random House.

Lovett, T., & Lovett, C. (1988). Suggestions for continuing legal education units in counselor training. Paper presented at annual meeting of American Association of Counseling and Development, Chicago; cited in Corey, G., (1991), *Theory and practice of counseling and psychotherapy.* Pacific Grove: Brooks/Cole Publishing Company.

Neufeld, V., & Norman, G. (Eds.) (1985). *Assessing clinical competence.* New York: Springer.

Norman, G. (1985). Defining competence: A methodological review. In V. Neufeld & G. Norman (Eds.), *Assessing clinical competence.* New York: Springer.

Overholser, J., & Fine, M. (1990). Defining the boundaries of professional competence: Managing subtle cases of clinical incompetence. *Professional psychology: research and practice, 21,* 462-469.

Rosenbaum, M. (1982). *Ethics and values in psychotherapy.* New York: The Free Press.

Sheldon-Wildgen, J. (1982). Avoiding legal liability: The rights and responsibilities of therapists. *The Behaviour Therapist, 5,* 165-169; cited in Overholser, J., & Fine, M. (1990), Defining the boundaries of professional competence: Managing subtle cases of clinical incompetence. *Professional Psychology: Research and Practice, 21,* 462-469.

Thompson, A. (1990). *Guide to ethical practice in psychotherapy.* New York: John Wiley and Sons.

Thoreson, R., Miller, M., & Krauskopf, C. (1989). The distressed psychologist: Prevalence and treatment considerations. *Professional Psychology: Research and Practice, 20,* 153-158.

Van Hoose, W., & Kottler, J. (1977). *Ethical and legal issues in counseling and psychotherapy.* San Francisco: Jossey-Bass.

Chapter Three

---------- ❖ ----------

Counselling
Relationships

---------- ❖ ----------

Counsellors must be aware that at all times
their primary obligation is to help their
clients. Counsellors must recognize that
they have limited confidentiality and must
always inform clients of counselling conditions.

❖ ❖ ❖ ❖ ❖ ❖ ❖ ❖ ❖ ❖ ❖ ❖ ❖

Ethical Articles on Counselling Relationships

B1 **Primary Responsibility**
Counsellors have a primary responsibility to respect the integrity and promote the welfare of their clients. They work collaboratively with clients to devise integrated, individual counselling plans that offer reasonable promise of success and are consistent with the abilities and circumstances of clients.

❖

B2 **Confidentiality**
Counselling relationships and information resulting therefrom are kept confidential. However, there are the following exceptions to confidentiality:
(i) when disclosure is required to prevent clear and imminent danger to the client or others;
(ii) when legal requirements demand that confidential material be revealed;
(iii) when a child is in need of protection.

❖

B3 **Duty to Warn**
When counsellors become aware of their clients' intent or potential to place others in clear or imminent danger, they use reasonable care to give threatened persons such warnings as are essential to avert foreseeable dangers.

❖

B4 **Client's Rights and Informed Consent**
When counselling is initiated, and throughout the counselling process as necessary, counsellors inform clients of the purposes, goals, techniques, procedures, limitations, potential risks and benefits of services to be performed, and other such pertinent information. Counsellors make sure that clients understand the implications of diagnosis, fees and fee-collection arrangements, record keeping, and limits to confidentiality. Clients have the right to participate in the ongoing counselling plans, to refuse any recommended services, and to be advised of the consequences of such refusal.

B5 Children and Persons With Diminished Capacity

Counsellors conduct the informed consent process with those legally appropriate to give consent when counselling, assessing, and having as research subjects children and/or persons with diminished capacity. These clients also give consent to such services or involvement commensurate with their capacity to do so.

❖

 B6 Maintenance of Records

Counsellors maintain records in sufficient detail to track the sequence and nature of professional services rendered and consistent with any legal, regulatory, agency, or institutional requirement. They secure the safety of such records and create, maintain, transfer, and dispose of them in a manner compliant with the requirements of confidentiality and the other articles of this *Code of Ethics*.

❖

B7 Access to Records

Counsellors understand that clients have a right of access to their counselling records, and that disclosure to others of information from these records only occurs with the written consent of the client and/or when required by law.

❖

 B8 Dual Relationships

Counsellors make every effort to avoid dual relationships with clients that could impair professional judgment or increase the risk of harm to clients. Examples of dual relationships include, but are not limited to, familial, social, financial, business, or close personal relationships. When a dual relationship cannot be avoided, counsellors take appropriate professional precautions such as informed consent, consultation, supervision, and documentation to ensure that judgment is not impaired and no exploitation occurs.

 B9 Respecting Diversity

Counsellors actively work to understand the diverse cultural background of the clients with whom they work, and do not condone or engage in discrimination based on age, colour, culture, ethnicity, disability, gender, religion, sexual orientation, marital, or socio-economic status.

❖

B10 Consulting With Other Professionals

Counsellors may consult with other professionally competent persons about the client. However, if the identity of the client is to be revealed, it is done with the written consent of the client. Counsellors choose professional consultants in a manner which will avoid placing the consultant in a conflict-of-interest situation.

B11 Relationships With Former Clients

Counsellors remain accountable for any relationships established with former clients. Those relationships could include, but are not limited to, those of a friendship, social, financial and business nature. Counsellors exercise caution about entering any such relationships and take into account whether or not the issues and relational dynamics present during the counselling have been fully resolved and properly terminated. In any case, counsellors seek consultation on such decisions.

B12 Sexual Intimacies

Counsellors avoid any type of sexual intimacies with clients and they do not counsel persons with whom they have had a sexual relationship. Counsellors do not engage in sexual intimacies with former clients within a minimum of three years after terminating the counselling relationship. This prohibition is not limited to the three-year period but extends indefinitely if the client is clearly vulnerable, by reason of emotional or cognitive disorder, to exploitative influence by the counsellor. Counsellors, in all such circumstances, clearly bear the burden to ensure that no such exploitative influence has occurred, and to seek consultative assistance.

B13 Multiple Clients

When counsellors agree to provide counselling to two or more persons who have a relationship (such as husband and wife, or parents and children), counsellors clarify at the outset which person or persons are clients and the nature of the relationship they will have with each person. If conflicting roles emerge for counsellors, they must clarify, adjust, or withdraw from roles appropriately.

❖

B14 Multiple Helpers

If, after entering a counselling relationship, a counsellor discovers the client is already in a counselling relationship, then the counsellor is responsible for discussing the issues related to continuing or terminating counselling with the client. It may be necessary, with client consent, to discuss these issues with the other helper.

❖

B15 Group Work

Counsellors have the responsibility to screen prospective group members, especially when group goals focus on self-understanding and growth through self-disclosure. They take reasonable precautions to protect group members from physical and/or psychological harm resulting from interaction within the group, both during and following the group experience.

❖

B16 Computer Use

When computer applications are used as a component of counselling services, counsellors ensure that:

(i) client and counsellor identity is verified;

(ii) the client is capable of using the computer application;

(iii) the computer application is appropriate to the needs of the client;

(iv) the client understands the purpose and operation of client-assisted and/or self-help computer applications;

(v) a follow-up of client use of a computer application is provided to assist subsequent needs.

In any case, computer applications do not diminish the counsellor's responsibility to act in accordance with the CCA *Code of Ethics*, and in particular, to ensure adherence to the principles of confidentiality, informed consent, and safeguarding against harmful effects.

❖

B17 Referral

When counsellors determine their inability to be of professional assistance to clients, they avoid initiating a counselling relationship, or immediately terminate it. In either event, members suggest appropriate alternatives, including making a referral to resources about which they are knowledgeable. Should clients decline the suggested referral, counsellors are not obligated to continue the relationship.

❖

B18 Termination of Counselling

Counsellors terminate counselling relationships with client agreement when possible, when it is reasonably clear that: the goals of counselling have been met, the client is no longer benefiting from counselling, when clients do not pay fees charged, when previously disclosed agency or institutional limits do not allow for the provision of further counselling services.

However, counsellors make reasonable efforts to facilitate the continuation of counselling services when services are interrupted by such factors as counsellor illness, client or counsellor relocation, client financial difficulties, and so forth.

CASE STUDIES
IN COUNSELLING
RELATIONSHIPS

B1 **PRIMARY RESPONSIBILITY**
Counsellors have a primary responsibility to respect the integrity and promote the welfare of their clients. They work collaboratively with clients to devise integrated, individual counselling plans that offer reasonable promise of success and are consistent with the abilities and circumstances of clients.

Respect for the Client (+)

The counsellor came highly recommended to a woman whose marriage was in trouble due to many factors, but most significantly, due to emotional and verbal abuse from her husband. The abuse had gone on for several years without the wife being able to persuade the husband to seek any kind of help. The counsellor recognized the hurt the woman was feeling and that she had a plan, which she seemed to have difficulty carrying out. The counsellor did not tell her what to do or question whether what she revealed to him were her true inner feelings. He seemed to accept what she was saying and to recognize that the feelings that she was displaying were real to her. This counsellor made the woman feel comfortable; the rapport between the two that was established during their first session was so positive that it left the door wide open for more revelations. The counsellor's genuineness was picked up by the woman early on in the first session. He showed understanding of the inner conflicts the woman had regarding whether or not she and her children should remain in the abusive situation. The counsellor was able to explain the cycle of abuse and the consequences of remaining in the situation, and to restate the alternatives the woman had decided were open to her. Most importantly, the counsellor helped her see that the time had come for her to make a decision.

Disclosure in a Group (+)

In a group session involving six students, all of whom come from non-abusive alcoholic homes, one of the students confides that he "cannot take any more." He is 16-years-old and is intending to take his father's car and run away to the nearest big city. He has no money, no skills, and no friends or relatives with whom to stay. It is his intention to live on the street. He is aware that many his age do and he feels it is better than the life he is living. Despite all arguments against this course of action from the other members of the group and the counsellor, the boy staunchly adheres to his position. Knowledge of the family situation leads the counsellor to believe that apart from the concern for the stolen car, little will be done for the student if parents were notified. The counsellor calls Child and Family Services and requests their help in working with the student and his family.

Alone (-)

A male teacher, Frank, who is in his early forties, came home one day and learned that his wife had taken their two children and left him. In the subsequent divorce case, his wife was given custody of the children. Frank has been seeing a counsellor for weekly sessions for several months. He continues to express much anger, pain and loneliness during his hourly sessions. During the last session, the counsellor stopped the session after 10 minutes and told Frank that he was "behind schedule" even though Frank had made his usual hourly appointment.

Doubting Counsellor (-)

In a small, remote community, a 14-year-old Grade 9 student, Mary, told her female school counsellor that she desperately needed to talk to her in confidence as soon as possible. The counsellor felt the student was probably over-reacting about something and did not meet with her immediately. A week later the student once again approached her counsellor and explained that she had been sexually abused by her stepfather. The counsellor was not convinced that the student was speaking the truth, and felt the student was out to attack her stepfather with these allegations. The counsellor told the student that she would look into the matter, but never reported it to the proper authorities for further investigation.

COMMENTS AND QUESTIONS

Counselling is a personal matter that involves personal relationships. Honesty, sincerity, acceptance, understanding, and spontaneity are basic ingredients for a successful relationship between the counsellor and counsellee. The degree of caring, counsellor interest and ability in helping the counsellee, and counsellor genuineness are all factors that influence this relationship and enhance the positive aspects of this ethical article. These characteristics were definitely lacking in the two negative cases.

Group counselling gives clients a place to express conflicting feelings, explore self doubts and come to the realization that they may share these concerns with their peers. A group may allow counsellees to openly question their values and to modify those that may need to be changed.

In a group setting, if members are to drop their defences and reveal their "selves," they need assurances that the group is a safe place in which to do this.

It is the responsibility of counsellors to make sure that they "promote the welfare of counsellees," whether this is in individual or group counselling. This article has been placed first in this counselling relationship section: first, because counsellors must never forget that their primary obligation is to help their clients. It is necessary that counsellors act in ways that will further the best interests of clients. Counsellors must:

a) be willing to consult with colleagues,

b) keep themselves informed about laws affecting counselling practice,

c) keep current,

d) reflect on the impact their values have on counselling,

e) be willing to engage in honest self-evaluation.

1. In the two cases "Alone" and "Doubting Counsellor," what would you have done as a counsellor?

2. What do you do when the school or agency that you work for has policies that do not appear to be helpful for your client?

3. What are some ways in which counsellors can enhance the welfare of clients?

4. Can you "promote the welfare" of a client by breaking confidentiality? Explain.

5. How can group leaders protect group members from "physical and psychological" harm?

B2 CONFIDENTIALITY

Counselling relationships and information resulting therefrom are kept confidential. However, there are the following exceptions to confidentiality:

(i) when disclosure is required to prevent clear and imminent danger to the client or others;

(ii) when legal requirements demand that confidential material be revealed;

(iii) when a child is in need of protection.

"What's Happening?" (+)

Fred Davis is a counsellor in a family counselling agency. One day he receives a phone call from the wife of one of the clients he is counselling. The wife indicates that she has seen some changes in her husband and asks the counsellor for information as to what her husband is saying during counselling. The counsellor, in a kind but firm manner, explains to the woman that the matters discussed during counselling are confidential.

Limited Confidentiality (+)

Fifteen-year-old Sally has been referred to the high school counsellor, Ms. Smith, by her English teacher because her grades are falling and she is very inattentive in class. She will end up failing the course if she doesn't do something to pull up her grades. During the course of the conversation between Sally and Ms. Smith, it becomes evident that Sally's performance in her other classes is similar to her performance in her English class, and that she will more than likely fail the year if she isn't able to improve her grades. Sally discloses that she has been feeling depressed lately and cannot seem to concentrate on her school work. After further probing, it becomes evident to Ms. Smith that Sally is being sexually abused by her father. Sally admits to the abuse but says she is afraid of what might happen to her if her father finds out she has disclosed this information to anyone. Ms. Smith tells

Sally that she is required to report the matter to a social agency (in Manitoba, this would be Child and Family Services) and assures her that it is in Sally's best interest that she do so. Ms. Smith then calls Child and Family Services and waits with Sally for the social worker to arrive.

Inappropriate Chatter (-)

An anger management group at a local high school was co-led by two counsellors. At a social gathering one evening, the one counsellor was the focus of attention as he shared antics and incidents that had occurred during the group sessions.

Breaking Confidentiality (-)

Sixteen-year-old Mary Lou made an appointment with Ms. Jones, the high school counsellor, to discuss what courses she should take in Grade 12 in order to prepare her for entering university the following year. During the course of their conversation, Mary Lou disclosed to Ms. Jones that she was having problems with her mother because her mother was always trying to control her life. Because she was of the belief that whatever she told Ms. Jones would be held in strictest confidence, she further disclosed that she has been lying to her mother, telling her that she was studying at the library in the evenings when in fact she was spending time with a young man whom, she felt, her mother would disapprove of. Shortly after the session was over, Ms. Jones made a call to Mary Lou's mother and informed her of Mary Lou's involvement with the young man and how she has been lying to her. Ms. Jones hoped she would be helping Mary Lou by informing her parents.

COMMENTS AND QUESTIONS

Confidentiality protects clients from unauthorized disclosures without informed consent. Confidentiality is crucial to establishing and maintaining a strong counsellor/client relationship. With confidentiality counsellors are not only respecting clients' ability to control their own lives, but also respecting all human relationships.

Counsellors will agree that the material of the counselling session belongs to the client. Confidentiality is, nevertheless, not absolute. There are times when confidentiality must be broken, and there are other times when breaking confidentiality remains unclear. Some of the exceptions to confidentiality include:

a) the client is a danger to self or others,

b) the courts order release of counselling information,

c) support staff who process information and papers,

d) legal and clinical consultation, and

e) during clinical supervision of counsellors.

1. What are additional exceptions to confidentiality?

2. How can we increase the chances of confidentiality in a group?

3. What is your responsibility as a counsellor when you hear other staff members discussing clients over coffee?

4. How should counsellors explain to clients that there are limits to their confidentiality?

5. How would you deal with the last two cases, "Inappropriate Chatter" and "Breaking Confidentiality"?

B3 DUTY TO WARN

When counsellors become aware of their clients' intent or potential to place others in clear or imminent danger, they use reasonable care to give threatened persons such warnings as are essential to avert foreseeable dangers.

The Client is Protected (+)

A 14-year-old Grade 9 student has been seeing her school counsellor for the past several months. She has not shared much information about her home life, but complains often about depression and a feeling of detachment from her peers. The counsellor has developed a good rapport with the young student, who has expressed that she feels much more comfortable lately in their counselling sessions. The young girl has recently revealed that she does not feel loved and does not have a good relationship with her parents. During one of the counselling sessions, she became tearful and expressed to the counsellor that she did not feel safe at home because she had been sexually abused by her father. The counsellor explained to her that his first priority was her safety and that he had an obligation to protect her. This obligation would mean that he would have to contact an agency that works to protect children from abuse (e.g. Child and Family Services in Manitoba). He assured her that she would now be safe and protected from any further harm and that her father would now get help with his problem.

Potential Suicide (+)

A suicide note was left by a Grade 7 student indicating her intention of suicide. The note was brought to the attention of the guidance department head since the girl's counsellor was out of the building at the time. Later, the counsellor spoke to the girl. The counsellor contacted her parents regarding the note. They did not seem too concerned but agreed to phone the counsellor or school principal if help was needed. Next, the counsellor met with the student and talked to her about her note and her suicide intention. It seemed that she had considered suicide, but had not thought of how to carry out the plan. She did have a very close friend, someone that she trusted and felt that she could talk to at all times. The counsellor gave the Grade 7 student the phone number of a suicide prevention centre, as well as her own home number to call.

Informing Others (-)

A 15-year-old student in a large high school had begun to see his school counsellor because of problems he was having with his girlfriend. The counsellor enjoyed the relationship he had with the students in the school and felt that he had gained their trust and respect. During one of these sessions, the boy expressed to the counsellor that many of the students trusted him and felt that he was really on their side. He also told the counsellor that he and his girlfriend had tried "crack" on several occasions. She had at first been hesitant to try the drug but after some pressure she gave in and in fact enjoyed it. The counsellor discussed the dangers of the drug as well as the strain the boy was putting on his girlfriend and their relationship.

The counsellor debated whether he should inform the girl's parents or the principal but felt that the trust he had gained among the students was very important. He decided to continue his sessions with the boy and did not inform the responsible authorities. He was informed several days later that the girl had nearly died of an overdose of drugs at a party on the weekend. The counsellor was given a short-term suspension from his position at the school for not following the school's policy on reporting drug use.

Selling Drugs (-)
Alan tells his counsellor that his friend Joe told
him about a big drug deal that is going to go
down that evening at the arcade. He mentions
Darryl, a good-looking, well-dressed, senior
student who is always surrounded by a group
of friends, as being the person who will purchase a large amount of "crack." Alan says
Darryl plans to sell the drugs to the other
students at school. The counsellor knows
Darryl's parents, his father is a teacher, and
feels that this could not be true. Alan, however, insists that he knows all of the details
of the transaction from Joe, and he wants
the counsellor to do something. The counsellor continues to listen to Alan and reflects
his concerns about the situation, but he tells
Alan that he can not get involved in something that is only hearsay evidence.

COMMENTS AND QUESTIONS
It is important for counsellors to inform clients, at the beginning of their sessions, of
their obligation and responsibility to break
confidentiality when counsellors feel that
their clients or others are in potential danger. By informing clients of their limited confidentiality, counsellors can alleviate the sense
of betrayal that clients may feel if they were
under the impression that anything said to
the counsellor would be kept confidential.
Warning of danger must be presented in such
a way that it is seen as a caring act on the
part of the counsellor.

The famous Tarasoff court decision has
helped counsellors understand how to act in
situations where there is danger to a third
party. Counsellors have a legal obligation to
third parties who are at risk from dangerous
clients. As with other situations where confidentiality must be broken, counsellors
should tell their clients that they have a responsibility to warn people in danger. Counsellors should then inform their supervisor,
the police and the intended victim.

Counsellors should be aware that there
may be certain repercussions that result from
informing responsible authorities. There is
the danger that other clients may feel that
the counsellor cannot be trusted, or the client may even feel a sense of anger or betrayal
toward the counsellor.

Counsellors must be aware of institutional
policies and the responsible parties to whom
they have an obligation to contact when they
feel the client or others are in danger. Parents have a right to be informed if their child
may be harmed, and parents should be informed of additional resources within the
community, or professional organizations,
that can help with a potentially dangerous
situation.

1. Do you agree with the Tarasoff decision
   that counsellors have a "duty to warn"
   people in danger? Discuss.

2. What can be done to alleviate a possible
   sense of betrayal that the students may feel
   if they become aware of the member breaking the confidentiality between the member and the counsellee?

3. Under what circumstances and in what
   situations should the counsellor assume
   responsibility for the counsellee's actions?

4. If there is a case in which the counsellor
   has been made aware of a possible danger
   to the client or others, but does not feel
   that the danger is probable, do they still
   have an obligation to inform responsible
   authorities?

5. Are counsellors legally obliged to inform
   responsible authorities of the clients' involvement in illegal activities if counsellors feel that it would be detrimental to
   the clients? Counsellors may feel they have
   a better chance of helping clients by encouraging them to stop their involvement
   in illegal activities within the framework
   of their counselling relationship.

B4 CLIENT'S RIGHTS AND INFORMED CONSENT

When counselling is initiated, and throughout the counselling process as necessary, counsellors inform clients of the purposes, goals, techniques, procedures, limitations, potential risks and benefits of services to be performed, and other such pertinent information. Counsellors make sure that clients understand the implications of diagnosis, fees and fee-collection arrangements, record keeping, and limits to confidentiality. Clients have the right to participate in the ongoing counselling plans, to refuse any recommended services, and to be advised of the consequences of such refusal.

A Plan of Action (+)

Jane is a 14-year-old Grade 8 student who comes to the school counsellor in a panic, thinking she is pregnant. The counsellor is a long-time staff member and well-liked by the student. Given the rapport between the two, it is not too long before the student is calm and rational enough to listen to the counsellor. The counsellor indicates there are ways in which a pregnancy can be confirmed and the plan of action would depend on the results. If negative, Jane would educate herself with regard to avoiding future unwanted pregnancies. If positive, Jane would have one of three choices: keep the baby, give the baby up, or abort, and the consequences of each choice would be discussed. Furthermore, Jane's parents would have to be informed. Should this moment arrive, the counsellor offered to either tell her parents himself or to be with her when she told them. Jane decided to work through her problem with the guidance of her counsellor.

Informed on Confidentiality (+)

Joyce meets with her school counsellor and tells the counsellor that she has a very serious concern, but before she will tell the counsellor, Joyce insists that the counsellor keep everything she says in strictest confidence. The counsellor carefully explains that she will keep matters confidential, but that there are limits to her confidentiality. The counsellor explains what these limits are. The counsellor then encourages Joyce to talk more about her demand for absolute confidentiality, and to then make a decision whether she wishes to tell the counsellor in spite of the limits that the counsellor has placed on confidentiality.

Secret Phone Call (-)

During the course of the counselling sessions, the counsellor discovers that part of the reason for the boy's aggression in class toward his teacher and peers is the fact that he has been physically abused by his father. The counsellor contacts a Child Guidance Clinic to give them this information. But because he is afraid the child and the child's mother will want to stop the counselling to protect the father, the counsellor does not indicate to either the boy or his mother that he has contacted the Child Guidance Clinic.

Principal's Orders (-)

Jocelyn, a Grade 11 student, was referred to the counsellor by a teacher who was having difficulty "controlling Jocelyn and her disruptive behavior in the classroom." Jocelyn and the counsellor established a good relationship, but the disruptive behavior continued and the principal was called in to take more severe action. The principal told the counsellor that he would be taking action in this situation and he asked the counsellor to turn any records of her meetings with Jocelyn over to him, so that he could get a better understanding of the situation. In spite of the fact that the counsellor had shown Jocelyn a counselling consent form that promised confidentiality (except when there was danger to the client and others), the counsellor gave the principal all her private documentation of her meetings with Jocelyn.

COMMENTS AND QUESTIONS

It is important that counsellors inform clients at or before counselling as to what they typically do in a counselling session. Counsellors should prepare a personal statement (informed consent) on their counselling. Such an informed consent form would contain a short statement about the counselling sessions, the nature of the counselling, the length and the type of follow-up used. This informed consent form would contain information on the counsellor's qualifications. There would also be a statement regarding confidentiality and the client's rights.

1. If it is true that the majority of school counsellors and employment counsellors do not have informed consent forms, what do you think are the reasons for this?

2. Besides the areas mentioned in the preceding comment, what other items should be part of a counsellor's personal statement?

3. Should group facilitators have different consent forms than individual counsellors?

4. What are some limitations that may result in the discontinuance of counselling? Should this information be part of the consent form?

5. Should the fee structure be part of the informed consent form?

B5   CHILDREN AND PERSONS WITH DIMINISHED CAPACITY

Counsellors conduct the informed consent process with those legally appropriate to give consent when counselling, assessing, and having as research subjects children and/or persons with diminished capacity. These clients also give consent to such services or involvement commensurate with their capacity to do so.

Research With Children (+)

A child psychologist at a university received a research grant to investigate the play behavior of children in kindergarten. The psychologist planned to observe children in three different schools in one school division. After receiving permission from the school division, school and teachers, the psychologist-researcher contacted all the parents and guardians with children in the three classrooms, and, after fully explaining her research, she asked parents and guardians to sign permission forms for their children to be involved in the study.

Special Needs Children (+)

The school psychologist was aware that there were many "special needs" children in the middle school in which she was working. She wanted to find out as much as possible about these children so that she could work with the teachers to help them in school. The psychologist explained to all the students in each classroom that she would be visiting regularly and observing their behavior. She also obtained permission from the parents and/or guardians of all the children for her proposed work.

No Consent (-)

A school psychologist, Frances Cooper, thought that she would be able to help two students that she was working with if she had a better idea of their behavior in the classroom and playground. The teachers involved told the psychologist to "come in anytime you want to," and so the psychologist did. When students in the classroom asked her why she was visiting, she said that she was interested in the classroom behavior of children.

Secret Data Gathering (-)

A counselling student worked at a crisis centre as part of his counselling practicum for his master's program. He realized that many of the clients coming for help were having emotional problems related to family relationships. He began to gather data with the intent of using the information for a paper that he planned to write.

COMMENTS AND QUESTIONS

Informed consent is a basic right for clients, and when counsellors are working with children and/or persons with "diminished capacity," they will need to conduct the informed consent process with parents or legal guardians. It is important that guardians have every opportunity to ask questions and that the information provided is totally understandable.

Counsellors are frequently faced with the dilemma of providing children with confidentiality, but also wanting to respect the legal responsibilities to parents and guardians. The ACA *Code of Ethics* asks that counsellors "act in the best interests" of children and that counsellors may include parents and guardians in the counselling process "as appropriate." In short, counsellors are expected to use professional judgment to act in the best interests of children and those of "diminished capacity."

1. What can be done to enhance the professional judgment of counsellors?

2. Is record keeping even more important when working with children or persons with diminished capacity?

3. In the case "No Consent," is it better to tell a "little white lie" than to let the class know she is observing one or two students?

4. How would you handle the situation in "No Consent"?

5. How would you deal with the situation in "Secret Data Gathering"?

B6 MAINTENANCE OF RECORDS
Counsellors maintain records in sufficient detail to track the sequence and nature of professional services rendered and consistent with any legal, regulatory, agency, or institutional requirement. They secure the safety of such records and create, maintain, transfer, and dispose of them in a manner compliant with the requirements of confidentiality and the other articles of this *Code of Ethics*.

Counsellor Files (+)

In a family counselling agency, records are kept of all the clients coming to the agency for counselling. These individual files contain only basic biographical information. Each counsellor at the agency keeps her or his own files on all clients that she or he is counselling. These personal counsellor files contain interview notes and are intended only for the use of the counsellor who is counselling a particular client.

Tape Recordings in a Practicum (+)

In a counselling practicum, students are required to submit audio and video tapes of counselling sessions with clients. The practicum instructor has developed appropriate forms that explain the purposes of the audio and video recordings. All clients and student counsellors sign the forms, giving permission for the practicum instructor and counselling student to view the tapes for learning purposes. After the viewing, the tapes are erased.

The Police Are Calling (-)

A marriage counsellor is contacted by the police regarding one of her clients. The police ask for any information the counsellor can give them from the interviews with this particular client. The counsellor, realizing the police are asking, goes to her files and tells the inquiring policeman the essence of the interviews.

The Principal's Policy (-)

The policy of one school principal is to have one set of files in his school. He insists that all counsellors write interview notes for each client that they see, and that these notes be placed in the school files. As a result of the protests from counsellors, the principal has "compromised" by telling counsellors that their interview notes "may be brief," but that they must submit a report on each student interviewed. In spite of the fact that the files are accessible to all the teachers, secretaries and clerks in the school, the counsellors continue to file their interview notes in the school files.

COMMENTS AND QUESTIONS

Client records belong to the client. These records include test data, letters of correspondence, any video or audio recordings and the counsellor's interview notes. These materials belong to the client and are for the use of the client and counsellor. These personal records "are not part of the official records of the institution or agency in which the counsellor is employed." Permission from the client is necessary before these "client records" are shared with others.

Standards of practice for maintaining records would suggest that interview notes should be recorded at the time service is provided, and they should be factual, objective, legible and well-organized. Any observations and personal impressions should be identified as those of the person producing the records.

1. What type of record-keeping policy is in place at your counselling centre?

2. Do some schools have records policies similar to those of the principal depicted in the last case?

3. Should counsellors-in-training be allowed to keep their audio or video recordings of clients?

4. Should counsellors give police or lawyers records of their interviews?

5. Should parents have access to the counselling records of their school-aged children?

B7 ACCESS TO RECORDS
Counsellors understand that clients have a right of access to their counselling records, and that disclosure to others of information from these records only occurs with the written consent of the client and/or when required by law.

Confidential Files (+)

A counsellor in private practice keeps detailed records of all her clients, including the dates of all sessions, a summary of the counselling session, commentary on counselling progress, and tentative plans for future sessions. All the records are kept in a locked file. Clients are informed at the beginning of counselling that the counselling records will be kept confidential unless ordered by the courts to release them.

Client Records (+)

After almost a year of counselling, Janice Z. began to wonder whether she should continue seeing the counsellor. She discussed the matter with her counsellor and felt she would be in a better position to make her decision if she could see all the records that the counsellor had made of their counselling sessions. After reading the records, Janice realized more clearly the progress that she was making was continuing, and so she made the decision to continue to come for counselling.

Provincial Mandate (-)

The Department of Education from one Canadian province sent out guidelines on the school records of students. The new guidelines said that all records, including those of counsellors, social workers and psychologists, were to be open to parents and guardians upon request. The Department of Education provided no guidelines for exceptions.

Releasing Counselling Records (-)

The police arrived at school and explained that they had arrested a student, Bob F., because they had suspected him of selling drugs to other students. Bob had indicated that he frequently spoke to his counsellor about many things. The police told the principal of the school that their case would be much stronger if they knew more about what Bob was saying to the counsellor. The principal told the counsellor to immediately provide the police with his counselling records. The counsellor gave the police his records.

COMMENTS AND QUESTIONS

Clients have a right of access to their counselling records. Records must be written so that clients can understand what the records say. What is less clear to counsellors is what they should do when parents or legal guardians want to see the counselling records of their children. Although parents may legally see the records of their children, counsellors must use their professional judgment as to whether the best interests of the child are being served by showing parents or guardians the records. Children, like adults, are protected by the Canadian Charter of Rights and Freedoms.

1. "Just because children are favoured in some areas of the law does not mean that they can't have the same rights as adults in other areas of the law." Discuss.

2. What do you think about the mandate presented in the "Provincial Mandate" case?

3. What would you do if you were the counsellor in the case "Releasing Counselling Records"?

4. Do you think that clients will understand the diagnosis and notes that counsellors record?

5. What should school counsellors do if administration insists that all records be kept in the school (cumulative) records?

B8 DUAL RELATIONSHIPS

Counsellors make every effort to avoid dual relationships with clients that could impair professional judgment or increase the risk of harm to clients. Examples of dual relationships include, but are not limited to, familial, social, financial, business, or close personal relationships. When a dual relationship cannot be avoided, counsellors take appropriate professional precautions such as informed consent, consultation, supervision, and documentation to ensure that judgment is not impaired and no exploitation occurs.

Referrals (+)

When two close friends of a marriage counsellor decide to divorce, they both seek their counsellor friend for counselling. The counsellor, knowing the ethical boundaries of dual relationships, decides it's best not to mix her personal relationship with a professional relationship. The member explains her dilemma to the couple and makes appropriate referrals to other marriage counsellors that she knows.

Counselling Students? (+)

A counsellor-educator is asked by one of her graduate students to help her with her severe depression. The counsellor-educator explains to the student that she is her teacher and evaluator of her work and that it would be inadvisable for them to have a counselling relationship as well. The counsellor-educator recommends several counsellors who she feels could help the graduate student.

Counselling a Relative (-)

A counsellor is approached by his niece regarding her personal problems. She is under all kinds of pressure from her family to leave the man she is dating, and who wishes to marry her. The man she is dating is of a different race, and her family strongly disapproves. The counsellor agrees to counsel his niece, since she has come to him with her concerns. Though he attempts to help his niece with her dilemma, his professional judgment becomes influenced. He tells his niece that she should leave her boyfriend and find a man from within her own race.

Counselling Co-Workers (-)

The director of a 10-counsellor counselling centre is approached by one of the counsellors at the centre regarding her own marital problems. The two counsellors are good friends, even though the director of the centre is required to send annual reviews of each counsellor to a board of directors. In spite of the different roles that the director has, she agrees to counsel her friend and co-worker.

COMMENTS AND QUESTIONS

Counsellors should be aware of the problems that can arise when dual relationships come into play. Frequently, dual relationships can impair counsellors' professional judgment and objectivity. School administrators who may have to discipline students are in a dual relationship if they also take on counselling responsibilities with the students. Marriage counsellors who work with couples who are their friends may encounter ethical dilemmas in their dual relationship. It is very difficult to balance a professional relationship during counselling with a personal relationship outside of counselling. For this reason, this ethical article clearly states that "dual relationships must be avoided."

1. Whose needs are being met when a counsellor counsels a close friend or relative?

2. What is the best way to avoid getting into a counselling relationship with friends?

3. When it is difficult or impossible to refer a potential client (with whom you have a supervisory or administrative relationship) to another counsellor, what are some pre-

cautions you should take in this counselling relationship?

4. Is it not possible that counselling a friend will enhance the friendship?

5. Should counselling students be allowed to have their counselling practicum in a school where they formerly worked as a teacher?

B9 **RESPECTING DIVERSITY**
Counsellors actively work to understand the diverse cultural background of the clients with whom they work, and do not condone or engage in discrimination based on age, colour, culture, ethnicity, disability, gender, religion, sexual orientation, marital, or socio-economic status.

Differences in Values (+)

Fred, a counsellor in private practice, is very aware of the general differences in values between "mainstream" Canadians and immigrants coming from Asia. He has found that many of his Asian clients are used to a more authoritarian relationship with parents and family, and are generally more compliant and co-operative. When an Asian client tells him about his unhappiness regarding his family's wishes for him to get an engineering degree, Fred realizes that both the family wishes and his client's interest must be considered. They spend many sessions discussing this dilemma and finally decide to have a session with key family members present.

Multicultural School (+)

A counsellor working in a middle school realized that there were literally dozens of ethnic and cultural groups in her school. She made every effort to learn more about the various minority groups and at all times attempted to demonstrate equal respect, warmth and genuineness to all the students she saw. She realized that she needed to carefully monitor any assumptions she made about students, no matter what their culture.

"Melting Pot" Philosophy (-)

Frank Weathers is tired of "all the multicultural awareness brainwashing" he is constantly receiving from his colleagues and the director of the counselling clinic where he works. He still has his 1970s "Perls Prayer" on the wall and relates to the line "I do my thing, and you do your thing..." He counters his colleagues' suggestions for multicultural education by telling them that his Rogerian attitudes of empathy, respect and genuineness for all clients is all he needs. "As well," Frank states, "immigrants have to learn how to fit into Canadian society."

Western Values (-)

Susan P. often complained to her counselling associates about clients from another culture who "take forever to say what they want or what's wrong." She says she can understand that these clients will have some trouble with the language, but dislikes the fact that she seldom can have eye contact with them, that she has to ask a lot of closed questions, and that she receives little positive feedback from them for her efforts to help. Often she suggests that the quiet, conforming, dependent clients join her evening group on assertiveness training.

COMMENTS AND QUESTIONS

Many research studies have shown that counsellor involvement with others, who are different in terms of "age, colour, culture, ethnicity, disability, gender, religion, sexual orientation, marital or socio-economic status," will result in greater respect for diversity. There is, therefore, a need for counsellors who come from a majority culture to learn more about other cultures and to be sensitive to cultural values and attitudes different than their own. Counsellors must educate themselves and learn how their own experiences, education, values and attitudes have affected them. They must look beyond North American counselling approaches and accept the fact that something can be learned from all ethnic and cultural groups.

1. In the third case, Frank Weathers feels empathy, respect and genuineness are sufficient. What do you think?

2. In the last case, what should Susan do to increase her multicultural acceptance?

3. Should counsellors help people from minority groups learn the normative behaviour of majority groups? If so, how?

4. What are some ways in which counsellors can learn more about diverse cultures?

5. Should counsellors work with clients against whom they have some biases or prejudices (e.g. gays, lesbians, seniors)?

B10 CONSULTING WITH OTHER PROFESSIONALS

Counsellors may consult with other professionally competent persons about the client. However, if the identity of the client is to be revealed, it is done with the written consent of the client. Counsellors choose professional consultants in a manner which will avoid placing the consultant in a conflict-of-interest situation.

Consultation With Consent (+)

David had been counselling Marty for several weeks without making much progress. He felt that Marty's home situation had much to do with Marty's problems in school. David felt it would be of benefit to him and to Marty if he consulted with another professional about Marty. David concluded that the social worker in the community would be a professionally competent person with whom to consult. David approached Marty with his intentions of consulting with the social worker. Marty gave his consent to this, and David then consulted with the social worker concerning Marty.

Consultation With Another Counsellor (+)

Janice has been counselling Miguel, a Grade 6 student, for several sessions. Miguel and his mother had recently moved to Canada to live with his aunt and uncle. Miguel liked his new home but he really missed his home and his family. School was very different for Miguel, and he was having some difficulty adjusting to this new environment. He had made no close contacts or friendships with other students. He maintained the distance between himself and others.

Janice was concerned about Miguel's situation. She had counselled clients similar to Miguel before, but Miguel had made little progress and she felt she needed advice from someone more experienced in this field.

Janice felt that it would be of benefit to her professionally, and of benefit to Miguel, if she consulted with another professional who had more experience with immigrant children.

Murray was a very experienced counsellor and had done much counselling of this type himself. Janice felt that he would be able to give some evaluation and advice on Miguel's situation and her counselling action.

Janice approached Murray and asked him if he would be willing to consult with her on one of her cases. Murray was willing to help. Janice explained Miguel's situation and her concerns to Murray. He gave Janice his opinions and ideas, and they discussed the situation. Miguel's identity was not revealed in this consultation.

Client Uninformed (-)

Through counselling sessions with Janice Wells, Tanya, a junior high student, had shown some improvements in her attitudes toward school. As counselling continued, Tanya began to disclose more, and she made reference to her involvement in "hanging out" with high school students and drinking and doing drugs. The counsellor felt that she should consult with Tanya's teacher concerning Tanya's situation. She felt that by consulting and collaborating with the teacher, she could get further insight into the client's situation and devise a plan of action that would best help Tanya.

Once Janice Wells decided that this consultation should be the next step, she went immediately to the teacher to discuss Tanya's situation. Tanya was not made aware of this consultation, and did not consent to such action.

Uninvolved "Client" (-)

An English teacher in an urban high school contacts one of the school counsellors about the strange behavior of one of her students. She also tells the counsellor that in a recent autobiographical paper that the student submitted, the student had written that it "would be wonderful not to be in this world anymore." Without stopping to talk to the student, the counsellor immediately informed his department head, the school principal and the parents of the student.

COMMENTS AND QUESTIONS

Consultation needs to be an integral part of counselling. Counsellors must realize their own attitudes and limitations in working with clients. Consulting with a professionally competent person can present new ideas and attitudes, and offer new ways of thinking to the counsellor. Often when working with a problem in a certain manner, counsellors may not easily recognize another effective approach. Consultation can provide a varied array of approaches and ideas. Counsellors may also receive needed reinforcement, support or evaluation of their ideas and practices through consultation.

Counsellors must remember that their primary obligation is to the client and any additional help from another professional may help the client.

It is crucial that when consulting another person, the counsellor maintain the highest ethical standards. In terms of ethical articles regarding consultation, the counsellor must not reveal the identity of the client unless the client is aware of the consultation.

1. What does a counsellor do if the client refuses consent for consultation?
2. Do you agree that with most consultation it is not necessary to reveal the name of the client?
3. How best can a counsellor avoid a conflict of interest situation when consulting with teachers?
4. What are some situations where a consultant can be put into a conflict-of-interest situation?
5. In the last case, "Uninvolved 'Client,'" what should the counsellor have done?

B11 RELATIONSHIPS WITH FORMER CLIENTS

Counsellors remain accountable for any relationships established with former clients. Those relationships could include, but are not limited to, those of a friendship, social, financial and business nature. Counsellors exercise caution about entering any such relationship and take into account whether or not the issues and relational dynamics present during the counselling have been fully resolved and properly terminated. In any case, counsellors seek consultation on such decisions.

Business Opportunity (+)

Several weeks after Louise Woodley's client had suddenly terminated counselling, she received a call inviting her to become involved in one of the businesses that her former client owned. The financial arrangements appeared attractive, and Louise knew her former client was a wealthy, successful business woman. Louise politely turned down the offer since she felt that not all the counselling issues had been resolved.

"Can't We Be Friends?" (+)

Approximately a year after completing his counselling with Alvin, George W. met Alvin in a shopping mall. They struck up a conversation and since they were next to a coffee shop, decided to have coffee together. Both of them were ardent hockey fans and when Alvin said that he had four season tickets and one of the men in their group couldn't come to the next game, and would George be interested in coming to the game, George gladly accepted. Later on, George thought about ethical articles related to seeing former clients, so he phoned a colleague to get his opinion regarding the invitation. Both agreed the counselling of the past was no longer an issue and George's colleague supported his acceptance of the invitation to a hockey game.

After Hours (-)

After group counselling sessions, the group facilitator would often go for a few drinks with some of the members of the group. Invariably, discussions began about some of the things that were happening in the group.

Personal Relationships (-)

Tanis H. was seeing a couple who were exploring the possibility of a marriage separation. After a few sessions, the woman stopped coming to counselling, feeling she wanted a marriage separation. Her husband, Eric, continued to see Tanis for counselling. Both Tanis and Eric soon realized that they had strong feelings for each other and Tanis stopped the counselling relationship. A few weeks later Tanis and Eric began seeing each other socially.

COMMENTS AND QUESTIONS

In Article B8, dual relationships were discussed and comments were made regarding the problems that can arise from dual relationships. Counsellors must always ask themselves whose needs are being met in dual relationships. The same question needs to be asked when considering relationships with former clients. It is difficult to discern when a past counselling relationship is no longer a factor. As suggested in this article, it is important that counsellors seek consultation regarding decisions to have financial, social or other relationships with former clients.

1. Is it acceptable to establish social or sexual contact with a former client?
2. In "After Hours," the group facilitator meets with some of the group members. What would make this situation acceptable?
3. Should individuals who have been clients always remain clients?
4. What guidelines would you establish regarding relationships with former clients?
5. With former clients, is there a difference among relationships that are financial, business, social or friendship?

B12 **SEXUAL INTIMACIES**
Counsellors avoid any type of sexual intimacies with clients and they do not counsel persons with whom they have had a sexual relationship. Counsellors do not engage in sexual intimacies with former clients within a minimum of three years after terminating the counselling relationship. This prohibition is not limited to the three-year period but extends indefinitely if the client is clearly vulnerable, by reason of emotional or cognitive disorder, to exploitative influence by the counsellor. Counsellors, in all such circumstances, clearly bear the burden to ensure that no such exploitative influence has occurred, and to seek consultative assistance.

Counselling Relationship Explained (+)

Bryan Adamar is an employment counsellor in a large employment-counselling centre. A woman, seeking to re-enter the workforce after having stayed home to raise three children, greatly appreciates the time and effort Bryan takes on her behalf. He spends many sessions with her, helping her to gain confidence in her ability to take on a job. Since the woman has recently left her husband, she feels she needs much emotional support. Thinking that Bryan Adamar is also attracted to her, she suggests they meet for dinner. Bryan, in a kind but firm way, explains that their meeting socially would interfere with their counselling relationship and that intimate behavior with clients was unethical.

"Just Say No" (+)

A female counsellor in a high school setting works regularly with a 17-year-old male student. During one session, the student places his hand on the counsellor's leg and leaves it there. The counsellor removes the student's hand, informs him that his action is inappropriate, and advises him that if it happens again she will have to terminate their relationship and refer him to another counsellor in the school.

Boundaries I (-)

A male elementary-school counsellor frequently gives his students pats on the back or hugs, recognizing how deprived of affection many of them are. One of his clients is an attractive 13-year-old, whose father has recently deserted the family. During one session, the girl breaks down and begins to cry. The counsellor attempts to comfort her and she ends up sitting on his lap as he strokes her back. Although the counsellor recognizes that he is being sexually stimulated by this contact, he does nothing to end it, and in fact encourages her to come back any time she needs a shoulder to cry on.

Boundaries II (-)

A male counsellor in private practice has a female client whose marriage has recently ended. He is seen to be a caring, compassionate counsellor, who regularly holds clients' hands or gives hugs when he feels it is helpful. On one occasion with this client, the hug becomes more than simply an affectionate gesture. At present, although they have not engaged in actual intercourse, a certain amount of sexual activity is now a regular part of each counselling session. The therapist justifies his actions by claiming that the client is a consenting adult and that his attention to her physical needs is part of the healing process for her.

COMMENTS AND QUESTIONS

This ethical article is an absolute mandate for counsellors to avoid any type of sexual intimacy or sexual relationship with clients. It is important that counsellors recognize and accept that sexual attractions are human responses, but it is just as important that coun-

sellors are aware of other options such as the following:

a) modelling sensitive but non-exploitive behavior,
b) willingness to consult with colleagues,
c) recognizing and dealing with their own issues of sexuality, and
d) recognizing the distinction between having sexual feelings and acting on them.

1. If you were aware that a counselling colleague was the male counsellor in "Boundaries I and II," what would you do?

2. What feelings or thoughts would be experienced if you was sexually attracted to a client?

3. What feelings or thoughts would you experience if a client was sexually attracted to you?

4. What approach would you take in either case?

5. What training would be helpful for you as a counsellor to assist you in this situation?

B13 MULTIPLE CLIENTS

When counsellors agree to provide counselling to two or more persons who have a relationship (such as husband and wife, or parents and children), counsellors clarify at the outset which person or persons are clients and the nature of the relationship they will have with each person. If conflicting roles emerge for counsellors, they must clarify, adjust, or withdraw from roles appropriately.

Clarifying Goals (+)

Five counsellors working at a crisis clinic had a number of issues that seemed to be getting in the way of a good working relationship among the five of them. They decided to all see a counsellor-mediator to discuss their concerns. Since one of the five counsellors also worked in the capacity of a part-time director of the small counselling unit, the counsellor-mediator carefully established the goals and relationships at the beginning of the first session. All the counsellors, including the director, agreed that they should be seen as five equal professionals in a crisis clinic.

Setting Common Goals (+)

A marriage counsellor had been meeting with Ted and Belinda Baxter for some time. As soon as she realized that Ted wanted to save his marriage, while Belinda wanted out of the marriage, she discussed this issue with Ted and Belinda. Eventually, the couple managed to agree on a compromise goal.

A Family Divided (-)

A family therapist was working with a family consisting of the parents and three adolescent children. Not much progress was being made, since the three children felt their parents would never change their autocratic and dictatorial ways of dealing with them.

The therapist decided he could help matters by working separately with the children for a while, and helping them plan a strategy that he felt would get the parents to be "less bossy" with their children. He told the children his plan would work best if the parents did not know about the strategy. He then called the family together, but did not inform the parents of his strategy.

Taking Sides (-)

At the beginning of the counselling, Bev outlined to the couple seeking marriage counselling that they would set goals together and that she felt her job was to help the two of them decide what was best for them. As she listened to each partner tell her and his side of the story, Bev could not help feel that the husband was the real villain in this marriage and that his wife had every reason to be very upset, and even get out of the marriage. Bev did not share her feelings, but it was obvious that she began to side almost exclusively with the woman's views on the marriage.

COMMENTS AND QUESTIONS

Many marriage and family counsellors are aware of additional issues when working with multiple clients, since the help given one client may be non-helpful or even detrimental to the other client. Conflicting roles can readily appear when working with multiple clients, and as this article suggests, counsellors must take the time to clarify, modify and adjust their roles. They need to have answers to questions such as the following:

- To whom do I have primary responsibility?

- What will I do if the goals of my multiple clients are different?

- Are family interests the most important, or the interests of individuals?

- What will I do if my values are very different from those of my multiple clients?

- Will I be able to keep from telling my clients how they should change?
1. Can the counselling goals be the same when working with multiple clients?
2. How do family counsellors deal with biases they might have regarding family life and child-rearing practices?
3. Can family and marriage counsellors be successful with others when their own commitment to marriage and family is not present?
4. What should Bev do in the "Taking Sides" case?
5. What should the counsellor have done in the "A Family Divided" case?

B14 MULTIPLE HELPERS
If, after entering a counselling relationship, a counsellor discovers the client is already in a counselling relationship, then the counsellor is responsible for discussing the issues related to continuing or terminating counselling with the client. It may be necessary, with client consent, to discuss these issues with the other helper.

Permission to Counsel (+)

Frank Owens has been seeing a counsellor in private practice for several months. Frank decides to go back to university to finish the last year of his degree, a degree program that he had interrupted for eight years. He learns of the counselling service at the university and sees a counsellor about some educational/career matters. When the university counsellor learns of Frank receiving counselling elsewhere, she says that she needs permission from the counsellor in private practice before she can continue counselling Frank. Frank agrees to this request and upon receiving permission the university counsellor and Frank continue their counselling relationship.

Group and Individual Counselling (+)

Freyda Elliott asks a group leader about joining her "confidence-building" group. In the ensuing screening interview the group leader learns that Freyda is currently under the care of a local psychiatrist. With Freyda's permission, the group leader contacts the psychiatrist regarding Freyda's joining her group. The psychiatrist feels that the group experience may be very helpful to Freyda and encourages her entering the confidence-building group.

Counselling Plus (-)

Joan and Bob have been seeing a marriage counsellor for over six months. One day Joan learns from her good friend about a counsellor who is very good. Besides seeing the marriage counsellor with her husband Bob, Joan also begins seeing the counsellor, Joyce Reynolds, that her friend recommended. When Joyce Reynolds learns that Joan is also seeing a marriage counsellor, she asks Joan for permission to discuss this dual counselling with the marriage counsellor. Joan tells Joyce that she does not want the other counsellor to know. She also tells Joyce how much she is gaining from their individual counselling sessions. Joyce decides to continue their counselling.

Two Counsellors for Bobby (-)

Bobby has been in trouble with the law regarding drug use, and his parents have arranged for him to see a counsellor with knowledge in working with adolescents using and abusing drugs. Since Bobby is on the volleyball team, he establishes a close relationship with the coach who is also the school counsellor. Bobby begins seeing the school counsellor. Even though both counsellors are aware that they are both counselling Bobby, neither counsellor makes any attempt to discuss the issue of "two counsellors for Bobby."

COMMENTS AND QUESTIONS

It is important that counsellors do not work at cross-purposes with a client. To help avoid any problems that might arise if two or more counsellors are working with the same client, it is vital that counsellors discuss issues related to dual counselling. The client must give permission for counsellors to contact each other, and if this permission is not granted, counselling by at least one of the counsellors should be terminated.

1. What are some of the problems that can arise if a client is seeing two counsellors at the same time?

2. If both counsellors agree, should a client see two counsellors?

3. Many counsellors would see the "Counselling Plus" case as an ethical "grey area." What do you think?

4. Is it the counsellor's responsibility to ensure that her or his client is not receiving other counselling?

5. What would you do as a counsellor if you were convinced that you were helping a client; the client said that you were being helpful; the client did not want to stop seeing another helpful counsellor; you discussed the issues with the other "first" counsellor, and he insisted that you stop seeing his client?

B15 GROUP WORK

Counsellors have the responsibility to screen prospective group members, especially when group goals focus on self-understanding and growth through self-disclosure. They take reasonable precautions to protect group members from physical and/or psychological harm resulting from interaction within the group, both during and following the group experience.

Screening Prospective Group Members (+)

A counsellor, about to start a social-skills group in her school, meets with the students individually to talk with them about the goals and expectations of the group. During the screening interviews, the counsellor and one of the students, Elaine, discuss areas Elaine wishes to focus on. It becomes evident that Elaine is having a major problem with another child also referred to the group. Elaine is reluctant to participate in the same group since she feels the conflict cannot be resolved at this time. Since several of these social-skills groups are being facilitated by the counsellor, it is possible to separate these two students yet allow them both to experience group counselling.

Prior Screening (+)

Several weeks before the group begins to meet, the counsellor interviews each member individually. He ascertains why the prospective members want to be a part of the group, if they have ever been involved with a group before, and how they think this group will benefit them. On one occasion the counsellor was challenged by a potential group member as to the need for a screening. The counsellor decided not to include this person in a group whose goals were self-understanding through self-disclosure.

Insufficient Screening (-)

A teacher referred a student, Susan, to a counselling group that was focussing on building empathy and anger control. Susan is an extremely angry acting-out student who has not learned to accept responsibility for her actions. Whenever she is in trouble, she diverts the blame elsewhere. Susan does not admit she has difficulty dealing with anger. Although a limited screening interview took place prior to placement of the child in this group, no discussion regarding goals of the group took place. Susan was unaware that she was expected to talk about her anger in this group setting. When she was confronted with her anger during one session, the results were traumatic for her and the other members of the group.

Group Follow-Up Counselling Needed (-)

A young boy in an elementary school refused to attend a counselling group after having a conflict with another member. The conflict arose as the boy was extremely angry due to rejection of his parents. He took it out on another group member who appeared to come from a stable, caring environment. The group leader felt rejected by this youngster's refusal to come to the group. As a result he ignored the child and did not arrange for counselling to assist the child in dealing with the rejection he was experiencing.

COMMENTS AND QUESTIONS

This ethical article denotes a responsibility for the counsellor to screen prospective group members, particularly when the group goals focus on self-understanding through self-disclosure, and for the counsellor to ensure that there is professional assistance available to any one who needs assistance, both during and following the group session.

Group members should be informed of their responsibility when entering the group. These responsibilities might include: taking risks, self-disclosure, giving and receiving feedback, and keeping confidentiality. Group members should be made aware of the possible advantages and disadvantages of participating in a group. They need to know the possible psychological risks and how the group might disrupt their lives. They need to be informed that often friends and families may not support the changes they make.

It is extremely important to ensure there is professional assistance available during and following the group experience. Individual group members may need assistance coming to terms with painful issues resulting from the group process or other events in their lives. Sometimes these issues are of a highly complex and personal nature, and it is not appropriate to deal with them in a group setting. Furthermore, upon conclusion of the group, referrals should be made when and if group members have issues they wish to discuss further.

1. What types of questions should be asked during a group screening interview?

2. What behaviors or comments in a screening interview would keep you from including a person in your group?

3. What type of professional assistance would you arrange if you were planning to lead a personal-growth group?

4. What types of follow-up activities are needed for group members?

5. What are the special issues related to confidentiality when doing group work?

B16 COMPUTER USE

When computer applications are used as a component of counselling services, counsellors ensure that:

(i) **client and counsellor identity is verified;**

(ii) **the client is capable of using the computer application;**

(iii) **the computer application is appropriate to the needs of the client;**

(iv) **the client understands the purpose and operation of client-assisted and/or self-help computer applications; and**

(v) **a follow-up of client use of a computer application is provided to assist subsequent needs.**

In any case, computer applications do not diminish the counsellor's responsibility to act in accordance with the CCA *Code of Ethics*, and in particular, to ensure adherence to the principles of confidentiality, informed consent, and safeguarding against harmful effects.

Computerized Career Information (+)

At one employment counselling centre, a computerized career-information system is used to help clients make career decisions. The director of this centre insists that all counsellors are thoroughly familiar with the computer system, and that all clients receive at least an initial and follow-up session so that counsellors can both explain the computer counselling tool and can discuss the results with the clients afterwards.

High School Career Information (+)

At a large high school in a large city in Eastern Canada, all the students in their final year of high school are given the opportunity of spending an hour or more on the computer terminal, and work with an interactive career-information program designed to help them explore future career directions. The high school has a full-time guidance technician who assists the students with the computerized program. Following this session with the computer, all the students are scheduled for an appointment with one of the counsellors of their choice to make any additional plans regarding their possible career directions.

Open Computer Access (-)

In a small remote northern town, the area employment office is equipped with the latest in computer equipment. The manager makes sure that all the information on each client – biographical, work history, and counselling interview information – is stored in the computer. All this data in the computer, including the counselling interview material, is accessible to all the staff members including secretarial staff and clerks.

Emotional and Career Needs (-)

In a career-counselling program designed to help 35- to 45-year-old women (with limited education and formal work experience) enter or re-enter the world of work, one counselling outreach program had designed a program that consisted mainly of computer interactions. Although some of the women were interested in "what the computer said," many others had other counselling needs that required attention prior to sitting in front of a computer terminal and examining career information.

COMMENTS AND QUESTIONS

As computer applications become more sophisticated there is the danger that the "computer becomes the counselling," rather than a tool, to help the counsellor help clients. Computerized career-guidance programs must be restricted to those clients that can truly benefit from such programs. Besides making sure that clients fully understand computer applications, counsellors must guarantee that follow-up counselling is provided after clients use the computerized career-guidance programs.

1. How do counsellors typically determine whether computer applications are appropriate to the needs of the client?

2. What are the implications of computers and the internet with reference to confidentiality, informed consent and records?

3. In a school or employment counselling centre, should counsellors store interview data in the computer?

4. What data is appropriate to store in a counselling computer system?

5. How long should client information be stored in the computer?

B17 REFERRAL

When counsellors determine their inability to be of professional assistance to clients, they avoid initiating a counselling relationship, or immediately terminate it. In either event, members suggest appropriate alternatives, including making a referral to resources about which they are knowledgeable. Should clients decline the suggested referral, counsellors are not obligated to continue the relationship.

Aggressive Client (+)

A counsellor has had four sessions with a client. With each succeeding session the client becomes more aggressive, hostile and verbally abusive towards the counsellor. The counsellor decides to terminate the counselling relationship after the client refuses to cease the verbal abuse directed toward the counsellor. The counsellor suggests further expertise is required and offers to make a referral. The client agrees and the case is appropriately referred.

Intoxicated Client (+)

A counsellor is working with a client concerning alcohol dependency. It becomes apparent after three sessions that the client attends the counselling sessions intoxicated. The counsellor informs the client he cannot work with him under these conditions, but suggests a referral to an agency skilled in the area of alcohol abuse. The client refuses to accept the referral. The counsellor then explains he must terminate the relationship and follows through with this.

Referral Refused (-)

After counselling a client for several months concerning issues of intense grief, loss, and abandonment, the counsellor decides that she can be of little further help and recommends that the client receive intense grief therapy with a specialist in this area. After discussing this decision with her client, the client refuses the suggestion and states she views this as further rejection and abandonment. She reproaches the counsellor for even suggesting a referral. The counsellor, not wishing to upset her client any further, forgets the referral and continues working with her client.

Unresolved Counsellor Issues (-)

A counsellor who is recently separated carries unresolved marital issues and over-identifies with a recently separated client. The counsellor is unable to be objective and is not performing her role competently. There is no clear differentiation of boundaries between client and counsellor. The counsellor continues the therapeutic relationship despite the circumstances.

COMMENTS AND QUESTIONS

This ethical article provides a clear mandate for counsellors to recognize their own boundaries of professional competence and personal limitations. It is necessary for counsellors to keep in mind that their primary obligation is to the client. Counsellors must maintain a relationship with the client only if it is beneficial to the client. Being always accountable to the client, counsellors must at all times evaluate their own abilities as counsellors. When, and if, counsellors are in situations where they lack competence, they must recognize this and refer the client to a specialist or terminate the therapy. Counsellors should be aware of the services and resources in their community in order to refer clients when necessary. Counsellors should also be aware of their own abilities and limitations and share their struggles with their supervisors and colleagues. Most importantly, they should realize that referring clients or terminating therapy when necessary is sound judgment. Ethically, members must admit to themselves and to their clients when they are not competent to continue the therapy.

When the client refuses the referral or termination, the counsellor is still obligated to terminate the relationship. This article makes counsellors accountable to clients and to themselves. Continual self-awareness is the key to effective counselling.

1. How can counsellors be sure that they are not referring too soon? Should counsellors "hang in there" a little longer than the client expects them to?

2. How can a counsellor know when to terminate counselling?

3. Would you continue counselling a client if he or she refused your referral?

4. Is counselling that does not seem to be accomplishing anything better than no counselling at all? (See "Referral Refused").

5. How can counsellors determine if they are being of "professional assistance"?

B18 TERMINATION OF COUNSELLING

Counsellors terminate counselling relationships with client agreement when possible, when it is reasonably clear that: the goals of counselling have been met, the client is no longer benefiting from counselling, when clients do not pay fees charged, when previously disclosed agency or institutional limits do not allow for the provision of further counselling services.

However, counsellors make reasonable efforts to facilitate the continuation of counselling services when services are interrupted by such factors as counsellor illness, client or counsellor relocation, client financial difficulties, and so forth.

Awareness of Skills (+)

A client that a counsellor has been counselling regarding a family matter (death of a parent) discloses that he is drinking heavily and realizes that it is a problem that is getting worse. Upon discussion with the client, the counsellor and client agree that referral to Alcoholics Anonymous would be advisable in order to monitor his progress in this area, and to set up a support group.

Strong Personal Bias (+)

A teenager comes for counselling and discloses that she is pregnant and wants an abortion. After discussion with the client, the counsellor refers the girl to a pregnancy and abortion clinic due to strong pro-choice feelings on the part of the counsellor and the inability to be objective in her professional assistance.

Referral Required (-)

A family counsellor had just moved to a new city and had joined a family counselling centre. He had worked with a client for several sessions when he learned of the client's problems of dealing with alcohol abuse in her family. The family counsellor, unaware of an excellent alcohol counselling program in the city, continued the counselling in spite of his total inexperience with "alcohol counselling."

Suicidal Tendencies (-)

Kayla Thompson had just graduated with a master's degree in counselling psychology. Her total counselling experience consisted of an eight-month field experience in an elementary school, working with an elementary-school counsellor. Kayla joined a three-person counselling service and began her private practice.

One of her first clients was a young man who told of his "useless life," his feelings of "hopelessness," and his envying his cousin who had recently committed suicide. Kayla, in her zeal to begin counselling, never questioned her own ability to help her client, in spite of her total lack of training in helping suicidal clients. She continued her once-a-week, Rogerian-like sessions, and after the third session she learned that her client had had an unsuccessful suicide attempt.

COMMENTS AND QUESTIONS

As stated in the first article in this section, "counsellors have a primary responsibility to respect the integrity and promote the welfare of their clients." This means that counsellors want clients to function without their help and, thus, when it appears that clients' goals have been met, counselling will be discontinued. This article also says that when the client is no longer benefitting from counselling, counsellors will terminate counselling, or will make efforts to have counselling or other services be done by other professionals.

This article also encourages counselling professionals to make every effort to have counselling continue for clients if they are relocated, cannot counsel due to illness, or when clients do not keep up with their financial obligations.

1. How can counsellors know if the goals of counselling have been met if they are using counselling approaches that are less cognitive and behavioural?

2. How would you determine if a client is no longer benefiting from your counselling?

3. Would you discontinue counselling for a client who has not paid her or his counselling fees for the last two sessions? Explain.

4. What do you think about the policy of some employee assistance programs that do not allow for more than four to six sessions of counselling?

5. Do most counsellors terminate counselling when research suggests other services may be superior to individual counselling (e.g. Alcoholics Anonymous has been shown to be more beneficial than one-on-one counselling)?

❖ ❖ ❖ ❖ ❖ ❖ ❖ ❖ ❖ ❖

ESSAYS ON COUNSELLING RELATIONSHIPS

Confidentiality: Dialogue and Discernment

John Sumarah, Ron Lehr, and Linda Wheeldon

Introduction

The promise of confidentiality is often the most important agreement between a client and a counsellor. The counsellor agrees to hold in confidence the revelations that the client discovers and shares during the counselling experience. Prior to counselling, a client can feel that her story has never been taken seriously and that the truth of her life has not yet been told. As the process of counselling opens and the relationship between the client and counsellor deepens, the responsibility and challenge associated with ethics and confidentiality become more complex.

The Oxford dictionary defines ethics as "relating to morals; treating of moral questions; honourable; set of principles of morals rules of conduct." Confidence is defined as "firm trust; assured expectation; telling of private matters; allowed to know private thoughts or affairs." Confidentiality, then, as related to ethics, espouses a set of principles assuring trust or confidence. Confidentiality assures trust or confidence in the person to whom private matters are shared.

The professional literature addresses the value, importance and limitations of confidentiality (Daniels & Ferguson, 1998; Jackman & Dobson, 1993; Rankin, 1990; Vandecreek & Knapp, 1984). In a discussion of the well-known Tarasoff case, Bersoff (1997) suggests that guarantees for privacy and confidentiality are decreasing; Herlihy, Healy, Cook and Hudson (1987) note the type of ethical violations made by counsellors and the need to improve ethics education; and Fly, Van Buck, Weinman, Kitchener and Lang (1997) suggest that an ethics course did not deter graduate students from making ethical violations. A number of researchers have also noted the importance of professional judgement in the field of ethics. Vandecreek and Knapp (1984) and Daniels (1999) suggest clearly that laws and codes of ethics provide guidelines for practitioners, and that good professional judgement is still in great demand. Betan and Stanton (1999) report that decision-making models take into consideration contextual awareness and emotionality, in addition to rational analysis. These researchers distinguish between knowing what to do and committing to doing it. The importance and timeliness of the issue of confidentiality to the profession of counselling is reflected in *The Manitoba Journal of Counselling*, which devoted its June 1998 issue to the topic.

In this essay we acknowledge the tension between the need for confidentiality and the issue of social control. We will reason that a counsellor's professional and ethical behaviour include a more proactive practice of confidentiality. Specifically, we offer two main points: first, that counsellors engage with their clients in an ongoing collaborative dialogue about confidentiality as part of the therapeutic process, and; second, that counsellors use a more informed process of communal discernment to assist them with their ethical dilemmas related to confidentiality. We agree with Prilleltensky (1994) that ethics need to be of prime concern in performing daily duties, rather than reflect our current attitude, where professional ethics are essentially equated with rules and regulations to be upheld, and called upon to discipline misconduct. The law, policies, codes of ethics, and ethical decision-making models provide useful guidelines for counsellors. Our hope in this essay is to extend the discussion of confidentiality and ethical education to include the client and others in a discernment process.

The essay is introduced by a short discussion of confidentiality and its relationship to the CCA *Code of Ethics*. We proceed then to a discussion of the relational context of confidentiality, which provides a rationale and

framework for a discussion of our central points about dialogue and discernment. We offer case examples to make more visible and concrete our discussion, and we end with a summary of our main points.

Confidentiality and Codes of Ethics

Codes of ethics are based on ethical principles, which state in one way or another the need to respect and care for the client, and the need to respect and care for others. When there is a conflict or dilemma, counsellors are asked to examine the principles to see if one takes precedence over the other. Section B of the CCA *Code of Ethics* addresses counselling relationships and the importance of confidentiality. B1 states that:

> Counsellors have a primary responsibility to respect the integrity and promote the welfare of their clients. They work collaboratively with clients to devise integrated, individual counselling plans that offer reasonable promise of success and are consistent with the abilities and circumstances of clients.

When a counsellor and client engage in a counselling relationship, the CCA *Code of Ethics* asserts that the counsellor should inform the client about confidentiality and its limits. Article B2, on confidentiality, states:

> Counselling relationships and information resulting therefrom are kept confidential. However, there are the following exceptions to confidentiality:
>
> (i) when disclosure is required to prevent clear and imminent danger to the client or others;
>
> (ii) when legal requirements demand that confidential material be revealed;
>
> (iii) when a child is in need of protection.

The duty to warn is covered in Article B3:

> When counsellors become aware of their clients' intent or potential to place others in clear or imminent danger, they use rea-

sonable care to give threatened persons such warnings as are essential to avert foreseeable dangers.

The *Code of Ethics* of the American Counseling Association (1995) devotes its Article B to the issue of confidentiality. The code begins with a statement about the client's right to privacy and then notes the exceptions stated similarly to the Canadian Code. In addition, Article B.1.g. of the American Code states:

> When counseling is initiated and throughout the counseling process as necessary counselors inform clients of the limitations of confidentiality and identify foreseeable situations in which confidentiality is breached.

These sections of the codes suggest to us very clearly that privacy and confidentiality are the primary basis of a counselling relationship, and that there are a few serious limitations to confidentiality. There is a tension between the private and the public, between the need for confidentiality and the social obligation to inform.

The counselling relationship is based upon the trust that what is communicated is confidential. Without this trust it is unlikely that the counselling experience would proceed very far. Most counsellors agree on this point. Some hold the first principle of respect for the client's privacy as sacramental in nature, a sign of the unique and special nature of this relationship. The limits to confidentiality cover harm, legal obligation, and the protection of children. While the limitations appear clear enough, they can often require interpretation. For example, if there is a "suspicion" of harm, sufficient reason is given to breach confidence.

While, as counsellors, we are happy with the emphasis on privacy and respect the need for limitations, we are less comfortable with the latter. We entered the counselling profession to facilitate private conversations not

to restrict them. Thus, we grapple with a serious ethical tension. If the counselling conversation is not private, then what is it? If it is private with limitations, then both the counsellor and the client work within a tension, which should concern them both. If, as counsellors, we encourage clients to be open, honest and truthful, and then divulge that we are obligated to inform another about a particular disclosure, we are cautioning them about being too open, honest and truthful.

To complicate matters the courts can disagree with one another. One court ruling can argue that public peril is a more important concern than confidential conversations, while another court can rule in the opposite direction. Some courts and some professionals, as in the Tarasoff case, argue that public concern takes precedence over respecting certain professional relationships (Bersoff, 1997). On the other hand, one can argue, as in the Zezulka case, that some professional relationships require that confidentiality takes precedence over the duty to warn (The Supreme Court of Texas, 1999). We are working, as professionals, with conflicted notions about the promise of confidentiality. At the moment, as the CCA *Code of Ethics* indicates, we are working with limited confidentiality.

Some counsellors are clear that the discussion of limitations needs to happen in the first session. Others are reluctant to begin the counselling process with such a discussion, especially if their perception is that trust is one of the presenting issues for the client. How this conversation about the limitations of confidentiality takes place is of considerable importance. As counsellors, we do not want to dissuade people from disclosing important aspects of their lives. While the judgement around when to discuss the limitations to confidentiality will vary, the codes and the laws are clear about when a breach of confidence is required.

An initial conversation between a counsellor and a client might sound similar to this:

> "Before we continue with our session today, I would like you to know that what happens between us is confidential. By that I mean that anything you tell me is held in strictest confidence and will not be communicated to anyone else without your permission. If I believe you were going to hurt yourself or someone else, or if I believe a child is in need of protection, I will need to break my confidence with you. In addition, you should know that I keep a written record of our meetings and if subpoenaed, I will have to release my records to others."

Though this is an abridged version, for most practising counsellors this statement would probably contain the essential elements of an acceptable standard of practice, and would explain how they would inform clients in order to obtain consent for counselling. Drosdowech (1998) believes that this consent should be obtained in advance, and cover not only the intervention but also any related issues regarding record keeping, reporting, and other disclosures of information" (p. 22).

The Relational Context of Confidentiality

What kind of relationship engenders trust or confidence? Often, a discussion of ethics and confidentiality takes into consideration the rights of the client. This is as it should be in a profession such as counselling. Equal in importance to the primacy of the individual is the relational. There is no "I" without a "You." Another way of acknowledging this notion is the assertion that the individual is part of a community of persons. Consequently, trust or confidence is embedded in the relational since it implies a dynamic between, at least, two people. The client's confidence in the counsellor relies upon trust in this particular relationship.

Confidentiality is a relational issue that has a context often much wider than the counselling environment. Is the school or the agency generally perceived as a safe place in which to make private disclosures? Does the atmosphere and environment speak of trust and confidence among its members? Can the community be trusted?

Promising anonymity rather than secrecy may actually engender trust. How this is done, of course, will say much about the counsellor and the professional community. Anonymity may not always be possible as in the case of a referral. The issue, here, however, is the kind and extent of the disclosure, and the commitment to client participation and consent. How the referral person or agency then treats the disclosure will determine whether the client will continue to see the counsellor as trustworthy, and whether the counsellor will have continued confidence in the referral agent.

In essence, the reason that confidentiality is such an important issue, is that, in counselling, relationships are important. The basis of any relationship is trust and confidence. Counselling relationships are particularly sensitive to concerns around trust and confidentiality since the disclosures are most often of a personal and private nature. Thus, particular care and concern with respect to confidentiality needs to be exercised in these relationships. Dialogue and discernment are ways of manifesting this care and concern.

Confidentiality and Dialogue

We believe that the current standard of informing the client about the limits of confidentiality is rather "limiting" in itself and may not sufficiently take into account an equitable client/counsellor relationship. Based upon what we see as a hierarchical model of counsellors as "all-knowing" and knowledgeable of what are in the "best interests of the client," this standard fails to take into account the trust upon which most counselling relationships are established. Rather than simply fulfilling the duty to inform clients, we believe counsellors need to be more proactive and mutually active in their approach to confidentiality. We believe, as does Prilleltensky (1994), that "A commitment to treating persons fairly, equitably and with respect demands that a collaborative approach be used" (p. 210). This is in opposition to traditional models of intervention, which have generally operated from an "expert knows best" point of view.

In a collaborative approach, the counsellor proactively engages in a therapeutic discourse with the client on the subject of confidentiality. It is the responsibility of the counsellor to actively revisit the issue of confidentiality on a regular basis with the client. Canter, Bennett, Jones and Nagy (1994) suggest that a discussion of confidentiality does not simply occur at the onset of counselling but "thereafter as new circumstances warrant."

Some disclosures from the client leave the counsellor with a personal and professional disquiet. The counsellor may sit with these concerns without discussion. As the concerns increase, there are choices around how to address these with the client and whether to share these concerns anonymously with a supervisor. Concern and choice may lead to professional duty. It also becomes difficult to uphold confidentiality, as the revelations of the client can require the counsellor to work with material that can be at once overwhelming, confusing, hurtful and difficult.

Counsellors, through reflective practice, experience the importance to consult and be guided by others. While sharing the difficulties may be of benefit, there is no clear standard to which a practising counsellor can appeal when the situation is not one of safety, legal or professional/educational concerns. There are times in counselling when either or both parties may want to disclose information about the session, since both want to make sense of and derive meaning from the session. On a continuum of sustained concern, the first line below suggests that there are different circumstances in which the counsellor may want to disclose information that has been communicated to him or her under the agreement of confidentiality. The experience for the counsellor is one of sustained disquiet, confusion or threat. The second line identifies that, according to the professional standards of practice, there are times when there is a choice, and other times when there is not a choice and one is obliged to disclose information.

Part of the responsibility of counselling is the requirement to discern where on the continuum the issue of conflict is situated, as well as how to approach the dialogue with the client about breaking the vow of confidentiality when it is the appropriate action to take.

The issue of ongoing dialogue may be especially true in our schools where parents and staff may want to know, at least in a minimal way, how a student is progressing. In this dialogue we should attempt to balance the "right to privacy" with the "need to know." Consider the following example:

COUNSELLOR RESPONSE TO CONFIDENTIAL INFORMATION
A Continuum of Sustained Concern

Professional/personal disquiet	Counsellor confusion	Professional supervision	Counsellor incompetence	Threat to self/others Protection of child

Counsellor Choice / **Professional Duty**

Counsellor:
Bob, I've really appreciated talking with you about how anger has been getting you into trouble with your Grade 7 teacher and your classmates. In our time together, you've worked really hard at not allowing it to have such an unhappy influence upon you. Today, your teacher, Mr. Sheppard, asked me to meet with him regarding your progress so I was wondering if you and I could talk about what is important for him to know, as well as things we talked about that you would prefer that he not know.

Bob:
Does he need to know that I don't like that he never asks me to answer questions in class? He always asks Melissa and Tommy, but never me, even when I raise my hand!

Counsellor:
You and I have discussed your disappointment about not being called upon to answer questions in class, and how this is one of those things that gives anger an edge over you. If Mr. Sheppard knew this, do you think that his co-operation might help you?

Bob:
Yeah. Well, okay but don't tell him that I am jealous of Melissa. Does he need to know things I told you about my family?

Counsellor:
You and I have talked a lot about your family. What are some of the things you would prefer that I not share with Mr. Sheppard?

One can see in this example the effort to dialogue about what should and should not be shared with the teacher. The counsellor needs to respect the wishes of his client and the concern of a colleague. His conversation with the teacher is also confidential. Both professionals need to exercise care and respect in how they share with each other. The relationship between the student and the counsellor, and the relationship between the student and the teacher are at stake, as well as the climate of trust in the school.

A similar situation arises when an adult is referred from an agency. The client has a right to know what will be shared and the referral source has a right to know, at least minimally, the results of the counselling. There are times when a breach of confidence is not required but may in fact be appropriate. Thus, there is a need for ongoing dialogue on the subject with the client.

It is difficult to tell a client that you believe that it is important and necessary to share with others the information that has been entrusted to you. To suggest that their secret is no longer safe brings up considerations that challenge the very foundation of trust. Consider the following example of a potentially serious situation where the counsellor works within the tension of protecting the right to privacy with the social obligation to inform.

Counsellor:
Suzanne, if I could, I would like to discuss with you something that happened at the conclusion of our last session with which I have been struggling. Something that occurred just a few moments ago has sent me a warning sign. During the session, yesterday, we discussed that you are feeling immense distrust of your partner and that you believed that he has been involved with someone else. You have also shared in former sessions that you have been unable to stop self-abusing when you're feeling threatened. This morning, where you were sitting, I found a note to your friend John asking if you could borrow his gun.

Suzanne:
Is this why you called and asked to see me right away today?

Counsellor:
Yes. Just a few minutes ago you stated that you would never feel threatened again, and you are sick of hurting your body because someone keeps hurting you. When I put all of these factors together with my experience

of you during our last session and today, I became concerned.

At this point, it would be wise for the counsellor to proceed with considerable caution. The client may be very distraught and disconnected. If the counsellor is wrong, all that occurs is a slow-moving session. If the counsellor is correct, then there is sufficient time to work with the possibility that the client may have a gun.

Suzanne:
What experience? I am fine.

Counsellor:
Good. But somehow I am not experiencing us to be as connected as we often can be.

Suzanne:
So?

Counsellor:
It is important for me to try and ascertain what has changed that.

Suzanne:
I don't have to tell you everything.

Counsellor:
You are right. It is up to you what you tell me.

Suzanne:
You got that straight.

Counsellor:
By saying "You got that straight" do you think that I accept your right to privacy? (Suzanne nods yes) Suzanne, you have stated that you are sick of hurting your body and have promised yourself that you would never feel threatened again. I believe that you are feeling very distraught right now.

Suzanne:
Maybe.

Counsellor:
It sounds like you want something to happen to make things change. Are you planning a big change?

Suzanne:
Perhaps.

Counsellor:
What is the kind of change that you are considering?

The counsellor is aware now that there may be a gun and an intention to use it.

In fact, in this real-life event, the client had borrowed a gun and the counsellor was able to diffuse the situation and get the client to leave it in the office. The counsellor was then able to discuss with the client who should know about the gun. With the client agreement, the counsellor called the husband and the client's family. Following the intervention of the family, authorities were notified and the counsellor was able to act in support of the client as she faced the consequences of her actions.

The counsellor discerned a number of ethical requirements while attempting to engage the client in the dialogue. There was the potential for dangerous behaviour, and one might argue that the first responsibility to her client was the prevention of harm. To ensure that the client felt sufficiently safe to disclose her plan to hurt her husband was the most moral reaction to the unfolding events. The counsellor saw that there was no harm done. However, as soon as the potential for danger was passed, she did engage the client in deciding what would be the best next step and renewed the commitment to support her client.

There is little question that these kinds of circumstances would require the counsellor to break confidentiality, and uphold the wellbeing and safety of all involved if the client refused to disclose. In this situation it would be more than the protection of anonymity that would be transgressed. There is a threat. It is imperative that the counsellor rise to the challenge of protecting life and limb of all involved. However, the counsellor was skilful and was able to guide the disclosure from the client. If she told the client that she was breaking confidentiality and planned to call the authorities, or that she thought that the client had already secured the gun and had plans to use it, this might not have occurred.

Counsellors want to work closely and carefully with clients. Dialogue and collaboration are key components in the confidentiality issue. If dialogue and collaboration can provide safety for both the client and the community, then other steps need not be taken. If they do not, then the professional guidelines are available.

Confidentiality and Discernment

Birky, Sharkin, Marin and Scappaticci (1998) studied how restrictions on disclosure affect relationships between counsellors and referral sources. Having the client's co-operation is one of the keys to success. Often enough the counsellor and client can work out issues that arise between them. Schulz (1994) makes this clear when he recommends the three " Rs" to help avoid ethical violations: good rapport, reasonable behaviour, and record keeping. There are other times when consultation is needed. Article A4 of the CCA *Code of Ethics* states it this way:

> Counsellors take reasonable steps to obtain supervision and/or consultation with respect to their counselling practices and particularly, with respect to doubts and uncertainties which may arise during their professional work.

Consultation and supervision regarding ethical issues such as confidentiality suggest a communal discernment that extends beyond the counsellor and client. Others are now included in the discussion about the "right thing to do."

This discernment process is involved for a reflective practitioner. Apart from the accepted ethical guidelines around required disclosures there are many questions around confidentiality. Do I believe the disclosure,

has the potential to help a client as in a consultation? That is, do I have confidence that the professional community present will be helpful? Sometimes we share anonymously with other significant people in our lives. What factors influence my sharing of information? Am I portraying myself as an effective practitioner? Why am I sharing even anonymously? If it is for my well being, is that a justifiable reason for sharing? It may or may not be. That is the discernment.

Discernment is the process used to arrive at a decision and in the case of confidentiality whether to share information or not. Discernment is a thoughtful process involving the mind and the heart, that is, both thoughts and feeling. It is the search for "the right thing for me to do" in this situation given these considerations. Some situations pose few questions and the discernment is straightforward. Other decisions are more involved and often require input from others so that the discernment is more comprehensive. Once the opinions of others are sought (and the opinions usually vary), the counsellor is left with making the decision.

The ethical decision-making models presented in the CCA *Code of Ethics* are useful guidelines. Ethical decision-making models imply the skill and ability to discern. Discernment in the context of confidentiality is the process that leads to an ethical decision. As a process, it searches for knowledge and truth as revealed to the counsellor during the process. Discernment involves a reflection and articulation of our experience in an effort to derive meaning, make decisions and take action. As such, discernment is an ongoing cyclical dynamic, and it takes into consideration an analysis of exterior and interior forces related to the issue. The exterior forces may include a knowledge of legal requirements, codes of ethics, and school or agency policies. Clients and other professionals also have views that we need to consider. The interior forces include a knowledge of our thoughts and feelings on the issue. What are my thoughts and feelings about my client, others and myself as related to a particular ethical issue? In particular, we are concerned about fears and anxieties that may restrict our freedom to decide what we believe is the right decision to make and then to act on it. What principle takes precedence over other principles, at least, in this situation? How will I know I am doing the "right" thing? What is the moral ambiguity and how do I resolve it or live with it? While there are often no easy answers to these questions, we believe that asking the questions honestly and openly are the first steps in the discernment process.

Codes of ethics allow for consultation for good reason. No one individual possesses all of the wisdom often needed in an ethical dilemma. We are not always certain how to deal with issues related to confidentiality. Others may offer suggestions, which have a definite influence on the decision and action. We consult because we are interested in knowing what other professional people would consider doing in this situation. We are attempting to uncover reason at a time when reason is somewhat elusive to us. We need, as counsellors, to be especially open to other considerations when we are emotionally involved. We are searching, through discernment, for ways to free us up to decide and act ethically and morally. We are not simply passing judgement on our situation. We are trying to decide a course of action that is often not so obvious. If it were, there would be very little need to consult or to discern.

Once we are as aware and knowledgeable as possible about the interior and exterior forces at work in our situation, we might conclude that we are still not free to decide, in which case more reflection and discernment are necessary. The question we ponder is why am I not free? What is the real issue here and how do I address it? Good communal discernment should help address these questions? We might also make a decision and conclude a short time afterwards that it is not the right decision and so the cycle continues. We might engage in the discernment process in the following way:

1. Decide in whom (1 or more persons) you have trust and confidence, persons who will ask good questions related to the issue.

2. Address the issue as you see it with the facts and feelings of which you are aware. This gives others some needed background information before they can be helpful.

3. Listen to yourself share with others to see what surfaces for you as you articulate your views.

4. Welcome now the questions of others. No one has a complete view of anything, so it is likely that you have missed something along the way. No other person has the complete view either.

5. Questions and comments should reflect concerns for the client, for others and for you. In this particular case, what surfaces as the priority? What are the views of others on this?

6. If you examine the positive and negative propositions of a confidentiality dilemma you might state it as, "I will do such and such" and "I will not do such and such." When you state it this way, you need to look at the perceived advantages and disadvantages for your client, others and you. What do you think the situation will be for your client, others and yourself if you disclose information or if you do not disclose information?

7. Other persons should not suggest what you should do. They might know what they would do if they were in the situation but you are the one in it.

8. You need to honestly address your fears and anxieties if you are to move towards freely deciding and acting ethically. Are you fearful of your client's reaction, public reaction, or other professionals' reaction? Are your feelings of insecurity and inadequacy getting in the way of a good decision?

9. Once you have made a decision, you need to live through the consequences and understand what happened. You want to learn from this process since you will have other decisions to make.

An example of confidentiality and discernment involves a high school student who has been referred to the counsellor by his parent. The student has been to see the counsellor on several occasions, and has spoken about his school work and university. The last visit was quite different. Kevin spoke about his awakening to homosexuality and the feelings that he had towards another male student.

Counsellor:
Welcome.

Kevin:
Thank you. Before we continue, I want to ask you again about whether or not what I say here is confidential.

The counsellor repeats the promise of respect for privacy and anonymity, and reminds the student about issues related to threat and danger as well as professional constraints. The student then discloses with the counsellor a sexual relationship he has with another 16-year-old male. Kevin's fear and principal concern is his parents' reaction. Through the discussion, it is revealed that Kevin's father has made overt heterosexist comments in public and has embarrassed the family.

Later in the day the counsellor receives a message from the school secretary that Kevin's father called and wants to know what's going on with Kevin. The father notes that Kevin's grades continue to slip. The father believes that Kevin is involved with someone and wants the counsellor to call him back.

There is a tension that arises in such situations. The counsellor has a counselling relationship with Kevin as well as an appreciation of the parent's concern. At this point, a number of questions arise for the counsellor. The counsellor, uncertain about how to reply to the father, shares the situation in confidence with two other professionals in whom she has confidence. A number of questions are posed. Who is the client here? What are the fears of the counsellor? The counsellor reflects on the parent's need to know about their son's involvement. The counsellor also reflects on the privacy needs of the other 16-year-old. Also, she recalls very clearly that the disclosure about sexual involvement was made only after the promise of confidentiality was provided. She does not want to betray Kevin or the other 16-year-old, but is unclear about what to say to the father. The counsellor is convinced that the father will get angry if she simply acknowledges the confidential nature of the conversation and encourages the father to address his concerns with his son. Other questions arise around disclosure. Would disclosure pose more of a threat than no disclosure given the circumstances? What other consequences are there to disclosure? Does Kevin's father have the right to know about the other student? Is there a school policy about such matters? What is the most anxiety-producing part of this dilemma for the counsellor? The counsellor is encouraged to meet with Kevin to notify him that his father has called and has requested a reply. The counsellor is also encouraged, as in an earlier example, to learn from Kevin what he believes should be shared with his father.

Again, we see the need for dialogue and discernment around confidentiality with the client and anonymously, at times, with others. Discernment is not something we simply engage in from time to time. It is a regular part of the therapeutic process. We discern often whether to ask this or that question, or whether to make this or that comment to a client. We discern, also, whether we think we can be helpful or not with a particular client. Dialogue with the client around matters related to confidentiality require ongoing discernment. Thus, we need to understand how we discern and what is most helpful to us as we discern. In ethical decision making we are engaged in a level of discernment that can affect the life of the client, the community and ourselves.

Summary

The issue of confidentiality is of obvious importance to the client, the counsellor, the public and the professional community. This essay provides an initial discussion of two main points to further the discussion of confidentiality. Ongoing dialogue with the client around issues of confidentiality, and a more informed communal process of discernment around ethical issues related to confidentiality were presented as important aspects of the overall discussion about ethics and confidentiality.

References

Bersoff, D. (1997). *Ethical conflicts in psychology.* Washington: American Psychological Association.

Betan, E., & Stanton, A. (1999). Fostering ethical willingness: Integrating emotional and contextual awareness with rational analysis. *Professional Psychology: Research and Practice,* 30(3), 295-301.

Birky, I., Sharkin, B., Marin, J., & Scappaticci, A. (1998). Confidentiality after referral: A study of how restrictions on disclosure affect relationships between therapists and referral sources. *Professional Psychology: Research and Practice,* 29(2), 179-182.

Canter, B., Bennett, B., Jones, S., & Nagy, T. (1994). *Ethics for Psychologists: A commentary on the APA Ethics Code.* Washington, DC: American Psychological Association.

Code of Ethics. (1999). Canadian Counselling Association: Ottawa, Ontario.

Code of Ethics.(1995). American Counseling Association. In *The Professional Counsellor* by H. Hackney & S. Cormier. Toronto: Allyn and Bacon.

Daniels, T., & Ferguson, D. (1998). Key ethical issues for counsellors. *Guidance and Counselling,* 14(2), 3-7.

Daniels, T. (1999). Ethical behaviour in counselling. *Guidance and Counselling,* 14(2), 1-2.

Drosdowech, N. (1998). Consent, negligence and confidentiality in the school system. *The Manitoba Journal of Counselling.* 24(3), 20-23.

Fly, B., VanBuck, W., Weinman, L., Kitchener, K., & Lang, P. (1997). Ethical transgressions of psychology graduate students: Critical incidents with implications for training. *Professional Psychology: Research and Practice:* 28, 5, 492-495.

Herlihy, B., Healy, M., Cook, E., & Hudson, P. (1987). Ethical practices of licensed professional counsellors. *Counsellor Education and Supervision:* 2, 1, 69-76.

Herlihy, B., & Sheeley, V., (1988). Counsellor liability and the duty to warn: Selected cases, statutory trends and implications for practice. *Counsellor Education and Supervision:* 27(2), 203-216.

Jackman C., & Dobson, K. (1993). Ethical and legal aspects for Canadian Psychologists. *Canadian Psychology:* 34, 345-353.

Oxford Dictionary and Thesaurus. (1995). Oxford: Oxford University Press.

Prilleltensky, I. (1994). *The morals and politics of psychology.* New York: State University of New York Press.

Rankin, W. (1990), *Confidentiality and clergy: Churches, ethics, and the law.* Harrisburg: PA. Morehouse.

Schultz, W. (1994). *Counselling ethics casebook.* Canadian Counselling Association. Ottawa, Ontario.

Supreme Court of Texas. No. 97-1208. (1999). *www.capitol.state.tx.us.*

Vandecreek, L., & Knapp, S. (1984). Counsellors, confidentiality and life engendering clients. *Counsellor Education and Supervision:* 24(1), 51-57.

The Counsellor as Custodian: Protecting Our Clients' Personal Information

Jo-Anne Sargent

At a very basic level, the practice of counselling consists of the exchange of information between two (or more) individuals. Typically, this exchange is weighted toward the client, who provides information verbally, or in other forms such as journal entries, letters, art, photographs, questionnaires, assessment forms. Because counselling services are based exclusively on information clients tell or convey about themselves, counsellors necessarily become the custodians, guardians, and managers of that information. This essay is intended to provide guidance for counsellors in the fulfillment of these roles. In the interest of expedience, I will focus on recorded information, as discussions of confidentiality and verbal information have been addressed elsewhere.

In order to orient ourselves to the issues of record keeping and management, it is necessary to define what it is we mean by "record." A record is a document in any form (e.g. paper, computer file, audio or visual recording) containing personal information about a client. This information may be recorded by either the individual himself or herself (e.g. letters, art work) or the practitioner (e.g. case notes), and may or may not contain identifiers such as name and address. It is generally considered in privacy law that although the record itself (e.g. the actual paper, computer file, video tape) belongs to the practitioner or agency, the information contained in it belongs to the individual (see for example the *Freedom of Information and Protection of Privacy Act* British Columbia, 1992). The fact that the client owns his or her information has important implications for issues such as access to records and record reten-

tion (to be discussed below). It also lends itself to a custodial definition of record keeping: that counsellors are, in essence, the guardians and caretakers of something (e.g. their clients' personal information) that does not ultimately belong to them, and therefore owe their clients the highest possible standards of privacy protection.

When viewed from this perspective, the rights afforded to clients, and the duties involved in record keeping and management, become more clear. Specifically, it becomes apparent that if the information contained in records belongs to the client, they have the right to know that such records exist (e.g. that notes are written after every session, or that sessions are being recorded), to know how those records are stored and secured, to have access to their information, and to know who besides themselves will have access to it. Each of these issues will be considered individually.

Informed Consent and Records

Clients have the right to know that their personal information is to be recorded. An important, underlying notion is that clients have the right to make choices about what kinds of information they disclose or withhold in counselling, and that these choices may be affected by whether or not they know that information is to be recorded. For example, a client who knows his or her information is to be recorded may be more reluctant to discuss feelings of frustration as a single parent, fearing that the ex-spouse might access the information and use it in an upcoming custody battle. Although counsellors are often very discriminating about recording potentially damaging information (more on that topic below), the point is that it is the client's fundamental right to make that decision, and that in order to make fully informed decisions about the disclosure of information, they need to know that it will be recorded.

This point is consistent with Article B4 of the CCA *Code of Ethics* which states that, "Counsellors make sure that clients understand the implications of ... record keeping...." The fact that information is to be recorded may carry implications for the client that cannot be anticipated by the counsellor in all cases. There are, however, implications of keeping records that counsellors can and should inform clients of, consistently and as a matter of good practice. These include the exceptions to confidentiality that are dictated by law or codes of ethics, such as the duty to report child abuse (exceptions to confidentiality been discussed elsewhere, and will not be treated here in detail).

Briefly, counsellors have a duty to know the situations in which they have a legal and/or ethical obligation to share clients' personal information with others. Consistent with the previous point about clients' right to know *before* they begin disclosing that information will be recorded, is the notion that clients have the right to know (again, *before* they begin disclosing) the circumstances under which confidentiality will be broken so that, given that understanding, they are free to choose the personal information they wish to share.

So what might the process of informing clients that their information will be recorded look like in actual practice? The simplest and most effective practice is for counsellors to include information about their record-keeping practices on their written consent forms. As well as listing the exceptions to confidentiality, counsellors should include a short paragraph explaining that notes about sessions will be kept, how they will be secured (e.g. locked filing cabinet), the length of the retention period, and that clients may see their records upon request (more on these latter three points below).

Using Discretion in Note Taking

In addition to giving clients control over the disclosure of information by informing them that a record will be made, counsellors can also use discretion about the types of information they record as a way of minimizing the potential negative implications of record keeping. In their discussion paper on record keeping practices, Soisson et al. (1987) state that although some members of the medical profession argue that "no amount of documentation is too much and no detail is too small" (p. 500), the same practice should not necessarily be applied to psychological records. Some counsellors, with all good intentions, try to minimize any potential harm to clients by not keeping records at all. Besides being unprofessional, this practice would be in direct violation of Article B6 of the CCA *Code of Ethics*, which states that "counsellors maintain records in sufficient detail to track the sequence and nature of professional services rendered...."

The question then becomes one of how to strike a balance between the need to create a record of services provided, while minimizing the potential harm to clients that that record could have. Based on the discussions of Soisson et al. and others in the field of psychology and counselling (Fulero & Wilbert, 1987; Eberlein, 1990; Kagle, 1984; Frank, 1995), it is recommended that the recording of information be limited as follows:

a) by giving due consideration to the types of information included on client records, and the present and future risks and implications involved for the client; and

b) by considering particularly the relevance of certain types of information before including them in records, such as illegal behaviour, sexual practices, hunches, speculations, or guesses, value judgements, emotional reactions/responses, and personal opinions.

Security of Records

As custodians of their clients' information, counsellors must safeguard records from loss or theft, as well as from unauthorized access, disclosure, copying, or use (see the Canadian Standards Association's *Model Code for the Protection of Personal Information*, 1996). Article B6 of the CCA *Code of Ethics* also speaks of the obligation to safeguard and dispose of records in a responsible manner. A general guiding rule is that the degree of security measures employed should increase with the sensitivity of the information. It can be argued that counselling information is very sensitive, given its personal nature, and therefore warrants a high degree of security.

Methods of record security can be divided into three categories: (a) physical measures, (b) organizational measures, and (c) technological measures (Canadian Standards Association, 1996). If counsellors address all three areas, they can be confident of having adequate security measures in place. The first, physical measures, includes such things as locked filing cabinets and restricted access to files. Paper records should be kept locked, in a room away from public access (e.g. waiting areas). The second, organizational measures, includes the use of security clearances (e.g. for repair persons), and limiting access of files to those persons who have a legitimate "need to know" in order to perform their duties. The last category, technological measures, addresses the use of computers, fax machines, e-mail, cordless phones, etc. in counselling practice, and warrants a lengthier discussion.

In noting that exchange and disclosure of information is far easier than ever, Bennett (1991) (see also O'Reilly, 1995; O'Toole, 1994) warns that data protection policies consistently fall behind technological capabilities for invading privacy. For example, counsellors who keep notes or information on computer files should be aware that computer files that have been deleted from either disks or the hard drive can be recovered, and that software programs exist that enable the recovery of files that have been accidentally erased. It is also possible with some programs to recover information in files that has been written over with new information, so this method is not entirely secure either. The best method available for ensuring the complete obliteration of information on either disks or the hard drive is to perform a low level format. This method should be used before a computer containing client information is sold, traded, or disposed of, and also before discarding disks. Counsellors should also use passwords and encryption programs to protect sensitive computer information.

There are a few guidelines available that address privacy concerns and technology. Canada's Health Informatics Association (COACH) has published *Security and Privacy Guidelines for Health Information Systems* (1995), targeted toward health service providers. The Office of the Information and Privacy Commissioner of British Columbia (1996) has also issued a set of guidelines for the secure transmission of personal information by fax (see also Capen, 1995). There are also guidelines in the use of cordless phones for doctors in a special report of the *Canadian Medical Association Journal* (Mouzar, 1995). All of these guidelines discourage health practitioners from using these forms of technology to transmit or receive personal information, except in emergencies. Sometimes exceptions must be made in order to expedite health services, however, in which case common sense procedures should be used.

For example, when transmitting information by fax, the sender should use a cover sheet, and call ahead to ensure that the person who is to receive the information is available to receive it. This will avoid the possibility that sensitive information sits on a fax machine or desk in open view of other personnel. Fax machines that regularly transmit or receive sensitive information should also be situated away from high-traffic areas, or equipped with mail boxes and encryption.

Counsellors should also, as a rule, refrain from using personal identifiers in e-mail, when using cordless or cellular phones, or when leaving messages on answering machines or voice mail unless absolutely necessary. And counsellors should always check with clients first before leaving phone messages, as clients may not wish for others in the home or at work to know they are seeing a counsellor.

Record Retention

Record retention, or the notion of how long one should keep client records, is an issue to which many practitioners give little thought. Often, decisions are based on convenience or opportunity (e.g. cleaning out old records when moving offices), or on vague notions that the longer records are kept, the better. However, in keeping with idea of a custodial nature of record keeping, (i.e. that we are caring for and safeguarding the valuable property of others), comes the notion that the longer records are kept, the greater the risk becomes of misuse or inadvertent disclosure (Canadian Standards Association, 1996). Logically, then, the maximum length of time to keep personal information is no longer than the length of time for which it is needed. This is not to say that records should be destroyed immediately after counselling ends; indeed, often there is a need to keep records longer. For example, clients might want to return to counselling at a later date, or may want to review their records later; or counsellors may want the information for consultation purposes with other health professionals the client is involved with, or may want to keep it for legal reasons. The generally accepted retention period for counselling records is seven years after the last client contact, or seven years past the age of majority for minor clients (Ruebesaat & Porteous,

1995; College of Physicians and Surgeons of British Columbia, 1998). Practitioners or agencies who wish to keep records longer for data collection purposes should remove all personal identifiers after the seven-year-time period has expired, and transfer the data into a summary or database.

Counsellors in private practice, who consult or contract their services, should clearly specify their record retention policy to the employer or other involved parties, in order to avoid conflict after the records have been destroyed. Counsellors in all settings should also inform clients about the length of time their information will be kept on file. Finally, counsellors should use adequate disposal measures to destroy records. There are horror stories about partially burned records or records in trash bins being found and read by the public. The surest method for disposal is shredding, with burning an alternative under carefully controlled conditions.

Access to Records

Access to records can be divided into two main categories: access by persons other than the client (known as "third-party access"), and client access to their own information contained in the record. Third-party access will be discussed first.

Third-Party Access

Article B7 of the CCA *Code of Ethics* says that counsellors must obtain "express consent" before revealing client information to others, unless required by law. Most ethical guidelines support this requirement (e.g. the Canadian Psychological Association *Code of Ethics*, 1991, standard I.40). Keith-Spiegel & Koocher (1985) recommend that psychologists use consent or release-of-information forms that include the following elements:

> Which records are to be sent; the purpose or intended use; the date the form was signed; an expiration date; any limitations on the data to be provided; the name and

signature of the person authorizing the releases, as well as that person's relationship to the client; and the signature of a witness (p. 67).

Presumably, the recommended use of an expiry date is to discourage use of "blanket" consent forms, or forms that could be used for multiple instances of release. Under "limitations on the data," counsellors might request that third parties refrain from further sharing the information without express permission, or that the data be destroyed after a certain length of time. Forms like this would be used when counsellors wish to share information with other health care providers (e.g. medical doctors, psychiatrists) or for consultation purposes. It cannot be stressed enough, however, that information should only be shared with those professionals who have a legitimate need to know the information in order to provide optimal health care, and that if written consent is not always practical or feasible, clients must be informed as quickly as possible of the release of their information.

Although the practice of obtaining consent for the release of information seems relatively straightforward, there are numerous situations that can pose challenges for counsellors. These situations often lie outside the usual information-sharing circumstances with other health care providers, and may not occur with frequency, but can be confusing when they do arise. The situations discussed here will include requests for access by parents of minor clients, requests by courts of law (subpoena), and requests for access to records of deceased clients.

Parental Requests for Access to Records

Difficulties can arise in at least two different ways when parents request access to the records of their children. First, the child or youth may not agree to let the parent see the records (i.e. may withhold consent), and second, one parent may oppose the request by the other parent to access records (which sometimes arises in the course of custody battles). There are few guidelines for counsellors about how to respond to these types of situations. In the first instance, one extant guideline states that minors who were deemed capable of consenting to the service are thereby also deemed capable of providing or withholding consent to release information to parents (College of Physicians and Surgeons of British Columbia, 1998). In other words, if the counsellor determined that the child was mature enough to understand the risks of treatment and to consent to treatment without the parents' approval, then the counsellor must also obtain consent from the minor for the release of information to third parties, including parents. Counsellors should familiarize themselves with any legislation in their province that speaks to minors consenting to health services; this law would contain guidelines for determining the maturity of the minor, which can be used by counsellors to guide decisions about allowing control over the release of information. One final point is that minor clients may need guidance in considering all the implications of either granting or withholding consent to release information, whether to parents or other third parties who may have their best interests in mind. Counsellors should do their best to present all sides of the situation and explore all possible implications with the client, so he or she can make the best possible decision for themselves.

In the second example, it was suggested that difficulties can arise when one parent requests access to records against the wishes of the other parent. Given the previous discussion, we will proceed on the assumption that the minor client was too young to give consent, and counselling had been obtained with the consent of a parent. First, counsellors should obtain the consent of the parent who consented to services before releasing information. If the consenting parent does not want the other parent to have access to the records, legal advice should be obtained. In some cases, there may be no obligation to release the information without a court order. Counsellors in these situations should keep in mind the best interests of the minor client, and try to work with the parents to reach an agreement that best serves the client's needs.

Subpoena of Records

Article B2 of the CCA *Code of Ethics* states that the request by a court of law for counselling records constitutes one of the exceptions to confidentiality, and in fact, counsellors have no choice but to release records or face legal consequences themselves. However, it should also be stated that official request for records by a court should not be confused with informal requests by lawyers, and that counsellors should confirm that their records have indeed been requested by a court of law before releasing them. Ogloff and Polvi (1998) recommend that "informal requests" (i.e. requests by telephone or letter) from lawyers should be given the same response as other informal requests, and that counsellors should not be intimidated into releasing information without express consent from the client (p. 380). If counsellors are unsure whether the request is informal or an official, court-ordered request, they should consult a lawyer.

There are a number of options for counsellors in the case of legal demands for records, and only a few will be mentioned here. First, counsellors could simply comply with the court's request, making sure that *only* that information that has been requested is released. Counsellors should remember that complying with court-ordered requests for information is one of the ethically and legally accepted exceptions to confidentiality, and will not be considered a violation of the client's rights. Second, counsellors can

file a motion to "quash" or cancel the subpoena, for which they will need legal counsel. Sometimes the motion to quash is only partially successful, in that the resulting review of the documents leads to the judge's decision to narrow the request to specific portions of the record. Third, counsellors can encourage the client to contest the subpoena, with the argument that his or her privacy rights should not be violated. Fourth, counsellors could consult with a lawyer about ways to negotiate the partial release of information (for a fuller description of these and other options, see Ogloff & Polvi, 1998). It is highly recommended that counsellors always obtain legal advice when records are requested by lawyers or a court of law, in order to ensure that their clients' rights to privacy are protected as much as possible under the circumstances.

Requests for Access to Records of Deceased Clients

When making decisions about the release of information belonging to clients who are deceased, counsellors should give the same due consideration as if the client was living, and proceed on the assumption that, "Privacy rights do not automatically end when a person dies" (Office of the Information and Privacy Commissioner, 1994, Order No. 27-1994). Unless the records are ordered released under the law for the purposes of an inquest or inquiry, counsellors should not release them to family members, friends, the spouse, etc., and when in doubt, should consult with their provincial information and privacy office and/or a legal expert.

In summary, instances in which third parties request access to records often pose difficulties for counsellors. Counsellors should discuss the implications with clients before obtaining consent for the release of information, should always proceed with the best interest of the client in mind, and should obtain legal advice when appropriate. Counsellors should also be aware that there may be provincial information and privacy legislation in their province that pertains to their place of employment, and should familiarize themselves with it.

Individual Access

The second primary category of access to information involves requests by clients to access their own information on record. The right to access and, if necessary, to correct one's personal information is seen as an integral aspect of privacy protection (see *Freedom of Information and Protection of Privacy Act,* British Columbia, 1992; Canadian Standards Association *Model Code for the Protection of Personal Information,* 1996). Gelman (1992) states that the right to access is, "rooted in the principles of a democratic society – freedom, self-determination, and privacy." He also notes that, "Access policies, when appropriately implemented, can result in improved record keeping and more responsible and accountable services" (Gelman, 1992, p. 75).

Counsellors who work for federal or provincial public bodies (e.g. Corrections, Mental Health Services, public schools) should be aware that federal or provincial privacy laws allow for access to records by clients. Counsellors working in private practice, however, are not covered by legislation (except in Quebec, where privacy laws apply to both private and public sectors), but should be aware that the Supreme Court has established a precedence for medical doctors in private practice, which would most likely be applied to other health professionals in private practice as well. In that ruling, the patient was allowed access to her information on file, including information provided by another health professional with whom her doctor had consulted (*McInerney v. MacDonald, 1992*).

The fact that access rights are firmly established in privacy and case law does not mean, however, that counsellors cannot use discretion when making decisions about access. Privacy laws usually include lists of exceptions to access, which allow the practitioner to make judgments about whether they think the release of the information would be harmful to the client. If counsellors think the information may have a harmful effect on the client, they should consult with another mental health professional. Counsellors should also withhold material that is copyrighted (e.g. test protocols). However, both privacy law and the *McInerney vs. MacDonald* ruling make it clear that the burden of proof for withholding information lies with the practitioner. In other words, counsellors would need to be able to strongly justify the decision to withhold client information.

Counsellors should also be aware that they have the duty to withhold information about individuals other than the client when it appears in the file, unless they have that person's express consent to release the information. This pertains to information about someone other than the client, which was obtained from someone other than the client. For example, if the counsellor included in his or her notes, information from a social worker about a client's family member, the client would not be allowed to see that information without the express consent of that family member. The counsellor would either try to obtain consent, or exclude that information from the copy shown to the client.

So what might the practice of client access to records look like for counsellors? First, clients should be informed that they have the right to access the information in their records at any time. This practice can contribute greatly to gaining client trust and building rapport. A sentence informing clients that they can request access to their records can be included on the initial consent/information form.

Some counsellors make record keeping a collaborative effort with clients at the end of sessions, as a way of summarizing and achieving closure. Together, the client and counsellor review the session and write down the salient or meaningful points. This is a nice way to integrate the work done in counselling, as well as making record keeping transparent and accessible for clients.

When requests for access are made, counsellors should review the record for information about third parties and assess for potential harm to the client. Counsellors can then either make a copy of the record (it is appropriate to have clients cover the cost of copying), or review the record with the client.

Conclusion

Good practice means that counsellors who work in public settings stay informed about and follow information and privacy policies that are in place. Often, those policies are dictated by federal or provincial privacy legislation, and counsellors should be aware of client rights and their own responsibilities under the law. Counsellors in public settings should make sure their clients are informed that records will be kept, who will have access to them, how long they will be retained, and their right to access their personal information. Counsellors in private practice would do well to devise an information policy that meets the same standards of privacy protection as the current legislation. Putting time and thought into the custodial relationship with our clients' information is not only good professional practice, but may help avoid confusion and mistakes down the road.

References

Bennett, C. J. (1991). Computers, personal data, and theories of technology: comparative approaches to privacy protection in the 1990s. *Science, Technology, and Human Values, 16*(1), 51-69.

Canadian Association for the Advancement of Computers in Health (COACH) (1995). *Security and privacy guidelines for health information systems.* Edmonton, Alberta: Healthcare Computing and Communications Canada, Inc.

Canadian Psychological Association (1991). *Canadian Code of ethics for psychologists.* Ottawa, Ontario: Author.

Canadian Standards Association (1996a). *Can/CSA-Q830-96 Model code for the protection of personal information.* Etobicoke, Ontario: Author.

Capen, K. (1995). Facts about the fax: MDs advised to be cautious. *Canadian Medical Association Journal, 153*(8), 1152-1153.

College of Physicians and Surgeons of British Columbia (1997). Privacy Code for Physicians' Offices in British Columbia. *British Columbia Medical Journal, 39*(12), 646-649.

Eberlein, L. (1990). Client records: ethical and legal considerations. *Canadian Psychology, 31*(2), 155-166.

Frank, M. L. (1995). *Privacy and access: new directions for counsellors' record keeping practices.* Unpublished masters thesis, Simon Fraser University, Vancouver, British Columbia.

Freedom of Information and Protection of Privacy Act S.B.C. 1992, c.61

Fulero, S. M., & Wilbert, J. R. (1988). Record-keeping practices of clinical and counseling psychologists: a survey of practitioners. *Professional Psychology: Research and Practice, 19*(6), 658-660.

Gelman, S. R. (1992). Risk management through client access to case records. *Social Work, 37*(1), 73-79.

Kagle, J. D. (1984). Privacy versus accountability: a health care dilemma. *Social Work in Health Care, 9*(3), 25-36.

Keith-Spiegel, P. C., & Koocher, G. P. (1985). *Ethics in psychology: Standards and cases.* Lincoln, Nebraska: University of Nebraska Press.

McInerny vs. MacDonald (1992), 2 S.C.R. 138

Mouzar, M. (1995). A warning to MDs: if you want to keep calls confidential, hang up the cordless phone. *Canadian Medical Association Journal, 153*(10), 1485-1488.

Office of the Information and Privacy Commissioner (1994). *Order No. 27-1994.* Victoria, British Columbia: Author.

Office of the Information and Privacy Commissioner (1996). *Guidelines for the secure transmission of personal information by fax.* Victoria, British Columbia: Author.

Ogloff, J. R., & Polvi, N. H. (1998). Legal evidence and expert testimony. In Uhlemann, M. R., & Turner, D. (Eds.), *A legal handbook for the helping professional,* 2nd edition (pp. 379-401). Victoria, British Columbia: The Sedgewick Society for Consumer and Public Education.

O'Reilly, M. (1995). Use of medical information by computer networks raises major concerns about privacy. *Canadian Medical Association Journal, 153*(2), 212-214.

O'Toole, A. W., O'Toole, R., Webster, S., & Lucal, B. (1994). Nurses' responses to child abuse: a factorial survey. *Journal of Interpersonal Violence, 9*(2), 194-206.

Ruebsaat, G., & Porteous, T. (1995). *Records management guidelines: Draft for field testing.* Victoria, British Columbia: British Columbia Association of Specialized Victim Assistance Programs.

Soisson, E. L., VandeCreek, L., & Knapp, S. (1987). Thorough record keeping: a good defence in a litigious era. *Professional Psychology: Research and Practice, 18*(5), 498-502.

The Duty to Protect

Edward N. Drodge

Canadian counsellors' duty to protect is most clearly enunciated in Article B3 of the CCA *Code of Ethics*: "When counsellors become aware of their clients intent or potential to place others in clear or imminent danger, they use reasonable care to give threatened persons such warnings as are essential to avert foreseeable dangers." This ethical position arises from the legal principle of the "duty of care," though in the professional ethical literature it is typically referred to as the duty to warn or the duty to protect. It is reasonable to expect that counsellors may encounter individuals who express violent fantasies or actions towards another individual that warrant consideration within the scope of the duty to protect. This essay will review the legal principles at stake with reference to several Canadian cases involving mental health practitioners and the duty to protect.

Litigation involving counsellors most often concerns an issue of negligence, and is therefore governed by tort principles rather than criminal law (Birch, 1992). A "tort" is "a civil wrong inflicted on one person by another for which damages may be awarded" (Wuester, 1991, p. 193). Liability is easier to establish under tort law than under criminal law because in tort law the establishment of liability need not be "beyond a reasonable doubt." What is required is that the preponderance of evidence should weigh in favour of the litigant (Birch, 1992). Negligence presupposes that a legal duty of care is owed (Schopp & Quattrocchi, 1985). This duty to a third person has sparked numerous civil suits resulting in a variety of interpretations, some more restrictive than others, but all forcing counsellors to be wary of the legal and ethical demands being made on them. However, in the majority of cases where duty to protect has been an issue, the defendant has been an institution rather than an individual. While most of the legal ramifications regarding the duty to protect in the mental health field emerged from cases involving psychiatrists (Greenberg, 1985; Leong, Eth & Silva, 1994; Mangalmurti, 1994; Mendelson & Mendelson, 1991; Slovenko, 1988), a psychologist was at the centre of the case that sparked most of the controversy: *Tarasoff v. Regents of the University of California.*

The Tarasoff Case

Current notions amongst mental health professionals about the "duty to protect" are generally linked to the Tarasoff case, which has been documented by a number of scholars within both the psychotherapeutic and the legal fields (e.g. Greenberg, 1985; Slovenko, 1988). In 1969, a 25-year-old graduate student from India, Prosenjit Poddar, was seeing a clinical psychologist, Dr. Lawrence Moore, as an outpatient at the mental health services clinic of the University of California at Berkeley. During several sessions, Poddar revealed to Dr. Moore that he had violent fantasies of harming (killing) a female undergraduate of a neighbouring college who he believed had betrayed him and forsaken his love. The young woman was 19-year-old Tatiana (Tanya) Tarasoff, the sister of Poddar's roommate at Berkeley.

Dr. Moore, realizing that he had a difficult situation on his hands, discussed several courses of action with two of his clinical peers. Moore believed that he should confront Poddar about a gun he had bought, and attempt to get the gun away from him. One colleague advised Moore that he should avoid that strategy because he thought that Poddar would terminate treatment and flee. Another colleague recommended that Moore should attempt to keep Poddar in therapy, by whatever means, for as long as he could, in order to diffuse the violent fantasies Poddar was displaying. Both colleagues advised

Moore that he did not have to take specific action other than the therapeutic efforts already in progress. But Moore did take action.

When Moore's request for the gun was denied, he concluded that Poddar was becoming more agitated and "psychotic at times." He reluctantly breached confidentiality and informed the campus police, both verbally and in writing, that in his opinion, Poddar should be involuntarily committed for 72 hours because Poddar was a danger to another individual. The police questioned both Poddar and other acquaintances, including Tarasoff's brother, who did not feel he was dangerous. However, the police released Poddar without further action after they concluded that he did not constitute the danger Moore had indicated. Poddar did not return to the university clinic for further sessions with Moore. Two months later, Poddar stabbed Tarasoff to death.

The civil action initiated by the slain girl's parents named three defendants: Dr. Moore, the campus police, and the University of California. The case eventually reached the Supreme Court of California, which brought down its initial ruling in 1974. The causes of action against three of the four plaintiffs were dismissed by virtue of immunity granted to the university regents and the campus police. However, Dr. Moore was found liable for his failure to warn the victim (Greenberg, 1985). This decision was subsequently vacated following a petition for rehearing.

In what is known as Tarasoff II (*Tarasoff v. The Regents of the University of California*, 1976), the California Supreme Court "modified its holding and imposed a duty to exercise reasonable care to protect the foreseeable victim" (Slovenko, 1988). Thus, Tarasoff II does not issue a directive to warn, but rather to use "reasonable care to protect." It has been pointed out (Slovenko, 1988) that most of the cases of negligence brought against hospitals, previous to the Tarasoff ruling, resulted from administrative or communication errors.

The counselling of Poddar may be termed "mal-therapy" because it could be argued that Dr. Moore and other staff did not exercise reasonable care in the treatment of Poddar. However, tort law does not require accuracy of perceptions, rather it is based upon reasonable foreseeability. In some cases where potential injury is serious, even if the likelihood of its occurrence is not great, reasonable steps to prevent it must be taken (Fleming, 1983). Dr. Moore's actions may be viewed as reasonable foreseeability, indeed actual foresight.

Duty of Care in Canada

Although there have been far fewer cases of the Tarasoff type in Canada, it appears that Canadian courts are following in the footsteps of their American counterparts, at least insofar as they have given a variety of rulings. Establishing a duty of care is typically problematic for courts because it involves an examination of a variety of policy considerations including responsibility for bearing the risk of injury, economic factors, and the social utility of a defendant's action (Smith, 1984).

As indicated previously, it is uncommon for individual counsellors to be found negligent in performing their duty of care to clients and the public. In fact, a thorough search of the legal literature by this author did not find any Canadian cases where counsellors were found negligent in their duty of care. On the other hand, other mental health practitioners and several Canadian institutions have been sued for negligence in this duty, and there has been one major verdict for the plaintiff.

One recent case (*T. S. v. Gaskell,* 1997) that bears notice concerns a social worker in Ontario, who was sued for professional negligence by her client. The client alleged that the social worker failed to recognize the potential harm that could result from having the client recount her history of childhood sexual abuse. Additionally, the client alleged that the social worker did not ensure that proper supportive measures were in place to allow the client to cope with the ensuing emotional upheaval that she alleged resulted from having the social worker conduct a thorough history taking. The plaintiff claimed that as a result of the counselling she received, she entered into a period of suicidal depression, drug abuse, and alcoholism from which she did not recover for five years. The court held that the defendant had not breached the appropriate standard of care in performing her counselling duties. It was demonstrated that the social worker and her client had a strong therapeutic relationship, that the defendent was aware that there was social support in place for her client (involvement with Alcoholics Anonymous), and most significantly, that the client expressed a desire to discuss the details of her past abuse and was not pressured in any way to recount such details. The judge made the observation that the standard of care expected of a therapist was not one of perfection. This is significant because it suggests that counsellors will not be held to unreasonably high standards of care. The case is illustrative because it demonstrates a general principle in cases of negligent duty of care cited in *O'Brien v. Michigan Central Railway*. "Negligence consists of two elements, namely, the duty to take care and its breach, with the burden of proving both originally resting upon the plaintiff."

A problematic issue for many counsellors is identifying to whom they owe a duty to protect apart from their clients. The legal principle of the duty of care extends to the wider public in cases where individuals pose a general danger as a result of their mental state. Most counsellors are aware of their legal responsibility to report incidents of abuse, particularly when it involves children. However, in at least one case, it was argued that

mental health practitioners may be negligent in the performance of this duty. In *S. (P). v. B. (S.K.)*, a psychiatrist informed the Children's Aid Society of his client's allegations of sexual abuse. This was consistent with the psychiatrist's standard of care to his client and with his duty under the provisions of the Family Services Act. However, his client's family sued him for negligence on the grounds that his formal report to Children's Aid contained erroneous information, and was therefore harmful to the family's reputation. The Ontario General Division Court held that the plaintiff's cause for action be dismissed on the grounds that the psychiatrist had a duty to protect only his client and not the client's family. This case is important for counsellors, who must recognize that in allegations of abuse, the duty to protect extends in the first instance to the client making the allegations, not to the party against whom the allegations are made.

The issue of foreseeability of danger is an important legal principle because it may be crucial in determining the extent of the duty of care. The general principle of foreseeability has been summarized in a number of cases of negligence outside the mental health sphere: "Caution must be exercised against a danger if such a danger is sufficiently probable so that it could be included in the category of contingencies normally to be foreseen" (*Mossop v. Gilmour*). In another legal statement about foreseeability, the opinion was expressed that, "If the possibility of the danger emerging is reasonably apparent, then to take no precautions is negligence" (*Smith Transport Ltd. v. Campbell*). Reasonable precautionary measures are central to the test of foreseeability. As *Mossop v. Gilmour* indicated, "The law does not require a prudent man (*sic*) to foresee everything possible that might happen." Several Canadian cases involving mental health practitioners are insightful regarding this issue, though again, counsellors were not central figures.

In 1977, *Wellesley Hospital v. Lawson* (Birch, 1992) concerned a violent inpatient who escaped a "secure ward" and assaulted another patient in the hospital. The plaintiff alleged that the hospital was liable because it did not take the necessary precautions to detain a known danger. The case ultimately reached the Supreme Court of Canada, which cited the Tarasoff case by way of finding the hospital negligent (Birch, 1992). Although the circumstances of this case did not involve the invocation to warn a third party, it was the hospital's duty to protect third parties through provision of secure wards.

Another Canadian case that made reference to the Tarasoff case is *Tanner v. Norys* (Birch, 1992), a case that occurred in Alberta in 1980. A psychiatrist was charged with false arrest and wrongful imprisonment after he notified the police of his patient's purchase of a gun and threats against a third party. The court found in favour of the defendant in this case, because it determined that the police acted independently of the therapist in making the arrest after they received an additional phone call from the plaintiff's wife.

Wenden v. Trikha (Birch, 1992) concerned a university student in Alberta, who was diagnosed with a major mental illness and was being treated with both medication and outpatient group therapy. However, because he did not take his medication regularly, he experienced persistent hallucinations and erratic behaviour. Despite warnings from his psychiatrist not to drive his car, he ran a red light in downtown Edmonton, crashing into another car and seriously injuring the driver of that car. A lawsuit alleging negligence was brought against the young man, the hospital, and the psychiatrist. The court found only the driver to be liable, noting that mental illness was not a defence against liability. The judge in this case stated that he paid close attention to Tarasoff's ruling, in particular whether a breach of duty occurred, and whether the psychiatrist owed a warning to

the public. He concluded that neither the hospital nor the psychiatrist had acted improperly.

A final Canadian example (*Haines v. Bellissimo*) of the duty of care owed by mental health practitioners, concerns a case of negligence against a psychologist, a psychiatrist, and the McMaster University Medical Centre. The widow of a client who had committed suicide sued the defendants for failure to take actions that might have prevented the suicide, specifically hospitalizing him. In making his ruling, the judge found no evidence that the defendants could have reasonably predicted their client's suicidal act, and therefore that they had no grounds to hospitalize him. The therapists involved exercised reasonable care and were prudent in their treatment actions.

Confidentiality and the Duty to Protect

Concern for the safety of others must be balanced by respect for the rights of the individual. Confronted with the prospect of a potentially dangerous client, all counsellors have a duty to warn the intended victim or victims, and the police. However, taking such action has negative consequences. Any breach of confidentiality that occurs jeopardizes the chances that the counsellor has of establishing a sound working relationship, based on trust, with the client. Birch (1992) suggests keeping the client in therapy may be a better means of averting danger (p. 100). Indeed, the most dangerous action might be to act in such a manner that would result in termination of the relationship. Schopp and Quattrocchi (1985) contend that while Dr. Moore, in Tarasoff, did expect his client to act violently, his actions curtailed therapy and may have increased the likelihood that his client would act out. However, whether warning an intended victim would increase or decrease the probability of danger remains empirically untested. Nevertheless, a counsellor, who has established a working alliance with a client, would be in an excellent position to effect change in that client's violent thoughts and behaviours by establishing a stable counselling relationship. The suggestion that the Tarasoff ruling leaves the single option of warning is erroneous: in fact, it could be the most detrimental option. Counsellors, who are too intimidated by the prospects of working therapeutically with a dangerous client, and who may wish to take a more direct response to avoid liability, could adhere to an alternative found in many ethical guidelines for mental health practitioners: referring the client to an appropriate specialist who can continue counselling. Counsellors, engaged in therapeutic efforts with a client, need to be vigilant to the potential for violence and prepared to act quickly to protect the interests of the public.

Dickens (1986) suggests that appropriate action to protect the likely victim also protects the patient (p. 776). There is some limited empirical evidence in a study by Beck (1982), showing that discussing a warning with the client strengthened the therapeutic relationship. It may be argued that a client who communicates to a counsellor, a threat against a third party, is indicating that he or she wants help, and in fact, does not want to follow through with the threat. Also, as Greenberg (1985) pointed out, it is unreasonable to expect a person to stand idly by while allowing another individual to inflict harm. These considerations raise the issue of whether all clients should be informed of the limits of the confidentiality privilege. A notable phrase emanating from the Tarasoff case is, "...the protective privilege (of confidentiality) ends where the public peril begins."

Conclusion

The Tarasoff case sparked an increased awareness of the ethical and legal responsibilities surrounding the duty to protect, while increased public alarm about violence has prompted a further shift towards policies and laws concerning public safety. The combination of these factors underscores the importance for counsellors to become knowledgeable about what constitutes a reasonable standard of care, to recognize whom the duty of care may be owed, and to exercise reasonable precautions when danger can be foreseen. Central to all of this is the therapeutic alliance between the counsellor and client. It seems fair to assert that when this relationship is developed optimally, there is more opportunity to have a standard of care that meets all of the ethical and legal requirements.

References

Beck, J.C. (1982). When the patient threatens violence: An empirical study of clinical practice after Tarasoff. *Bulletin of the American Academy of Psychiatry and the Law, 10*, 189-201.

Birch, D.E. (1992). Duty to protect: Update and Canadian perspective. *Canadian Psychology, 33*, 94-101.

Canadian Counselling Association. (1999). *Code of ethics*. Ottawa: Author.

Dickens, B.M. (1986). Legal issues in medical management of violent and threatening patients. *Canadian Journal of Psychiatry, 31*, 772-780.

Fleming, J.G. (1983). *The Law of Torts*, 6th Ed. Toronto: Carswell.

Greenberg, L.T. (1985). The evolution of Tarasoff: Recent developments in the psychiatrist's duties to warn potential victims, protect the public, and predict dangerousness. *The Journal of Psychiatry and Law, 12*, 315-348.

Haines v. Bellissimo (1977) 82 D.L.R. (3rd) 215.

Leong, G.B., Eth, S., & Silva, J.A. (1994). Silence or death: The limits of confidentiality when a psychotherapist is threatened by the patient. *The Journal of Psychiatry and Law*, 235-243.

Mangalmurti, V.S. (1994). Psychotherapist's fear of Tarasoff: All in the mind. *The Journal of Psychiatry and Law*, 379-409.

Mendelson, D., & Mendelson, G. (1991). Tarasoff down under: The psychiatrist's, duty to warn in Australia. *The Journal of Psychiatry and Law*, 33-61.

Mossop v. Gilmour (1950), 1 W.W.R. (N.S.) 29, [1951] 1 D.L.R. 440 (B.C. C.A.), affirming [1950] 2 W.W.R. 77, [1950] 4 D.L.R. 218 (B.C. S.C.), reversed on other grounds (*sub nom. Gilmour v. Mossop*) [1951] S.C.R. 815, [1951] 4 D.L.R. 65.

O'Brien v. Michigan Central Railway (1909), 19 O.L.R. 345 (C.A.).

Schopp, R.F., & Quattrocchi, M.R. (1985). Tarasoff, the doctrine of special relationships, and the psychotherapist's duty to warn. *The Journal Psychiatry and Law*, 12, 13-37.

Slovenko, R. (1988). The therapist's duty to warn or protect third persons. *The Journal of Psychiatry and Law*, 16, 139-209.

Smith, J.C. (1984). *Liability in negligence.* Toronto: Carswell.

Smith Transport Ltd. v. Campbell (1951), [1952] O.R. 479 (H.C.).

S. (P.) v. B. (S.K.) (September 25, 1997), Doc. 95-CU-93625 (Ont. Gen. Div.).

T.S. v. Gaskell (1997), 147 D.L.R. (4th) 730 (Ont. Gen. Div.).

Tarasoff v. Regents of the University of California, 118 Cal. Rptr. 129, 529 P.2d.533 (Cal. 1974).

Tarasoff v. Regents of the University of California, 113 Cal. Rptr. 14, 551 P.2d.334 (Cal. 1976).

Wuester, T.J. (1991). Legal liability. In D. Turner & M.R. Uhlemann (Eds.), *A legal handbook for the helping profession* (pp 193-208). Victoria,BC: University of Victoria.

Boundary Violations in Counsellor-Client Relationships

Glenn W. Sheppard

Boundary violations are acts that breach the core intent of the professional-client association. They happen when professionals exploit the relationship to meet personal needs rather than client needs. Changing that fundamental principle undoes the covenant, altering the ethos of care that obliges professionals to place clients' concerns first. In fact, all of the boundaries in a professional-client relationship exist in order to protect this core understanding (Peterson, 1992, p. 75).

Peterson uses the term "boundary violations" to refer to a wide range of behaviours all of which constitute a violation of the ethical codes of conduct, which are intended to set boundaries for relationships between human service professionals and their clients. In her book, *At Personal Risk: Boundary Violations in Professional-Client Relationships,* she elaborates on four broad categories of relationship violations. They are:

- *A reversal of roles.* This refers to situations in which the professional helper, in order to satisfy his or her personal needs, switches places with the client so that the client becomes, to a significant degree, the caregiver. Such role reversals violate the primary ethic of care in which the client's needs must remain paramount. They also blur the relationship boundaries between the client and helper, and leave the client vulnerable to abuse.

- *The secret.* Here, Peterson is referring to the professional's withholding of information that is vital to the client and the concealment of which may be damaging to the client's well-being in the relationship. The lack of disclosure may also compromise the client's ability to exercise informed con-

sent. Typically, in such circumstances, the helper has dual agendas, which contribute to maintaining the secret.

- *The double bind.* This type of boundary violation occurs whenever the client is placed in a "no-win" situation because of some request or demand by the professional helper. These are situations that present a conflict of interest for the client, who feels trapped as a consequence of such a request because there is uncertainty as to implications for the therapeutic relationship of refusing or acceding to it.

- *The indulgence of personal privilege.* Violation of this nature occurs whenever the professionals decide to use their authority or position in the relationship to fulfil a personal agenda. This could range all the way from using information gained from the client to pursue some personal benefit outside the relationship, to establishing a sexual relationship with a client.

Whether or not one accepts precisely Peterson's conceptualization of ethical boundaries and their violations within professional relationships, it is clear that it is grounded on the fundamental principles on which a professional code of ethical conduct is based. These ethical principles, according to Kitchener (1984, 1985), who has analyzed many human service ethical codes, are: do no harm; benefit others; respect autonomy; be fair; and be faithful. In the Canadian Counselling Association *Code of Ethics* these fundamental ethical principles are stated as follows:

a) respect for the dignity of persons,
b) not willfully harming others,
c) integrity in relationships,
d) responsible caring,
e) responsibility to society and
f) respect for self-determination.

Most human-service professional associations give supremacy to the ethical concept of *non-malefience,* which has its origins in the history of medical ethics (Childress, 1981; Beauchamp & Childress, 1979). This principle is more commonly stated as "above all do no harm." It obligates professional helpers not only to avoid inflicting harm intentionally, but to refrain from engaging in any activities in which there is a high risk of harm to their clients without any offsetting benefits. Clearly, when professional relationship boundaries are violated, clients are vulnerable to abuse, and helpers may fail to keep their ethical obligation to "do no harm."

These ethical principles and concepts are now receiving increased attention within the counselling profession and are reflected in the various ethical codes or standards of practice of national counselling associations (American Counseling Association (ACA), 1995; British Association of Counselling (BAC), 1990; Canadian Counselling Association (CCA), 1999). Also, many scholars are making a significant contribution to advancing our understanding of this critical dimension of professional life (Corey, Corey, & Callahan, 1998; Eberlein, 1988; Herlihy & Corey, 1997; Kitchener, 1988, 1996; Koocher & Keith-Spiegel, 1998; Pope & Vasquey, 1998; Tymchuk, 1986). This may be an indication of the growing maturity of the profession as well as a response to the public demand for accountability in the provision of quality mental health services. Whatever its origin, it is consistent with Gibson and Mitchell's (1990) observation that, "A profession's commitment to appropriate ethical and legal standards is critical to the profession's earning, maintaining, and deserving the public's trust" (p. 45).

Historically, the counselling profession was quick to publicly express an understanding of its legal and ethical obligations. The American Personnel and Guidance Association produced the first code of ethics for counsellors in 1961, just 10 years after its founding. In fact, it established an ethics committee just one year following its forma-

tion as a professional association (Gibson & Pope, 1993). This first code has been published in three revised editions since 1961 (American Association for Counseling and Development (AACD), 1988) and recently as the American Counseling Association it has published a *Code of Ethics and Standards of Practice (1995).* The much younger Canadian Guidance and Counselling Association adopted its first code of ethics in 1981 and approved a revised code in 1989 (CGCA, 1981, 1989). This Association has also taken a new name, and as the Canadian Counselling Association (CCA), it approved a new code of ethics in 1999.

The CCA *Code of Ethics (1999)* acknowledges that the determination of appropriate ethical behaviour must frequently be made when issues are not clear-cut and in circumstances in which conflict between several competing ethical principles must be resolved. For this reason, the Code contains a brief introduction to the process of ethical decision making by providing an abbreviated six-step sequence, which counsellors may follow as an aid to resolving ethical dilemmas. An ethical decision-making approach has considerable utility for assisting counsellors with the sometimes difficult issues associated with those circumstances likely to lead to the boundary violations highlighted by Peterson (1992).

Although all professional ethical codes address boundary violations, maintaining clear and appropriate boundaries around relationships with clients continues to challenge helping professionals (Johnson & Farber, 1996; Vallally, 1995). Lamb and Catanzaro (1998) define boundary behaviors as, "...those behaviors or activities that mark the limits or parameters of appropriate, good, and ethical practice, including both structural (e.g. roles, time, place-space) and process (e.g. gifts, language, self-disclosure, physical contact, interactional patterns) dimensions" (p. 498). Smith and Fitzpatrick (1995) point out that there can be at least two aspects to non-sexual boundary concerns. They are boundary crossings and boundary violations. A boundary crossing is a departure from usual counselling practice but may not necessarily place a client at risk. However, violations are those behaviors that place the client and the counselling process at risk of harm. Nevertheless, all boundary crossings should be of concern to counsellors and kept to a minimum, since some researchers have concluded that sexual misconduct by helping professionals is typically preceded by a number of inappropriate non-sexual behaviors. This, they believe, contributes to the gradual erosion of a commitment to the maintenance of an ethical professional relationship (Folmon, 1991; Simon, 1989; Somer & Saadon, 1989; Strasburger, Torgensen, & Sutherland, 1992).

The determination of appropriate boundary behavior within professional helping relationships can be quite complex and may be influenced by factors such as counsellors' theoretical perspective, presenting problem, and client behavior. Despite this complexity, the competent management of relational boundaries is essential to the maintenance of professional safety and integrity in the counselling process (Epstein, 1994). Boundaries must be established within a process, which, by its nature, is intimate and private, and includes all the challenges associated with balancing closeness and maintaining appropriate physical and psychological distance (Wilmer, 1991).

Clients are often in their most vulnerable state when they seek out counselling. As clients share the most private details of their lives, counsellors listen empathically to their clients' pain, confusion, anxieties, and failures as well as to their hopes and dreams. Such sharing can result in feelings of intimacy and closeness. The individual attention and understanding of a counsellor may be unique in the life of a client. It is not surpris-

ing then that this may engender strong feelings that may distort the client's view of the counsellor. In fact, some theoretical constructions of counselling acknowledge such distortions as an expected and normal *transference* phenomenon (Corey, 1996; Miller & Stiver, 1997; Pope & Vasquey, 1998).

Transference usually means the transfer by the client to the counsellor and to the counselling relationship of emotions, needs, and conflicts experienced with significant others in their lives. These writers believe that counsellors must learn to recognize the many manifestations of transference and manage this phenomenon for the benefit of client insight and growth. Transference, it is assumed, can be evident in a wide range of strong client feelings towards the counsellor, such as love, anger, and ambivalence. Clients, for example, may develop an excessive need to please their counsellors in order to feel liked or valued by them.

From this theoretical perspective, there is also the complementary counsellor process of *countertransference*. This refers to the counsellor transferring to the client feelings, thoughts, and behaviours, which stem from the counsellor's life experiences. Such transfer might result from unresolved personal issues or from unmet needs in the counsellors' life. Gerald Corey (1986) talks about the potential in counselling for countertransference to occur:

> I found that when I began counselling others, old wounds opened and feelings that I had not explored in depth came to the surface. Being a therapist forces us to confront our unexplored blanks related to loneliness, power, death, sexuality, our parents and so on (p. 362).

Counsellors who work with children and adolescents may face unique challenges with respect to the maintenance of appropriate professional boundaries. Children and young adolescents share concerns with adult counsellors, which often center around interpersonal conflicts and hurtful experiences with parents, teachers and other adults. Counsellors may violate relationship boundaries by an excessive need to be overprotective of their young clients. Children may also distort the counselling relationship out of their need to receive from the counsellor nurturance and care that is lacking from other adult caregivers in their lives. Clearly, it is the responsibility of counsellors to protect children from abusive experiences. However, this responsibility can be extended beyond acceptable relational boundaries when counsellors, out of their unmet needs, unwittingly develop unhealthy dependency upon their clients, and the dynamics of their counselling are transformed into those of a needy, overprotective parent.

Eliana Gil (1991) cautions about the strong risks of countertransference when counsellors work with abused children:

I have alluded to countertransference issues throughout the book but deal with them at length here to emphasize the relevance of countertransference to work with abused children. These children are extremely vulnerable, with tumultuous histories of abuse, neglect, and deprivation. Consequently, they elicit a multitude of responses from the therapist, including intense hostility, sadness, protective impulses, and/or feelings of helplessness.

Occasionally, a child's plight demands special attention, and highly qualified professionals may find themselves behaving in unexpected ways. For example, one clinician treating an abused child got herself licensed as a foster parent and entered into a dual role with the child. Another clinician, whose rescuing instinct was strongly evoked, adopted a child. While these may be extremes, the clinician must carefully assess any personal conduct that threatens to develop outside the boundaries of a strict therapeutic relationship (p. 192).

Of course, working with adult clients who have been sexually abused as children may be just as challenging. Briere (1992), author of a number of publications dealing with therapy for sexually abused adults, is cognizant of the risks of boundary violations when doing this work. It is his view that:

Perhaps the most dangerous form of abuse-related countertransference is that of boundary violation. Examples of therapist boundary confusion include any type of sexual behaviour with clients, obviously inappropriate personal disclosures during therapy, excessively intrusive questions or statements, and most generally, the therapist's use of the client to gratify the therapist's own needs (p. 160).

Whether or not one accepts the theoretical constructs of transference and countertransference, most counselling practitioners and theorists would agree that the counsellor's unmet needs can sometimes be so enmeshed in the counselling relationship as to obstruct his or her objectivity. Most individuals who enter the counselling profession have a strong motivation to help others, and they receive satisfaction from being instrumental in helping others to make positive personal changes. These are acceptable and even desirable motivations, but it requires that counsellors be "...aware of their own needs, areas of unfinished business, potential personal conflicts, defenses and vulnerability" (Corey, 1996, p. 369). By continuing to develop their self-understanding, counsellors minimize the risks of relationship violations and avoid abuse of their power within counselling.

Erickson (1993) succinctly captures just why avoiding boundary violations is so important for those seeking counselling;

Perhaps the main problem with boundary violations is that they replicate for the most susceptible their experiences with role reversal in their families of origin. Thus, instead of a corrective emotional experience, our conduct with those clients offers a replication of these early, familiar, very damaging encounters. It should be noted that many boundary violations are initiated by clients who consciously or unconsciously try to reduce the window of their own vulnerability by equalizing the power differential in the relationship. These situations, too, are our responsibility to manage appropriately to prevent the client's having yet another experience with being hurt by those who are supposed to help (p. 87).

One of the most serious boundary violations, which continues to be of grave concern to counsellors, clients and the general public is sexual contact between helpers and their clients. Such unethical behaviour continues to occur despite the fact that ethical codes of conduct for all the helping professions explicitly prohibit it (Haspel, Jorgenson, Parsons, & Wincze, 1997; Somer & Saadon, 1999; Vasquey & Kitchener, 1988). Very early in the history of the helping professions, sexual contact between helpers and their clients was considered to be unacceptable. In fact, the medical profession has had this prohibition since it was included in the Hippocratic Oath over two thousand years ago (Edelstein, 1943). Despite this long-standing taboo, sexual exploitation continues to occur within all helping professions (Gabbard, 1989; Lamb & Catanzaro, 1998; Layman & McNamara, 1997; Somer & Saadon, 1999; Pope, 1990; Screenivasan, 1989; Wilson, 1993).

The *CCA Code of Ethics* (1999) states the prohibition against sexual contact between counsellors and clients in *Section B, Article B12* as follows:

Counsellors avoid any type of sexual intimacies with clients and they do not counsel persons with whom they have had a sexual relationship. Counsellors do not engage in sexual intimacies with former clients within a minimum of three years

after terminating the counselling relationship. This prohibition is not limited to the three year period but extends indefinitely if the client is clearly vulnerable, by reason of emotional or cognitive disorder, to exploitative influence by the counsellor. Counsellors, in all such circumstances, clearly bear the burden to ensure that no such exploitative influence has occurred, and to seek consultative assistance.

This ethical clause is similar in intent to those found in the ethical codes of other professions. For example, in its position paper (Screenivasan, 1989), the Canadian Psychiatric Association states, "Erotizing the physician/patient relationship is unacceptable under any circumstances and cannot be rationalized as therapy" (p. 234). The Code of Ethics (1996) of the National Association of Social Workers stipulates, "The social worker should under no circumstances engage in sexual activities or sexual contact with current clients, whether such contact is consensual or forced." In several additions to the principles of medical ethics adapted by the American Psychiatric Association (APA, 1985), practitioners are alerted to the potential for sexual misconduct, "...the necessary intensity of the therapeutic relationship may tend to activate sexual and other needs and fantasies on the part of both patient and therapist, while weakening the objectivity necessary for control" (p. 4). Also, like most codes, it states that, regardless of the behaviour of the client, it is the clear and unequivocal responsibility of the professional under all circumstances to maintain this fundamental relationship boundary.

Article B12 also addresses the issue of post-termination sexual relationships between counsellors and their former clients. There is not an absolute prohibition against such a possibility. However, it does set a time limit of three years after the ending of the counselling relationship and presents a general criterion, which must be met in order to make any such sexual contact ethically acceptable. Also, the counsellor is held responsible for ensuring that there is no risk of exploitation and other psychological harm because of the previous professional contact and/or the mental health status of the former client.

This position is similar to that taken by the American Psychological Association (1995), but which sets a shorter time limit of two years. Professional contact between a counsellor and a client can be for any of a wide range of services, which can vary considerably with respect to duration and intensity. A contact can be as brief as one session with limited client self-disclosure and little possibility for the development of a transferential relationship. In such a circumstance, it may be inappropriate to have an absolute prohibition against any future non-professional contact between the counsellor and client. However, this point of view remains controversial and the American Psychiatric Association has an absolute ban on sexual contact with former patients (Gabbard, 1994; Lamb & Catanzaro, 1998).

According to a study by Gibson and Pope (1993), as well as others (Borys, 1994; Anderson & Kitchener, 1996), counsellors continue to support this basic ethical standard, and disapprove of a wide range of behaviours that they consider to be a violation of this relationship boundary. These researchers report that one-quarter of the 21 behaviours judged to be unethical by the 579 certified counsellors in their study were of a sexual nature. These findings are encouraging, however, since they indicate a growing public and professional awareness of the disturbing extent of sexual abuse within society in general, including abuse within professional-client relationships.

The prevalency rates for this most serious boundary violation are difficult to establish. However, a number of national surveys based on self-reports conducted in the U.S. have been summarized by Pope and Bouhoutsos (1986). They conclude that sexual intimacies between clients and male therapists happen at a rate of from nine to twelve per cent and from two to three per cent between female therapists and their clients. Another U.S. study, conducted by Bajt and Pope (1989), reports that an alarming proportion of sexual contact between therapists and clients include children and adolescents. They report that 56 per cent of the victims in this study were young clients, including girls between the ages of three and seventeen years with a mean age of thirteen years and boys ranging from seven to sixteen years with an average age of twelve years. In a study by Parsons and Wincze (1995), therapists were asked whether they had treated in the past three to four years, any clients who reported having sexual contact with a previous therapist. As many as 22 per cent reported that they had done so.

Somer and Saaden (1999) conducted a study in which they "undertook to enhance our understanding of the process of leading to sexual boundary violation in psychotherapy from the perspective of former exploited patients" (p. 504). They concluded that the offending psychologists were well regarded but typically worked alone and that there was a gradual sequence of ethical boundary crossings eventually leading to the sexual misconduct. Many of the clients had been sexually abused as children. Their initial positive response to the sexual activity was later seen by those clients as exploitation and revictimization. The authors make the very well-founded recommendation that professionals working with sexual abuse victims not work in isolation from other colleagues, and that they seek out peer consultation and support.

Some feminist therapists have expressed the view that sexual contact within counselling, the victims of which are largely female clients, can only be properly understood within the context of larger societal problems that result in the abuse of women (Gartell, Herman, Olarte, Feldstein, & Localio, 1986). Others believe that counsellors and counsellor-educators should be particularly well-qualified and committed to the advancement of our recognition, understanding, and change of the societal structures and processes that lead to the victimization of women (Frazier & Cohen, 1992).

Regardless of the reasons advanced or debated to explain the sexual misconduct by professional helpers, clearly this critical problem requires urgent attention. In the counselling profession, as in other human service groups, it demands increased recognition as an issue of immediate concern and requires the attention of individual practitioners, counsellor-educators and professional organizations.

One strategic element in an overall initiative to address the risks of sexually based boundary violations has been proposed by Corey (1991). He argues that counsellor education programs do not adequately prepare counsellors to deal appropriately with sexual feelings that they may experience towards their clients. Corey proposes that, "Educational programs must provide a safe environment in which trainees can acknowledge and discuss feelings of sexual attraction. If counsellors do not learn how to deal with these feelings, they are more likely to become involved in seductive exchanges. Ideally, practitioners will be able to accept their sexual feelings and desires toward certain clients, and at the same time see the distinction between having these feelings and *acting* on them" (p. 68).

Counsellors may experience feelings of sexual or romantic attraction towards clients more frequently than has been previously acknowledged (Gottlieb, Sell, & Schoenfeld, 1988). In a U.S. survey, 87 per cent (95 per cent of men, 75 per cent of women) of the 575 psychotherapists responding to a ques-

tionnaire reported that they had been sexually attracted to their clients on at least one occasion (Pope, Keith-Spiegel, & Tabachnick, 1986). Pope and his associates (Pope, Sonne, & Holyroyd, 1993) have published a book entitled *Sexual Feelings in Psychotherapy: Explorations for Therapists and Therapists-in-Training.* This publication is based on the author's research on sexual attraction in therapeutic relationships. It should serve as a useful resource in responding to Corey's call to deal with this important dimension of counselling in graduate training and in continuing professional development programs.

Some professionals, (e.g. Gartell, Herman, Olarte, Feldstein, Localio, 1986) advocate that professional human-service associations should adopt a policy of mandatory reporting to ethics committees or licensing boards of all complaints heard from clients of being sexually abused by their counsellors. In fact, a number of U.S. states have legislated such mandatory reporting (Appelbaum, 1990). In Canada, two provincial commissions examining sexual misconduct in the medical profession have each recommended mandatory reporting by medical practitioners whenever a patient alleges that they were sexually abused by a member of that profession (Hardy, 1993; Wilson, 1993).

In the United States, five states have enacted legislative prohibitions against therapists sexual misconduct. The Minnesota statute, for example, provides the following conditions for civil action against any offending therapist:

> A cause of action against a psychotherapist for sexual exploitation exists for a patient or former patient for injury caused by sexual contact with the psychotherapist, if the sexual contact occurred: (1) during the period the patient was receiving psychotherapy from the psychotherapist; or (2) after the period the patient received psychotherapy from the psychotherapist if (a) the former patient was

emotionally dependent on the psycho-therapist; or (b) the sexual contact occurred by means of therapeutic deception.

The patient or former patient may recover damages from a psychotherapist who is found liable for sexual exploitation. It is not a defense to the action that sexual contact with a patient occurred outside a therapy or treatment session or that it occurred off the premises regularly used by the psychotherapist for therapy or treatment sessions. (Minn. Stat. 148A.02. 1996). (In Haspel et al., 1997, p. 64).

In addition to the increased attention to sexual dual relationships between counsellors and clients, there has been a dramatic increase in professional concerns over non-sexual dual relationships (Anderson & Kitchener, 1996; Borys, 1994; Gibson & Pope, 1993; Kagle & Giebalhausen, 1994; Pearson & Piazza, 1997; Pope et al., 1987; Pope, 1991). Dual or multiple relationships are present whenever counsellors have non-professional relationships with clients, supervisees, research participants, or students. Such relationships can occur before, during and after professional relationships and many of them have the potential to compromise counsellors ethical obligations to their clients.

The CCA *Code of Ethics* (1999) addresses dual relationships in a number of articles of the Code.

B8. Dual Relationships

Counsellors make every effort to avoid dual relationships with clients that could impair professional judgment or increase the risk of harm to clients. Examples of dual relationships include, but are not limited to, familial, social, financial, business, or close personal relationships. When a dual relationship can not be avoided, counsellors take appropriate professional precautions such as informed consent, consultation, supervision, and documentation to en-

sure that judgment is not impaired and no exploitation occurs.

B11. Relationships With Former Clients

Counsellors remain accountable for any relationships established with former clients. Those relationships could include, but are not limited to those of a friendship, social, financial, and business nature. Counsellors exercise caution about entering any such relationships and take into account whether or not the issues and relational dynamics present during the counselling have been fully resolved and properly terminated. In any case, counsellors seek consultation on such decisions.

C7. Conflict of Interest

Counsellors who engage in consultation avoid circumstances where the duality of relationships, or the prior possession of information could lead to a conflict of interest.

F7. Relational Boundaries

Counsellors who work as counsellor-educators, trainers, and supervisors establish relationships with their students, trainees, and supervisees such that appropriate relational boundaries are clarified and maintained, and dual relationships avoided.

Anderson and Kitchener (1996) report that psychologists identify a number of distinct types of non-sexual, non-romantic relationships with clients. They are: personal-friendship, collegial-professional, supervisory-evaluative, religious, collegial-professional plus social, and workplace. These contacts they further divide into those that are circumstantial and others that are intentional.

Pearson and Piazza (1997) have made a very helpful contribution to this challenging ethical area by proposing a comprehensive classification of dual relationships based on their review of previous efforts appearing in the literature, including Anderson and Kitchener's analysis. As they point out, often well-meaning and ethically motivated counsellors and other professionals can be unaware of the ethical implications inherent in the duality of relationships. The following excerpt from their classification system can help to heighten awareness of this problematic area:

Circumstantial Multiple Roles
At times, dual relationships occur out of pure coincidence. Examples would include a counselor who is returning defective merchandise to a store where the only clerk is a current client, or a counselor whose child befriends the child of a client. As noted by Smith and Fitzpatrick (1995), such incidents are inevitable in small communities. The risk in these cases seems to be primarily a misinterpretation of which relationship is in effect at the time, and therefore which relationship "rules" are in effect. For example, the aforementioned store clerk could interpret his or her customer's complaints or demands as personal attacks, thereby affecting the client-counselor relationship.

Structured Multiple Professional Roles
Dual relationships often occur because they are integral to a professional's job. They can occur between professional colleagues or between a professional and a nonprofessional, such as a student or a client. What is essential to this type of dual relationship is that the nature of all the relationships is professional. Structured multiple professional roles are prevalent in counselor education and supervision. Kurpuis, Gibson, Lewis, and Corbet (1991) pointed out that faculty and supervisors can hold multiple roles simultaneously, including those of instructor, advisor, supervisor, administrator, employer, and mentor. These roles are typically perceived as complementary and are not necessarily thought to create conflicts of interest for

the professional. However, problems can arise if the professional loses sight of, or takes advantage of, the power differential inherent in his or her role (e.g. the faculty member who requests first authorship of an article when the student co-author deserves it). The supervisee or student may given in to the professional's wishes due to the power differential of one relationship, even if the nature of the other relationship is peer-like.

Shifts in Professional Roles
Dual relationships can occur when there is a change or shift in organizational structure, thereby changing the relationships of those within the organization. An example of such a shift would be two therapists in an agency who have developed a close friendship. Because there is no power differential (they are both at the line staff level), this creates no difficulty. The supervisor of their program then resigns, and one of them successfully bids for the position, gaining supervisory authority over the other. Other examples of this are when clients become co-workers or former students are hired as faculty in programs from which they graduated, suddenly becoming educators to former peers and peers with former educators.

Personal and Professional Role Conflicts
In this type of dual relationship, there may be a pre-existing professional relationship that is followed by a personal relationship, or the parties may have already developed a personal relationship that is followed by a professional one. Circumstances in which a professional relationship becomes complicated by the development of a subsequent personal relationship seem to have received the most notoriety, primarily because of increasing attention to sexual dual relationships between professionals and their clients, students, or supervisees. However, this type of dual relationship does not have to be sexual or romantic in nature. Social or peer-like dual relationships, such as collaborating on publications or engag-

ing in a shared pastime (such as a sport or a hobby), are also examples of mixing personal and professional roles.

The Predatory Professional
This final type of dual relationship occurs "when professionals exploit the relationship to meet personal needs rather than client needs" (Peterson, 1992, p. 75). Predatory professionals deliberately seduce or exploit others, unconcerned with anything but their own needs.
(Pearson & Piazza, 1997, pp. 92-97).

The dual relationship clauses in the CCA *Code of Ethics* implicitly recognize that counselling relationships are characterized by a significant power differential. Clients are typically at their most vulnerable state when seeking help. They are expected to be open and self-focussed in the counselling encounter. This is not the emotional status or behaviour expected of the counsellor. Indeed, such openness and self-preoccupation by the counsellor could very well constitute ethical misconduct. It is this inherent power imbalance that can make dual relationships so challenging to the maintenance of appropriate relational boundaries.

Typically, studies of the beliefs and experiences of helping professionals with respect to dual relationships have involved asking participants to respond to an inventory of behaviors presented by the researchers (Anderson & Kitchener, 1996; Borys, 1988; Gibson & Pope, 1993). The results of these studies suggest a lack of consensus with respect to some of the behaviors at the lower end of the duality scale, but there appears to be an agreement that certain behaviors are never acceptable, such as: selling a product to a client; engaging in sexual activity with a client during counselling or after termination; inviting a client to a personal party or social event; accepting more than a small token gift from a client; accepting an invitation from a client to attend a social event;

and, inviting a client to an office party or open house. A Canadian study is now being conducted by a graduate student at the University of Victoria in which members of the CCA in British Columbia are being asked what their beliefs and experiences are with respect to dual relationships (Tracey Nigro, personal communication, November, 1999).

With our heightened awareness of this area of ethical concern, it is not surprising that a variety of behaviors are consistently identified because of their problematic duality. St. Germaine (1993) has added to this list of counsellor behaviours, which, in her view, constitute a dual relationship with clients:

• buying a product or service from a client,
• selling a product to a client,
• entering into a business or financial arrangement with a client,
• attending social events of a client or inviting a client to social events,
• developing a friendship or social relationship with a client or former client,
• accepting gifts from a client,
• counselling a client's close friend, family member, or lover,
• counselling a close friend or family member, or the lover of a friend or family member,
• counselling an employee or student, or a close friend or family member of an employee or student (p. 29).

During the past decade, there has been increased attention to dual relationships within higher education (Bowman, Hatley & Bowman, 1995; Rupert & Holmes, 1997). Some writers have focussed, in particular, on the multiple roles integral to the work of those educators in professional preparation programs (Congress, 1996; O'Conner, Slimp & Burian, 1994). Counsellor-educators and others are urged to increase their attentiveness to the multiple roles that they might be expected to fulfil, and whenever possible to avoid the duality of relationships, which might result in contradictory goals and expectations, and have the potential for harm to their students. In addition to *Article 7 in Section F* of the CCA *Code of Ethics*, this obligation is addressed in two additional articles, namely,

F4. Clarification of Roles and Responsibilities

Counsellors who engage in counselling supervision of students or trainees take responsibility for clarifying their respective roles and obligations.

F8. Obligation to Inform

Counsellors who work as counsellor-educators, trainers, and supervisors take steps to inform students, trainees, and supervisees, at the beginning of activities associated with these roles, of all reasonably foreseeable circumstances under which confidentiality may be breached during such activities.

Counsellor-educators may be particularly at risk of unwittingly entering into dual relationships since they often fill many roles, including supervisor, administrator, teacher and mentor. As others have pointed out (Bowman et al., 1995; Congress, 1996; Corey et al., 1998; O'Conner et al., 1994; Pearson & Piazza, 1997), counsellor-educators and supervisors need to be alert to the potential ethical pitfalls of dual relationships before they engage in counselling with their students or supervisees. The risks of blending these roles, according to Kitchener (1988), are, "...confidentiality may be compromised, student autonomy sacrificed, the therapy process impaired, and objectivity damaged..." (p. 217).

The British Association of Counselling (BAC) in its various codes of ethics addresses the ethical concern over dual relationships (BAC 1986, 1990). For example, in its *Code*

of Ethics and Practice for the Supervision of Counsellors (1986) it states:

> Supervisors and counselors are both responsible for setting and maintaining clear boundaries between working relationships and friendships or other relationships, and making explicit the boundaries between supervision, consultancy, therapy and training (BAC, 2.3, p. 175).

The British codes recognize the potential for a conflict of interest when those with managerial responsibility for counsellors also serve as supervisors. It sets out the following ethical guideline to avoid the potential risks in such duality of roles:

> Counsellors who have line managers owe them managerial accountability for their work. The counselling supervisor role should be independent of the line manager role. However, where the counselling supervisor is also the line manager, the counsellor should also have access to independent consultation support (BAC, B.3.3, 1990).

There is also a growing recognition of the potential for boundary violations associated with the experiential components of programs to prepare group counsellors as well as with the personal growth experiences required in some counsellor education programs (Forester-Miller & Duncan, 1990). There is the concern that the multiple roles of counsellor-educators who teach and supervise these important components of counsellor education programs can unwittingly have a negative consequence for students. Therefore, the CCA *Code of Ethics* (1999) contains the following two clauses intended to alert counsellor-educators, trainers, and supervisors to these concerns and of the need to take the necessary precautions.

F10. Dealing with Personal Issues

Counsellors responsible for counsellor education, training, and supervision recognize when such activities evoke significant personal issues for students, trainees, and supervisees and refer to other sources when necessary to avoid counselling those for whom they hold administrative, or evaluative responsibility.

F11. Self-Growth Activities

Counsellors who work as counsellors educators, trainees, and supervisors ensure that any professional experiences which require self-disclosure, and engagement in self-growth activities are managed in a manner consistent with the principles of informed consent, confidentiality, and safeguarding against any harmful effects.

In addition, counsellor-educators and others would do well to heed the advice of Bowman et al. (1985) who state the following based on their study of this complex ethical area:

The findings of this study support the need for continuing professional debate and research regarding ethics within the area of faculty-student relationships. More important, the focus should be expanded to include more student input, because mentoring, friendship, and social interaction often have a profound influence on a student's overall graduate training experience. Students and faculty can benefit from exploring the issues of what constitutes a dual relationship, what unethical behaviors are, and how the abstractness of any ethical code on faculty-student relationships should be interpreted (p. 241).

The Association for Specialists in Group Work (ASGW) also addresses the dual relationship issues in its *Ethical Guidelines for Group Counselors* (1989). To minimize the risks to students, it set the following standard of conduct for counsellor-educators:

Students who participate in a group as a partial course requirement for a group course are not evaluated for an academic grade based upon their degree of participation as a member in a group. Instructors of group counseling courses take steps to minimize the possible negative impact on students when they participate in a group course by separating course grades from participation in the group and by allowing students to decide what issues to explore and when to stop. (#9 [g])

School counsellors need to be particularly cognizant of the ethical challenges associated with the duality of roles, since they frequently have to balance their responsibilities to students, parents, colleagues and the community (Hardy, 1986). Ethical dilemmas can emerge when the expectations of these groups are in conflict. For example, if school counsellors are expected to accept school disciplinary functions, it may compromise their obligations to place the welfare of clients first, since it is difficult to reconcile the dual roles of disciplinarian or informant and counsellor. If possible, school counsellors should avoid disciplinary roles such as lunchroom or bathroom monitor, substitute teacher, or hall supervisor.

School counsellors can avoid some of those ethical dilemmas by being sensitive to and anticipating the potential complications arising from attempting to fulfil multiple roles. They can, in collaboration with their professional colleagues, reach a shared view of their role and responsibilities and ensure that it is clearly communicated to students, teachers, administrators, and parents.

Of course, as many authors acknowledge, helping professionals who work in small communities and in institutions, such as schools and hospitals cannot always avoid multiple relationships with clients (Brownlee, 1996; Keith-Spiegel & Koocher, 1985; Schank & Skovholt, 1997). Schank and Skovholt (1997) conducted a study of the dual relationship dilemmas experienced by psychologists working in rural and small communities. They concluded that:

> Overlapping relationships are inevitable in rural and other small communities where community involvement lessens suspicion and increases approachability and where "denying help to a potential client because of a pre-existing relationship could mean that the person gets no help at all" (p.44).

Kitchener (1988) has proposed a number of guidelines, which might help counsellors, counsellor-educators, and other helpers, regardless of type of work environment, to recognize those dual relationships that have a high probability of leading to ethical difficulties. She suggests the use of these three guidelines:

> First, as the incompatibility of expectations increases between roles, so will the potential for misunderstanding and harm; for example, the incompatibility of the expectation of a therapist and a supervisor.

> Second, as the obligations of different roles diverge, the potential for divided loyalties and loss of objectivity increases.

> Last, as the power and prestige between the professional's and consumer's roles increases, so does the potential for exploitation and an inability on the part of the consumers to remain objective about their own best interests.

> These three taken together suggest that the relationship has a high potential for misunderstanding, confusion and damage (p. 219).

Herlihy and Corey (1997) conclude their comprehensive treatment of dual relationships in counselling with the following succinct thematic summary of the state of our current understanding of this complex area of ethical concern:

- Multiple relationship issues affect virtually all mental health practitioners, regardless of their work setting or clientele.
- All professional codes of ethics caution against dual relationships, but newer codes acknowledge the complex nature of these relationships.
- Not all multiple relationships challenge us to monitor ourselves and to examine our motivations for our practices.
- Whenever you consider becoming involved in a dual or multiple relationship, seek consultation from trusted colleagues or a supervisor.
- There are few absolute answers that can neatly resolve dual or multiple relationship dilemmas.
- The cautions for entering into dual or multiple relationships should be for the benefit of our clients or others served, rather than to protect ourselves from censure.
- In determining whether to proceed with a dual or multiple relationship, consider whether the potential benefit outweighs the potential for harm.
- It is the responsibility of counsellor preparation programs to introduce boundary issues and explore multiple relationship questions. It is important to teach students ways of thinking about alternative courses of action.
- Counsellor education programs have a responsibility to develop their own guidelines, policies, and procedures for dealing with multiple roles and role conflicts within the program (pp. 223-228).

This inventory of key beliefs about the nature of role duality in counselling is a cogent reminder of the dynamic and emerging nature of our ethical strivings within the counselling profession. It also underscores the necessity for counsellors to exercise a high level of ethical reasoning and concern in fulfilling their obligation to maintain appropriate relational boundaries with clients. In fact, most instructional models advocated for the teaching of professional ethics emphasize the need to teach a process of ethical reasoning and decision making (Gawthrop & Uhlemann, 1992; Elliot, 1991; Kitchener, 1984).

The CCA *Code of Ethics* now declares that members, counsellor-educators, as well as others, have a responsibility to induct students into the ethical standards of the profession. It states:

F3. Ethical Orientation

Counsellors who are responsible for counsellor education, training, and supervision have an obligation to make their students, trainees, and supervisees aware of their ethical responsibilities as expressed in the CCA *Code of Ethics,* and Standards of Practice.

This ethical requirement is intended to ensure that the counselling profession meets a fundamental condition of professionalism: having a membership with a thorough understanding of and adherence to a shared code of ethical conduct. Although such codes are essential to the maintenance of the integrity and accountability of the profession, boundary violations as well as other ethical misconduct, can only be prevented when counsellors have the ability and courage to exercise a high level of ethical judgement. As Pope and Vasquey (1991) express it:

Such codes...cannot do our thinking, feeling and responding for us. [They] can never be a substitute for the active process by which the individual therapist or counselor struggles with the sometimes bewildering, always unique, constellation of responsibilities, contexts, and competing demands of helping others (p. xi).

References

Adler, J., & D. Rosenberg (1992). *Psychotherapy.* Newsweek, April 13, 53-58.

American Counseling Association (1995). *Code of ethics and standards of practice.* Alexandria: VA: Author.

American Counseling and Development Association (1988). *Code of ethics.* Alexandria: VA: Author.

American Psychiatric Association (1985). *Principles of medical ethics with annotations especially applicable to psychiatry.* Washington, DC: Author.

American Psychiatric Association (1995). Ethical principles of psychologists and code of conduct. Washington, DC: Author.

American Psychological Association, Ethics Committee (1988). Trends in ethics uses, common pitfalls, and published resources. *American Psychologist,* 43(7), 564-572.

American Counseling Association (1995). *Code of ethics and standards of practice.* Alexandria: VA: Author.

Anderson, S.K., & Kitchener, K.S. (1996). Nonromantic, nonsexual post-therapy relationships between psychologists and former clients: An exploratory study of critical incidents. *Professional Psychology: Research and Practice,* 27(1), 59-66.

Appelbaum, P.S. (1990). Statutes regulating patient-therapist sex. *Hospital and Community Psychiatry,* 41, 15-16.

Association for Specialists in Group Work (1989). *Ethical guidelines for group counselors.* Alexandria, VA: Author.

Bajt, T.R., & Pope, K.S. (1989). Therapist-patient sexual intimacy involving children and adolescents. *American Psychologist.*

Beauchamp, T.L. & Childress, L.F. (1979). Principles of biomedical ethics. Oxford: Oxford University Press.

Beck, M., K. Springen, & Foote, D. (1992). *Newsweek,* April 13, 53-58.

Borys, D.S. (1994). Maintaining therapeutic boundaries: The motive is therapeutic effectiveness, not defensive practice. *Ethics and Behavior,* 4, 267-273.

Bowman, V.E., Hatley, L.D., & Bowman, R.L. (1995). Faculty-student relationships: A dual role controversy. *Counselor Education and Supervision,* 34, March, 232-242.

Briere, J.N. (1992). *Child abuse trauma: Theory and treatment of the lasting effects.* Newbury Park, CA: Sage Publications.

British Association for Counselling (1990). *Code of ethics and practice for counselors.* Rugby: England. Author.

British Association for Counselling (1986). *Code of ethics and practice for the supervision of counsellors.* Rugby: England. Author.

Brownlee, K. (1996). Ethics in community mental health care. *Community Mental Health Journal,* **32**, 5, 497-503.

Canadian Counselling Association (1999). *Code of ethics.* Ottawa, Author.

Canadian Guidance and Counselling Association (1989). *Guidelines for ethical behavior.* Ottawa: Author.

Canadian Guidance and Counselling Association (1981). *Guidelines for ethical behavior.* Ottawa, Author.

Canadian Psychological Association (1986). *A Canadian code of ethics for psychologists.* Old Cheben, Quebec: Author.

Childress, L.F. (1981). Priorities in biomedical ethics. Philadelphia: Westminister Press.

Congress, E.P. (1996). Dual relationships in academia: Dilemmas for social work educators. *Journal of Social Work Education,* **32**, 3, 329-338.

Corey, G. (1996). *Theory and practice of counseling and psychology.* Pacific Grove, CA. Brooks/Cole Publishing Company.

Corey, G., Corey, M.S. & Callahan, P. (1998). Issues and ethics in the helping professions (5th ed.). Pacific Grove, CA: Brooks/Cole.

Eberlein, L. (1988). The new CPA code of ethics for Canadian psychologists: An education and training perspective. *Canadian Psychology,* 29(2), 206-212.

Edelstein, L. (1943). The Hippocratic Oath: Text, translation and interpretation. *Bulletin of the History of Medicine, Supplement 1.* Baltimore: John Hopkins Press.

Elliot, M.M. (1991). *Ethical Decision Making and Judgements of Psychologists: An Exploratory Study.* Unpublished doctoral dissertation, University of Alberta, Edmonton.

Epstein, R.S. (1994). *Keeping boundaries: Maintaining safety and integrity in the psychotherapeutic process.* Washington, DC: American Psychiatric Press.

Erickson, Beth M. (1993). *Helping men change: The role of the female therapist.* Newbury Park, CA: Sage Publications Limited.

Folman, R.Z. (1991). Therapist-patient sex: Attraction and boundary problems. *Psychotherapy,* **28**, 168-173.

Forester-Miller, H., & Duncan, J.A. (1990). *The Ethics of Dual Relationships in the Training of Group Counselors: The Journal for Specialists in Group Work,* 15(2), 88-93.

Frazier, P.A. & Cohen, B.B. (1992). Research on the sexual victimization of women: Implications for counselor training. *The Counseling Psychologist,* 20, 141-158.

Gabbard, G.O. (1994). Reconsidering the American Psychological Association's policy on sex with former patients: It is justifiable? *Professional Psychology: Research and Practice,* 25, 329-335.

Gabbard, G.O. (1989). *Sexual exploitation in professional relationships.* Washington, D.C.: American Psychiatric Press, Inc.

Gartell, N., Herman, J., Olarte, S., Feldstein, M. & Localio, R. (1986). Psychiatrist-patient sexual contact: Results of a national survey. I: prevalence. *American Journal of Psychiatry,* 143, 1126-1131.

Gartell, N., Herman, J., Olarte, S., Feldstein, M., & Localio, R. (1986). Reporting practices of psychiatrists who knew of sexual misconduct by colleagues. *American Journal of Orthopsychiatry,* 57, 287-295.

Gawthrop, J., & M. Wilemann (1992). Effects of the problem-solving approach in ethics training. *Professional Psychology: Research and Practice,* 23, 1, 38-42.

Gibson, W.T., & Pope, K.S. (1993). The ethics of counseling: A national survey of certified counselors. *Journal of Counseling and Development,* 71, 330-336.

Gibson, R.L., & Mitchell, M.H. (1990). *Introduction to counseling and guidance* (3rd. ed.). New York: Macmillan.

Gil, E. (1991). *The healing power of play: Working with abused children.* New York, NY: Guildford Press.

Gothell, T.G., & Gabbard, G.O. (1993). The concept of boundaries in clinical practice: Theoretical and risk-management dimensions. *American Journal of Psychiatry,* 130, 188-196.

Gottlieb, M.C., Sell, J.M., & Schoenfeld, L.S. (1988). Social/romantic relationships with present and former clients: State licensing board actions. *Professional Psychology: Research and Practice,* 19, 459-462.

Green-Vasan, U. (1989). Sexual exploitation of patients: The position paper of the Canadian Psychiatric Association. *Canadian Journal of Psychiatry,* 34, 234-235.

Hardy, G. (1993). Mandatory reporting of sexual abuse: Physicians say regulations go too far. *Evening Telegram,* January 7, p. 12.

Haspel, K.C., Jorgenson, L.M., Parsons, J.P., & Wincze, J.P. (1997). Legislative Intervention Regarding Therapist Sexual Misconduct: an Overview. *Professional Psychology: Research and Practice*, February, 28, 1, 63-72.

Herlihy, B., & Corey, G. (1992). Dual relationships in counseling. Alexandria: VA. *American Association for Counseling and Development*.

Herlihy, B., & Corey, G. (1997). *Boundary issues in counseling: Multiple roles and responsibilities*. Alexandria, VA: American Counseling Association.

Hermansson, G. (1997). Boundaries and boundary management in counselling: The never-ending story. *British Journal of Guidance and Counselling, 25*, 133-143.

Hines, A.H., & Charg, A.S. (1998). Dual agency, dual relationships, boundary crossings, and associated boundation violations: A survey of military and civilian psychiatrists. *Military Medicne, 163*, 826-833.

Horst, E.A. (1989). Dual relationships between psychologists and clients in rural and urban areas. *Journal of Rural Community Psychology*, 10, 15-23.

Huey, W.C. (1986). Ethical concerns in school counselling. *Journal of Counseling & Development*, 64, 321-322.

Hyattsville, M.D. *American Psychological Association.*

Johnson, S.H. & Farber, B.A. (1996). Maintenance of boundaries in psychotherapeutic practice. *Psychotherapy*, 33, 391-402.

Kagle, J.D., & Giebelhausen, P.N. (1994). Dual relationships and professional boundaries. *Social Work, 39*, 2, 213-220.

Keith-Spiegel, P., & Koocher, G.P. (1985). *Ethics in psychology*. Hillsdale, N.J.: Lawrence Eribaum.

Kitchener, K.S. (1996). There is more to ethics than principles. *The Counseling Psychologist*, 24(1), 92-97.

Kitchener, K.S. (1988). Dual role relationships: What makes them so problematic? *Journal of Counseling & Development*, 67, 217-221.

Kitchener, K.S. (1985). Ethical principles and ethical decisions in student affairs. In H.J. Canon & R.D. Brown (eds.), *Applied Ethics in Student Services*. San Francisco: Jossey-Bass.

Kitchener, K.S. (1984). Intuition, initial evaluation and ethical principles: Foundation for ethical decisions in counseling psychology. *The Counseling Psychologist*, 12, 43-55.

Koocher, G.P., & Keith-Spiegel, P. (1998). *Ethics in psychology: Professional standards and cases*. New York: Oxford University Press.

Koocher, G.P. (1994). The Commerce of Professional Psychology and the New Ethics Code. *Professional Psychology: Research and Practice, 25*, 4, 355-361.

Kurplus, D., Gibson, G., Lewis, J., & Corbet, M. (1991). Ethical Issues in Supervising Counseling Practitioners. *Counselor Education and Supervision*, 31, 48-57.

Lamb, D.H., & Catanzaro, S.L. (1998). Sexual and Non-sexual Boundary Violations Involving Psychologists, Clients, Supervisors, and Students: Implications for Professional Practice. *Professional Psychology: Research and Practice*, October 29, 5, 498-503.

Layman, M.J., & McNamara, J.R. (1997). Remediation for ethic violations: Focus in psychotherapists' sexual contact with clients. *Professional Psychology: Research and Practice*, 28, 281-292.

Lerman, H., & Rigby, D.N. (1990). Boundary violations: Misuse of the power of the therapist. In H. Lerman and N. Porter (Eds.), *Feminist ethics in psychotherapy* (pp. 51-59). New York: Springer Publishing.

Miller, J.B., & Stiver, I.P. (1997). The healing connection: How women form relationships in therapy and in life. Boston: Beacon Press.

National Association of Social Workers (1996). *Code of ethics*. Washington, DC: Author.

O'Conner Slimp, P.A., & Burian, B.K. (1994). Multiple relationships during internships: Consequences and recommendations. *Professional Psychology: Research and Practice, 25*, 1, 39-45.

Parsons, L.P., & Wincze, J.P. (1995). A survey of client-therapist sexual involvement in Rhode Island as reported by subsequent treating therapists. *Professional Psychology: Research and Practice*, 26, 171-175.

Pearson, B., & Piazza, N. (1997). Classification of dual relationships in the helping professions. *Counselor Education and Supervision, 37*, December, 89-99.

Pettifor, J., & Pitcher, S. (1982). Ethics training in Canadian graduate schools. *Canadian Psychology*, 23(4), 235-242.

Peterson, M.R. (1992). At personal risk: Boundary violations in professional-client relationships. New York, NY: W.W. Norton and Co., Inc.

Pope, K.S., (1985). How clients are harmed by sexual contact with mental health professionals: The syndrome and its prevalence. *Journal of Counseling & Development*, 67, 222-226.

Pope, K.S., (1990). Therapist-patient sexual involvement: A review of the research. *Clinical Psychology Review*, 10, 477-490.

Pope, K.S., & Bouhoutsos, J.C. (1986). *Sexual intimacy between therapists and patients*. New York: Praeger Press.

Pope, K.S., & Vasquey, M.J.T (1998). *Ethics in psychotherapy and counseling*, (2nd. ed.). San Francisco: Jossey-Bass.

Pope, K.S., Sonne, J.L., & Holyroyd, J. (1993). *Sexual feelings in psychotherapy: Explanations for therapists and therapists-in-training*.

Pope, K.S. (1994). Sexual involvement with therapists. Washington, DC: American Psychological Association.

Pope, K.S., Keith-Spiegel, P., & Tabachnick, B.G. (1986). Sexual attraction to clients: The human therapist and the (sometimes) inhuman training system. *American Psychologist*, 41, 147-158.

Rupert, P.A., & Holmes, D.L. (1997). Dual relationships in higher education. *Journal of Higher Education, 68*, 6, 660-678.

Ryan, C.J., & Anderson, J. (1996). Sleeping with post: The ethics of past-termination patient-therapist sexual contact. *Australian and New Zealand Journal of Psychiatry*, 30, 171-178.

Salisbury, W.D., & Kinnier, R.T. (1996). Post-termination friendship between counselors and clients. *Journal of Counseling & Development*, 74, 495-499.

Sell, J.M., Gottlieb, M.C., & Schoenfeld, L. (1986). Ethical considerations of social/ romantic relationships with present and former clients. *Professional Psychology: Research and Practice*, 17(6), 504-508.

Schank, J.A. (1998). Ethical issues in rural counselling practice. *Canadian Journal of Counselling, 32* (4), 270-283.

Schank, J.A., & Skovholt, T.M. (1997). Dual-relationship dilemmas of rural and small-community psychologists. *Professional Psychology: Research and Practice, 28* (1), 44-49.

Screenivasan, U. (1989). Sexual exploitation of patients: The position of the Canadian Psychiatric Association. *Canadian Journal of Psychiatry*, 34, 234-235.

Simon, R.I. (1989). Sexual exploitation of patients: How it begins before it happens. *Psychiatry Annual, 19*, 104-112.

Smith, D., & Fitzpatrick, M. (1995). Patient-therapist boundary issue: An integrative review of theory and research. *Professional Psychology: Research and Practice, 26*, 499-506.

Somer, E., & Saadon, M. (1999). Therapist-Client Sex: Clients' Retrospective Reports. *Professional Psychology: Research and Practice*, 30, 5, 504-509.

St. Germaine, J. (1996). Dual relationships and Certified Alcohol and Drug Counselors: A National Study of Ethical Beliefs and Behaviors. *Alcoholism Treatment Quarterly,14*, 2, 29-44.

St. Germaine, J. (1993). Dual relationships: What's wrong with them? *American Counselor, 2*, 25-30.

Stadler, H.A. (1986). To counsel or not to counsel: The ethical dilemma of dual relationships. *Journal of Counseling and Human Service Professions*, 1(1), 134-140.

Strasburger, L.H., Jorgensen, I., & Sutherland, P. (1992). The prevention of psychotherapist sexual misconduct: Avoiding the slippery slope. *American Journal of Psychotherapy, 46*, 544-55.

Thoreson, R.W., Shaughnessy, P., & Frazier, P.A. (1995). Sexual contact during and after professional practices and attitudes of female counselors. *Journal of Counseling & Development*, 74(1), 84-89.

Tymchuk, A. (1986). Guidelines for ethical decision making. *Canadian Psychology, 27*(1), 36-43.

Vallally, S.E. (1995). Defining professional boundaries in therapeutic relationships. Unpublished master thesis, University of Calgary, Calgary, Alberta.

Vasquey, M.J.T., & Kitchener, K.S. (1988). Introduction to special issue. *Journal of Counseling & Development*, 67, 214-216.

Wilmer, H.A. (1991). *Closeness in personal and professional relationships*. Boston, Mass: Shambhala publications, Inc.

Wilson, D. (1993). B.C. doctors to adopt sex-abuse proposal. *The Globe and Mail*, July 9, p. 10.

Chapter Four

❖

Consulting and
Private Practice

❖

Counselling is a business and as such is
governed by legal and ethical regulations
and guidelines. Counsellors, both in private
practice and as part-time consultants, need
to be aware of their additional responsibilities in relationship to advertising, contracts
and business.

❖ ❖ ❖ ❖ ❖ ❖ ❖ ❖ ❖ ❖ ❖ ❖ ❖

ETHICAL ARTICLES ON CONSULTING AND PRIVATE PRACTICE

 C1 **General Responsibility**
Counsellors provide consultative services only in those areas in which they have demonstrated competency by virtue of their education and experience.

❖

 C2 **Undiminished Responsibility and Liability**
Counsellors who work in private practice, whether incorporated or not, must ensure that there is no diminishing of their individual professional responsibility to act in accordance with the CCA *Code of Ethics*, or in their liability for any failure to do so.

❖

C3 **Accurate Advertising**
Counsellors, when advertising services as private practitioners, do so in a manner that accurately and clearly informs the public of their services and areas of expertise.

❖

 C4 **Consultative Relationships**
Counsellors ensure that consultation occurs within a voluntary relationship between a counsellor and a help-seeking individual, group, or organization, and that the goals are understood by all parties concerned.

❖

 C5 **Informed Consent**
Counsellors, who provide services for the use of third parties, acknowledge and clarify for the informed consent of clients, all obligations of such multiple relationships, including purpose(s), entitlement to information, and any restrictions on confidentiality. Third parties include courts, public and private institutions, funding agencies, employees, and so forth.

C6 Respect for Privacy

Counsellors limit any discussion of client information obtained from a consulting relationship to persons clearly involved with the case. Any written and oral reports restrict data to the purposes of the consultation and every effort is made to protect client identity and to avoid undue invasion of privacy.

❖

C7 Conflict of Interest

Counsellors who engage in consultation avoid circumstances where the duality of relationships, or the prior possession of information, could lead to a conflict of interest.

❖

C8 Sponsorship and Recruitment

Counsellors present any of their organizational affiliations or membership in such a way as to avoid misunderstanding regarding sponsorship or certification. They also avoid the use of any institutional affiliation to recruit private-practice clients.

❖ ❖ ❖ ❖ ❖ ❖ ❖ ❖ ❖ ❖ ❖ ❖ ❖ ❖

CASE STUDIES IN CONSULTING AND PRIVATE PRACTICE

C1 GENERAL RESPONSIBILITY
Counsellors provide consultative services only in those areas in which they have demonstrated competency by virtue of their education and experience.

Referral Resources (+)

John Smith, a member of a small consulting firm, was asked to help a large electrical and electronics wholesaler with a research project that demanded both a knowledge of complex statistical procedures and an understanding of a number of standardized group tests. John Smith, who is quite knowledgeable in the area of testing, accepted the job, with the provision that he would be using the statistical expertise and computer software of another consulting firm.

Skill Awareness (+)

Joan Sutherland, a career consultant, has many contacts in business and industry. She has been asked to be a consultant for a firm owned by a good friend of hers. The work is mainly in conflict management. Ms. Sutherland informs her friend that although her knowledge of career counselling and consulting has made her familiar with conflict management, she does not feel she has enough expertise in the area to take on this job.

Mediation Services (-)

A counsellor-educator at a university accepted a consulting contract to work with a large insurance company to help management and workers establish a program for mediation of disagreements. The counsellor-educator has very little knowledge about mediation services.

Lacking Resource Knowledge (-)

A counsellor-consultant moved to a new city and opened a one-person counselling and consulting firm. Because of past associations with several national firms, he was able to obtain a lucrative consulting contract from one of the firms. Much of the work consisted of community liaison, and a knowledge of community resources was a definite asset to any consultant taking on this job. The consultant, although new to the city, felt he would quickly learn about available resources and made no mention of his limited knowledge of the city's community resources.

COMMENTS AND QUESTIONS

The first case illustrating this ethical article shows a consultant who is aware of his own competencies (in this case, a knowledge of tests), who is not at all reluctant to admit to his limited resources in computer software for statistical analysis, and who is willing to use the expertise of another firm that has the appropriate resources. Consultants may have a great deal of expertise in many areas, but few consultants can be knowledgeable in all areas related to counselling. It is sound practice for consultants to admit shortcomings, but also to look for further education and supervision as they develop additional areas of expertise.

1. In the "Mediation Services" case presented, what can the consultant do to make her or his consulting contract more ethical?

2. Is "on the job" training acceptable for consultants?

3. Is it appropriate for consultants to accept contracts from former employers?

4. How should consultants advertise their skills or competencies?

5. Will it be seen as a shortcoming if and when a consultant uses the services of other consultants?

C2 UNDIMINISHED RESPONSIBILITY AND LIABILITY

Counsellors who work in private practice, whether incorporated or not, must ensure that there is no diminishing of their individual professional responsibility to act in accordance with the CCA *Code of Ethics*, or in their liability for any failure to do so.

Values Awareness (+)

Joseph Overland, a consultant in a large Canadian city, was approached to help a provincial agency make decisions regarding funding for several pregnancy-information organizations. Joseph was very aware of his values regarding abortion and other issues, and felt his strong "anti-abortion" stance would get in the way of his being fair to organizations appealing for funds for abortion counselling. He did not take the job.

Getting Set (+)

Richard has retired from his job as a counsellor with a mental health agency, and has decided to see clients privately in his home. He has checked the zoning by-laws with the city, and purchased the necessary licence to operate. He has also purchased liability insurance, and a locked filing cabinet for client files. He has ensured that clients have a private room off the main entrance in which to wait for appointments, where they will not be readily seen by clients who are leaving. He has prepared consent forms listing the ethical and legal exceptions to confidentiality and his fee schedule, consent forms for the release of information (for when he needs to consult with other professionals), and an information sheet on how client information will be kept secure and how clients can access their personal information. Richard has contacted professionals in his community with whom he can consult, when necessary, about challenging cases within his area of expertise.

Too Little, Too Late (-)

Susan is a counsellor in private practice whose training and experience is working with couples. A couple Susan has been working with refers another couple to her, but Susan finds out when they call that they want her to work with their teenage son. Susan has no experience or training in working with adolescents, but because she would like to expand her practice, she accepts. Susan sees the boy for five sessions before realizing that her work is having little effect with him, and she finally refers him elsewhere.

Unprofessional Practice (-)

Dan has left his job as a child and youth counsellor to open a private practice. One of the things Dan disliked the most about his job was the bureaucracy and red tape, which he felt constrained him in his work. Dan wants a more relaxed approach, so he doesn't use consent forms, doesn't have a fee schedule, and doesn't issue receipts to clients. Generally, Dan thinks that "being his own boss" means he can run his private practice with very little in the way of structure and protocol.

COMMENTS AND QUESTIONS

The last of the four cases presented under this article illustrates how this article can be abused. Dan, who has begun a private practice, needs to be all the more vigilant regarding ethical practice now that he has full responsibility for all professional decisions regarding confidentiality, informed consent, record-keeping, duty to warn, diversity issues and so forth. All professional counsellors in private practice must adhere to the CCA *Code of Ethics.*

1. Should liability insurance for counsellors in private practice be higher than for counsellors working for agencies, schools or institutions?

2. Is it ethical for consultants to take contracts for work they do not know much about, but hope to prepare by contacting other professionals with expertise in the required area?

3. Who is liable for counsellors or consultants working for a large organization with many counsellors and/or consultants?

4. What do you think of Susan's behaviour in the third case, "Too Little, Too Late"?

5. Should all consultants be required to be members in a professional organization like CCA?

C3 ACCURATE ADVERTISING
Counsellors, when advertising services as private practitioners, do so in a manner that accurately and clearly informs the public of their services and areas of expertise.

Business Card (+)
A recent graduate from a doctoral program in general and family counselling established his own private counselling service. After joining CCA, he applied for Canadian Counsellor Certification and was accepted. His business card read as follows:

John Smith, PhD
Certified Counsellor (CCA)
111 Chestnut Road
Winnipeg, Manitoba R1A 2B3
(204) 123-4567 (residence)
(204) 765-4321 (business)
- personal counselling
- family counselling

Private Practitioner (+)
A private practitioner had received a master's degree in counselling psychology, and had specialized in family counselling. Both in his advertising and his informed consent forms, he carefully pointed out that typical counselling sessions would consist of relationship building, discussion of concerns, decision-making, and formulating plans of action.

False Advertising (-)
A counsellor in private practice had received her master's degree from a faculty of education, in the department of educational psychology. Many of the courses she had taken in her master's program were in school counselling. In her advertising for her private counselling services in the Yellow Pages, she indicated that her degree was in "counselling psychology." The faculty of education that she graduated from offered no degree in counselling psychology.

Deceptive Advertising (-)
A recent advertisement in a paper read, in part, as follows:

...trained counsellor specializing in family counselling...

This counsellor had received a degree in theology from a non-accredited university and his total counsellor training consisted of a weekend workshop on "family reconstruction."

COMMENTS AND QUESTIONS
The gist of this ethical article is that members accurately inform the public of their "services, expertise and techniques of counselling." Too often the expertise of the member is glowingly described or implied through the listing of paper credentials, but the detailed description of services and techniques are neglected.

Members are implored not to advertise information that is "false, inaccurate, misleading, partial, out-of-context, or deceptive." In the last two cases, the members presented either false or misleading advertising.

1. What are some examples of misleading advertising of counsellor services of which you are aware?

2. What is your responsibility once you become aware of misleading or false advertising of counsellor services?

3. How should counsellors advertise their "techniques of counselling"?

4. Since so much of advertising exaggerates positives, can we expect counsellors to inform accurately or realistically?

5. Should counsellors advertise the fact that they are members of professional organizations such as CCA?

C4 CONSULTATIVE RELATIONSHIPS
Counsellors ensure that consultation occurs within a voluntary relationship between a counsellor and a help-seeking individual, group, or organization, and that the goals are understood by all parties concerned.

Collaborative Action (+)

A guidance and counselling co-ordinator in a British Columbia school district has been asked by the principal in another school division to help the counsellors in his school reorganize a guidance and counselling program that will meet the needs of students, teachers, parents and administrators. The co-ordinator meets with students, teachers, parents and administrators and then verifies the goals and techniques with the principal in order to affirm continuing support. He then begins the work of reorganizing the program, making sure that counsellors, parents, teachers, administrators and students are consulted.

Group Leadership Skills (+)

A few years ago Human Resources Development Canada decided to begin a program whereby all their employment counsellors would be trained in group leadership skills. The final goal was to have personnel from within the organization provide the training to other employment counsellors. Several university counsellor-educators were hired as consultants to work with Human Resources to get the project under way and to provide the initial group leadership training. After a few years, the training program was well established and the consultants were no longer directly involved.

Further Consulting Offered (-)

A counsellor-consultant was hired to help prepare counsellors to organize and train students in their schools for peer-helper programs. After a two-week program, the consultant indicated that his services were available to each of the participants in the program to help them actually start peer-helper programs in the schools. The consultant explained that his years of experience were needed to start the programs effectively. The counsellors had been led to believe that the two-week program would prepare them to do the organizing of the peer-helper programs by themselves.

Ready for Self-Direction (-)

A consultant is hired by an employment agency to help employment counsellors with the skills of conflict management. The counsellors are eager and skillful counsellors, and after a few days of professional development appear ready to use their newly developed skills. The consultant, knowing she is being paid a per diem of $500, decided to spend another five days of professional development with the employment counsellors, going over much of the same material once more.

COMMENTS AND QUESTIONS

In this article, counsellors are reminded that consultative relationships are voluntary, and that the goals established should be fully understood by all participants. It is important that all the people involved in a consultative relationship have the opportunity to ask any questions, and have all pertinent information given to them in language they can fully understand, so that informed decisions can be made by all. Generally, goals, aspects of the relationship, and limits relating to confidentiality will be put in writing.

1. How can consultants make sure that all participants are involved voluntarily?

2. What happens when there is a disagreement regarding the goals among participants?

3. Should the interventions that the consultant may use be approved by the participants?

4. Discuss how you would have dealt with the case "Further Consulting Offered."

5. What should the consultant have done in "Ready for Self-Direction"?

C5 **INFORMED CONSENT**
Counsellors, who provide services for the use of third parties, acknowledge and clarify for the informed consent of clients, all obligations of such multiple relationships, including purpose(s), entitlement to information, and any restrictions on confidentiality. Third parties include courts, public and private institutions, funding agencies, employees and so forth.

Directives to the Consultant (+)

A large company has counselling services for their employees, and they most frequently use the services of one consulting counsellor, Norman Atwell. The company is having real difficulty with one employee who frequently gets into arguments with his co-workers. The manager of this employee phones Norman Atwell and strongly suggests to him that he see the employee for counselling and to encourage him to seek a job elsewhere. Norman Atwell realizes that the possible client has not received sufficient information and he informs the manager that he would be violating his code of ethics regarding services for a third party by not informing him of the goals and/or purposes of the counselling.

Confidentiality (+)

A psychologist was hired by Human Resources Development Canada to provide education and training for any employees who were experiencing burnout or stress on the job. The psychologist informed all the participants that he would be reporting back to management aspects of their work that they felt contributed to their burnout or stress. He also informed the participants that he would describe the stressful situations but that no names will be revealed to management. The psychologist also explained these conditions to management.

Consultant's Report (-)

A consultant, eager for additional business, had been asked by a school division to make recommendations for several schools that were renovating classrooms into guidance and counselling areas, with individual offices for counsellors, and a waiting room/resource area for students. The consultant, who was very familiar with guidance and counselling areas, drew up a tentative plan, but then asked building consultants for their advice regarding structure, lighting and heating. The building consultants indicated that building codes had changed and there would be many additional costs if the whole area was brought to present-day electrical standards. The consultant talked to the school division superintendent about this. The consultant agreed not to mention the coding deficiencies in his report, after the superintendent assured him their divisional electricians would look after things.

Not Enough Consulting (-)

A consultant's report showed what she thought would be a good design for arranging counselling space for a number of employment counsellors working in a career centre. She had been hired to design the area after counsellors had gone to their manager and asked him to do something about the currently poor arrangement. The consultant had listened to the manager's ideas but had not arranged any meetings with the counsellors before submitting her report.

COMMENTS AND QUESTIONS

When counsellors act as consultants to third parties, they must remember that obtaining informed consent from all people involved is a basic right of third parties. Sometimes it is difficult to anticipate all the goals, procedures, relationships and restrictions that might arise, but with thorough, careful planning many of the obligations of informing third parties can be met.

Consultants working with third parties can be put into conflicts with regards to issues of confidentiality. The degrees or limits of confidentiality must be discussed beforehand. There must be protection for participants, and there may be times when it is not the best practice to say that everyone involved should receive feedback.

1. When would a consultant likely limit her or his feedback to all participants?

2. Are there times when informed consent is not needed?

3. How can consultants deal most effectively with differences in status and power among participants?

4. Is a consultant justified in trying to change the people who hired her or him?

5. What are the special conditions of informed consent as it pertains to the courts and funding agencies?

C6 RESPECT FOR PRIVACY
Counsellors limit any discussion of client information obtained from a consulting relationship to persons clearly involved with the case. Any written and oral reports restrict data to the purposes of the consultation and every effort is made to protect client identity and to avoid undue invasion of privacy.

Conscientious Consultant (+)
Terry is a trauma counsellor and has been contracted by a school district to do some trauma counselling with students after a shooting incident at a high school. Terry is given a small office in which to see individual students privately. She makes it clear to students before they begin that a summary of their work together will be forwarded to the school counselling office, but that no one other than the counsellors will have access to it. When Terry writes her summary reports after sessions, she makes sure to include only those details relevant to the incident.

Confidential Consulting (+)
Sam is hired to do conflict-resolution work with the staff and management of a local company. After completing the contract, Sam asks whether he can list the company name on his curriculum vitae. Sam is told that the company would prefer to not have it known that they hired someone to do conflict-resolution work with them, and they would prefer not to be included on his list. Sam respects their wishes.

Idle Speculation (-)
Alex is hired as a consultant to work with the management of a private business college to improve their communication and active listening skills. On the second day of the workshop, Alex is having lunch with a member of the teaching staff who expresses interest in the workshop. The person begins to speculate about which management members would have the most difficulty learning the communications skills and asks for Alex's opinion. Alex says he can't go into detail, but that the teacher's guesses were "very accurate."

Invasion of Privacy (-)
Heather is hired to do a workshop on stress management for the staff of a local company. In a discussion about the stresses of parenting, one participant announces that she and her husband are ending their marriage, and that she is finding their discussions of custody of the children very stressful. Without asking the participant's permission, Heather makes a point of taking a member of the management aside after the workshop to tell her about the pending divorce, in case the woman needs "extra support through her difficult time."

COMMENTS AND QUESTIONS
This ethical article, much like the articles on confidentiality, clearly states that counsellors and consultants need to keep client information private. Counsellors and consultants are encouraged to adapt existing guidelines on privacy to their own practice. The Canadian Standards Association's *Model Code for the Protection of Personal Information* consists of ten principles related to privacy:
- accountability
- identifying purposes
- consent
- limiting collection
- limiting use
- accuracy
- safeguards
- openness
- individual access
- challenging compliance

For a fuller treatment of how these principles can be used by counsellors and consultants, the reader is referred to the essay, "Putting the 'Privacy' into Private Practice" by Jo-Anne Sargent, which is at the end of this section.

1. Is there a "grey area" between counsellors talking about clients with other professionals over coffee and when they request a more formal consultation?

2. In the case "Confidential Consulting," is it all right for Sam to tell possible future clients that he has done consulting work for the "local company"?

3. Should Alex in "Idle Speculation" be censored for his comments? What would you say to Alex?

4. In "Invasion of Privacy," Heather wanted to be helpful. Do her obvious attempts to be helpful supercede the participant's right to privacy?

5. Where and when in your counselling organization is privacy not always observed?

C7 CONFLICT OF INTEREST
Counsellors who engage in consultation avoid circumstances where the duality of relationships, or the prior possession of information, could lead to a conflict of interest.

Avoiding Conflicts of Interest (+)

A counsellor-consultant with a small but thriving practice was also a member of the local school board. The board decided to offer leadership training for all the administrators in the school division. The counsellor-consultant, who had offered similar types of workshops throughout the province, excused himself from the board meeting while any discussions or decisions were made regarding who would provide the leadership training.

Referrals (+)

Jane Sullivan, a consultant specializing in family counselling, was very aware of the competency requirement for her profession, and knew that counsellors should not work outside their particular field of competence. Whenever she received contract offers that were not related to family counselling, she referred the possible clients to other experts.

Recruiting Clients (-)

A consultant was hired by a university to offer a counselling skills course for the continuing education division of the university. Students were strongly encouraged to seek their own counselling in order to experience the feelings clients might have. The part-time instructor was also a partner in a private counselling service and suggested that the practicum students might wish to receive counselling at his counselling service. He would see to it that his partners would offer students favourable counselling fees.

Dual Role (-)

A counselling foundation received a large contribution. Part of the money was to be used to offer career-development workshops throughout Canada. One member of the foundation board knew about this requirement and without letting others know, took on the work himself.

COMMENTS AND QUESTIONS

More ethical guidelines are needed for consultants since they work in many different areas and are affiliated with a wide range of professional organizations (or none at all). Consultants must be particularly careful with regards to multicultural considerations and the varying expectations from clients regarding consultants' roles. As well, consultants are often seen as having more power, and they must be careful that they develop independence in clients rather than dependence.

Conflicts of interest can also arise when there are hidden agendas or dual relationships. For example, the manager of a firm hires a consultant to improve relationships among staff, but then after the workshops asks the consultant to supply the names of the employees who seem to be detrimental to his firm's climate. All of these potential problems underscore the importance of confidentiality and informed consent in consulting.

1. In the case "Avoiding Conflicts of Interest," should the consultant accept a contract if the board offered him one?

2. What are some ways that the power imbalance between consultant and client can be diminished?

3. Where might you experience a conflict of interest if you were asked to be a consultant?

4. How could the conflict outlined in "Recruiting Clients" be resolved?

5. What elements would you include in an informed consent form to help avoid conflict-of-interest situations?

C8 SPONSORSHIP AND RECRUITMENT

Counsellors present any of their organizational affiliations or membership in such a way as to avoid misunderstanding regarding sponsorship or certification. They also avoid the use of any institutional affiliation to recruit private-practice clients.

Non-Faculty Member (+)

A counselling consultant, who has a four-person consulting firm, frequently teaches courses at a nearby university. Even though the consultant is frequently introduced as teaching at the university, she quickly clarifies by saying she has her own consulting firm, has on occasion taught a course for the university, but is not a faculty member at the university.

CCA Member Only (+)

Bob Reynolds, a counsellor in a rural high school, recently became a member of the CCA. At a divisional meeting of counsellors, where counsellor certification is being discussed, most of the counsellors assume Bob is certified since he has been accepted for membership by CCA. Bob points out that he is only a member of CCA and has not applied for counsellor certification through CCA.

Recruiting Clients (-)

A part-time instructor at a university was hired to offer a counselling practicum in the continuing education division of a university. Students were strongly encouraged to seek their own counselling in order to experience the feelings clients might have. The part-time instructor was also a partner in a private counselling service and suggested that the practicum students might wish to receive counselling at his counselling service. He would see to it that his partners would offer students favourable counselling fees.

Misleading Business Cards (-)

Tom Anderson, a counsellor in a high school, was hired by the university in his city to teach a summer-school course for beginning counsellors. While at the university, he had 1000 business cards made up with the university logo. He felt this university affiliation would help him in future consulting and counselling work.

COMMENTS AND QUESTIONS

In 1993, the American Counseling Association (See ACA Legal series) made the following observations regarding the advertising of professional counselling services:

a) The advertisement should conform both in form and content to lawful licensing board regulations and ethical standards published by professional associations, national certifying boards and regulatory boards.

b) The advertisement should both be truthful and accurate, and make no unverifiable claims as to quality of service.

c) The advertisement should be reviewed by an attorney experienced in both mass media law and the law of mental health regulations.

It is obvious that in the case of Tom Anderson and his "Misleading Business Cards," little or no attention was paid to the above advertising guidelines. As this article suggests, members must not imply inaccurate sponsorship.

1. Many counsellors do not have their business cards reviewed by a lawyer. Are there other ways to review business cards that would result in greater accuracy in advertising counselling services?

2. Can you provide some examples of inaccurate sponsorship?

3. Is there a "fine line" between being a member of a university and recruiting clients for private practice?

4. Should counsellor-educators at universities involved in practicum supervision have their own private counselling practice?

5. How can consultants best avoid any implied affiliation with a professional organization or an institution?

❖ ❖ ❖ ❖ ❖ ❖ ❖ ❖ ❖ ❖ ❖ ❖ ❖

Essays on Consulting and Private Practice

Competency and the Private Practitioner
Thomas Kerr

Maintaining professional competence and practising within one's limits is a challenge all counsellors must contend with. For the counsellor in private practice this challenge can border on the formidable. Without institutional standards or peers in close proximity, the temptation to wander into the unknown in the name of "keeping up the practice" may be overwhelming. Furthermore, hazards such as isolation and burnout are common in private work, often have devastating effects on the quality of practice, and can place the public at risk. For the counsellor working in a public or agency setting, there are often an array of means for maintaining and improving competence "in house" (e.g. case conferencing, supervision, continuing education opportunities). The counsellor in private practice, however, must typically go beyond the work place and its hours of operation to access these types of activities. Maintaining and practising within the boundaries of competence requires an understanding of: the dimensions of competence; the methods commonly used to establish, maintain, and improve competence; and the inherent limitations of these methods. For the counsellor in private practice, peer supervision and critical self-assessment may be the most effective means of ensuring that practice remains within the bounds of competence. It is also essential that counsellors be aware of the appropriate choice of actions when situations exceed their boundaries of competence.

The CCA *Code of Ethics* has five standards (A1, A3, C1, D3, F2) that specifically address the issue of competence, while several other standards (e.g. A2, A4) relate more indirectly. Standard A1 and A3 are perhaps most relevant:

A1. General Responsibility

Counsellors maintain high standards of professional competence and ethical behaviour, and recognize the need for continuing education and personal care in order to meet this responsibility.

A3. Boundaries of Competence

Counsellors limit their counselling services and practices to those which are within their professional competence by virtue of their education and professional experience, and consistent with any requirements for provincial and national credentials. They refer to other professionals when the counselling needs of clients exceed their level of competence.

The Problem of Competence

These standards describe clearly a counsellor's obligations with respect to competence and go further to suggest avenues for maintaining competence (e.g. continuing education) and dealing with situations that are beyond one's ability (e.g. referral). However these standards, similar to others found in professional codes, do not specify what constitutes competent practice. The work of counselling may seem so broad and varied that a singular definition of competence is impossible to attain. The academic literature examining competence in counselling practice is diverse in its focus and addresses topics as varied as multicultural competence (Pedersen, 1985; Sue, 1990), multi-person therapies (Lakin, 1994), counsellor self-efficacy (Larson & Daniels, 1998), and clinical diagnosis (Hamann, 1994). The problem of defining competent practice is further complicated by the ongoing debate concerning which counselling approaches are most efficacious. Some writers have argued that developing an eclectic approach based on empirical evidence is the best way to ensure competent practice. Treatment-outcome studies, however, are often limited by methodological shortcomings and produce inconsistent findings. As the debate continues, it is the responsibility of each counsellor to assess on a daily (or perhaps case-by-case) basis his or her level of competence and the best counselling approach to employ. Given the private practitioner's isolation and limited access to peer consultation, self-assessments of competence must be exceptionally conservative.

Professional associations have struggled to establish criteria for competence and have reported difficulties in detecting and dealing with incompetence among its membership (Koocher & Keith-Spiegel, 1998). Certain experiences and qualifications have nonetheless been associated with established competence, the most obvious of which are academic training, professional experience and recognition (e.g. licensing, certification, accreditation and registration). Some authors have criticized academic training in counselling, arguing that training programs are not eclectic enough in orientation to prepare students to deal with the variety of situations encountered in the work context (Lazarus, 1990). Another concern is that the skills and knowledge acquired during training quickly fade from memory or become outdated. According to Dubin (1972) the half-life of a doctoral degree in psychology is about 10 to 12 years (cited in Berven & Scofield, 1987); in other words, half of the knowledge acquired during training is lost or obsolete after 10 years.

More controversial means of establishing competence include licensing, certification, accreditation, or registration. Professional licensing, certification, etc., have long been justified as a means of establishing competence and protecting the public (Claiborn, 1982). These methods, however, typically serve as an indicator of a minimal level of training and only tend to reflect an assessment of an individual at a specific point in time. There are few, if any, effective means of ensuring that counsellors maintain competence or practice within their limits beyond initial licensing (Koocher & Keith-Spiegel, 1998). Considerable disagreement concerning specific assessment criteria has likewise clouded the debate on licensing. Requirements vary, and can include academic degrees, board exams, letters of reference, and specified years of experience. Regardless of the criteria used to assess candidates, these methods rarely specify with which clients or problems practitioners are competent to work (Corey, Corey & Callanan, 1993). Given the diversity of clients and the issues they bring to counselling, it is unlikely that any counsellor is competent to work with all types of clients.

Dimensions of Competence

Several authors have developed models of competence that apply to counselling or the practice of psychology (Abeles, 1994; Berven & Scofield, 1987; Norman, 1985; Pope & Brown, 1996; Peterson & Bry, 1980). These models typically specify two or three key dimensions of competence. Among the more comprehensive specific to the work of counselling is the model developed by Berven and Scofield (1987), which emphasizes three domains of competence: knowledge, skill, and affective domains. The knowledge domain refers first and foremost to what one knows. This typically includes knowledge of behavioural sciences, counselling techniques, therapeutic-change processes, professional ethics, and any other information that contributes to competent practice. According to Pope and Brown (cited in Koocher & Keith-Spiegel, 1998), knowledge competence should ideally consist of "knowledge based on empirical research and sound clinical scholarship regarding practice with a particular population" (Koocher & Keith-Spiegel, 1998, p. 54). Another important aspect of knowledge competence involves recognizing what one does not know. This awareness helps establish individual limitations and consequently serves to reduce risk to the public.

There may be limitations, however, to placing too much emphasis on the acquisition of knowledge. According to Larson and Daniels (1998), a counsellor who possesses a breadth of knowledge is only effective when the appropriate knowledge is accessed and acted upon in the immediate context. What is required then is competence in the skill domain, which simply refers to what is done in the course of counselling work. For most counsellors this domain includes a variety of techniques, decision-making skills, and counsellor-process variables (e.g. warmth, respect). As in the knowledge domain, however, competence in this domain typically refers to skills for which there are established standards. For the private practitioner with limited access to peer consultation, developing areas of specialization is the easiest route to competence in both the knowledge and skill domain.

The third domain described by Berven and Scofield (1987) is the affective domain, which has also been referred to as emotional competence (Pope & Brown, 1996). This domain encompasses general emotional health, and the ability to tolerate clinical material and detect one's own biases as they emerge during the course of counselling. Self-care and healthy life-style are frequently cited as the primary means of maintaining competence in the affective domain. Affective competence has received considerable attention in the literature on burnout and impairment, and has special implications for the counsellor in private practice. Koocher and Keith-Spiegel (1998) point out that the impaired psychologist is most often an individual who is professionally isolated, and that social support in the workplace, an experience rarely enjoyed by private practitioners, is a key factor in preventing burnout.

It seems that current models of competence have neglected a fourth dimension that is integral to effective practice. In order to be fully competent a counsellor must also possess an ability to engage in complex conceptual processing during counselling sessions. This domain could be referred to as the cognitive domain. Although this domain may be regarded as a collection of skills, discussions of the skill domain have typically focussed on technical prowess. Competence in the cognitive domain requires an ability to be present, interpersonally speaking, in a counselling session, while simultaneously reflecting on the content of the session, applying relevant knowledge, and considering a range of possible understandings and actions. This area of competence has been referred to as "cognitive processing" (Larson & Daniels, 1998) and "cognitive counseling skills" (Borders, 1991). It has been noted that while this activity is critical to counsellor competence, it is rarely taught in counselling training programs (Larson & Daniels, 1998).

The Challenge of Maintaining Competence

Counsellors have traditionally accessed a variety of methods for maintaining and improving competence. The more common methods include continuing education and supervision. Other approaches include participation in peer supervision, using self-assessment and the dimensions of informed consent as a means of self-regulation, and professional disclosure (for a complete explanation of professional disclosure see the essay by Pawlovich in this edition titled "Establishing and Maintaining Competence: An Ethical Responsibility"). While the methods for improving and maintaining competence have merits, each, including some of the more common approaches, has limitations. It seems that certain methods are more appropriate for certain people than others. The counsellor in private practice must be exceptionally conservative in assessing his or her learning needs, and determining which methods of maintaining competence are most

appropriate. The private practitioner must also accept responsibility for actively pursuing appropriate methods for maintaining competence, as many of the means will not be readily available in the workplace. One approach to assessing limits and learning involves considering the population and related problems one expects to encounter in practice, and then reviewing one's competence using the previously discussed domains of competence by Berven and Scofield (1987).

Continuing Education Activities

Professionals of many disciplines rely on continuing education activities as a means of maintaining competence. For counsellors these activities come in a variety of forms. Houle (cited in Berven & Scofield, 1987) has developed three categories for distinguishing continuing education activities. The "instruction" category is the most commonly recognized and includes formal learning activities such as workshops, seminars, inservices, and institute training. The "inquiry" category refers to learning that occurs as by-products of participation in activities such as research, professional presentations, class instruction, committee work, and reading of journals, textbooks, and other professionally relevant materials. The third category is referred to as "performance," which includes activities involving the day-to-day application of a skill or idea. This type of learning is usually enhanced if supervision and feedback follow the performance.

Certain learning activities may be more useful than others for particular practitioners. For example, the instruction and inquiry categories may be especially useful for the veteran counsellor whose academic training has become outdated. Exposure to new ideas and techniques is likely the best method of keeping knowledge and practices current. For counsellors in private practice the instruction category and certain types of inquiry-based learning (e.g. classroom teaching, committee work) may have a secondary benefit of reducing feelings of isolation that can occur as a result of working alone. These two categories are also essential for the counsellor in private practice who is considering changing or acquiring a new specialty. In this case relying on performance learning alone would be considered by most as unethical.

For the new graduate or novice counsellor the first two types of learning may be useful. However the performance category may be most important, especially when supervision is accessed to enhance learning. Others have argued that sustained performance is invaluable for counsellors as it fosters development of cognitive and conceptual processing skills (Larson & Daniels, 1998; Borders, 1991).

The limitations of these learning approaches should be acknowledged. One problem concerns skills and techniques learned in instruction situations. Berven and Scofield (1987) point out that for many there is a tendency to rely on familiar methods to the exclusion of newer practices. Many counsellors have experienced the initial excitement that comes with exposure to a new technique during a conference presentation. Unfortunately, this initial excitement is too often followed by a reluctance to employ the technique once one returns to daily practice. It seems that new and unfamiliar techniques can stimulate discomfort and intimidation, and fear of exposing one's weakness or ignorance can lead the counsellor to resort to familiar practices. The literature on counsellor self-efficacy may provide ideas for facilitating integration of information learned in workshops and seminars. Larson and Daniels (1998) note that modelling, role-playing, and visual imagery have all been found to increase counsellor self-efficacy. Private practitioners may wish to seek out workshops that incorporate these methods, or alternatively, integrate activities such as role-playing into peer supervision meetings.

A second problem concerns the ambiguity surrounding the amount of training required to apply a technique or theory competently. Does a half-day workshop render one competent to perform a highly evocative technique? How much supervised practice is required? Can this technique or theory be used with any population? In situations in which these questions are not easily answered, counsellors may take the advice of Koocher and Keith-Spiegel (1998) who recommend consulting a colleague who has expertise in applying the approach.

As mentioned above, the performance-learning category may be invaluable to new graduates or novice counsellors. Problems can however arise when counsellors, especially those who have long since completed their academic training, rely exclusively on this type of learning. While practical experience is valuable, training quickly becomes outdated, and new ideas and approaches (likely gained through instruction and inquiry-based methods) are then needed.

Peer Supervision

Peer supervision is something that often occurs informally, if not formally, in most agency or public settings. Unfortunately, the private practitioner rarely enjoys peer supervision or consultation unless he or she actively pursues it outside of work. Peer supervision can be invaluable for the private practitioner, as it is often the only source of inter-professional contact. Greenberg, Lewis and Johnson (1985) reported on a peer supervision group consisting of private practitioners. The group found that meeting with peers helped them deal more effectively with difficult clients, ethical and professional dilemmas, and served to mitigate burnout and feelings of isolation.

Borders (1991) states that not all peer-supervision groups are effective and helpful. She points out that peers can be "overly supportive and prone to giving advice" (p.248), and that groups sometimes struggle with staying focussed on the task at hand. A further problem that can limit the benefits of peer supervision is theoretical rigidity. Feedback from particular individuals may be limited to a single theoretical viewpoint, or groups of individuals who are like-minded may spend considerable time "preaching to the already converted." In this situation, fresh ideas and suggestions may quickly run out.

Borders (1991) has presented a format for peer supervision that may be especially effective for private practitioners, as it reduces the likelihood that aforementioned problems will occur. In this format the ideal group size is three to six members, including one member who has experience providing supervision. The group initially identifies learning goals, and then individual members take turns presenting videotapes of counselling sessions to the group. In her article, Borders elaborates on six steps that define the format. These steps are as follows:

1. The counsellor identifies questions about the client or videotape session and requests specific feedback about his or her performance.

2. Peers choose or are assigned roles, perspectives, or tasks for reviewing the videotape segment.

3. The counsellor presents the pre-selected videotape segment.

4. Peers give feedback from their roles or perspectives, keeping in mind the goals and questions that were specified by the counsellor.

5. The supervisor facilitates the discussion as needed, functioning as a moderator and process observer.

6. The supervisor summarizes the feedback and discussion, and the counsellor indicates if the supervision needs were met (p. 249).

Borders lists a variety of roles and perspectives that peers can take in reviewing the tape, including assuming the role of the client or client's parent, viewing the tape from a particular theoretical perspective, or creating a metaphor for the client, counsellor, or counselling process. Borders emphasizes that these peer reviews have the added benefit of facilitating development of cognitive counselling skills, as individuals work to consider and integrate the many perspectives and critical viewpoints of group members.

Self-Assessment and Informed Consent as Useful Heuristics

Given the absence of established definitions of competence, Koocher and Keith-Spiegel (1998) argue that the most reliable method of maintaining competent practice is to strive for a sensitive awareness of one's boundaries of competence and the limitations of applied techniques. Once limitations have been assessed, counsellors can begin to seek constructive remedies. While these authors acknowledge the usefulness of formal methods of retraining, they also state that it is impossible to determine the most useful means of maintaining competence when the defining criteria have not been established.

A problem commonly encountered by counsellors involves determining when or when not to use a particular technique or counselling approach. An array of questions must be answered before a technique is applied. Examples of such questions include, "Is this the right technique for this client or problem?" or "Do I really know how to apply this technique and see it through to a therapeutic end?" Again, when these questions are difficult to answer, it would be ideal to consult a colleague with expertise in applying the technique before proceeding, especially when considering a technique for which formal standards have not been established. Unfortunately for the private practitioner, this can sometimes be a challenge as colleagues are not always immediately accessible, and a busy practice can leave the practitioner with little time for consultation.

One heuristic that private practitioners can use to assess competence involves contemplating the dimension of informed consent prior to applying a technique. Counsellors often discuss these same dimensions with clients at the beginning of therapy, and ideally revisit them before proceeding with a novel technique. However, counsellors rarely contemplate these dimensions as a means of assessing their own competence. This method involves a prudent and conservative process of self-reflection and questioning on the part of the counsellor. The questions counsellors ask themselves will differ slightly from those they ask clients when assessing informed understanding, although some similarities exist. The most critical questions counsellors can ask themselves include:

- Do I understand fully the purpose and nature of this activity, including the reasons for which it would be applied in this situation for this particular client?

- Do I understand fully all the mutual responsibilities involved in this task, including all the tasks and skills required of me and my client?

- Do I understand, and can I explain, all of the likely risks and benefits that could occur as a result of applying this technique in this situation?

- Do I know how to assist a client in withdrawing from this activity in a therapeutic manner?

While this approach is not meant to replace other methods such as peer consultation or supervision, it may serve as a useful complement, especially in situations where a counsellor has difficulty accessing a colleague with the appropriate expertise. This approach may also be useful when a counsellor has gained some exposure to a particular method (e.g. through a workshop) but is questioning the extent to which the learning has been fully integrated.

What to Do When the Boundaries of Competence are Challenged

Practicing competently requires that counsellors take appropriate action when their boundaries of competence are challenged. Doing the right thing in this situation may be especially difficult for a private practitioner who is trying to develop or maintain a practice. Knowing how to respond can make a decision to act appropriately easier. The CCA *Code of Ethics* identifies four possible responses to situations that test the boundaries of competence. The responses include: seeking continuing education (Article A1); referring to other professionals (Article A3); seeking supervision or consultation (Article A4); and terminating when service is no longer benefiting the client (Article B17). The individual practitioner must carefully weigh the risks and benefits of continuing or terminating treatment and act accordingly. In some situations, it may be in the client's best interest to continue treatment while seeking supervision or peer consultation. In other situations, the risk of harm may make termination or referral a more appropriate response. If weighing the risks or benefits becomes difficult, or if a counsellor recognizes that there may be a competing interest at work, he or she should seek consultation from a colleague or supervisor who has experience both with the client and the presenting problem.

While these responses listed in the CCA *Code of Ethics* are appropriate, some circumstances may require more careful consideration. For example, when alternative resources are not available, a private practitioner may elect to stretch her or his boundaries to accommodate a client in exceptional need. This circumstance is not uncommon to practitioners practicing in rural setting. Koocher and

Keith-Spiegel (1998) recommend a "three-step process" (p. 68) for dealing with situations like this. First, the counsellor should make sure he or she is aware of every possible referral source in the community. Second, the counsellor can elect to treat the client and seek ongoing telephone consultation and support from a colleague with the appropriate competencies. Third, if there is so much discrepancy between the needs of the client and the skills of the counsellor that the client is placed at risk for greater harm, the counsellor would refuse to provide treatment or terminate treatment if it was already started.

Another difficult situation involves applying practices for which established training standards do not exist. In such situations a counsellor may have difficulty determining whether or not she or he has the required competencies to apply the technique or approach. In addition to seeking consultation, the counsellor can inquire about the expected success rate for the population being treated. This information may assist the practitioner in determining whether or not he or she has adequately applied the technique.

Conclusion

Given the many unresolved issues surrounding competence, it is clear that maintaining competence and practising within one's limits is a challenge for all counsellors. Private practitioners face exceptional challenges in this regard, as they must take full responsibility for maintaining their own competence. Additional difficulties may arise when competing interests tempt the counsellor in private practice to stretch the boundaries of competence. Understanding the dimensions of competence, one's own limitations, the methods for establishing and maintaining competence, and the appropriate actions to take when one's boundaries are challenged, can help ensure that ethical responsibilities are fully met.

References

Abeles, N. (1994). Competency in psychology. In R. J. Corsini (ed.), *Encyclopedia of Psychology* (Vol. 1, pp. 275-276). New York: Wiley.

Borders, L. D. (1991). A systematic approach to peer group supervision. *Journal of Counseling & Development,* 69, 248-251.

Berven, N. L., & Scofield, M. E. (1987). Ethical responsibility in establishing & maintaining professional competence. *Journal of Applied Rehabilitation Counseling,* 18 (4), 41-43.

Claiborn, W. L. (1982). The problem of professional incompetence. *Professional Psychology,* 13 (1), 153-158.

Corey, G., Corey, M. S., & Callanan, P. (1993). *Issues and ethics in the helping professions* (4th ed.). Brooks Cole: California.

Dubin, S. S. (1972). Obsolescence or lifelong education: A choice for the professional. *American Psychologist,* 27, 486-496.

Greenberg, L. S., Lewis, G. J., & Johnson, M. (1985). Peer consultation for groups for private practitioners. *Professional Psychology: Research and Practice,* 16, 437-447.

Hamann, E. E. (1994). Clinicians and diagnosis: Ethical concerns and clinical competence. *Journal of Counseling and Development,* 72, 259-260.

Koocher, G. P., & Keith-Spiegel, P. (1998). *Ethics in psychology: Professional standards and cases.* Oxford University Press: New York.

Lakin, M. (1994). Morality in group and family therapies: Multi-person therapies and the 1992 ethics code. *Professional Psychology: Research and Practice,* 25, 344-348.

Larson, L. M., & Daniels, J. A. (1998). Review of the counseling self-efficacy literature. *The Counseling Psychologist,* 26(2), 179-218.

Lazarus, A. A. (1990). Can psychotherapists transcend the shackles of their training and superstitions? *Journal of Clinical Psychology,* 46(3), 351-358.

Norman (1985). Defining competence: A methodological review. In V. Neufeld and G. Norman (Eds.), Assessing clinical competence, *Professional Psychology: Research and Practice.*

Pedersen, P. (1985). Intercultural criteria for mental-health training. In P. Pedersen (Ed.), *Handbook of cross-cultural counseling and therapy* (pp. 315-321). Westport, CT: Greenwood Press.

Peterson, D. R., & Bry, B. H. (1980). Dimensions of perceived competence in professional psychology. *Professional Psychology,* 11 (6), 965-971.

Pope, K. S., & Brown, L. S. (1996). Recovered memories of abuse: Assessment, therapy, forensics. Washington, DC: American Psychological Association.

Sue, D. (1990). Culture in transition: Counseling Asian-American men. In D. Moore and F. Leafgren (Eds.), *Problem solving strategies and interventions for men in conflict* (pp. 153-168). Alexandria, VA: American Association for Counseling and Development.

Putting the "Privacy" Into Private Practice

Jo-Anne Sargent

Being a counsellor in private practice sometimes means struggling with issues, which in a public work setting, would be quickly settled by consulting the policy and procedures manual. What do we do, or more importantly, how do we decide what is best, when faced with issues for which we're not prepared? Questions from clients such as, "Can I see my records?" or "Do you charge for missed appointments?" can catch us off guard if we haven't put thought into the "how-to" of private practice.

According to Article C2 of the CCA *Code of Ethics*, counsellors in private practice are held to the same ethical standards of conduct as their peers in public work settings. However, they often do not have the advantage of a clearly defined policy that translates ethical conduct into action. The intention of this essay is to help private practitioners develop guidelines for one area of practice in particular–the protection of clients' personal information. Researchers of psychological practice have noted that codes of ethics and general standards of practice are notably vague regarding information-handling procedures (Fulero & Wilbert, 1988), while other research shows that the public is very concerned about the privacy of personal health information (Louis Harris Canada, 1994). As more and more counsellors in private practice work as consultants as well, issues of privacy and consulting will also be addressed. Readers will note that they will be referred from time to time to the essay titled "The Counsellor as Custodian: Protecting Our Clients' Personal Information" in Chapter Three of this book, in order to avoid repetition on closely related topics.

Privacy

First, it is important to clarify what is meant by privacy and how it relates to counselling practice. Privacy can be thought of as a large, umbrella concept that encompasses a number of related sub-topics. For example, physical privacy and the concept of a private, personal space are included under the topic of privacy. For counsellors, confidentiality has always been an important aspect of privacy. Counsellors have long recognized the importance of privacy and confidentiality in therapy as essential to promoting autonomy (Kupfer, 1987; Melton, 1983) and for the "execution of effective psychotherapy" (Corcoran, 1988, p. 194). (See also Nowell & Spruill, 1993; Robinson, 1991). And most, though not all, counsellors realize that keeping client records secure is important as well. However, there are other issues involved in protecting the privacy of client information that should be addressed in order for private practitioners to uphold adequate standards in this area.

Bennett (1992) points out that despite the fact that most authors have given up attempting to define privacy in its broadest sense, there is a fundamental concern about which virtually all experts agree. This is "the loss of human dignity, autonomy, or respect that results from *a loss of control over personal information*"(p. 26). We can probably be safe in assuming that most clients would share the same concern: that once their personal information has passed from their lips or hand to the counsellor, control over it is no longer in their possession. By looking at counselling records (notes, assessments, reports, artwork, journals, etc.) from this perspective (i.e. through the eyes of our clients), we might be able to imagine their concerns: "Where will my information be kept?" "Who else besides you will see it?" "How long will you keep my information on file?" "Can I see what you've written about me?"

When we combine the notion of concern about the loss of control of information with the notion that clients *own* the information in their records (although they do not own the record itself), we see the wisdom of having in place a comprehensive set of guidelines for protecting that information. This would also allow us to answer clients' questions and concerns when they arise, and to be ready for situations that might otherwise cause problems.

Canadian Standards Association's *Model Code for the Protection of Personal Information*

So how would a counsellor in private practice go about devising a comprehensive privacy policy? Rather than re-inventing the wheel, so to speak, it makes sense to look for existing guidelines and adapt them to the needs of the practice. As comprehensive guidelines for privacy do not exist in the psychology and counselling literature (Sargent, 1998), we have to look farther afield. Counsellors are encouraged to find out whether their province has information and privacy legislation, and if so, to familiarize themselves with it. Provinces that have such legislation will also have a privacy commissioner's office, which can be found in the government pages of the phone book. This office can help counsellors obtain a copy of the legislation, or find it via the Internet. Although the legislation will apply to counsellors in public settings such as mental health agencies, schools, and women's shelters, counsellors in private settings can get an idea of the standards required in those settings.

The problem with using a legislative document as a guideline, however, is similar to using a code of ethics: legislation is broadly written, with the intention that public bodies will develop policy based on it, according to the needs of the setting. So while it can give counsellors in private practice a sense of standards, it may not answer the question of, "How do I put this into practice in real life?"

Fortunately, there exists "an instrument in the toolkit of privacy advocates" (Bennett, 1995, p. 4) that is both specific and adaptable to counselling practice. It is the Canadian Standards Association (CSA) *Model Code for the Protection of Personal Information* (1996a). This will be referred to as the CSA *Model Code* and was developed as a voluntary, national standard that adheres closely to Canadian federal and provincial information and privacy legislation. The intention of the CSA *Model Code* is to provide a standard of privacy protection for businesses and organizations not covered by federal or provincial privacy legislation. The CSA *Model Code* is designed (as is most information and privacy legislation) to strike a balance between the privacy rights of the individual (i.e. customer, client, patient), and the information requirements of the private organization. The CSA has also published a workbook, which says that the CSA *Model Code* "can be applied to all types of organizations, from small sole proprietorships to large corporate enterprises" (Canadian Standards Association, 1996b, p.v.).

The CSA *Model Code* is based on the concept of "fair information practices," that is, a set of principles that are common to most access and privacy laws wherever they are found in countries throughout the world (Bennett, 1996). The CSA *Model Code* is made up of 10 principles, which are:

1. accountability
2. identifying purposes
3. consent
4. limiting collection
5. limiting use, disclosure, and retention
6. accuracy
7. safeguards
8. openness
9. individual access
10. challenging compliance

Counsellors can use the principles as a blueprint for creating their own privacy-protection policy, knowing that it will be sufficiently comprehensive and comparable to standards used by their peers in public settings.

Counsellors who are interested in using the CSA *Model Code* as a guideline should consider obtaining a copy of it and the workbook, which provides step-by-step guidance for creating a privacy policy. The CSA's contact information is included in the references at the end of this essay. The remainder of this essay will provide a brief overview of the 10 CSA principles as they might be applied to counselling practice. Some of the concepts in the principles were discussed in the previously mentioned essay, and the reader will be referred to that piece for details.

1. Accountability

The first principle states that, "An organization[1] is responsible for personal information under its control and shall designate an individual or individuals who are accountable for the organization's compliance with the following principles." The principle on accountability might apply to counsellors in a few ways. First, the principle implies that counsellors should have an established information-handling policy. Second, the principle clearly states that the practitioner is responsible for the information collected from individuals. This responsibility raises a few related issues. Practitioners who work as consultants should be able to explain their privacy-protection procedures to their clients, so no confusion arises about responsibilities for security, record retention, access, etc. Further, a sub-section of this principle states that information shared with third parties remains the responsibility of the organization or person who collected it, and therefore "a comparable level of protection" should be arranged by contractual or other means. In their study of ethical dilemmas in psychology, MacKay and O'Neill (1992) reviewed a case in which an assessment report sent to a

medical doctor found its way into court, the psychologist never having been notified, consulted, or his records officially subpoenaed. The authors concluded that psychologists should work to minimize the possibility of similar occurrences.

In practice, counsellors can implement this principle by:

(a) formulating an information privacy policy;

(b) inquiring about the security measures used by third parties before forwarding information; and

(c) requesting that third parties refrain from further sharing client information without obtaining express consent (i.e. explicit consent, either verbally or in writing) from the client.

2. Identifying Purposes

The second CSA *Model Code* principle states that, "The purposes for which personal information is collected shall be identified by the organization at or before the time the information is collected." The principle goes on to recommend that individuals be informed about the purposes for which the information will be used "at or before the time of collection." For counsellors, this means informing clients at the outset about situations such as supervision, consultation, teaching, or research, in which their information will be disclosed. It is important for counsellors to respect the right of their clients to refuse to consent to their information being disclosed in all instances except when it is required by law or the counsellor's code of ethics. For example, a client may not want his or her information used in a case presentation for a conference, even if no identifying information is included. There may be a fear, especially in small communities, that the details would be sufficient for identification of the individual.

The most common use of client information by counsellors, however, is when consultation is required. Again, clients should be informed at the outset of services that in order to provide a high standard of service, the counsellor may consult with another professional when appropriate, but that identifying information will not be used.

It is also important for counsellors working as consultants, in accordance with Article C5 of the CCA *Code of Ethics*, to explain clearly to clients exactly who will have access to their personal information. For example, if a counsellor is asked to provide services in conflict resolution for a group of staff members, and is expected to submit a report to the employer, the staff members have a right to know that before the process commences.

3. Consent
According to this principle, "The knowledge and consent of the individual are required for the collection, use, or disclosure of personal information, except where inappropriate." The CSA *Model Code* also states that *express* consent (either verbal or written) should be obtained when the information "is likely to be considered sensitive." Given that counselling involves information that is highly personal and sensitive, it is reasonable to expect that counsellors would always obtain express consent before disclosing personal information. The phrase "except where inappropriate" can be applied to the exceptions to confidentiality common in counselling practice (i.e. when a child is being harmed or is in danger of being harmed, when a person is in danger of harming themselves or someone else, when records are ordered released by a court of law). For a detailed discussion of consent for the release of information to third parties, including a list of suggested elements to include on consent forms, see the previously mentioned essay, under the heading "Third Party Access." That section also includes discussions of access to records by parents of minor clients, access to records of clients who are deceased, and court-ordered requests for access.

For counsellors working as consultants, Article C6 of the CCA *Code of Ethics* states that "counsellors limit any discussion of client information obtained from a consulting relationship to persons clearly involved with the case." Let us use the previous example of a counsellor who is hired to do conflict-resolution work with a group of staff members. The employer(s) would be clearly involved with the case, whether they were present for the work or not, because they are responsible for staff and for implementing any changes. Other staff members who were not involved in the conflict, however, are not "clearly involved with the case," and the counsellor should not answer questions or divulge information without consent.

Another issue faced by counsellors in their role as consultants is the confidentiality of the consultation itself. Clients who hire a counsellor, again using the previous example of conflict-resolution work, may not want members of the public to know about the consultation. Counsellors may be tempted to list their work with clients on a curriculum vitae, or talk about it with potential clients. Counsellors need to give their consultation clients the same right to confidentiality as their counselling clients; just as we wouldn't talk about having worked with a specific person, we shouldn't talk about having worked with organizations or businesses without their consent. Many consulting clients may be happy to provide a reference, or to let it be known that the counsellor provided services for them, but the choice to release that information is theirs, not the counsellor's.

4. Limiting Collection
The fourth CSA *Model Code* principle states that "The collection of personal information shall be limited to that which is necessary for the purposes identified by the organization. Information shall be collected by fair and lawful means." An implication of this principle would be that counsellors should not use

deception in obtaining information (e.g. secretly recording phone calls or sessions, using deception in research). The notion of limiting the information collected to that which is necessary raises issues about the types of information included and excluded from counsellor notes. Counsellors should have a clear idea of how they make decisions about note taking, and the reader is referred once again to the previously mentioned essay, under the heading "Using Discretion in Note Taking."

Counsellors in the role of consultants need to use discretion about the information that is included in reports to third parties. Article C6 of the CCA *Code of Ethics* states that "Any written and oral reports restrict data to the purposes of the consultation, and every effort is made to protect client identity and to avoid undue invasion of privacy." If the counsellor is to submit a report after the consultation to a third party such as an employer, he or she should provide a general report about the process and the outcome, without divulging any personal information that arises during the consultation.

5. Limiting Use, Disclosure, and Retention

This principle states that "Personal information shall not be used or disclosed for purposes other than those for which it was collected, except with the consent of the individual or as required by law. Personal information shall be retained only as long as necessary for the fulfillment of those purposes." For counsellors, the issues under this principle have already been captured in previous discussions under Consent and Identifying Purposes. A detailed discussion of record retention is found in the previously mentioned essay, *The Counsellor as Custodian*, under the heading "Record Retention."

Counsellors working as consultants should have a clear record-retention policy, and should inform clients as to how long they will keep a record of the consultation before

it is destroyed. The generally accepted record-retention period is seven years, or seven years past the age of majority for under-age clients. Counsellors and consultants should also have a plan for the custody of their records in the event of death or withdrawal from practice.

6. Accuracy

This principle states that "Personal information shall be as accurate, complete, and up-to-date as is necessary for the purposes for which it is to be used." Subsection 4.6.1 of the principle goes on to advise that "Information shall be sufficiently accurate, complete, and up-to-date to minimize the possibility that inappropriate information may be used to make a decision about the individual." This section is relevant to counselling practice, in that records of clients are sometimes used to make decisions that have a great impact on the life of the client and his or her family, such as in the following situations:

- in custody and access decisions
- as the basis for awarding benefits to victims
- in making decisions about taking children out of the home into the custody of the state.

Given the far-reaching impact that counselling records can have, it is important that counsellors and consultants are accurate in their record-keeping practices. The reader will be reminded, however, of the discussion under the principle "Limiting Collection," where it was recommended that counsellors record only that information that is relevant to the procedure being provided, and especially refrain from recording information that is both irrelevant and potentially harmful to the client. The notion of completeness in record keeping must therefore be balanced with the previous discussion about limiting the collection of information.

Some guidelines offer specific methods for achieving accuracy in record-keeping practices. For example, in his book *Documentation in Counseling Records* (1991), Mitchell advises counsellors to follow these key points:

- Make notes grammatically clear and correct.

- Use precise language: reduce the potential for misinterpretation.

- Use only adjectives that are defined, necessary, and clinically appropriate: when possible, replace an adjective with a verb that describes behavior.

- Avoid cliches like the plague!

Other sources of guidance for accuracy in record-keeping practices include the British Columbia Association of Specialized Victim Assistance Programs *Records Management Guidelines* (Ruebsaat & Porteous, 1995), and the *Legal Handbook for Helping Professionals*, (Uhlemann, M. R., & Turner, D., 1998). The American Psychological Association (APA) (1993) also has guidelines that instruct psychologists to be attentive to disclosure of outdated records, which "might cause adverse effects" for clients. The APA recommends that when disclosing out-dated information, psychologists warn the recipient of its "outdated nature and limited utility."

Based on these guidelines, it is recommended that counsellors should

- Follow guidelines such as Mitchell's (1991) for note taking.

- Update client records as soon after sessions as possible, so the information is as accurate as possible.

- Warn third parties if information is outdated before forwarding.

7. Safeguards

This principle states that "Personal information shall be protected by security safeguards appropriate to the sensitivity of the information." As previously mentioned, the information kept by counsellors is extremely personal and sensitive, and should therefore be safeguarded by stringent security measures. Again, please see the essay *The Counsellor as Custodian* in Chapter Three for details, under the heading "Security of Records." It will simply be noted here that the information on clients in consulting work is to be protected according to the same standards as that of counselling clients.

8. Openness

Principle eight states that information about an organization's information policies and practices should be made readily available to individuals. The principle also lists the types of information that should be made available, including:

- The person(s) within the organization who is(are) responsible for implementing the information policies and practices,

- The means of gaining access, a description of the type of personal information held,

- Copies of the organization's information policies,

- The names of organizations to whom personal information is made available.

Counsellors who have formulated an information-privacy policy may want to have a written outline readily available for clients. Knowing about how their personal information is to be handled can go a long way toward building a trusting relationship with clients.

9. Individual Access

This principle states that

Upon request, an individual shall be informed of the existence, use and disclosure of his or her personal information and shall be given access to that information. An individual shall be able to challenge the accuracy and completeness of the information and have it amended as appropriate.

The notions that individuals own the information in their records, have the right to access it, and the right to correct it when necessary, are important aspects of privacy protection. This principle is discussed in detail in the previously mentioned essay, under the heading "Individual Access." For counsellors working as consultants, the same principle would apply. The client should have access to any personal information that he or she provided to the counsellor, and which the counsellor included in the record. The counsellor would have to be careful, when handling requests for access, to restrict access to only those portions that pertain to that individual, and to withhold information about others.

10. Challenging Compliance

The last principle of CSA *Model Code* states that individuals should be "able to address a challenge concerning compliance with the above principles to the designated individual or individuals accountable for the organization's compliance." For counsellors, good practice would mean providing clients and consultees with the information necessary to challenge the counsellor's information practices or policies. This may mean, in the event of a conflict over any of these practices, that the practitioner would provide information about filing a complaint with the professional association or governing body with whom the counsellor is affiliated.

Conclusion

The CSA *Model Code for the Protection of Personal Information* has been reviewed as a possible guideline for counsellors in private practice who would like to develop an information-privacy policy. The CSA *Model Code* is a good choice for practitioners in private practice, because it is based on well-accepted, internationally recognized principles, is widely used as a privacy standard by businesses and private organizations in Canada, and is consistent with Canadian privacy legislation.

By giving some thought to each of the principles, counsellors should be able to devise practices for handling their clients' information that provides maximum privacy protection for their clients, and a sense for the counsellor that they are practicing in a highly professional and responsible manner.

Endnote

[1] The reader should note that "organization" can be read as "private practitioner" throughout the essay.

References

American Psychological Association (1993). Record Keeping Guidelines. *American Psychologist, 48*(9), 984-986.

Bennett, C. J. (1992). *Regulating privacy.* London: Cornell University Press.

Bennett, C. J. (1995). Standards for privacy. *The International Privacy Bulletin, 3*(2), 4-6.

Bennett, C. J. (1996). Protecting privacy on the Canadian information highway: policy developments and regulatory options. *Canadian Journal of Information and Library Science, 21*(3/4), 2-3.

Canadian Standards Association (1996a). *Can/CSA-Q830-96 Model code for the protection of personal information.* Etobicoke, Ontario: Author. 178 Rexdale Boulevard, Etobicoke, Ontario M9W 1R3.

Canadian Standards Association (1996b). *Plus 8300 Making the CSA privacy code work for you.* Etobicoke, Ontario: Author.

Corcoran, K. J. (1988). The relationship of interpersonal trust to self-disclosure when confidentiality is assured. *Journal of Psychology, 122*, 193-195.

Fulero, S. M., & Wilbert, J. R. (1988). Record-keeping practices of clinical and counseling psychologists: a survey of practitioners. *Professional Psychology: Research and Practice, 19*(6), 658-660.

Kupfer, J. (1987). Privacy, autonomy, and self-concept. *American Philosophical Quarterly, 24*(1), 81-89.

Louis Harris and Associates, and Westin, A. F. (1994). *The Equifax Canada report on consumer and privacy in the information age.* New York: Louis Harris and Associates.

MacKay, E., & O'Neill, P. (1992). What creates the dilemma in ethical dilemmas? Examples from psychological practice. *Ethics & Behavior, 2*(4), 227-244.

Mitchell, R. W. (1991). Documentation in counseling records. In T. P. Remley, Jr. (Series Ed.), *The AACD Legal Series: Vol. 2* (pp. 1-75). Alexandria, Virginia: American Association for Counseling and Development.

Nowell, D., & Spruill, J. (1993). If it's not absolutely confidential, will information be disclosed? *Professional Psychology: Research and Practice, 24*(3), 367-369.

Robinson, I. (1991). Confidentiality for whom? *Social Science and Medicine, 32*(3), 279-286.

Ruebsaat, G., & Porteous, T. (1995). *Records management guidelines: draft for field testing.* Victoria, British Columbia: British Columbia Association of Specialized Victim Assistance Programs.

Sargent, J. M. (1998). Psychologists' information practices: An empirical investigation. Unpublished master's thesis, University of Victoria, Victoria, British Columbia.

Uhlemann, M. R., & Turner, D. (1998). Core legal knowledge for the helping professional. In Uhlemann, M. R., and Turner, D. (Eds.), *A legal handbook for the helping professional,* 2nd edition (pp. 2-35). Victoria, British Columbia: The Sedgewick Society for Consumer and Public Education.

Chapter Five

---------- ❖ ----------

Evaluation and Assessment

---------- ❖ ----------

In the guidelines presented in this section, counsellors are encouraged to familiarize themselves with proper test administration and interpretation procedures.

❖ ❖ ❖ ❖ ❖ ❖ ❖ ❖ ❖ ❖ ❖ ❖ ❖ ❖

ETHICAL ARTICLES
ON EVALUATION
AND ASSESSMENT

D1 General Orientation

Counsellors adequately orient and inform clients so that evaluation and assessment results can be placed in proper perspective along with other relevant information.

❖

D2 Purposes and Results of Evaluation and Assessment

Counsellors take responsibility to inform clients about the purpose of any evaluation and assessment instruments and procedures, and the meaning of evaluation and assessment results.

❖

D3 Evaluation and Assessment Competence

Counsellors recognize the limits of their competence and offer only those evaluation and assessment services for which they have appropriate preparation and which meet established professional standards.

❖

D4 Administrative and Supervisory Conditions

Counsellors ensure that evaluation and assessment instruments and procedures are administered and supervised under established conditions consistent with professional standards. They note any departures from standard conditions, and any unusual behavior or irregularities which may affect the interpretation of results.

D5 Use of Technology

Counsellors recognize that their ethical responsibilities are not altered, or in any way diminished, by the use of technology for the administration of evaluation and assessment instruments. Counsellors retain their responsibility for the maintenance of the ethical principles of privacy, confidentiality, and responsibility for decisions regardless of the technology used.

❖

D6 Appropriateness of Evaluation and Assessment

Counsellors ensure that evaluation and assessment instruments and procedures are valid, reliable, and appropriate to both the client and the intended purposes.

❖

D7 Reporting Evaluation and Assessment Results

Counsellors ensure that when reporting evaluation and assessment results to clients and other individuals, care is taken to provide, in an appropriate manner, accurate and sufficient information for an understanding of any conclusions and recommendations made, and to identify the basis for any reservations which might exist.

❖

D8 Release of Evaluation and Assessment Data

Counsellors ensure that evaluation and assessment data are released only to persons qualified to interpret and use them properly.

D9 Integrity of Evaluation and Assessment Instruments and Procedures

Counsellors who use psychological tests and other assessment instruments, the value of which depends on their novelty to the client, ensure that they are limited to and safeguarded by, those with the professional interest and competence to do so.

D10 Sensitivity to Diversity When Assessing and Evaluating

Counsellors proceed with caution when judging and interpreting the performance of minority group members and any other persons not represented in the group on which the evaluation and assessment instruments and procedures were standardized. They recognize and take into account the potential effects of age, ethnicity, disability, culture, gender, religion, sexual orientation, and socio-economic status on both the administration of, and the interpretation of data from such instruments and procedures.

❖

D11 Security Maintenance

Counsellors ensure the integrity and security of evaluation and assessment instruments and procedures consistent with any legal and contractual obligations. They refrain from appropriating, reproducing, or modifying established evaluation and assessment instruments without the expressed permission and adequate recognition of the original author, publisher, and copyright holder.

❖ ❖ ❖ ❖ ❖ ❖ ❖ ❖ ❖ ❖ ❖ ❖ ❖ ❖

CASE STUDIES IN EVALUATION AND ASSESSMENT

D1 GENERAL ORIENTATION
Counsellors adequately orient and inform clients so that evaluation and assessment results can be placed in proper perspective along with other relevant information.

Recognizing Language Differences (+)

Mr. Richard D. is an immigrant who recently decided to leave his home in France and move to Winnipeg. He is fluent in the oral communication of English and is able to communicate well verbally. However, he has a problem in interpreting written English. He was requested to take a job evaluation test at a placement center for the unemployed. Both a written and oral form of the test were available. The counsellor, who was informed of Richard's weakness, administered the test orally to Richard and wrote exactly what Richard said for each test question.

Orientation (+)

A counsellor decided that in order to help his client, Heather, she needed a personality assessment. Before conducting the test, the counsellor held an orientation meeting with Heather. During this meeting, Heather was told the purpose of the test, ways in which the counsellor would use the test, and some of the limitations of personality testing. During this meeting, the counsellor answered any questions or concerns Heather had about the test. At the end of the meeting, the counsellor felt Heather was comfortable with taking the test.

Standardized Tests for Placement (-)

An American aptitude test battery is used for the placement of students at an inner-city high school. There are no Canadian, national or local norms for the tests. Based on the results of these tests, as well as school grades, students are placed in various educational streams in the school. There are large numbers of recently immigrated students in this school. Most score very low in the aptitude test and most have not achieved well in school, due to their weaknesses in English. As a result of low scores, most of these immigrant students are placed in "high school leaving" streams.

"The Test Says..." (-)

In a private career-counselling office, one counsellor regularly uses the Strong-Campbell Interest Inventory to help clients make career decisions. After clients have completed the inventory and the computer print-out of results has been returned, the counsellor tells clients, "The test says you should go into one of the following occupations..." Little or no time is taken to consider other relevant factors in career decision-making; factors such as aptitude, personality, socio-economic and job outlook.

COMMENTS AND QUESTIONS

Certain guidelines and procedures must be followed when administering a test and interpreting test results. Before a counsellor administers a test to a client, the following matters should be considered:

a) the counsellor previews in advance the language, ethnic and culture differences of the client and selects the appropriate assessment, or makes necessary adjustments to ensure differences are recognized;

b) the counsellor obtains consent from the client before any test is administered or information about the examinee is shared;

c) the client is informed as to the purpose of testing and confidentiality and limitations are explained;

d) the client is informed of the availability of test results, interpretations made and explanation of interpretations;

e) the counsellor ensures the client understands that these test results are only one factor from a variety of data used when making a counselling or personnel decision.

1. If you were a client, what questions might you want to ask about the nature of the test?

2. Should standardized tests be the main criterion used for placement and college/university selection?

3. What would you do to make a client feel more at ease prior to taking the test, especially if you noticed outward signs of being over-anxious?

4. How will the client be notified of test results? How will the test results be given to the client (written or verbal)?

5. As a member who administered the test, how will the test results be used and will anybody else in your department have access to them?

D2 PURPOSES AND RESULTS OF EVALUATION AND ASSESSMENT

Counsellors take responsibility to inform clients about the purpose of any evaluation and assessment instruments and procedures, and the meaning of evaluation and assessment results.

The Purpose of Testing (+)

The counsellor informs students, class by class, of the purposes of a group aptitude test. The counsellor carefully explains the information booklet making sure all the students taking the test understand the process. The test administration is explained by the counsellor. Students are made aware of the test's possible significance and how the results can be used in helping to make future educational and career decisions. Students are also informed that all test interpretations will be done on an individual basis so that other relevant information can be considered.

Test Orientation (+)

At the counselling centre of a Canadian university, the counsellors organize and teach regular testing orientation sessions. Every effort is made to help clients understand the purposes and uses of any standardized tests that will be used. In addition, clear instructions are given regarding the individual interpretation that will follow.

Results for the Files (-)

Frank Newman, a high school counsellor, found out that most of the high schools were administering the Differential Aptitude Tests (DAT) to Grade 9 students. With administration's agreement, he scheduled two morning meetings in the gymnasium for all Grade 9 students to complete the DAT. Students were simply asked to complete the test in order that the school would have their scores on file.

Unstated Purpose for Testing (-)

As a regular practice, a school principal asks the teachers in her elementary school to administer the Canadian Tests of Basic Skills to all Grade 4 and Grade 5 students. One year, after the scores were known, two of the Grade 5 teachers received very negative reports on their teaching from the principal. Upon inquiring about these negative reports, these were told that the students in their classes had not progressed sufficiently (one grade equivalency higher) since their testing in the previous year when the students were in Grade 4.

COMMENTS AND QUESTIONS

This ethical article requires those who are in charge of testing to delineate the purpose of testing, the criteria of the examinees' welfare and explicit prior understanding with tests, the examinees' right to know the testing results, the interpretations made, and other aspects of the testing results. In other words, clients need informed consent. Informed consent implies that clients understand the full purpose of testing as well as how the interpretation will be done and how the results will be used. Testing provides clients and counsellors with additional information so that more realistic decisions can be made. It is very important that counsellors realize that it is their responsibility to see that tests serve the best interests of clients.

1. What are some things a counsellor can do to make the testing experience a more collaborative venture?

2. How could a counsellor explore examinees' reasons for taking tests, as well as their past experience with tests?

3. What are the major purposes of testing?

4. Who should introduce the idea of standardized testing, the client or the counsellor? Why?

5. What are some ways in which the counsellor can explain beforehand how interpretations, conclusions and recommendations will be made for interest and personality inventories, intelligence tests, diagnostic tests, achievement batteries and aptitude tests?

D3 EVALUATION AND ASSESSMENT COMPETENCE

Counsellors recognize the limits of their competence and offer only those evaluation and assessment services for which they have appropriate preparation and which meet established professional standards.

Art Therapy (+)

A beginning counsellor sees that the art work of one student consistently depicts scenes of violence involving children and adults. Recognizing that there may be psychological significance in this art work, and acknowledging the limitations of his own expertise, the counsellor hands over the collection to the guidance department head, a counsellor with many years of experience, and some knowledge of art therapy.

Staff Orientation (+)

At the beginning of a school year a counsellor at a high school holds an orientation workshop with school administration and teaching staff, at which the counsellor's education background, training, experience and competencies are outlined. Participants become familiarized with the range of tests that can be accessed and ones that are beyond the competence of the counsellor to administer. The counsellor makes it clear that for these situations the services of a school psychologist should be enlisted.

Score Misinterpretation (-)

A procedure of one small community high school is to administer the Canadian Test of Basic Skills to all new students entering the school with a view to determining an estimate of functional levels in language and mathematics. The school counsellor administers the tests and makes available to teachers the grade-equivalent scores. No attempt is made to interpret the scores with the teachers nor to make conversions to percentile ranks. Teachers take the grade-equivalent scores into account in assessing functional levels and developing individual programs, often misinterpreting both the meaning and intent of grade-equivalent scores.

Limited Information (-)

Art interpretation happens to be a recently discovered interest of this department head through some journal articles she has read. She has even discovered a neatly packaged technique including a test to verify the findings. She then applies the test to the client. From the test results, she concludes family violence to be the root cause of the problem. Based on her findings, she proceeds to get social workers involved to start the necessary investigations.

COMMENTS AND QUESTIONS

It is incumbent upon the counselling practitioners to engage in constant self-scrutiny and self-evaluation regarding knowledge of skills and competence in testing.

It is both a duty and a responsibility to remain current on test availability, the latest testing techniques, the norming schemes, and the accurate interpretation of results. This can be achieved through professional reading, attendance at seminars and workshops, maintaining contact with colleagues, and enrolling in upgrading and refresher courses.

Counsellors should convey to clients the range of testing services within and outside their sphere of competence. There must be a willingness to refer to a more competent authority when cases arise requiring services outside counsellors' levels of ability or training.

1. What are some of the pitfalls of certain types of inventories and tests being offered on the computer internet?

2. What set of criteria might one have to determine the degree of comfort and competence in providing a testing service to clients?

3. To what extent should a practitioner attempt to upgrade and keep current on up-to-date test availability, techniques, and results interpretations?

4. What specific information about one's background and competencies should one divulge to prospective clients?

5. What guidelines might one follow in determining at which stage a referral to another authority is made?

D4 ADMINISTRATIVE AND SUPERVISORY CONDITIONS

Counsellors ensure that evaluation and assessment instruments and procedures are administered and supervised under established conditions consistent with professional standards. They note any departures from standard conditions, and any unusual behavior or irregularities which may affect the interpretation of results.

Counsellor Competence (+)

A counsellor has decided to use a test designed to measure attitudes and values with a particular client. The counsellor has extensive knowledge about this type of test and about whether it is suitable and appropriate for his client. The counsellor is qualified to give this test. He carefully administers the test exactly as prescribed in the administration manual.

Irregularities Noted (+)

John Elder is qualified to administer a large number of standardized tests. During the administration of a group aptitude test, the electricity in the room goes off for three or four minutes.

John carefully notes this irregularity since he feels the test results and subsequent interpretations could be affected.

Consultant Job Placement Through the Mail (-)

A counsellor with a career-consulting firm sends out brochures advertising career-aptitude inventory tests, which can be purchased through the mail from his firm. The advertisement claims that if you buy the test you can give yourself the test and find out what career you are best suited for. These tests have not been designed or standardized to be self-administered or self-scored.

Prescribed Material Shortage (-)

A counsellor in a high school is administering a test to a group of students. Due to budget cuts the counsellor was unable to purchase the prescribed computer answer sheets that go with the test booklets. Therefore, the counsellor has the students write out the answers on a sheet of paper and then marks and scores them himself.

COMMENTS AND QUESTIONS

This ethical article is a mandate for counsellors and any other qualified professionals who administer tests, to do so only as prescribed in the administration manual. The only exception to changing test-administration regulations would be for research, and then only if the changes are in accord with professional standards. The counsellor must note and report any unusual behaviour or irregularities during the testing session, which may affect the interpretation of the test scores. Tests done through the mail are unethical, the only exceptions being those designed for self-administering and self-scoring, such as some interest inventories.

1. What qualifications would you expect to have as a counsellor before giving any tests or battery of tests?

2. Besides understanding the prescribed methods in any given administration manual, counsellors first need to be able to clarify the purposes of the test and point out any limitations for any particular client. How could this be done?

3. What are some irregularities that might occur during testing and that should be reported?

4. Do you believe it is all right to self-administer and self-score interest inventories?

5. Would you allow a person who has difficulty with the language on the test more time?

D5 USE OF TECHNOLOGY
Counsellors recognize that their ethical responsibilities are not altered, or in any way diminished, by the use of technology for the administration of evaluation and assessment instruments. Counsellors retain their responsibility for the maintenance of the ethical principles of privacy, confidentiality, and responsibility for decisions regardless of the technology used.

On-Line Counselling (+)
Sara B. had prepared carefully before deciding to do a limited amount of on-line counselling for clients in remote areas. She was a certified counsellor with many years of experience. She made sure all data received during counselling would be secure. As well, she allowed herself adequate time to process on-line counselling interactions after each session. When testing was a part of the counselling, Sara made sure that tests were valid and reliable, and that time was spent on qualitative data as well.

Sending Confidential Faxes (+)
The counsellor, Adrian C., realized that the fax machine in their counselling centre was centrally located and many people had access to all the faxes that were sent daily. Before receiving confidential information by fax, Adrian made sure that a phone call was made just before sending the fax so that he could immediately pick up the confidential fax.

Secret Password (-)
Joe, a college senior, noted the word HELPER taped to the side of the computer of one of the counsellors in the college counselling centre. He had already seen the computer account number left on the desk of the counsellor. When Joe got back to his own computer, he used this information to look

at the case notes that the counsellor had made on her clients.

Computer Test Results (-)
A very busy counsellor decided he could see more clients in a shorter period of time if he relied more on his personal computer, particularly when he was counselling clients with career concerns. Clients sat at the computer and completed a battery of tests. They also received computer-generated results of the tests. Counsellor and client then discussed the test results. The counsellor made no attempts to check the data entries of the client, nor to add qualitative data to the computer-generated data.

COMMENTS AND QUESTIONS
The use of technology in counselling continues to increase at a rapid pace. Computers are now being used not only to score tests but also to administer tests, provide statistical comparisons and to print out computer-generated assessments. Computerized assessment is now possible on highly sophisticated tests such as the Wechsler Adult Intelligence Scale, the Wonderlic Personnel Test, the Minnesota Multiphasic Personality Inventory and the 16 Personality Factor Test. The benefits of computerized tests include rapid retrieval of information and easy storage of data. As well, with computers it is possible to tailor tests for the test-taker.

Counsellors must, however, also be aware of limitations of technology and assessment. Sound testing practices include observing clients during test taking. Will counsellors rely too much on the computer, and not take the time for observation? Furthermore, there is the danger of the computer-generated assessment results and reports becoming the major focus of the counselling, rather than an adjunct to the counselling. There may also be a need for new information on validity, reliability and normative data for using well-known standardized tests on the computer.

1. What safeguards should be put in place to guarantee tests and records confidentiality?

2. Should test results be placed on a college- or university-wide computer network?

3. What are some of the strengths and limitations of computer-generated assessment results and reports?

4. How frequently should passwords be changed?

5. What can counsellors do to make sure that clients do not buy into the perceived "magic" of computer-generated results and suggestions?

D6 APPROPRIATENESS OF EVALUATION AND ASSESSMENT

Counsellors ensure that evaluation and assessment instruments and procedures are valid, reliable, and appropriate to both the client and the intended purposes.

Placement Policy (+)

A school division has a policy that all senior high students who transfer in from out-of-province must complete a standardized achievement test battery. Much time was taken by division counsellors and psychologists in selecting a test battery that was appropriate for out-of-province students. Each year the appropriateness of the test was re-evaluated.

Test Appropriateness (+)

The manager of an employment centre asks the counsellors in his office to recommend an aptitude test that will be helpful in determining the mechanical aptitude of clients. After careful examination of O.K. Buros' *Mental Measurements Yearbook* and the examination of the technical data available on several aptitude tests, the counsellors recommend an aptitude test that appears to be appropriate, reliable and valid.

Language Deficiencies (-)

A high school student, Sophie, has recently moved from predominantly French-speaking Quebec City to an English-language high school in Edmonton. Although Sophie can read and speak English, she is not at the same level as other students in her grade. When Sophie completes an aptitude test, the counsellor uses the regular normative data and makes no allowances for Sophie's language deficiencies.

Finding the Gifted Students (-)

A program for educating "gifted" children is being rushed into place by a school division that seems to be responding more to parental pressure than to any clearly defined educational goal or research to substantiate the advisability of such a program. To select students for the "gifted" program, the school superintendent asks counsellors to use a group intelligence test that measures verbal ability, numerical ability, and abstract reasoning. The test is 20-years-old and no data is available suggesting that the test is appropriate for the selection of "gifted" students.

COMMENTS AND QUESTIONS

This ethical article clearly states the importance and need to be knowledgeable and skilled in test selection and use. There must be a purpose for giving tests and standards should be followed for evaluating tests. The publication, *Standards for Education and Psychological Tests*, is a comprehensive guide for both test developers and test users. These standards set out information that should be included in test manuals: information on technical adequacy and information on how to use the test. As well, test users will find an extensive review of tests in O.K. Buros' *Mental Measurements Yearbook*.

Several factors should be considered when selecting either norm- or criterion-referenced tests. Validity is the most important factor. This means that the test must measure what it claims to measure and what the user wants it to measure. Reliability coefficients must meet acceptable standards and there should be a relatively small standard error of measurement. To make sure the test is appropriate, the population on whom the test was normed should include people like the ones to be tested. These and other considerations are to be adhered to before selecting tests for use.

1. What questions would you be prepared to discuss with your administrator if the required tests did not show evidence of sufficient validity in their test manuals?

2. If a test is a "big seller," does this imply that the test is valid? Explain.

3. How would you counter the argument, "The use of an inadequate device is better than the use of no test at all"?

4. Explain why it is realistic to demand very high standards of reliability when using tests for decision-making?

5. How can you ensure greater test appropriateness with clients from minority groups?

D7 REPORTING EVALUATION AND ASSESSMENT RESULTS

Counsellors ensure that when reporting evaluation and assessment results to clients and other individuals, care is taken to provide, in an appropriate manner, accurate and sufficient information for an understanding of any conclusions and recommendations made, and to identify the basis for any reservations which might exist.

Tests and Counselling (+)

Bob, a first-year engineering student, is not enjoying his program of studies. He decided to take an interest inventory at the university counselling centre to see if his interests really were in engineering. After the results of the interest inventory were known, the counsellor discussed the results with Bob. The interest inventory scores did not support his field of study, but the counsellor pointed out that a standardized interest inventory was only one factor among many others that should influence his career decision. The counsellor and Bob then discussed some of the other factors.

Effective Test Interpretation (+)

A school counsellor telephoned the parents of one student in order to communicate a concern about the student's behavioural change over the last several months. The student appeared sullen, non-communicative with all school personnel and the number of classes he was skipping was increasing. After talking with the counsellor, the student revealed that he felt hopelessly lost in most of his subjects. The student agreed to some diagnostic testing in order to find out more specifically what the major problems might be. Since the parents were very concerned and willing to help, the counsellor asked the student's permission to include them in the discussion of the test results and in future remedial learning plans.

Parental Request for Information (-)

In November of Jamie's Grade 6 year, her parents noticed she appeared to be regressing in mathematics and not progressing in her reading ability. The parents knew that special testing was done for some students at the beginning of each year by the resource teacher and counsellor. After learning that Jamie had been tested several months earlier, the parents requested the results of the tests. The results indicated dramatic drops in performance, yet the results had not been communicated to the parents and remedial action was not implemented to correct or work with Jamie. The present classroom teachers were not informed of the child's problems or what teaching strategies might help her learning.

Inadequate Test Interpretation (-)

A counsellor is trying to do some research in the area of self-concept and adolescent females. A standardized test on self-concept was administered to all students in one middle school. After test results were interpreted, the counsellor intended to meet with the students individually to discuss the test results. Due to lack of time, only half of the students were provided with this opportunity. With the rest of the students, the results were handed back to each classroom, generally to groups of 35, with a short period of time made available to answer any questions students might have. As there were no questions asked, no further interpretation was provided.

COMMENTS AND QUESTIONS

Test results must be accompanied by adequate interpretation, and where it is felt to be necessary by counselling as well. Many of the tests that counsellors use are fairly easy to administer and interpret. This is true for a number of interest inventories and some aptitude tests. Nevertheless, clients will usually not be familiar with the scores provided and counsellors need to take the time to make sure that results are communicated in an understandable way. If possible, test interpretations should be provided as only one piece of information and be related to other information available to the counsellor and client.

1. Is it appropriate for interpretation of test results to be done in small groups, or should all interpretation be done individually?

2. Should all tests be subject to a "User Qualification Form" to ensure that only qualified people are administering the tests?

3. Who is qualified to determine whether or not a test administrator is in fact qualified to interpret the results of the test? Does a particular degree really determine whether or not the user is qualified to interpret the results and communicate them in an ethical fashion?

4. Should test-interpretation practica or workshops be required for all counsellors-in-training?

5. What needs to be done in the last two cases presented to make the behaviour of the counsellor more ethical?

D8 RELEASE OF EVALUATION AND ASSESSMENT DATA

Counsellors ensure that evaluation and assessment data are released only to persons qualified to interpret and use them properly.

Discussion of Test Results (+)

Mrs. Jones, the parent of an elementary-school student, asked to know the results of the WISC-R taken by her daughter. The psychologist set up an appointment and carefully interpreted the test results so that Mrs. Jones understood the scores from the WISC-R.

Student Cumulative Files (+)

Cumulative files are kept on all students attending public schools. These cumulative files include pertinent medical data (e.g. medication, allergies, medical conditions), past grades, inventory results, and other information. Psychological test results are placed in the psychologist's private files, and are only released to counsellors and others who are qualified to interpret the results of each specific psychological test.

Access to Test Scores (-)

In this middle school, all students' cumulative files can be accessed by teachers, the student, and his or her parents. When psychological assessments are sent to the school, they are also placed in the students' cumulative files.

Reporting to Outside Agencies (-)

Counsellors are in frequent contact with agencies such as Child and Family Services and Child Guidance Services regarding particular students. These outside agencies may request further information about psychological tests performed in the school. One busy counsellor gave the school secretary the job of sending test results to outside agencies. Since the school secretary had a good friend at one of the outside agencies, she frequently reported test results verbally over the phone to her friend.

COMMENTS AND QUESTIONS

The Supreme Court of Canada has ruled that every person has the legal right to know what is written about them. This includes government documents, school files and medical records. The records must be written in such a manner that the person can understand the information, as in the case of school cumulative files. If the records are not written as such, a qualified person should be on hand to interpret the information.

1. How does one determine if the person to whom test scores are released is truly qualified to interpret and use the test scores properly?

2. What is the difference between "psychological test scores" and "interpreted test results"?

3. What are your organization's regulations regarding the storing of test results in clients' files?

4. Should secretaries have access to psychological test scores?

5. Where should psychological reports and standardized test scores be kept?

D9 INTEGRITY OF EVALUATION AND ASSESSMENT INSTRUMENTS AND PROCEDURES

Counsellors who use psychological tests and other assessment instruments, the value of which depends on their novelty to the client, ensure that they are limited to and safeguarded by, those with the professional interest and competence to do so.

Test Security (+)

Professor Jonathan Stewart was quite concerned that many standardized tests in the faculty of education, where he worked, were not being properly safeguarded. He received permission from the dean of the faculty and his department head to draft a policy on the "safeguarding of tests." This policy resulted in some inventories being kept in the library and some tests in locked filing cabinets in professors' offices.

Graduate Record Examinations (+)

Joan Fisher was concerned about all the manuals that were available to help potential graduate students prepare for their Graduate Record Examinations (GRE). As well, several workshops were advertised purporting to help students score higher on their GRE. She contacted the GRE office and was reassured to find that the GRE tests were constantly being revised and that GRE preparation manuals and special workshops might help students somewhat, but this preparation was taken into consideration when norms were established.

Test Item Coaching (-)

In one urban school, students are placed into a "gifted" program if they have demonstrated outstanding achievement in earlier grades or if they score at the 98th percentile or above on several sub-tests of the Differential Aptitude Test (DAT). One counsellor, whose daughter attends this school, takes the DAT home and has her daughter familiarize herself with some of the test items. Not surprisingly, her daughter gets into the gifted program based on her DAT scores.

Test Reproduction (-)

One professor, who teaches a unit on John Holland's career theory, has graduate students familiarize themselves with Holland's "hexagonal" model by having them complete Holland's interest inventory, the "Self-Directed Search." He reproduces copies of the original for each member of the class.

COMMENTS AND QUESTIONS

The first case is used to demonstrate ethical behaviour. Test users are responsible for safeguarding the use of tests. If tests are to be valid and reliable, they must be "new" to the person taking the test. Any prior information or coaching that clients receive invalidate test results and normative data.

1. What safeguards for tests are in place in your organization?

2. Should professors or teachers be allowed to reproduce interest inventories when the inventories are only being used to explain a model? (See the last case.)

3. This article states that psychological tests be given by persons with professional competence. How can counsellors best attain this competence?

4. How are special manuals with sample questions and preparation for testing workshops different from the "prior information" and "coaching" mentioned in this article?

5. Should some adjustment be made to scores for students who have taken many standardized tests during their school years? Or for students who are taking their first-ever standardized test?

D10 SENSITIVITY TO DIVERSITY WHEN ASSESSING AND EVALUATING

Counsellors proceed with caution when judging and interpreting the performance of minority group members and any other persons not represented in the group on which the evaluation and assessment instruments and procedures were standardized. They recognize and take into account the potential effects of age, ethnicity, disability, culture, gender, religion, sexual orientation, and socioeconomic status on both the administration of, and the interpretation of data from such instruments and procedures.

Student Placement (+)

An immigrant student, who has only lived in Canada for a year, recently completed several standardized tests to help school officials make placement decisions. The test results suggested placement in the stream for "slower learners." The homeroom teacher said she would develop other, more appropriate ways of determining this immigrant student's academic potential. She did this, and after the student performed at an above-average level, the student was placed in the appropriate educational stream.

Score Adjustments (+)

Several counsellors, in a school division that has many students who are from minority groups, decided to do something about the fact that many of these students did not perform well on a particular standardized test. They carefully researched the literature on this issue and learned how to adjust the scoring on their standardized test so that a more accurate score was derived for minority-group students.

Miller's Analogies Test (-)

The Miller's Analogies Test was used as a major criterion for admission to one university graduate program. Many foreign students who applied did not have a strong English background and because of low scores were not admitted to the graduate program.

Non-Representative Norm Group (-)

A counsellor, working in a remote northern community, administered tests of mental ability (I.Q.) to all the students in the school. He used an American group I.Q. test and used the American norms. When interpreting the test scores, the counsellor paid no attention to the fact that most of the students spoke English as their second language, and that most of the students were not represented in the norms.

COMMENTS AND QUESTIONS

Counsellors and researchers should examine carefully the performance of minority groups on standardized tests. The following issues should be kept in mind:

a) Standardized tests provide only an estimate of an individual's performance in standard English as compared to a cross-section of American (sometimes Canadian) persons of the same age or grade.

b) Culturally diverse populations are typically under-represented in normative data.

c) Are there culturally appropriate tests available?

d) Testing is one aspect of counselling. Members must acquire competencies in multicultural counselling when interpreting tests for minority groups.

1. What provisions are made for school counsellors, agency counsellors, career counsellors and counsellors in private practice to acquire competencies in multicultural counselling to help them with minority clients?

2. Since culture is not fair, can we or should we expect counsellors to use "culture-fair" tests?

3. Even though minority groups are under-represented in normative data, can we expect counsellors to develop their own norms?

4. Is what we expect of minority groups in Canada different than in the United States (cultural mosaic or melting pot)?

5. Do minority-group members want special consideration?

D11 SECURITY MAINTENANCE
Counsellors ensure the integrity and security of evaluation and assessment instruments and procedures consistent with any legal and contractual obligations. They refrain from appropriating, reproducing, or modifying established evaluation and assessment instruments without the expressed permission and adequate recognition of the original author, publisher, and copyright holder.

Reproducible Interest Inventories (+)

Every year Frank Nubold, a senior-school counsellor, is faced with a limited budget. He finds it very worthwhile to use several self-scoring interest inventories when helping students with their future career planning. To help offset the costs of buying a new supply of the standardized tests each year, Frank Nubold asks the students to contribute a portion of the costs of the readily reproducible interest inventories.

Aptitude Tests (+)

During high school, students often take an aptitude test to give them ideas as to which careers relate to their abilities. Before the test, the counsellor explains to the students that the test measures aptitude in areas such as verbal reasoning, mechanical, abstract reasoning and so forth. These aptitudes are later related to possible careers. It is stressed to the students that the results of the test are to be viewed as suggestions. Students are made aware that just because the aptitude test does not suggest a certain career does not mean that the student would not do well in it, or should not consider it.

Canadian or American Social Studies? (-)

A board of education made the decision to test the basic knowledge of middle school students in the area of social studies. A number of standardized tests were reviewed for this purpose and the one chosen was American and used American norms. When the testing was announced to the public, as well as when the results were given, teachers stated that the test was intended to measure students' knowledge of social studies, and that the students were being compared to students in the same age bracket. There was no reference to the fact that the tests were American and that a few of the "most glaring" American questions had been changed. (For example, a question about George Washington was changed to a question about Laura Secord). The lack of information given would leave most parents with the impression that the test scores reflected their child's knowledge of Canadian social studies.

New Norm Group (-)

A Canadian test publisher decides to enlarge the norm group for one popular Canadian achievement test. These changes are carefully explained in the technical manual. As a result of the new norm group, students in many school divisions score considerably higher. Since the publisher does not include the technical manual with the package of materials sent to schools, teachers and counsellors are left with the impression that students are scoring higher.

COMMENTS AND QUESTIONS

This ethical article is similar to Article D9, "Integrity of Evaluation and Assessment Instruments and Procedures," in that counsellors must see to it that procedures for test-taking are similar for all people taking the standardized instrument. In addition, changes should not be made to any standardized test "without permission and adequate recognition of the original author, publisher, and copyright holder." Changing an instrument without permission is not only unethical, but also has the effect of changing the validity, reliability and normative data of the standardized test.

1. What can counsellors do to increase the likelihood of administering tests consistent with published procedures?

2. What are your ethical obligations when you notice that a colleague has copied an interest inventory for her or his class?

3. Are local norms necessary in order to provide test-takers with accurate information? Explain.

4. Should teachers and professors be allowed to duplicate standardized tests for instructional purposes only for the classroom?

5. Should students in school pay for the costs of standardized tests used in counselling?

❖ ❖ ❖ ❖ ❖ ❖ ❖ ❖ ❖ ❖ ❖ ❖ ❖ ❖

ESSAYS ON
EVALUATION
AND ASSESSMENT

Ethical Perspectives on the Use of Psychological Tests in Counselling

Beth E. Haverkamp and Jaye Wald

As the preamble to the CGCA *Guidelines for Ethical Behavior* (1989) states, "The specification of ethical standards enables a professional association to clarify for its present and future members and to those served by its members, the nature of their professional and ethical responsibilities." Viewed from the client's or society's perspective, these responsibilities become legitimate expectations that individuals have of the counselling profession. With respect to psychological testing, there are three groups that can be described as having expectations of how we practice. Our clients certainly have expectations of us, as does the society in which we work. Also, implicit in the development of an ethics code is the requirement that we have expectations of ourselves. This framework — what clients expect of us, what society expects of us, and what we must expect from ourselves — provides a way to examine the CCA *Code of Ethics* in the area of psychological testing.

What Clients Have a Right to Expect From You

While some counsellors have held the belief that testing automatically creates an impersonal, diagnosis-based approach to clients, we conceptualize it as an collaborative process embedded within the counselling relationship. As numerous authors (Duckworth, 1990; Hood & Johnson, 1997; Pope, 1992; Tinsley & Bradley, 1986) note, testing is best viewed as one component of the counselling process and not as a separate, disconnected activity. From this perspective, tests can be used to facilitate client self-awareness and knowledge, identify and clarify concerns, provide a vehicle for further exploration, guide decision making, and assist in treatment planning (Ben-Porath, 1997; Butcher, 1997; Campbell, 1990; Finn & Tonsager, 1997; Hood & Johnson, 1997). Furthermore, Duckworth (1990) has described what she views as a counselling approach to the use of tests, in which the goal of testing is empowerment of the individual. As Carl Rogers (1942) stated:

> "It is when tests are used to meet a felt need of the client, rather than merely as information for the counselor, that they function therapeutically....From the point of view of effective therapy, tests are of value when they can be used constructively by the client in making decisions or in taking positive actions." (p. 251).

A "how to" for embedding test use within a facilitative counselling relationship is presented within the CCA *Code of Ethics*, although it is not labelled as such. There are four general principles that underlie many of the specific articles describing legitimate client expectations and characteristics of an effective counselling relationship:

a) developing a collaborative therapeutic partnership;

b) viewing the client as a unique individual;

c) facilitating client awareness and integration of self-knowledge; and

d) having client welfare as one's first priority.

An understanding of how these principles are reflected within the individual articles can illuminate how ethical test use is also effective counselling.

Clients come into counselling expecting that their counsellor will be caring, knowledgeable, supportive, and honest. These same expectations extend to the counsellor's use of tests. As counsellors, we are responsible for establishing the therapeutic relationship and eliciting the client's active participation.

Article B1, which requires collaboration, implies that clients are not just passive "testees;" rather, they should participate and contribute to the entire testing process. Engaging their participation can facilitate clients' motivation and interest, thereby increasing the likelihood that they will respond non-defensively and ultimately find the testing experience personally meaningful.

The concept of informed consent, as highlighted in Article C5, is critical to using tests in a manner consistent with establishing a therapeutic partnership and, more broadly, the principle of respect for the dignity of persons. A common misperception relative to test use, views informed consent as simply gaining client permission for testing and disregards the possibility of active collaboration. Collaboration is a necessary aspect of informed consent because both elements, giving consent and receiving information, are necessary to be an informed participant. Informed consent implies that the client is a knowledgeable participant in counselling decisions that affect him or her. It is a process that should reflect the ongoing reciprocal nature and interaction between testing and counselling (Spengler, Strohmer, Dixon, & Shivy, 1995).

Article D2 states that counsellors inform clients about the purposes and results of tests. Specifically, clients should expect an explanation of the purposes and procedures of testing as part of the informed consent process. Informed consent requires that clients be involved in the decision to use tests, identify areas where testing may be helpful and, where possible, participate in test selection (Campbell, 1990; Duckworth, 1990; Hood & Johnson, 1997). The choice of tests should always consider clients' specific needs and wishes by asking, "What does the client hope to obtain from testing?" This decision-making process can be facilitated by providing clients adequate information about specific tests (e.g. test purposes) and giving clients ample opportunities to ask questions and raise concerns. As part of informed consent, clients have a right to be informed of the potential risks of testing, such as the possibility of experiencing conflict-arousing information. Counsellors can also promote client welfare, as mandated in Article B1, by providing adequate information, conveying that client input is valued, and facilitating their full participation in decision making.

With regards to using tests with children and adolescents, written consent of parents or legal guardian is required. However, counsellors should also try to obtain consent from clients under 18-years to the extent of their abilities. Children and adolescents are commonly referred for testing because of a "problem" identified by parents or teachers. As a result, testing situations can elicit a range of reactions in children, including fear or anger. As counsellors, it is important to help these clients explore and discuss their feelings. Establishing rapport and safety will greatly ameliorate their fears or concerns. Similar to adults, counsellors need to answer children's questions honestly and directly. This becomes critical when working with older children or adolescents.

Similar to Article D2, Article D7 also addresses the client's right to receiving an accurate interpretation of his or her test results. Test interpretation is the most important, and one of the most difficult aspects, of psychological testing. As with other phases of testing, sharing the results with a client should be an interactive and collaborative process (Pope, 1992). Test feedback should be seen as an opportunity to facilitate client awareness and integration of self-knowledge.

In the interpretation phase of testing, the counsellor must integrate test data with the client's presenting concern and relevant biographical information. This information is synthesized into meaningful patterns, which then is clearly communicated to the client, using understandable language (Campbell,

1990; Duckworth, 1990; Hood & Johnson, 1997; Sattler, 1992). In order to fully benefit from the information, clients must first understand it. When communicating the results, counsellors should focus on the main points and avoid overloading the client with too much information. Inconsistencies across test scores, or between test scores and biographical information, should be explored with the client.

This approach to test interpretation applies equally to children and adolescents. Children as young as 10-years can benefit from basic test interpretation. To facilitate their understanding, counsellors should provide simple and concrete information. In communicating test results to younger people, highlight main findings, use examples, or relate results to the child's real life experiences. Ideally, all adults significantly involved with the child (e.g. parents, teachers) should also receive an accurate interpretation of the test results, as well as practical and attainable recommendations to address the presenting concern.

Research has demonstrated that, "Assessment feedback is itself therapeutic for clients." (Finn & Tonsager, 1992, p. 278). Goodyear (1990), in a review of research on the effects of test interpretation, found that, "Clients who receive test interpretation—regardless of format or of the particular outcome criteria employed—do experience greater gains than do those in control conditions" (p. 243). In another study, Finn and Tonsager (1992), observed that, after receiving test feedback, college students reported decreased distress as well as increased self-esteem and hope about the future.

Some counsellors succumb to the temptation to "soft pedal" test results when they believe the information will be unwelcome or unpleasant. The risk is that this decision serves the counsellor's interests more than the clients; the client receives potentially inaccurate or incomplete information about himself or herself. If the test's reliability or validity is questionable, it should not be used at all. Just as counsellors must make decisions about whether to confront a client on behavior observed in a counselling session, they must decide whether negative test interpretation is relevant to the client's concern.

A final issue that impacts how counsellors and clients use tests is that tests do carry a certain mystique. Research on "bogus" personality inventories suggests that test-takers may attribute credibility to results that contradict their self-perceptions (Dickson & Kelly, 1985). The perceived mystique of tests can enhance their effectiveness as interventions (Duckworth, 1990), but also heightens the responsibility to use them ethically. As Pipes and Davenport (1990) note, "To many clients there is a certain amount of magic in tests; however, your specialty is psychology, not magic. Therefore, avoid describing tests in mysterious terms" (p. 122).

Another valid client expectation relates to Article D10, which requires counsellors to be sensitive to client diversity. This article requires us to examine a test's appropriateness, particularly in working with special groups or culturally diverse clients. In using tests with clients from distinct cultures or minority groups, we must exercise great caution in test selection and interpretation (Betz, 1990; Hood & Johnson, 1997; Merrell, 1999). It would be unfair to use a test for members of groups who may not be well-represented in the tests' norm groups. Counsellors also need to be aware of culturally specific test content, in that individuals from other cultures may lack familiarity with certain items or questions. It is also important to consider whether a test is gender-biased, either by unequal representation in the norm groups or in the test items themselves.

The most carefully developed test will not apply equally to all clients. Treating clients as unique individuals means we must ask the guiding question, "What is the appropriateness of this test for this client?" To be sensitive to client diversity relative to test use, we should always obtain appropriate background and cultural information. Furthermore, awareness and knowledge of cultural differences and test biases is essential in using tests ethically and fairly.

The obligation to be sensitive to diversity is also reflected in Article D1, which reminds us that test data is only one of many pieces of information that should be considered in decision making. Clients have a right to expect that we will help them place test information in perspective, relative to other aspects of their lives and experience. The requirement that psychological testing involve multiple measures and sources of information (Hood & Johnson, 1997; Sattler, 1992; Subich & Billingsley, 1995) is based on the fact that tests provide current samples of behavior within a given context; such samples cannot reflect the entire picture (Sattler, 1992). A multiple assessment approach allows for the synthesis of several sources of quantitative and qualitative information and can help create an overall and unique portrait of the client.

Test interpretation requires the counsellor to integrate all sources of information based on the entire assessment. Test scores should never be interpreted in isolation, nor should they be used to make decisions. As Hood and Johnson (1997) state, "Tests do not provide a magic answer, instead they should be looked at as one additional source of information that may be helpful in problem solving" (p. 10). For example, a college student who requests vocational testing should not make major career decisions based on test results alone. In this situation, the counsellor should help this client integrate test results with other aspects of his or her life in order to make vocational choices.

Consider the example presented in this case-studies chapter where a counsellor uses the Strong Interest Inventory to help clients make career decisions. This counsellor simply uses the computer printout of results to suggest what occupations the client should consider. A multiple assessment approach would consider other sources of information to aid in career decision making, such as aptitude, ability, and personality, as well as considering contextual factors such as background information, training requirements, job outlook, or geographic mobility.

In some circumstances, modification or adaptation of a test may be necessary (Geisenger, 1994). Consider the example of test adaptation as illustrated in the case of Mr. Richard D. in this case-studies chapter. In this case, the counsellor recognized that, because of Richard's limited ability in interpreting written English, a written form of a job evaluation test would not fairly represent his abilities. Hence, the counsellor made an appropriate decision to administer an oral version of the test.

Another fundamental client expectation is that we protect our client's welfare through maximizing benefits and minimizing harm in using tests. This guideline is embedded within the larger domain of general client rights of Article B4, subsumed under the principles of respect for client dignity. Psychological testing does have an impact on the lives of others and has the potential to cause harm if misused. The right to confidentiality and privacy, highlighted in Articles D5 and D8, is fundamental in both counselling and testing. Clients expect that test results will be confidential and will not be misused. As a result, it is our responsibility to inform clients about who will receive results and psychological reports and how they will be used. For example, the written psychological report should not include information that might compromise the individual's self-respect or integrity. As indicated by Article C6, ethical practice also directs counsellors to avoid undue invasion of the client's privacy. The choices of what information to obtain

from testing must be relevant to the purposes of counselling. Finally, as required by Article D11, we are obligated to properly safeguard and store tests and results.

There are several ways counsellors can uphold the principles of general caring and respect, as well as minimizing harm to our clients. Counsellors should avoid using psychological or statistical jargon in communicating test results. When relevant, care should be taken to explain diagnostic labels (e.g. learning disability) or test terminology that may cause negative reactions for the client. A potential misuse of results includes focussing on the client's weaknesses or negative findings rather than realizing that he or she has a range of competencies and strengths. Consistent with Article C5, additional counselling may be required when communicating test results to parents or otherwise appropriate persons. After testing, it is important to provide clients with an opportunity to discuss the testing experience and raise concerns.

For example, it would be potentially harmful to tell a client, "You scored very high on the impulsivity scale of the 16PF test." In addition to the results not being explained in understandable and meaningful terms, this statement could possibly be distressing for the client. A more ethical approach would be to use tentative language to explore whether the result is consistent with the client's experience as in stating, "The results suggest that you may act or decide before you've thought things through...Does that fit your experience?" If the client concurs the counsellor can pursue further, by asking, "Does it occur so often that you would describe yourself as impulsive?" If so, that would be consistent with the test scores. Describing the 16PF scales in everyday language rather than with their scale names, and eliciting client reactions, can minimize any distress or confusion for the client.

Another way to minimize harm to clients is to ensure that we, as counsellors, are competent and trained to administer psychological tests. As counsellors, we may be responsible for the entire testing process, which includes pre-testing session(s), administering the test, scoring, interpreting, writing the report, and post-assessment or debriefing session(s), all of which require a high degree of competency. Psychological testing, similar to other aspects of counselling, requires a blend of technical skill, knowledge and clinical judgment that can only develop through supervision and practical experience. Another important aspect of ethical test use is self-knowledge, specifically of our own errors of judgment, biases, and limitations of competence (Hood & Johnson, 1997; Spengler, et al., 1995).

What Society Expects From Testing Professionals

Counsellors have approached psychological testing with attitudes ranging from enthusiasm to skepticism to distrust. As such, they reflect attitudes of the larger society where, as Keith-Spiegel and Koocher (1985) note, "Tests have seemed to be powerful tools for advancing human welfare, but occasionally great concern about the real, imagined or potential abuses of tests has become a public policy issue" (p. 87). Ethical articles and guidelines outline counsellors' responsibilities to act as informed "gatekeepers" and "caretakers" of tests. The debate cited above revolves around the issue of whether or not tests are "trustworthy." The label "trustworthy" overlaps the notion of test validity, but better reflects the inescapable fact that most of the public must rely on professionals to provide the information needed to decide if a test is trustworthy. Given that most clients, parents, or newspaper reporters do not understand technical aspects of tests, it falls to the test user to make informed decisions

about appropriate test selection, use, and interpretation.

There are four articles that address the issue of the test user's responsibilities to the larger society; these standards address the ways in which counsellors are expected to use their specialized knowledge of tests to protect the public from inaccurate information and protect the integrity of the tests themselves.

Articles D8 and D7 are concerned with issues of accuracy. The first article, states that test scores are to be, "released only to persons qualified to interpret and use them properly" (p. 12). Inherent in this article is the recognition that counsellor's responsibilities extend beyond the client-counsellor relationship where the results may have been generated. This article also relates to the issue of access to client records in Article B6, which requires that any information identifying a client be released only with the client's expressed consent. (See Tranel, 1994, for a thorough discussion of the release of test data).

Article D7, which addresses how test results need to be reported, also recognizes that counsellors are sometimes called upon to comment on the use of tests. It requires that any statements made will give accurate information and avoid any exaggerated claims of benefits or unsubstantiated criticisms. As noted above, members of the public rely on testing professionals to help them make informed decisions about whether testing is in their best interests. Irresponsible, unsubstantiated statements effectively erode the public's ability to make thoughtful decisions about testing.

Articles D9 and D11 address the counsellor's relationship to the test-development industry in addition to the general public. Article D9, which requires that counsellors maintain the integrity of test instruments, highlights that the validity of many tests becomes seriously compromised if their items or format are revealed to test takers. It directs counsellors to avoid providing advance information, modifying the test, or coaching test takers.

While not stated explicitly, this article also protects clients; any time the validity of a test has been compromised, the test taker is in danger of receiving false or misleading information about himself or herself. While a student who has been coached may feel momentary pleasure at receiving a higher ability test score, the ultimate outcome may be potentially harmful if decisions are made based on a distorted sense of one's abilities. Disclosure of protected test information, which invalidates test results, is ultimately disrespectful of clients; it contradicts the norms of honesty and respect, which are meant to characterize the counselling relationship.

A similar Article, D11, requires "Counsellors ensure the integrity and security of evaluation and assessment instruments..." (p. 12). This article mandates counsellors to observe copyrights by not appropriating, reproducing, or modifying tests without permission. This protects the test author's or developer's interests but also serves clients and counsellors as well. In addition to conforming to public copyright laws, it helps ensure that available versions of the test will represent the levels of reliability and validity that were achieved in the original test development. A portion of a test, or another modification, does not have the same reliability and validity characteristics as the original. Without additional research on the modified version, you cannot be confident that the new version will produce useful, accurate information (Geisinger, 1994).

A second benefit of observing copyrights through the purchase of test materials is that the test developer is supported in conducting continued research and revision for the measure. The task of developing a sophisticated, well-validated test is expensive and time consuming, as are revisions that ultimately result in improvements. Respect for copyrighted material helps preserve the unspoken contract between test developer and test user, in which the test developer agrees to continue research that will make the test the best measure possible.

What You Should Expect From Yourself

As the preamble to the *CGCA Guidelines for Ethical Behavior* (1989) notes, these guidelines are "intended to inspire each member to engage in professional behavior of the highest order." Like other aspects of counselling, test use requires a specialized knowledge base; and ultimately, each counsellor must evaluate whether his or her breadth of knowledge constitutes competence in a given area. The willingness to monitor one's own competence, and to make responsible decisions based on that self-knowledge, is one of the hallmarks of professional conduct. In defining one's boundaries of competence, ethical practice also involves knowing when to refer a client to another mental health specialist. Consider the example in the case-studies chapter of a beginning counsellor who sees the art work of one student consistently depicting scenes of violence. Acknowledging the limits of his experience, he refers the student to the guidance department head. This demonstrates ethical practice in evaluating one's competency.

Article D3 mandates that counsellors not exceed the limits of their competence in using tests. Ultimately, this article is linked to promoting the client's welfare, as counsellors who administer or interpret tests for which they have not been trained are placing their clients at risk. Similarly, selecting tests without consideration of their established reliability and validity places clients in the position of making decisions based on faulty information.

For some counsellors, competence in test evaluation and use presents a challenge that differs from their sense of competence in evaluating other counselling interventions. Test evaluation requires a knowledge of psychometrics, which for some, may seem to have only a limited relationship to "the business of counselling." Many counsellors know that validity is a desirable quality for tests to have, but may not be aware that validity does not exist "in general." The counsellor must know how to evaluate this for himself or herself, for a given situation.

As Article D6 indicates, counsellors are directed to consider the validity, reliability and appropriateness (e.g. norms or standardization samples) of tests before using them with clients. While most counsellors are aware that these are important aspects of test quality, it is also important to understand how to assess reliability and validity for specific testing situations. Even a test as well-respected and carefully researched as the Strong Interest Inventory (Harmon, Hansen, Borgen, & Hammer, 1994) is not valid or appropriate in all testing situations.

Another factor that is essential to deriving valid and useful test information is the administration of the test. Article D4 also requires that standardized administration procedures be observed. Scores derived from non-standard testing conditions are not trustworthy reflections of the client's abilities or characteristics and, again, puts the client at risk for receiving false feedback. When a counsellor is evaluating a traditional standardized test, the task of evaluating the test's characteristics is relatively straightforward. The test manual and test reviews by experts in the field can provide information on reliability, validity, and norms. However, there are two situations where evaluation may be more difficult. The first of these is the expanding use of computerized testing; the second concerns newly developed measures for which little information exists.

Professional newsletters are filled with advertisements for computerized career-choice programs and computer versions of well-known inventories. Ease of scoring and potential savings in time, make these attractive options for many agencies and schools. What is sometimes overlooked, however, is that the computerized version of an established test must meet the same criteria of reliability and validity as its paper and pencil counterpart. This is most easily seen if we consider the above discussion of standardized administration procedures that relates to Article D5. This article reminds counsellors of their responsibility for the use of technology in testing. Changing from a paper and pencil to computer administration of a test has altered the standardized administration format, and psychometric properties of a new computerized version must be independently assessed. Publishers of computerized versions should provide evidence of their measure's reliability and validity.

Another area for caution is the selection or use of newly developed measures. Every year, dozens of new instruments are introduced and our mailboxes are filled with advertisements that claim to offer the very best way to identify depression, sales ability, reading problems, or eating disorders. The advertisement often shows how your clients or students will be classified on a multicolored chart or will be given a personal profile analysis. Such promotional materials often look professional and convincing, and produce what can be called the "Glossy Brochure Syndrome." It is possible to read through 10 slick pages of glowing praise for a new measure without once coming across a description of research underlying the claims being made such as, "Used by hundred of schools!" and "Praised by experienced practitioners!" The ethical counsellor's response to this should only be "So what?" Responsible test developers conduct research as part of their test development and know that reporting on validity and reliability enhances the credibility of their tests. Responsible test publishers may use glossy brochures, too, but will include information that supports the claims being made.

What resources exist for the counsellor who wants to make informed, ethical decisions about test selection, but lacks confidence interpreting validity coefficients and factor-derived scores? In addition to test manuals, two excellent sources which contain reviews of specific tests are the *Mental Measurements Yearbook* series and *Test Critiques*. The *Mental Measurements Yearbook* series, published by the Buros Institute of Mental Measurements, contains descriptive information about tests as well as critical reviews by experts in that field. *Test Critiques*, published by the Test Corporation of America, is a multi-volume series of reviews, which discuss both technical and practical aspects of many tests.

The American Counseling Association (ACA), CCA's counterpart in the United States, has published two resource books, which are designed for the practicing counsellor. An overview of testing practices and measures typically used in cognitive, career and personality assessment is found in Hood and Johnson's (1997) *Assessment in Counseling: A Guide to the Use of Psychological Assessment Procedures (2nd Edition)*. Cichetti (1994) also provides guidelines for evaluating tests and Lyon's (1998) *Test Scores and What They Mean (6th edition)* offers non-technical information and descriptions of test "terminology" and statistics.

If asked what activities characterize their work with clients, few counsellors would include testing at the top of their list. However, surveys indicate that tests are widely used (Watkins, Campbell, & McGregor, 1988), and the extensive use of tests can be attributed to the role they play in providing clients with information that is useful in making important life decisions. As Duckworth

(1990) states, "People are likely to change in ways therapeutic to themselves and others if they have accurate information about themselves, their strengths and weaknesses, and ways they are currently dealing with life. Testing is one method of getting that information and conveying it, through test interpretation, to the client" (p. 199). Our adherence to the CCA *Code of Ethics* will help insure that the information we communicate is accurate and useful, minimizes negative consequences, and serves the best interest of our clients, our profession, and the society in which we live.

The following provides a summary of general guidelines for using tests with adults, as well as adolescents and children within counselling psychology practice. The case-studies chapter also provides more concrete examples of how to implement ethical practice into test use.

General Testing Guidelines.

1. Approach testing as a collaborative process embedded within the counselling relationship. Elicit the client's active participation and feedback to make it a personally meaningful and positive experience.

2. Informed consent is a process that should reflect the ongoing reciprocal nature and interaction between testing and counselling. An informed decision requires that the client understand the potential risks/benefits of testing, testing options, limitations of tests, and test descriptions. In deciding to use tests, ask the client, "What do you hope to obtain from testing?"

3. Use multiple measures and sources of information when using tests.

4. Consider cultural and contextual factors (e.g. gender, socio-economic status, age, ethnicity) that are relevant in test selection and interpretation.

5. Test results and interpretation must be communicated in a meaningful, under-

standable, and collaborative manner. Involve the client in interpreting the test results.

6. Exercise caution when releasing test results. Results should only be released with the client's expressed consent and only to qualified persons who can properly use and interpret the results.

7. If requested to comment on the use of tests, present accurate information and avoid any exaggerated claims of benefits or unsubstantiated criticisms.

8. Maintain the integrity of test instruments by not revealing test items or format to test takers. Avoid providing advance information, modifying the test, or engaging in coaching.

9. Observe copyrights by not appropriating, reproducing, or modifying tests without permission.

10. Do not exceed the limits of one's competence and qualifications in using tests.

11. It is important to be able to evaluate a test for a given client. Always consider the validity, reliability and appropriateness (e.g. norms or standardization samples) of a test before administering it.

12. Always observe standardized administration procedures. If there are deviations from the standardized conditions, it is essential those changes are reflected in the test interpretation and final written report.

Guidelines for Testing Children and Adolescents

1. Children, as young as 10-years, can benefit from basic test interpretation. To facilitate their understanding, provide simple and concrete information. Highlight main findings, use examples, or relate results to the child's real life experiences.

2. Testing situations can elicit a range of reactions in children from curiosity to fear. It is important to be aware of potential feelings that may arise. Establishing rapport and safety will greatly ameliorate their fears or concerns.

3. Answer children's questions honestly and directly. This is even more critical when working with older children or adolescents.

4. Children and adolescents are commonly referred for testing because of a "problem" identified by parents or teachers (e.g. "Billy is immature for his age.") In this example, the problem "immaturity" must be defined in behavioral terms. It is the counsellor's responsibility to ask the referral source specific questions (e.g. "What is Billy doing when he is acting immature? What is he specifically doing? When does the behavior occur and doesn't occur?).

5. Ideally, all adults significantly involved with the child (e.g. parents, teachers) should be actively involved in the testing process. This includes their participation in interviews, completing self-report measures, and receiving test results within the parameters of parental permission.

6. For younger or less-verbal children, drawing tests may be more appropriate.

7. Watch for signs of fatigue or boredom and incorporate breaks as necessary.

8. If the test is performance-based (e.g. intelligence testing), encourage children to put forward their best effort, rather than commenting on specific test items, or comparing them to other children's performance.

9. Structure the physical environment so that it is conducive to obtaining the child's best performance (e.g. minimize distractions, ensure the child is sitting comfortably).

10. One important aspect of your self-knowledge is to be aware of potential biases or expectancy effects you may have when working with children, such as the well-known halo-effect.

11. Always obtain informed consent by parents or legal guardians. However, involve the child or teen in the informed consent process to the extent of their abilities.

References

Ben-Porath, Y. S. (1997). Use of personality assessment instruments in empirically guided treatment planning. *Psychological Assessment, 9,* 361-367.

Butcher, J. N. (1997). Introduction to the special section on assessment in psychological treatment: A necessary step for effective intervention. *Psychological Assessment, 9,* 331-333.

Butcher, J. N., Dahlstrom, W. G., Graham, J. R., Tellegen, A., & Krammer, B. (1989). *Minnesota multiphasic personality inventory-2 (MMPI-2): Manual for administration and scoring.* Minneapolis: University of Minnesota Press.

Canadian Guidance and Counselling Association (1981, 1989). *Guidelines for ethical behavior.* Ottawa: Author.

Cicchetti, D. V. (1994). Guidelines, criteria, and rules of thumb for evaluating normed and standardized assessment instruments in psychology. *Psychological Assessment, 6* (4), 287-290.

Dahlstrom, W. G. (1993). Tests. Small samples, large consequences. *American Psychologist, 48* (4), 393-399.

Dickson, D. H. & Kelly, I W. (1985). The "Barnum Effect" in personality assessment: A review of the literature. *Psychological Reports, 57,* 367-382.

Duckworth, J. (1990). The counseling approach to the use of testing. *The Counseling Psychologist, 18,* 198-204.

Finn, S. E., & Tonsager, M. E. (1992). Therapeutic effects of providing MMPI-2 feedback to college students awaiting therapy. *Psychological Assessment, 4* (2), 278-287.

Finn, S. E., & Tonsager, M. E. (1997). Information-gathering and therapeutic models of assessment: Complementary paradigms. *Psychological Assessment, 9,* 374-385.

Geisinger, K. F. (1994). Cross-cultural normative assessment: Translation and Adaptation issues influencing the normative interpretation of assessment instruments. *Psychological Assessment, 6* (4), 304-312.

Goodyear, R. K. (1990). Research on the effects of test interpretation. *The Counseling Psychologist,* 18, 240-257.

Handler, L. (1996). The clinical use of drawings. In C. S. Newmark (Ed.) *Major psychological assessment instruments (2nd ed.),* pp. 206-293. Boston: Allyn & Bacon.

Harmon, L. W., Hansen, J. C., Borgen, F. H., & Hammer, A. L. (1994*). Strong Interest Inventory application and technical guide.* Palo Alto, CA: Consulting Psychologists Press.

Hood, A. B., & Johnson, R. W. (1997). *Assessment in counseling. A guide to the use of psychological assessment procedures (2nd ed.).* Alexandria, VA: American Counseling Association.

Kapes, J. T., & Mastie, M. M. (1988). *A counselor's guide to career assessment instruments (2nd ed.).* Alexandria, VA: National Career Development Association, a division of the American Association of Counseling and Development.

Keith-Spiegel, P., & Koocher, G. P. (1985). *Ethics in psychology: Professional standards and cases.* Hillsdale, NJ: Lawrence Erlbaum.

Keyser, D. J., & Sweetland, R. C. (Eds.). (1984-1990). *Test critiques: Volumes I - VIII.* Kansas City, MO: Test Corporation of America.

Lyon, H. B. (1998). *Test scores and what they mean (6th ed.).* Boston: Allyn & Bacon.

Meirer, S. T. (1999). Training the practitioner-scientist: Bridging case conceptualization, assessment, and intervention. *The Counseling Psychologist, 27* (6), 846-869.

Merrell, K. W. (1999). *Behavioral, social, and emotional assessment of children and adolescents.* Mahwah, NJ: Lawrence Erlbaum.

Mitchell, J. V., Jr. (Ed.). (1985). *The ninth mental measurements yearbook.* Lincoln, NE: Buros Institute of Mental Measurements.

Moreland, K. L., Eyde, L. D., Robertson, G. J., Primoff, E. S., & Most, R. B. (1995). Assessment of test user qualifications: A research-based measurement procedure. *American Psychologist, 50,* 14-23.

Nevo, B., & Jager, R. S. (Eds.). (1993). *Educational and psychological testing: The test taker's outlook.* Toronto: Hogrefe & Huber.

Pipes, R. B., & Davenport, D. S. (1990). *Introduction to psycho-therapy: Common clinical wisdom.* Englewood Cliffs, NJ: Prentice-Hall.

Pope, K. S. (1992). Responsibilities in providing test feedback to clients. *Psychological Assessment, 4,* 268-271.

Prediger, D. J., & Garfield, N. (1988). Testing competencies and responsibilities: A checklist for counselors. In J. T. Kapes and M. M. Mastie (Eds.), *A counselor's guide to career assessment instruments (2nd ed.).* Alexandria, VA: National Career Development Association, a division of the American Association of Counseling and Development.

Rogers, C. R. (1942). Counseling and Psychotherapy. Boston: Houghton-Mifflin.

Sattler, J. M. (1992). *Assessment of children (3rd ed.).* San Diego: Jerome M. Sattler, Publisher, Inc.

Spengler, P. M., Strohmer, D. C., Dixon, D. N., & Shivy, V. A. (1995). A scientist-practitioner model of psychological assessment: Implications for training, practice, and research. *The Counseling Psychologist, 23,* 506-534.

Tranel, D. (1994). The release of psychological data to nonexperts: Ethical and legal considerations. *Professional Psychology: Research and Practice, 25,* 33-38.

Tinsley, H. E. A., & Bradley, R. W. (1986). Test interpretation. *Journal of Counseling and Development, 64,* 462-466.

Watkins, C. E. Jr., Campbell, V. L., & McGregor, P. (1988). Counseling psychologists' uses of and opinions about psychological tests. A contemporary perspective. *The Counseling Psychologist, 16,* 476-486.

Wodrich, D. L. (1997). *Children's psychological testing. A guide for nonpsychologists (3rd ed.).* Baltimore: Paul H. Brookes Publishing.

Womer, F. B. (1988). Selecting an instrument: Chore or challenge? In J. T. Kapes and M. M. Mastie (Eds.), *A counselor's guide to career assessment instruments (2nd ed.).* Alexandria, VA: National Career Development Association, a division of the American Association of Counseling and Development.

Ethical Principles and the Use of Standardized Tests in Counselling

John Stewart

Despite the criticisms levelled against the use of standardized tests (Goldman, 1994a, 1994b; Zytowski, 1994), Gregory (1996) maintains that, "When used ethically and professionally, tests help users make fair and sound decisions about individuals and groups" (p. 592). This essay is based on this assumption. When test users respect ethical guidelines and competencies learned in professional education, standardized test instruments can be used effectively to provide information that may not easily be obtained using other methods. Indeed, as Anastasi (1992) indicated, test users should be criticized more than the tests.

The purpose of this essay is to draw test users attention to ethical principles (Canadian Counselling Association, 1999) as they relate to the use of standardized test instruments. Recognizing that standardized tests can be used in program evaluation as well as for group assessment, the content of this article will focus on formal assessment techniques as they might be used within the counselling process. Assessment is defined as a process used to collect information (Hohenshil, 1996; Hood & Johnson, 1991). The assessment process consists of a number of components including: deciding if standardized instruments will yield the desired information, the qualifications of the test user, instrument(s) selection, administration procedures, scoring and interpretation, and communicating the results (American Counseling Association, 1989).

The Decision to Test

The main purpose of testing should be to efficiently obtain information about a client,

which cannot be easily obtained via other means (Hohenshil, 1996). The decision to use standardized instruments should be directly related to the reason(s) why the client requested the services of a professional counsellor (Corey, 1996). Counsellors should look for any unreasonable expectation such as the wish for magical answers or misunderstanding of testing, and clarify such information. Another issue concerns the invasion of a client's privacy (Cohen, Swerdlik & Phillips, 1996). Counsellors ought to consider the kinds of information clients need to give about themselves and under what conditions. The information collected should relate directly to the client's reason for seeking counselling. Collecting more information than necessary might be deemed an invasion of client privacy.

The principles "general orientation" and "purposes and results" of evaluation and assessment suggest that counsellors provide the client with an orientation in plain language to the purposes of assessment, the types of instruments to be considered, the procedures to be followed, and how the results will be used within, and possibly outside, the counselling relationship. This orientation enables the client to give informed consent (Cohen et al., 1996). The client should be an active participant in the selection of the instrument(s) to be used. This participation should be restricted to the type of instruments used, not the specific instruments. The decision of what instruments to use should be left to the counsellor's expertise. Further, in some instances, if a client is prone to excessive anxiety and self-doubt, counsellors may choose not to use an appropriate test due to the possibility of the client misunderstanding the results.

The principle, "respect for rights," obligates counsellors to respect the civil, legal and moral rights of all clients, especially in deciding and selecting which instrument(s) to use. For example, counsellors need to obtain informed consent from their clients prior to using any assessment instrument. Counsellors should ensure that clients understand the implications of testing, and of their right to decline participation at any point in the process. Additionally, test users should inform their clients about the legal limits of confidentiality regarding test results. If in the course of testing, a counsellor learns of abuse or possible injury to others, the counsellor is obligated to break confidentiality. Another principle involves "computer use." If the assessment involves the use of computers, clients need to be capable of using the computer application and understanding its purpose. Furthermore, the computer application should be appropriate to the clients' needs. Counsellors need to be aware that while computerized testing is cost-efficient, free from scoring errors and presentation bias, computerized interpretations are a poor substitute for a psychological assessment, typically lack validity and are unsigned. These characteristics raise ethical questions about interpretation competence and responsibility (Gregory, 1996).

Qualifications of the Test User

This component focusses on test users and implies that they self-assess to determine their psychometric competence to use the particular instrument(s) under consideration (Garfield & Prediger, 1994). Test users should consider the purpose of testing, characteristics of the instrument(s), the context within which the testing will take place, and their role in the selection, administration, scoring and interpretation of the instrument.

The ethical principles, "general responsibility," "boundaries of competence," and "evaluation and assessment competence" address the issues of high standards of professional competence, competence to administer, score and interpret instruments, and the need for continuing education. Counsellors should be aware that competence is not necessarily indicated by academic degrees and/

or diplomas. Counsellors ought always to keep abreast of research on the psychometric properties of assessment instruments (Anastasi, 1992) and use those that represent best practice (Gregory, 1996). Additionally, they need to pursue further educational experiences periodically to guard against skill deterioration. By following these guidelines counsellors respect the integrity and promote the welfare of their clients. They ought to work collaboratively with clients concerning the type of instrument(s) to use, and choose ones that are consistent with the abilities and circumstances of clients. The principle, "integrity of instruments and procedures," indicates that counsellors ought to respect the novelty of assessment instruments. This means that counsellors do not allow clients or individuals in relation to the client, such as teachers or parents, to become familiar with assessment instruments. Such familiarity enhances the possibility of test pollution (Haladyna, Nolen & Haas, 1991).

Selecting the Instrument(s)

The decision to use an instrument should be based on a careful analysis, including the characteristics of the client, the construct(s) to be assessed, the purpose of testing, and the interpretation and use of the assessment results (Mehrens, 1994). This analysis involves the validity and reliability of the instrument(s), the purposes for which they were developed, their technical characteristics, and the appropriate involvement of the client in the selection process.

The ethical principle, "appropriateness of evaluation and assessment," indicates that counsellors ought only to use instruments that are valid, reliable, and appropriate to the client and the intended purpose of testing. Additionally, the principle, "security maintenance," indicates that counsellors ought not to modify or copy instruments in any way without the expressed permission of the author, publisher and copyright holder.

Administration Procedures

This component deals with the standardized procedures developed by the instrument author(s). By following these procedures, counsellors help to promote their clients' optimal performances. Clients must have a proper orientation, including an explanation of what the instrument is designed to measure, the tasks involved in completing the instrument, how the instrument is to be administered, and how the scores will be reported and used. Clients should be provided with practice items, and an illustration of how to mark the answers, particularly if a separate answer sheet is being used. Counsellors ought to give verbatim directions, provide for appropriate timing, and follow the exact sequence of tasks as prescribed in the administration manual. They should strive for good rapport with their clients and demonstrate calmness and empathy, but act impartially during the testing. Such counsellor behaviour enhances motivation and promotes a positive attitude as clients attempt each item on the instrument.

The ethical principle, "administration and supervisory conditions," directs counsellors to ensure that the testing context is consistent with the context as set out in the administration manual of the instrument. However, counsellors ought to note any deviation from the prescribed administration procedures and consider this deviation in their scoring and interpretation of the test results.

Scoring and Interpretation

Scoring and interpretation requires the counsellor to follow the procedures as outlined in the administration manual to ensure consistency and accuracy of the scores. Counsellors ought to recheck the scoring by selecting random items for their scored accuracy. They need to verify the accuracy of the raw scores and their conversion to norm scores. As well, counsellors ought to check the date of testing and label the scoring results appropriately.

Indirectly the ethical principle, "administrative and supervisory conditions," speaks to the proper administration and scoring of instruments.

Interpretation involves giving meaning to the raw scores. Counsellors must understand the procedures used to translate scores into verbal descriptions (eg. pass/fail) or into derived scores (eg. standard score). Any departures from these procedures will result in error. To interpret the results of an instrument correctly, the counsellor must understand the instrument(s) validity and reliability, as well as the current research on the instrument. The counsellor must consider issues like reliability to assess test stability, the standard error of measurement to assess random error in individual scores, the variance components attributed to error in the reliability scores, and what factors may have artificially raised or lowered the scores such as "test speededness" (Anastasi, 1992).

Additionally, counsellors must consider the intended use of the results of standardized tests when interpreting them. Counsellors must consider the instrument's validity since tests should never be used for purposes for which they were never intended. For example, if the instrument(s) is used for placement, then predictive validity is important to consider. Counsellors must consider the relationship between the test scores and an independent criterion measure as the basis of predictive validity. Further, if description is the purpose, then the comprehensiveness of information is important, since no set of scores can adequately describe an individual. In addition to instrument properties, counsellors need to explore clients' biographies within which to interpret the assessment results (Anastasi, 1992). Further, they should be cognisant of the most recent research results regarding the construct(s) being assessed (Anastasi, 1992). When counsellors combine instrument characteristics, the past and current background information from the client, and recent research on the construct being assessed, they enhance the rigor of their interpretation of test results.

An issue surrounding the interpretation of standardized instruments is the role of ethnic and cultural factors in behaviour (Corey, 1996). Counsellors ought always to recognize the limitations of standardized instruments and be aware of social and cultural factors that influence behaviour. In addition to instrument limitations, counsellors need to be sensitive to the possibility of examiner bias (Taylor, 2000), which may not be conscious and could include the influence of the test-user's ethnicity, culture and language. If such a bias exists, counsellors need to refer their clients to another professional. The ethical principle, "sensitivity to diversity," indicates that counsellors must consider the diversity of the individuals they work with (Pedersen, 1997). Counsellors must recognize and consider the potential effects of age, ethnicity, disability, culture, gender, religion, sexual orientation, and socio-economic status on both the administration and interpretation of the test results. These factors, if not considered, can increase the possibility of test-score pollution (Haladyna et al., 1991).

Communicating Test Results

Counsellors must report the results to clients in a manner that enables them to understand (Hood & Johnson, 1991), such as the use of graphics (Strahan & Kelly, 1994). Counsellors should encourage clients to discuss their impressions and feelings about the assessment process. Further, they need to indicate to clients how the test results will be used, and how they will respect the confidentiality of the results and who will have access to them. Counsellors must obtain permission from their clients prior to releasing any information to a third party. Counsellors must indicate to their clients the limitations of the test scores including the limits of interpretation, any abnormalities in the testing procedure,

and that the test data represents one source of information and should rarely be used alone to make decisions. Counsellors ought to inform their clients about the length of time the results will be retained and how they may be released.

The ethical principle, "maintenance to records," indicates that counsellors will maintain records consistent with any legal, regulatory, agency or institutional requirements. Also, this principle indicates that counsellors will maintain the safety of such records in compliance with the requirements of confidentiality and other articles of the CCA *Code of Ethics*. Further, the ethical principle, "access to records," indicates that counsellors should reveal the results of the counselling record only with the expressed consent of the client or when required by law. And the principle, "reporting evaluation and assessment results," indicates that counsellors must take care in reporting the results such that their clients are able to understand the conclusions and recommendations made. Lastly, the principle, "release of evaluation and assessment data," indicates that counsellors ought only to release assessment data to individuals who are qualified to interpret the results.

Conclusion

The components of the assessment process have been discussed with the view of contextualizing them within relevant ethical principles. The ethical principles are helpful to guide assessment procedures and to ground decision making about the use of instruments and their results. When used ethically and professionally, standardized test results can help clients to understand their problems, make responsible decisions, behave more effectively, maximize their potential, and hence live more satisfying lives (Hood & Johnson, 1991).

References

Anastasi, A. (1994). What counselors should know about the use and interpretation of psychological tests. *Journal of Counseling Development, 70*(5), 610-616.

American Counseling Association, (1989). *Responsibilities of users of standardized tests.* Alexandria, VA: American Counseling Association.

Cohen, R. J., Swerdlik, M. E., & Phillips, S. M. (1996). *Psychological testing and assessment.* Chapter 2. Toronto, ON: Mayfield Publishing Company.

Canadian Counselling Association (1999). Code *of ethics.* Ottawa, ON.

Corey, G. (1996). *Theory and practice of counseling and psychotherapy.* Toronto, ON: Brooks/Cole Publishing Co. Chapter 3.

Garfield, N. J., & Prediger, D. J. (1994). Assessment Competencies and Responsibilities: A Checklist for Counselors. In J. T. Kapes, M. M. Mastie, & E. A. Whitfield. *A counselor's guide to career assessment instruments.* (3rd ed. pp. 41-48). Alexandria, VA: National Career Development Association.

Goldman, L. (1994a). The marriage between tests and counseling redux: Summary of the 1972 article. *Measurement and Evaluation in Counseling & Development, 26*(4), 214-217.

Goldman, L. (1994b). The marriage is over...for most of us. *Measurement and Evaluation in Counseling & Development, 26*(4), 217-219.

Gregory, R. J. (1996). *Psychological testing: History, principles, and application* (2nd Ed.) Chapter 15. Toronto, ON: Allyn and Bacon.

Haladyna, T. M.., Nolen, S. B., & Haas, N. S. (1991). Raised standardized achievement test scores and the origins of test score pollution. *Educational Researcher, 20*(5), 2-7.

Hohenshil, T. H. (1996). Editorial: Role of assessment and diagnosis in counseling. *Journal of Counseling & Development, 75*(1), 64-68.

Hood, A. B., & Johnson, R. W. (1991). *Assessment in counseling: A guide to the use of psychological assessment procedures.* Chapters 16, 17, 18. Alexandria, VA: American Association for Counseling and Development.

Mehrens, W. A. (1994). Selecting A Career Assessment Instrument. In J. T. Kapes, M. M. Mastie, & E. A. Whitfield. *A counselor's guide to career assessment instruments.* (3rd ed. pp.23-30). Alexandria, VA: National Career Development Association.

Pedersen, P. B. (1997). The cultural context of the American Counseling Association code of ethics. *Journal of Counseling & Development, 76*(1), 23-28.

Strahan, R. F., & Kelly, A. E. (1994). Showing clients what their profiles mean. *Journal of Counseling & Development, 72*(3), 329-332.

Taylor, R. L. (2000). *Assessment of exceptional students: Educational and psychological procedures.* (5th ed.). Chapter 3. Toronto, ON: Allyn and Bacon.

Zytowski, D. G. (1994). Test and counseling: We are still married and living in discriminant analysis. *Measurement and Evaluation in Counseling & Development, 26*(4), 219-224.

Chapter Six

---------- ❖ ----------

Research and
Publication

---------- ❖ ----------

There are critical ethical issues in the area
of research and publication. Some of the
issues considered relate to qualitative research, the ethics of caring, informed consent, publication, and cultural diversity in
research.

ETHICAL ARTICLES ON RESEARCH AND PUBLICATION

E1 Researcher Responsibility

Counsellors plan, conduct, and report on research in a manner consistent with relevant ethical principles, professional standards of practice, federal and provincial laws, institutional regulations, cultural norms, and standards governing research with human subjects.

❖

E2 Subject Welfare

Counsellors are responsible for protecting the welfare of their research subjects during research, and avoid causing injurious psychological, physical or social effects to persons who participate in their research activities.

❖

E3 Principal Researcher Responsibility

Counsellors, when in the role of principal researcher, are responsible for ensuring that appropriate ethical research practices are followed and, with respect to research involving human subjects, they obtain an independent and appropriate ethical review before proceeding with the research. Research associates involved in the research activities share ethical obligations and full responsibility for their own actions.

❖

E4 Voluntary Participation

Counsellors ensure that participation in research is voluntary. However, involuntary participation may be appropriate when it can be shown that participation will have no harmful effects on subjects, is essential to the research, and meets ethical review requirements.

E5 Informed Consent of Research Subjects

Counsellors inform all research subjects of the purpose(s) of their research. In addition, subjects are made aware of any experimental procedures, possible risks, disclosures and limitations on confidentiality. Subjects are also told they are free to ask questions and to discontinue at any time.

E6 **Research Confidentiality**
Counsellors ensure that research information on subjects is confidential, and the identity of participants is protected unless otherwise authorized by them, consistent with all informed consent procedures.

❖

E7 **Further Research**
Counsellors have an obligation to collaborate with colleagues by making available original research data to qualified researchers who may wish to replicate or verify the research.

❖

E8 **Research Sponsors**
Counsellors, when conducting research, obtain informed consent from sponsors and institutions, and ensure that sponsors and institutions are given feedback information and proper acknowledgment.

❖

E9 **Review of Manuscripts**
Counsellors who review material submitted for publication, research or other scholarly purposes respect the confidentiality and proprietary rights of those who submitted the research.

❖

E10 **Reporting Results**
In reporting research results, counsellors mention any variables and conditions that might affect the outcome of the investigation or the interpretation of the results, and provide information sufficient for others who might wish to replicate the research.

❖

E11 **Research Contributions**
Counsellors give due credit through joint authorship, acknowledgment, footnote statements, or other appropriate means to those who have contributed significantly to the research and/or publication, and to those who have done previous work on the topic. For an article that is based mainly on a student thesis or dissertation, the student is listed as principal author.

E12 **Submission for Publication**
Counsellors do not submit the same manuscript or one essentially similar in content for simultaneous publication consideration by two or more journals. In addition, manuscripts published in whole or in substantial part in another journal or published work should not be submitted for publication without acknowledgment and permission from the previous publication.

❖ ❖ ❖ ❖ ❖ ❖ ❖ ❖ ❖ ❖ ❖ ❖ ❖ ❖

CASE STUDIES IN RESEARCH AND PUBLICATION

E1 **RESEARCHER RESPONSIBILITY**
Counsellors plan, conduct, and report on research in a manner consistent with relevant ethical principles, professional standards of practice, federal and provincial laws, institutional regulations, cultural norms, and standards governing research with human subjects.

Responsible Practice (+)

A department of counselling psychology has established an ethics committee to evaluate all research proposals, and particularly those proposals involving research with human subjects. In one research proposal, university student volunteers will be used to compare the results of three treatment processes for dealing with depression. Before approving the research proposal, the ethics committee consults with experts on each of the treatment processes to consider possible harmful side effects to student subjects.

Research in Schools (+)

Several university researchers plan to study the possible effects single parent families have on the school success of their children. They need the co-operation of many schools to obtain anecdotal information, standardized test scores and school grades. They plan meetings with school superintendents, school principals and teacher representatives to explain their research, the possible benefits for educators and their plans for confidentiality and publishing of results.

Protecting the Client (-)

One private counselling centre receives many referrals for counselling from various large companies that provide counselling services as part of their employee benefits. One of the companies asked for an evaluation report on all the counsellors in the counselling centre so that they could determine whether or not they would continue to refer employees to the centre. The head of the counselling centre asked for a videotaped counselling session from each counsellor so that she could show examples of good counselling to the company asking for feedback on counsellor effectiveness. The counsellors at the centre each submitted a videotape.

Obtaining Research Approval (-)

Several school counsellors in a large city school division agreed to administer a questionnaire to their guidance classes in order to help a colleague, Sally Strunk, collect data for her master's thesis. The questions on the questionnaire were very "low key" (to use the words of the researcher) and did not invade the privacy of any of the students. Sally realized that her school division had a policy on getting school board approval for her research, but because of the many weeks delay anticipated to get approval, and because of the totally harmless nature of her questionnaire, she collected the data with the help of her colleagues in counselling.

COMMENTS AND QUESTIONS

Counsellors doing research must be educated in research methodologies and should, at all times, attempt to answer research questions professionally and ethically. Research subjects should have confidence in researchers and their ability to "plan, conduct, and report" research with high professional standards of practice.

Confidentiality and informed consent are key responsibilities of the researcher. There must be:

a) detailed explanations of the purposes and procedures of the research,

b) identification of any experimental procedures,

c) identification of risks and benefits of the research,

d) willingness to discuss any questions that participants pose,

e) confidentiality of all tape recordings, verbal disclosures, records, and tests, and

f) an understanding that participation is voluntary at all times.

1. What are the research guidelines for the organization or institution where you work?

2. Is it a violation of research ethics when student teachers complete a university assignment that calls for some classroom observation? Discuss.

3. In the case "Protecting the Client," what needs to be done to make this situation ethical?

4. Are there times (see "Obtaining Research Approval") when it should not be necessary to go through all the channels for obtaining research approval?

5. What cultural norms might effect how a research project would be conducted?

E2 SUBJECT WELFARE
Counsellors are responsible for protecting the welfare of their research subjects during research, and avoid causing injurious psychological, physical or social effects to persons who participate in their research activities.

Ethics Committee (+)
All graduate students and professors conducting research must submit any research proposal dealing with human beings to an ethics committee. Part of the responsibility of this ethics committee is to ensure that proper procedures are in place to safeguard the welfare of all the subjects in the research experiment.

Research on Streaming (+)
One school principal has asked the divisional researcher to study the advantages and disadvantages of streaming in the school. After observing many of the classes in the school and talking to the teachers, the researcher is convinced that the procedures needed to examine streaming will be highly disruptive to students and teachers. The researcher informs the principal that the research design that they had hoped to use will have to be changed in order to better protect students and teachers from any harmful effects.

Strenuous Exercises (-)
A physical education teacher, Butch Cassidy, was working on his master's research thesis and gathered information on his study from students in his physical education classes. One part of his study included checking the amount of time it took students' heartbeats to return to normal after a strenuous series of exercises. No mention was made to students of the study and no precautions were taken with regards to the strenuous exercises before the study began.

Confidentiality Missing (-)
Although students enrolled in an introductory psychology course were given a detailed handout of what will be expected from them when volunteering for any experiment, there was no mention made that names of people who participated in the experiments would be included in the results. When experiment results were released, each student was identified by first name and student number.

COMMENTS AND QUESTIONS
This ethical article states that subjects who participate in research experiments should not be exposed to injurious psychological, physical or social effects. This article needs to be considered each time a subject participates in an experiment or research situation. It should not be assumed that subjects know this article. The article needs to be discussed fully with all subjects. As well, parental permission is necessary for students to be research subjects.

Prior to participating in a research experiment, each subject should receive a detailed outline of what to expect. Some of the information contained in the outline would include:

- a description of the research experiment,
- the purpose of the research,
- that participation was voluntary,
- permission for subjects to withdraw from the research at any time,
- the date, time and how long the research would take,
- where the experiment would be held,
- that each student that participated in the test situation would receive results and that their names would not be identified,
- assurances of confidentiality of all information gathered, and
- explanations of research results for subjects.

1. Besides presenting ethical articles, what are some other ways to prevent harm to research subjects?

2. What are some well-known research experiments that have caused psychological or physical harm to the subjects?

3. Should the availability of counselling for subjects after the research be part of all research designs?

4. When new counselling techniques or methods are used in research, can the psychological and social effects on clients be predicted?

5. The social effects of certain research practices are sometimes overlooked by researchers. What are some negative social effects that might result from certain research practices?

E3 PRINCIPAL RESEARCHER RESPONSIBILITY

Counsellors, when in the role of principal researcher, are responsible for ensuring that appropriate ethical research practices are followed and, with respect to research involving human subjects, they obtain an independent and appropriate ethical review before proceeding with the research. Research associates involved in the research activities share ethical obligations and full responsibility for their own actions.

Divisional Research Study (+)

The co-ordinator of guidance and counselling for a school division organized a task force to do research on the issue of AIDS education in junior and senior high schools in her division. The task force consisted of parents, teachers, counsellors, administrators, and family-life educators. Some of the issues discussed by the task force were age appropriateness, content, availability, and presentation of the material. Before the research on AIDS education was begun, the co-ordinator discussed the various ethical issues related to the study and the need for everyone to look out for the welfare of students.

Mainstreaming Research (+)

The superintendent of a large urban school division allowed a researcher and his team to study the effects of mainstreaming of students in all classrooms. Teachers were asked for their help and co-operation with the study. Before agreeing to work with the researcher, the teachers invited a professor from the university, who was very knowledgeable about research and ethics, to help them examine the ethical and practical issues related to the study.

Videotaping Interviews (-)

The head of a counselling psychology department allows all counsellor-educators in the department to have counsellors-in-training record both audio- and video-tape sessions with clients. Although clients are aware they are being taped, and that the tapes will be seen by others, no guidelines or regulations have been established by the department head regarding who has access to the tapes, where they will be stored, or when they will be erased.

Minimal Direction (-)

A researcher obtained a large grant to study cross-cultural counselling. Several of his graduate students were interested in doing the research. The researcher was extremely busy on several other projects he was involved in, and so he gave the graduate students complete control of subject selection, interview questions and safeguards for confidentiality. He did insist on being the principal researcher.

COMMENTS AND QUESTIONS

All members involved in a research project have the responsibility of being familiar with guidelines related to research, and the obligations of adhering to the guidelines. Graduate students doing research under the supervision of a professor are responsible for their own ethical actions. When research is being done with human subjects, the principal researcher must receive an independent ethical review of the research proposal before proceeding with the research. The principal researcher has the added responsibility of making sure that all participation in research is voluntary, that no harm will be done to research subjects, that research subjects are fully informed of the purposes of the research, and that the identity of research subjects is disguised.

1. What should the process be in an independent review of a research proposal involving human subjects?

2. What can the principal researcher do to ensure ethical research practice?

3. Should there be more explicit guidelines on videotaping? What might these guidelines be?

4. In the last case presented, what should the principal researcher have done?

5. What other guidelines should be included for researchers?

E4 **VOLUNTARY PARTICIPATION**
Counsellors ensure that participation in research is voluntary. However, involuntary participation may be appropriate when it can be shown that participation will have no harmful effects on subjects, is essential to the research, and meets ethical review requirements.

Identity Protected (+)

A research counsellor in a large Canadian urban centre was gathering information on sexual abuse/incest obtained from records of adult survivors of such abuse. Information required was age of onset, gender, perpetrator's status in the family/community, intervention (if any), years span between last incident and seeking of help, marital history of survivor, etc.

Clients' permission was not sought for use of this information, but no identification of individuals was attached to the statistics gathered. The purpose of the research was initial information gathering on sexual abuse/incest survivors. This information was to provide a base for further study of such abuse, which would hopefully lead to the development of early intervention strategies.

The long-term educational plan was the development of workshops by school counsellors for the in-servicing of school personnel division-wide on the issues/concerns of child-abuse intervention strategies.

Voluntary Participation (+)

Elementary and junior high counsellors in a large Canadian urban centre where grade structure was K-6, 7-9, and 10-12, developed a longitudinal study on children with learning disabilities. The purpose of the study was to research factors that contributed to a positive or negative transition from elementary school to the junior high level.

Information gathering began at the Grade 4 level and the study continued to Grade 9.

The framework was both objective and subjective. Criteria for entry into the study was established by the resource team who determined the definition of learning disability.

The study involved family (parents/siblings) and student participation. The research instruments were surveys and interviews. Participants were solicited through presentation of accurate information of the study including interviews, and written explanations. Written consent from both parents and students was mandatory. In addition, participants were free to withdraw from the study at any time.

The desired outcome was the development of intervention strategies, which would promote successful social transitions from one school level to the next, and the maintenance of this success throughout the upper level for students with their particular defined special needs.

Non-Voluntary Participation (-)

A research project on the reaction of teenagers to their parent's separation and divorce was being conducted at a university by a candidate for a PhD in counselling psychology. The purpose of the study was to provide information and analysis for teachers, counsellors, and social workers, who work with teenagers. The premise of the study was that the information:

a) would help to highlight individuals who are at risk from the experience, and

b) would lead to intervention before crisis.

Names of prospective participants were attained randomly from the divorce dockets. Sixty teens and either one of their parents were required for the study. The committed time requested was four individual sessions of 45 minutes over a six-month period.

One interviewer, a counselling student in the department of counselling psychology, became aware at a first session that one individual, a 15-year-old male, was very reluctant to be in the study. He was verbally abusive to his father during the initial session, and distant and abrupt in his communications with the interviewer. The interviewer did not suggest that they consider withdrawing from the study. The reluctant behaviour continued for the remaining three sessions.

Unaware Participants (-)
A middle school counsellor initiated a small group on the developmental issues of peer pressure relating to sexuality. The group consisted of six girls, ages 12 to 14. These students were not aware that they were being videotaped by a research counsellor. This particular researcher had requested the taping for the purpose of presenting it to counselling students who were studying adolescent sexual development.

COMMENTS AND QUESTIONS
This ethical article underscores that:

   a) Written consent of all voluntary participants in research studies must be mandatory.

   b) Written explanation of the research, including purposes of the study and techniques to be used, must be presented to all voluntary participants.

   c) Voluntary participants must be clearly advised that they can choose to refuse to participate in the research.

   d) Voluntary participants must be advised in writing that they can withdraw from the study at any time.

1. Can involuntary research participation ever be justified?

2. Should explicit rights of participants (voluntary/involuntary) be protected legally by legislation?

3. What type of consequences should be in place for researchers who:

   a) knowingly cause psychological/emotional or physical damage to participants,

   b) do not honestly inform participants about essential components of the study, which could influence their consent to participate,

   c) deliberately mislead the participants?

4. In what types of counselling research would it be advantageous to have non-voluntary participants?

5. In the last case presented, "Unaware Participants," can a case be made that this taping will "have no harmful effects" on the middle school girls?

E5 INFORMED CONSENT OF RESEARCH SUBJECTS

Counsellors inform all research subjects of the purpose(s) of their research. In addition, subjects are made aware of any experimental procedures, possible risks, disclosures and limitations on confidentiality. Subjects are also told they are free to ask questions and to discontinue at any time.

New Approach to Family Life (+)

A guidance counsellor decided to use his class for a research project as a part of a university course in which he was enrolled. The project involved testing a new approach to teaching a unit in family life. The teacher and professor set up the project together.

A letter was composed to parents describing the project in general. The letter was sent home at the beginning of the family-life unit and the students were informed about the project and its purpose. Parents and/or students were given the option of being part of the project. At the completion of the project, and following an analysis of the results, a summary was composed and sent to students and parents. Several parents responded with telephone calls to the counsellor and also made comments at the parent-teacher conference that followed the project. Parents were interested in the nature and results of the study.

Discipline Project (+)

A school principal and guidance counsellor set up a project in which "reality therapy" was taught to a whole school staff as a discipline approach. Teachers were informed of the purpose of the study and were given a chance as staff to opt into the program. Parents were also informed of the project and training sessions were provided for them as well. Students were taught the major tenets of "reality therapy." Throughout the year records were kept of the discipline infractions and comparisons made to the year before. Following the completion of the project, a summary of the results was published and circulated along with the results of a survey given to teachers, parents and students.

Self-Concept Research (-)

In a research project, some guidance counsellors and parents were trained to work directly with students in the school and in the home on enhancing students' self-concept. Magic circle, active listening, and classroom meeting were some of the procedures taught. There were three groups involved. The first group of students included training for both counsellor and parents. The second group involved the training of the counsellor only. The third group was a control group in which no training was involved. A series of tests designed to measure improvement in self-concept were administered to all three groups.

No plan was in place to inform students or their parents of this research, either before or after the completion of the project. Parents of the first group were exposed to the information, but neither parents or students of the second group were aware of the project. Nothing was planned to inform the control group of the research project.

Uninformed Students (-)

A high school counsellor, John Smith, invited Grade 12 students to participate in a research project involving the research of students' backgrounds, and relating this information to their academic success throughout their high school years. Students were asked to participate in this project, and were given credit in the form of term marks for participating. No mention was made of the purpose of the study to the students.

The questionnaire took from one to two hours to complete and included specific items related to family background. These items, if answered in the affirmative, would indicate criminal acts of abuse. The purpose of the project was intended to parallel research on the effects of abuse and its relationship to academic progress.

COMMENTS AND QUESTIONS
This article states that all research subjects should be informed of the purpose of the study or project. Researchers must take the time to carefully explain these purposes before subjects volunteer to be part of the study.

In the two positive cases presented, all parties involved were informed of the purposes of the projects. As well, results of the studies were made available. In the last case presented, the researcher, John Smith, placed himself in a very difficult position if an actual case of abuse was revealed by the questionnaire. To use marks as an incentive for participation in a project of this type is placing pressure on students to participate and reveal personal information that they might not otherwise disclose.

1. As a counsellor, how might you participate in or initiate research on abuse in your school?

2. How would the counsellor have carried out his project if family life were a controversial topic in his community?

3. How should counsellors handle resistance to research projects from other teachers?

4. What are some research projects where "withholding information" about the project is necessary?

5. To capture the spirit of informed consent, what can researchers do to encourage subjects to feel "free to ask questions and to discontinue at any time"?

E6 RESEARCH CONFIDENTIALITY
Counsellors ensure that research information on subjects is confidential and the identity of participants is protected unless otherwise authorized by them, consistent with all informed consent procedures.

Subject Disclosure (+)
A researcher in counselling psychology is studying, through direct observation and videotaping, the anxiety subjects may show when asked to elaborate on traumatic childhood experiences. Before the first session with each subject begins, the researcher informs the subjects of the purpose of the research study and counselling session. The researcher makes sure that each subject fully understands the purposes and obtains written consent from each subject willing to participate and be videotaped. At the end of the study, all videotapes of sessions are erased.

Case-Study Research (+)
A university researcher contacts a large child-guidance centre for information on reports of child abuse. The researcher asks that these reports be given to him without any identifying material regarding the subjects.

Videotaping (-)
Gayle Jones has had second thoughts about a videotape of a session that she initially consented to, and now she is asking that the researcher erase the tape of the session. Gayle is concerned about having other people see the tape and learn about her personal problems. The researcher weighs the options of erasing the tape for the subject's benefit or keeping it because it could prove useful research for the researcher's benefit. He decides to meet his own needs and keeps a copy of the subject's videotaped session. The researcher feels safe because he still has the sub-

ject's initial written consent form. The researcher allows others to see the videotape.

Subject Confidentiality (-)

A counsellor-researcher walks into the university cafeteria and overhears four of his counsellor trainees discussing counsellee subjects by name. He decides to ignore the students' conversation.

COMMENTS AND QUESTIONS

Before supplying data to others or reporting the results on specific subjects, researchers must get informed consent from the subjects involved or else disguise the identities of these subjects. If these measures are not taken, researchers can be held ethically and legally liable by their professional organization, employer, or the court system. The foremost questions researchers should ask themselves before disclosing information on specific subjects are:

a) Can the research subject be hurt in any way in this study?

b) Is the subject aware of the research and has she or he given consent to participate?

c) Has every effort been taken to disguise the identity of the research subjects?

1. What are the added difficulties of research confidentiality when doing research in schools and with students?

2. Should a subject's identity be disguised if she or he is found to have been abused?

3. Should a subject's identity be disguised if he or she disclosed a criminal act?

4. Should researchers disguise the identity of subjects in a qualitative research study? Why? Why not?

5. Is it ever possible to disguise the identity of subjects who are part of a study while they are "attending" an institution (e.g. prison, school, group home)?

E7 FURTHER RESEARCH
Counsellors have an obligation to collaborate with colleagues by making available original research data to qualified researchers who may wish to replicate or verify the research.

Collaboration With Colleagues (+)

A professor in this university reports on her study, which refutes some commonly held ideas regarding learning theory. The study is published in a highly regarded professional journal. A professor in educational psychology from another university requests to see a copy of the original data. A copy of the data is provided the following week, along with some additional comments.

Available Raw Data (+)

The head of this department of educational psychology established a policy that all the data for each thesis or dissertation published by graduate students in the department be made available to any interested faculty member or graduate student. This policy also included guidelines on confidentiality issues related to research subjects.

Non-Collegial (-)

A well-known Canadian counsellor-educator publishes an article that strongly supports a particular counselling technique that he favours. In this article he also points out how this technique is far superior to many other well-established counselling techniques. When several counsellor-educators contact him regarding the more detailed original data, he ignores their requests for more information.

Confidentiality Lacking (-)

A high school counsellor was in the process of completing her master's thesis on teenage pregnancy and abortions. She was using the school records and her position as one of the school guidance counsellors to obtain data for her research. She had received the school administration's permission and her fellow counsellors' support in doing her study. The girls were made aware of her study and were promised complete confidentiality. She successfully defended her thesis, and her work was made available to other university faculty and students. It was also reported in the education section of the local newspaper. Mrs. O'Shea, the chairperson of the Pro-Life Council and a powerful school board member, who was trying to shut down the local abortion clinic, indicated that she wanted to examine the data some more and needed to know the names of the students. The counsellor, in fear of losing her promotion, supplied the names to Mrs. O'Shea.

COMMENTS AND QUESTIONS
This ethical article indicates that members have an obligation to collaborate with colleagues by making original research available to qualified others. There is no place for selfishness, secrecy and petty jealousies in the pursuit of knowledge. An open, collegial, cooperative attitude will provide the greatest benefit to the profession and to the knowledge base.

Collaboration with colleagues encourages:

a) a high level of scientifically verifiable research,

b) use of acceptable research methods,

c) honesty and accuracy in interpreting and reporting research, and

d) a faster pace of knowledge acquisition.

1. What effect does this article have on client confidentiality and informed consent?

2. Do cost and time factors, and a concern for the use to be made of the data, enter into the decision to make original research available?

3. Do personal feelings about your colleagues influence decisions about making research available?

4. What, if any, effect does reputation, power, position or money have on decisions to request or provide original research? Who is to be considered a qualified other?

5. How can university tenure and promotion guidelines effect research collaboration with colleagues?

E8 RESEARCH SPONSORS
Counsellors, when conducting research, obtain informed consent from sponsors and institutions, and ensure that sponsors and institutions are given feedback information and proper acknowledgement.

Acknowledgment of Sponsors (+)

A counsellor in a high school requires additional funding for a research project she is doing. She writes to several local businesses, explains her project, and asks for some funding. All contribute small amounts to her project. She explains the sponsorship to all her research subjects, and then undertakes her research. When the research is completed and the paper is written, the sponsors are included in the acknowledgments.

Informed Consent of Sponsors (+)

Fourteen colleges and universities in one Canadian province decided to support a study that would provide high school students with more information about each of the colleges or universities. The major researcher informed each college and university as to the type of questions she would be asking and that comments would be solicited from present college/university students. She received written permission to use the data collected, and at the end of the project all the colleges and universities were given full details on the results of the study, and were all acknowledged as contributing sponsors of the study.

Unacknowledged Sponsor (-)

A university professor receives a small grant from a university's innovations grants to develop a new course in counselling. In his promotional material for the course, the professor does not acknowledge the money received from the university's innovations grants.

Neither does he acknowledge the work done by a graduate student who was paid from the grant money.

Inappropriate Feedback (-)

A parents' group in a wealthy suburban area felt that newspaper reports of alcohol and drug use in the city were not relevant for their area. They decided to ask the schools to conduct a survey of alcohol and drug abuse in the two divisional high schools. Alcohol and drug abuse were found to be quite widespread. Since this information was bound to upset the parents' group, the researchers reported the results as being "inconclusive."

COMMENTS AND QUESTIONS

In a recent newspaper account the journalist pointed out the real ethical dilemma faced by researchers, who had found that users of a certain product had slightly more incidence of cancer. The makers of the product had recently contributed 10 million dollars to the university where the researchers worked. This case, and other similar cases, point to the importance of informed consent for sponsors, the need for clear directions on feedback, and the publishing of all research results. Sponsors and institutions should be given the same respect as individual participants in research: namely, the opportunity for giving informed consent.

On the other hand, sponsors or institutions should not expect any control over research results simply because they have funded the research. As with all research, whether sponsored or not, results of research should be reported accurately and clearly, and acknowledgement should be given to all contributors.

1. Should a sponsor who funds an entire research study have control over the results of the study?

2. If sponsors request that their financial contributions be kept anonymous, should

this request be honoured? Are there exceptions?

3. Are there situations where research results should not be given to sponsors or institutions? Clarify.

4. What would you have done in the case study entitled "Inappropriate Feedback"?

5. Is it adequate to give sponsors and institutions verbal feedback? Should researchers always attempt to publish their results, even though they are being discouraged from doing so by sponsors or institutions?

E9 REVIEW OF MANUSCRIPTS
Counsellors who review material submitted for publication, research or other scholarly purposes respect the confidentiality and proprietary rights of those who submitted the research.

Reviewing Manuscripts (+)

Professor Jones, a member of the CCA, published widely and successfully. He was asked to be a reviewer for the *Canadian Journal of Counselling*. When he received manuscripts from the editor, he promptly reviewed the manuscripts following all the guidelines provided by the editor on confidentiality, feedback and process.

Editorial Review Board (+)

In establishing a board of reviewers for a major counselling journal, Sue Thomas, the editor, made sure she had reviewers with expertise in a wide range of counselling areas. Manuscripts for review were then sent only to reviewers with specific expertise related to the research topic of the manuscript.

Breaking Confidentiality (-)

A professor in a university, who regularly reviewed manuscripts for journals, received a manuscript that dealt with a novel approach to using solution-focused brief therapy. Receiving the manuscript was very timely, since the professor was speaking on "innovations in solution-focussed counselling" in the next week. In his speech the next week, the professor included some of the ideas from the manuscript.

Reviewing the Manuscripts of Known Writers (-)

The manuscript Dr. John Johnson received for reviewing purposes could only have come from his good friend at another university in the same city. John Johnson was very familiar with the research and the many obstacles his friend had encountered in finally getting his results written up. There were both procedural errors and some gaps in the data in the manuscript under review. Dr. Johnson decided his friend needed all the help he could get and spent the majority of his review emphasizing the positive aspects of the study.

COMMENTS AND QUESTIONS
In smaller research communities it is sometimes difficult to disguise the identity of researchers. This puts all the more emphasis on the need for confidentiality of manuscripts submitted for publication. Until a manuscript is published, the contents of the manuscript, as well as the identity of the authors, should remain confidential. The authors of manuscripts have all proprietary rights to their manuscripts, and any and all use or reference to the manuscripts belongs to the authors.

1. In the case on "Breaking Confidentiality," what should the professor have done if he wanted to use the ideas from an unidentified writer?

2. "I'm about ready to give up submitting research for publication. The last two times I submitted something, I had to wait 18 months the first time and about a year the second time." What can and should be done to process manuscripts quicker?

3. Should manuscripts for journals resulting from thesis or dissertations be evaluated the same way as other submissions?

4. What are some safeguards that can be put into place to guard the "proprietary rights" of unidentified writers?

5. What needs to be done in the last case to change the behaviour of John Johnson to more ethical behaviour?

E10 REPORTING RESULTS
In reporting research results, counsellors mention any variables and conditions that might affect the outcome of the investigation or the interpretation of the results, and provide information sufficient for others who might wish to replicate the research.

Ethnic Variables (+)
The school psychologist recognized the ethnic diversity of the student population at a high school he was to test as a whole. When reporting the results, he included a detailed description of the school population. He described the number of recent immigrant students, the many transfer students, their ages, grade levels, and length of time living in Canada.

Sex Survey (+)
A very powerful parent committee in a small rural town of 10,000 people sought the assistance of the guidance department to survey the students at the local high school to determine their degree of sexual activity. The counsellor reported that the results were significantly lower than the national average and of those neighbouring towns and city. In writing his report, the counsellor explained that the results might reflect the students' awareness that the survey was prompted by the parents' committee and that the results would be given to them. Possibly, students were not entirely forthcoming due to anxiety, or possible stricter curfews, of restrictions to social functions, and of the possibility of parents finding out who was sexually active.

Superficial Study (-)
The head of a divisional counselling association has conducted a study to examine students' social values. He obtained the assistance of one counsellor from each of the high schools to help him administer the study to

a number of students in each school. The results were then compiled representing the school division as a whole. The results were published in the divisional newsletter. Absent from the report were any details on the number of subjects from the vastly different high schools in this large school division. As well, no mention was made of the fact that no attempt at random selection of students was made.

"Jumping the Gun" (-)

At a "case conference" meeting, which included all the counsellors of the high school, the school social worker and the psychologist, an 18-year-old male student became the focus of attention. The student in question had become an increasing behaviour problem at school as well as exhibiting decreased academic performance. A personality test had been administered to the student by the psychologist and the report was being shared at this meeting. The team made recommendations based on the test without consideration of the effects that the recent break-up of the student's parents and the death of a grandparent in a car accident might have had on results of the personality test.

COMMENTS AND QUESTIONS

If research is to be of any real value and benefit, researchers must report any conditions or variables that may have affected the outcome of interpretation of the results. Not reporting a variable that may have affected the research results leaves the research impotent, and casts a shadow on the validity of the research findings. A few of the conditions or variables that could affect the outcome and interpretation of results are:

a) the cultural backgrounds (e.g. norms, values, beliefs) of the subjects,

b) socio-economic influences especially if results are being grouped or compared to another social class,

c) religious influences of the subjects, (e.g. customs, values, beliefs)

d) the personal, social and medical histories of the subjects, where appropriate and ethical.

1. In the "Sex Survey" case study, the counsellor explained that the results of the study may have been influenced by the knowledge that the students' parents would get the results. Knowing this to be the case, how could this research study have been improved?

2. Do you feel that it is a realistic expectation that all variables and conditions that may affect results be identified?

3. Under what circumstances, if any, do you feel it is ethical to disclose a subject's medical or personal history when reporting variables and conditions that may affect results?

4. Do you feel that our own values, beliefs and biases are variables and conditions that may affect research results?

5. What are some additional variables that could affect research results?

E11 RESEARCH CONTRIBUTIONS
Counsellors give due credit through joint authorship, acknowledgment, footnote statements, or other appropriate means to those who have contributed significantly to the research and/or publication, and to those who have done previous work on the topic. For an article that is based mainly on a student thesis or dissertation, the student is listed as principal author.

Appropriate Acknowledgment (+)
A counsellor in a relatively small high school requires additional data for a research paper she is writing. She writes to three nearby schools who can help her with the data collection. When the research is completed and the paper is written, the three schools and their counsellors are included in the acknowledgments.

Joint Authorship (+)
A counsellor is asked to write an article explaining the school's guidance program. Recently, the school principal and the counsellor had written a similar paper for another organization. After receiving the principal's approval and making some minor adjustments to the paper, the counsellor asked for permission, from the publisher of the original article, to submit this similar article. After receiving permission, the counsellor submitted the adapted manuscript for publication. Both the principal and counsellor were listed as authors.

Unethical Behaviour (-)
During a conversation with a colleague, a counsellor is given significant information pertaining to a paper he is writing. The counsellor uses the discussion as the basis for the paper and includes many of his colleague's ideas. When the paper is completed, the colleague's name is not acknowledged in any way.

Footnoting (-)
A counsellor uses an entire section of a colleague's unpublished paper within the body of a manuscript she is writing. The unpublished work is not referenced and is used as the counsellor's own ideas.

COMMENTS AND QUESTIONS
It is important to give due credit to any person or group who gives information, written or verbal, or significantly assists a researcher. Knowing where information comes from gives researchers credibility and helps to substantiate their ideas and statements. Another reason for giving due credit is to assist future researchers. It helps them to find background information and check specific data.

Major contributions to research should be given joint authorship. This includes help with writing a paper, or with the actual research or testing. For example, an assistant who helps to design a test and formulates procedures should be given joint authorship. Minor contributions should be acknowledged through references or footnotes.

1. If, for business reasons, a major sponsor asks not to be credited for sponsoring your research, do you abide by the sponsor's wishes? Discuss.

2. When do the ideas of others become your own? Many ideas come from someone, whether they are known or not. Where is the line between one's own idea and someone else's?

3. Is it unethical to use what you think are your own ideas if you have not checked to see whether these ideas have not been presented elsewhere?

4. If you pay someone to collect data for you, does he or she need to be acknowledged in a subsequent research article?

5. When graduate students publish parts of their theses or dissertations as articles, should they acknowledge the members of their thesis or dissertation committee?

E12 SUBMISSION FOR PUBLICATION

Counsellors do not submit the same manuscript or one essentially similar in content for simultaneous publication consideration by two or more journals. In addition, manuscripts published in whole or in substantial part in another journal or published work should not be submitted for publication without acknowledgment and permission from the previous publication.

Single Submission (+)

A graduate student in this department of counselling psychology wrote her thesis on reasonable behaviour on the part of counsellors in dealing with confidentiality in a counselling situation. After having her advisor read the thesis, she was encouraged to submit it for publication. The student obtained a list of the current journals on counselling psychology, and reviewed the most recent publications. The author chose to submit the thesis to one counselling journal that had recently published other articles related to confidentiality and other ethical issues.

Acknowledgment and Permission From Previous Publication (+)

A professor in a department of educational psychology submitted a lengthy manuscript to a professional journal. The editors of the journal agreed to publish one major part of the manuscript. Various colleagues advised the professor that they found the article useful to their courses, and wished to read more about the subject. The professor was advised to submit the article in whole to another publication. He subsequently contacted the previous publisher and requested acknowledgment and permission to submit the manuscript to another publisher in order that it might be published in whole.

Publisher Does Not Respond (-)

At this university, one professor wrote a manuscript regarding the timely issue of AIDS education in the schools. He felt that time was of the essence for publication due to the rising epidemic of sexually transmitted diseases among our youth. The professor was aware that it could take up to three months for a publisher to respond to a manuscript submission. Due to time constraints, the author chose not to wait for an answer to his submission, and after a six-week period, he submitted the work to another publisher.

Embarrassment Caused (-)

An author submitted the same manuscript to three publications simultaneously. Two of the three publications accepted the manuscript. The author contacted the editors of the less prestigious journals and informed them that he was withdrawing his manuscript for publication. The other journal published the manuscript.

COMMENTS AND QUESTIONS

This ethical article states that an author must not submit a manuscript to two or more journals simultaneously for publication consideration. As well, when an author chooses to submit for publication a manuscript that has been published in part by another publisher, it is his or her obligation to get permission from the previous publisher to allow the manuscript to be published in another journal.

Due to the costs incurred and the time required to read all the manuscripts that are submitted to a publication, there are no journal publishers who will accept a manuscript from an author if it comes to their attention that there were multiple submissions. Counsellors and researchers should be aware of the validity of this concern by editors. It is not ethical practice to have a manuscript, or portion thereof, submitted to, or published in, more than one journal without acknowledgment. Even in the event of a time constraint, which the author may deem to be unreasonable, it would not be ethical to submit the work again at any time, without the written notification to, and the permission of, the first publisher.

1. What are some ways in which the whole review process of manuscripts can be improved?

2. Should reviewers of manuscripts be paid a small honorarium on the condition that they review a manuscript within one week?

3. Do you believe that a letter stating "multiple submissions" should be allowed, and manuscripts could be sent to more than one publisher, if in fact they have been so advised?

4. What are the advantages and disadvantages of allowing for multiple submissions of manuscripts?

5. Is it realistic to expect a publication to respond to you regarding acceptance or refusal of your submitted manuscript within a reasonable and agreed-upon time limit, for example, a period of six to eight weeks?

❖ ❖ ❖ ❖ ❖ ❖ ❖ ❖ ❖ ❖ ❖ ❖ ❖ ❖

Essays on Research and Publication

Collaborative Narrative Inquiry and the Ethic of Caring

Renate Schulz

Traditionally, research has been based on a positivist paradigm that can be characterized by the dominance of the researcher as expert knower doing research on subjects, all the while seeking objectivity, and invoking strict controls for bias or extraneous effects. Such circumstances carry the connotations of rigidity and precision that have historically been associated with scientific rigour and credibility.

Over the past two decades, however, this paradigm has come under increased scrutiny, as various forms of qualitative research have emerged to transform the research landscape. Current notions about the nature of reality, about what counts as knowledge, and about what research is most relevant to the theory and practice in a field, have brought about associated changes in the process of research, as well as in the relationship between researcher and researched. The objectivity of traditional research, with its distanced third person and passive voice, no longer predominates the field.

Instead, more and more frequently, practitioners are engaging in research on their own. Or, using a variety of qualitative research methodologies, they are working in partnership with researchers to explore their experiences as counsellors. Collaborative narrative inquiry is one such research method where researcher and practitioner share responsibility in the research process, and where the relationship between the practitioner and the researcher is central to the research design and to the kind of information that the research yields.

Collaborative Narrative Inquiry

In collaborative narrative inquiry, the practitioner is a partner in the research endeavour. Narrative inquiry proceeds over time, and a wide range of data is collected through participant observation, interviews, and document analysis. These data are then arranged in such a way that an account of practice is given in the form of a narrative. The point of the narrative is an understanding of the persons being studied from the perspective of their own situation, rather than judgmentally from afar. Counsellors and researchers involved in narrative inquiry describe their work, explain their actions, and express their thoughts. The structure of the story they tell, its narrative line, gives form to their ideas. Connelly and Clandinin (1990) describe the relationship in narrative inquiry as one in which both partners in the research feel they have a voice with which to tell their stories, for the telling or shaping of stories is an activity that orders meaning.

Storytelling is at the heart of human conduct. The novelist, Singer (1976) points out that, "Today we live, but by tomorrow today will be a story. The whole world, all human life, is one long story" (p. 11). And Britton (1982) tells us that, "Our memories of past experiences are in story form, are narratives. We so readily construct stories out of our past experiences that it is difficult to perceive that anything has been 'constructed' at all" (p. 153). Narrative research is about validating practitioners' stories. As such, it parallels the familiar centrality of storytelling in counsellor-client interactions. In valuing the stories counsellors tell, narrative inquiry validates counsellors' experiences and the ways they learn from their practices.

The narratives of all of us are complex and particular orderings of our prior experiences, woven together bring a kind of unity to our professional lives. The structure of the stories we tell about our experiences as counsellors, their narrative line, gives form to our ideas and meanings. An examination of the way in which we order our tellings, the way in which we foreground certain aspects or marginalize others, can yield new understandings of who we are as counsellors and how it is that we are doing what we are doing. Connelly and Clandinin (1990) write that stories "function as arguments in which we learn something essentially human by understanding an actual life or community as lived" (p. 8). In this way, narrative discourse contributes to knowing.

Collaborative narrative inquiry as a research method is gaining increasing recognition as a powerful way of understanding the professional lives of practitioners and the complexities of their lived experiences (Casey, 1996). It is research *with* rather than *on* a practitioner. The emphasis is on partnership between the researcher and the participant, or co-researcher. Therefore, references to the counsellor as subjugated "subject," acted upon by the researcher, are not appropriate. Within a collaborative inquiry relationship, the traditional role of researcher as expert knower disappears. The researcher as objective, distant, or detached observer gives way to the researcher as engaged, involved co-participant in the community of study. Because collaboration requires both a shared affinity and an interdependence, the lines separating researcher and researched blur. The hierarchical distinctions dissolve and the relationship moves to a partnership of equals.

Each collaborative investigation is relational and begins by recognizing the time it takes to build the trust that allows participants to take risks, and reveal beliefs and values to each other. The breakdown of the traditional compartmentalization of researcher and researched is both dependent upon and encourages the development of trust and dialogue characterized by openness. It is also this greater level of trust and openness between research partners that allows dialogue to develop into the deeper kind of conversational sharing that so richly informs the texts of narrative inquiry. The researcher-counsellor and counsellor-researcher work together to understand the meanings of their stories of practice, and help each other with what they know and how they know what they know. As collaborators or co-labourers in the research, both counsellor and researcher share interpretive responsibility, and the findings of the research explain phenomena from the jointly constructed understandings of both partners in the research.

As more researchers adopt the methods of narrative inquiry, where new practices are situated within reconfigured relationships between researchers and practitioners, it becomes increasingly important that we develop a dialogue of inquiry into the ethical issues of collaborative narrative research. Much of the power and persuasiveness of collaborative narrative inquiry can be traced to the close, long-term and trusting relationship between research partners. But it is also this closeness that raises some of the most difficult ethical issues.

The Ethic of Caring

Noddings' (1984, 1987, 1991, 1992) ethic of caring and her notions of fidelity provide a framework within which to situate an examination of some of these issues. Relationship lies at the heart of Noddings' ethic of caring. The relationship that is so fundamental to our being induces caring. Natural caring, explains Noddings (1987), "establishes the ideal for ethical caring, and ethical caring initiates this ideal in its efforts to institute, maintain, or re-establish natural caring" (p. 385). How we relate to family and friends should therefore become our model for a caring relationship, and a primary fidelity to persons should guide our thinking during research. Noddings emphasizes the importance of genuine mutuality, truly collaborative inquiry, and research practices informed by a caring attitude toward others. She argues that the quality and depth of research on practice would be enhanced if the virtue of fidelity were placed at the center of this work. She defines fidelity not as faithfulness to duty or principle, but rather as faithfulness attached to those with whom we are in relation. Noddings writes that an ethic of caring takes fidelity to persons as primary, and when faced with a research decision, she suggests that we make our decision on the basis of answers to these questions: "What effect will [this decision] have on the present relation? What effect will it have on the development of this person as a caring person? What effect will it have on our community of caring?" (Noddings, 1987, p. 390).

Research on practice that is grounded in an ethic of caring would not make counsellors the objects of research. Instead, Noddings suggests that problems that are of interest to both parties should be chosen as the object of research. When both parties are meaningfully involved in the same problem or the same inquiry, the relationship between researcher and researched is fundamentally changed. Then the process of inquiry can become truly collaborative.

Although Noddings, in her work, addresses the teacher-researcher relationship, the principles of her ethic of care are equally applicable to counselling. Thus she maintains that collaborative inquiry into issues of mutual interest, conducted in an atmosphere of trust and respect, would be more meaningful "research *for* teaching [counselling] instead of simply research *on* teaching [counselling]" (p. 394).

A code of ethics is necessary to establish standards for research practices. But within any project where people work together closely over long periods of time, the complexity and diffuseness of the ethical dimensions are such that rules cannot guide us infallibly. In the American Educational Research Association Code of Ethics Revisions, 2000, it is suggested that rules should be held loosely and tentatively for consideration. We must know when to discard rules in order to deal in caring ways with the needs of others with whom we are in relation.

Anticipating the dilemmas of researchers torn between fidelity to persons and fidelity to the research, to a funding body, or to an institution, Noddings posits the following case.[1] After having worked with a counsellor only to find that he or she is either incompetent, sexist, or racist, how should we respond? Can we address our concerns about this person's practice and still remain faithful to the counsellor as a person, as well as to the trusting relationship we have built together? Noddings reminds us that the principle of fidelity or faithfulness to persons must remain inviolate, but that the problem of the counsellor's incompetence, sexism, or racism must also be dealt with, and that it can be dealt with in a manner compatible with the tenets of an ethic of caring. We are asked to deal with the issues by affording our research partner "special treatment," much as we would offer it to each of our friends, and as we would wish it to be offered to us. Noddings (1987) uses the term "confirmation" to describe this aspect of a caring relationship. She writes, "As we work, talk, and debate together, we begin to perceive the ethical ideals that each of us strives toward. Then we are in a position to confirm — to help the other to actualize the best image" (p. 393). Confirmation asks that we attribute to the other the best possible motives, take into consideration what the counsellor is trying to achieve, and, as with a friend, support his or her best qualities. Instead of creating a negative research portrait about the counsellor's practice, Noddings recommends that counsellor and researcher enter into genuine dialogue, examining the issue together by checking interpretations and exploring meanings. In short, Noddings recommends talk. Just as friends turn to conversation as a way of dealing with problems and coming to understand each other, conversation is also the characteristic method of research that seeks to understand people's understandings.

Reciprocal Self-Disclosure

Within a partnered research context where we work together over a long period of time and have many conversations, it is through sharing and storytelling in conversation that our relationship develops. In conversation with friends we tell a story, and they in turn share one, which brings us closer together. It's a process that builds relationships. Within a genuine relationship of mutuality, we spontaneously share personal ideas, experiences, thoughts, and feelings. This may involve a degree of risk taking on our part, but it is also the way we reveal ourselves as individuals. Talking about details of our daily life sends a message of rapport and caring and is a way of getting to know others better as individuals. Self-disclosures serve the function of establishing intimacy, and act as a form of modelling whereby the research partner is encouraged to respond in a similar vein. By the way in which we engage in conversation and show interest in and share our thoughts, ideas, and understandings, we nourish a friendship. By opening ourselves up to others, we invite a conversational balance; we create a symmetry in our conversation and open the way for our partner in conversation to feel comfortable about disclosing more.

Is it ethical within a research relationship to tell stories or reveal things in order to elicit a reciprocal self-disclosure that will further the data gathering for our inquiry? Alternatively, is it ethical to remain silent about some things for fear that speaking out might shut down the conversation and thus jeopardize our data gathering? Is it acceptable at times to sacrifice the relationship for data?

The practice of ethical and moral compromises in research is common. Punch (1994) argues that in the interests of collecting meaningful data and ensuring the validity of participant response, "... it may be unavoidable that there is a degree of impression management, manipulation, concealment, economy with the truth, and even deception" (p. 95).

But deception and exploitation are diametrically opposed to research methods wherein the researched is viewed as a full partner in a collaborative enterprise. When our research is based on principles of collaboration, we can anticipate a reciprocal relationship with our research partner. We can expect a relationship in which we share stories, share risks, and share in the research design from beginning to end. We can expect to become partners in the generation of knowledge. Adopting such a position has implications for what counts as ethical in our practice. An ethic of caring would suggest that self-disclosure should be a natural part of the process of building a relationship, not a gambit. And because reciprocal self-disclosure promotes intimacy, we have a responsibility to maintain the climate of caring and confirming that encouraged this intimacy. When our research practices are informed by a caring attitude toward others, our decisions are based on what effect our actions will have on the relationship, on the development of the other as a caring person, and on our community of caring.

Informed Consent

Caring is exercised in a traditional sense through adherence to the concept of informed consent, whereby individuals involved in a study completely understand not only what is expected of them, but also the possible consequences of having taken part in the study. It is not possible when working with emergent themes to try to satisfy the demands for the kind of clear-cut statements of intent and consequence that are traditionally associated with informed consent. A more appropriate ethical guideline in narrative research is the concept of ongoing, continual

negotiation in conversation, characterized by honesty and candor, and built on mutual trust and respect. As with friends, within a collaborative research relationship, participants enter into discussion with an open agenda, guided not by rules and standards or by proper signatures on a standardized consent form, but by the relationship at hand.

The significance of relationship for the research also alerts us to consider the ethical consequences of that relationship. Richert (Brody, Schroeder, Webb, Schulz, & Richert, 1994,) cites change as one of the most compelling of these ethical issues. Although clear-cut statements of intent and consequence, as they have traditionally been defined, are not possible within a collaborative research framework, Richert suggests that change, however, is a predictable outcome of any research process. Both researcher and participant change in the course of their work together. Richert contends that in a relationship that occurs within the context of a research project where the purpose is to understand a phenomenon, the people working together on the inquiry will change as a result of their inquiry. They will come to know more, and to understand more about what they are studying. But these changes in their knowledge and understanding can also be negative. Participants might come face-to-face with ideas and understandings that are disquieting and that they would rather not encounter. Through the research they might be confronted with images of themselves that, like it or not, remain with them. Richert (Brody et al., 1994) suggests that, "As people begin to examine what they do and why they do it — a natural outcome of the research relationship — new doors open whether or not they are invited to open." For this reason, it is important to examine the nature of the research relationship and the responsibility of the one who initiated the research, to inform research colleagues, before they consent to enter into a research partnership, about the possibility of change occurring.

If we wish to do our research in a mindful way, let us give thought to the responsibilities we have within the research relationship to begin conversations with our colleagues about anticipated change. When our research practices are grounded in beliefs about the importance of relationship, fidelity, and caring, these beliefs guide our thinking and the ways in which we engage our co-researchers in conversation.

Confidentiality

The centrality of relationship and conversation to successful collaborative narrative inquiry invites a reconsideration of the notion of confidentiality. In research activities where identities are buried under numbers and within statistical formulae, guarantees of privacy, anonymity, and confidentiality are more easily met than within research activities characterized by face-to-face interactions. And issues of privacy and confidentiality loom even larger when descriptive studies are done closer to home and identities become more difficult to disguise. Traditionally, our response to these issues has been to provide pseudonyms for participants and to change place names. But as Lincoln (1990) reminds us, "It must be remembered that laws and regulations regarding confidentiality, privacy, and anonymity for research respondents were framed under epistemologies and ontologies (i.e. logical positivism and post-positivism) that are now believed to be *inadequate* and indeed, *misleading* for human inquiry" (p. 279).

As we move further and further away from paternalistic research paradigms, we begin to question more and more the need for the old rules governing confidentiality, privacy, and anonymity. When we begin to see research participants in a new way — no longer as subjects needing protection — then we also begin to rethink the rules that govern our relationship. The word *subject* can be traced to the Latin *sub jugere*, meaning to place under the yoke, or to enslave. When the term "subject" is no longer a part of our research language, then we can begin to view our research relationships with practitioners differently. When we think of the counsellors we work with as collaborators and full partners in the research endeavor, we enter into a new working relationship. And within the framework of this new professional relationship, our understanding of what constitutes ethical behavior also changes.

We might begin by examining the way in which we identify both the participants in our studies and the published authors from whose works we have drawn insights. While we identify published authors and researchers in full in our reference list, this courtesy is not extended to the counsellors from whom we have gained as much, if not more, insight as we have gleaned from those whose writing has been published. While we are careful to cite correctly in our references the names of university researchers, writers and others whose works we have used, we are equally careful to hide the names of the counsellors we work with, to ensure confidentiality and to protect their identities. Power is both exercised and acknowledged in the naming or withholding of names in a bibliography. And practitioners, unacknowledged in the references and referred to throughout the text by pseudonyms only, become, as it were, half-objects.

But as the hierarchical relationships of traditional methods of research give way to more collaborative forms of inquiry, where the researcher is no longer seen as having interpretive authority over the persons studied, then it becomes a matter of ethics not to ensure anonymity, but rather to give full naming credit to the co-participants in a study.

Caring Research Practices

It is difficult to predict the moral and ethical quandaries that we might wander into in our research. It is also difficult to know which small decisions will lead to larger dilemmas. Each research setting is bound to give rise to slightly different ethical issues. Although we have a responsibility to attempt to anticipate ethical problems and to conduct ourselves with integrity in the face of problems, we cannot possibly articulate in advance all the ethical dilemmas that might emerge during a study. Neither can we rely on rules and regulations to solve dilemmas arising unexpectedly out of the complex interactions of human relationships. It is the values that undergird our research methods and behaviors toward research participants that can guide us through the complexities of a situation. The ethical guidelines we follow in our personal lives as we deal in caring ways with family and friends can also guide us in our professional work. The ethic of caring, as Noddings (1987) suggests, can become an anchor to throw out whenever we find ourselves in danger of drifting away from persons, relations, and the principles of collaboration in our research work.

Endnotes

[1] Reprinted by permission of the publisher from Schulz, R., Interpreting teacher practice: Two continuing stories, (New York Teachers College Press, c 1997 by Teachers College, Columbia University. All rights reserved.) Selected excerpts from Ch. 5, pp. 81-106.

References

American Educational Research Association, Code of ethics revisions (2000). *Educational Researcher,* 29(3), 40.

Britton, J. (1982). *Language and learning.* Middlesex, England: Penguin.

Brody, C., Schroeder, D., Webb, K., Schulz, R., & Richert, A. (1994, April). *Collaborative narrative inquiry: Fidelity and the ethics of caring in teacher research.* Paper presented at the annual meeting of the American Educational Research Association, New Orleans.

Casey, K. (1996). The new narrative research. In M. W. Apple (Ed.) *Review of Research in Education,* 21, 211-254.

Christiansen, H., Goulet, L., Krentz, C., & Maers, M. (Eds.) (1997). *Recreating relationships: Collaboration and educational reform.* New York: SUNY.

Clandinin, D. J., & Connelly, F. M. (1994). Personal experience methods. In N. K. Denzin & Y. S. Lincoln (Eds.), *Handbook of qualitative research,* 413-427. Thousand Oaks, CA: Sage.

Connelly, F. M., & Clandinin, D. J. (1990). Stories of experience and narrative inquiry. *Educational Researcher,* 19(5), 2-14.

De Marrais, K. B. (Ed.) (1998). *Inside stories: Qualitative research reflections.* Mahwal, New Jersey: Laurence Erlbaum Associates.

Hollingsworth, S. (1992). Learning to teach through collaborative conversation: A feminist approach. *American Education Research Journal,* 29(2), 373-404.

Lincoln, Y. S. (1990). Toward a categorical imperative for qualitative research. In E. Eisner & A. Peshkin (Eds.), *Qualitative inquiry in education: The continuing debate.* New York: Teachers College Press, 277-295.

Noddings, N. (1984). *Caring: A feminine approach to ethics and moral education.* Berkeley: University of California Press.

Noddings, N. (1987). Fidelity in teaching, teacher education, and research for teaching. In M. Okazawa-Rey, J. Anderson, & R. Travers (Eds.), *Teachers, teaching and teacher education.* Cambridge: Harvard Educational Review, 384-398.

Noddings, N. (1991). *Stories in dialogue: Caring and interpersonal reasoning.* In C. Witherell & N. Noddings (Eds.), Stories lives tell: Narrative and dialogue in education. New York: Teachers College Press, 157-170.

Noddings, N. (1992). *The challenge to care in schools: An alternative approach to education.* New York: Teachers College Press.

Punch, M. (1994). Politics and ethics in qualitative research. In N. K. Denzin & Y. S. Lincoln (Eds.), *Handbook of qualitative research.* Thousand Oaks, CA: Sage, 83-97.

Schulz, R. (1997). *Interpreting teaching practice: Two continuing stories.* New York: Teachers College Press.

Singer, I. B. (1976). *Naftali the storyteller and his horse, Sus.* New York: Farrar, Strauss & Giroux.

Stuart, C. A. (1998). Care and concern: An ethical journey in participatory action research. *Canadian Journal of Counselling,* 32(4), 298-313.

The Question of Ethics in Qualitative Research

Paul R. Madak
Sandra L. MacDonald

The Canadian Counselling Association (CCA) in 1999 published a *Code of Ethics* that provides guidance to counsellor practice in clear and concise language. One of the critical areas covered in the ethical code is research. However, the "preamble," recognizes that:

> Although a Code of Ethics is essential to the maintenance of ethical integrity and accountability, it cannot be a substitute for the active process of ethical decision making. Members increasingly confront challenging ethical demands and dilemmas in a complex and dynamic society to which a simple and direct application of this code may not be possible (CCA 1999, p. iii).

Therefore, the purpose of this article is to discuss some of the more complex dilemmas that can occur for the counsellor-researcher when using qualitative methodologies in his or her research. We will discuss these dilemmas rather than offer solutions. The reason for this is that for many of these dilemmas there are no clear-cut solutions. Each ethical dilemma encountered by the counsellor-researcher will be unique depending upon the topic being studied (e.g. sexual abuse, counsellor/client relationships, and group counselling techniques), the informants under study (e.g. clients, parents, teachers, or elementary students), and the context in which information is collected (e.g. classroom, home, playground, or counsellor's office). It is therefore each counsellor-researcher's responsibility to "...develop the ability and courage to exercise a high level of ethical decision making" (CCA 1999, p.iii).

Qualitative research methods establish a much closer working relationship with the individuals under investigation than do quantitative methods. In the quantitative research models the "subjects" are to be viewed from afar with uninvolved objectivity, while in the qualitative models the "informants" are individuals to be observed up close and interacted with (Bogdan & Biklen, 1997; Eisner, 1991; Patton, 1990). It is this closeness to the informants in the qualitative research study that creates "gray areas" that complicates a straightforward interpretation of a code of ethics. Therefore, the uses of qualitative research methods require a more diligent approach to the topic of ethical behavior.

> Because qualitative methods are highly personal and interpersonal, because naturalistic inquiry takes the researcher into the real world where people live and work, and because in-depth interviewing opens up what is inside people — qualitative inquiry may be more intrusive and involve greater reactivity than surveys, tests, and other quantitative approaches (emphasis in original, Patton, 1990, p. 365).

While codes of ethics clearly state the basic guidelines (e.g. informed consent, no harm to the subjects, confidentiality of identity and scores/responses, and honesty in reporting the data), these codes are general in nature and do not deal with ethical issues in any depth, and none provide direction about how to deal with problems that fall in the "gray areas" that are associated with qualitative research practices.

In this article we will identify a few of the ethical dilemmas that should be taken into consideration by the counsellor-researcher before, during, and after the first piece of information is collected. That is, while it is important to attempt to identify possible ethical concerns in the planning stages of a research project, the counsellor-researcher must be prepared to deal with issues that arise during data collection for which an immediate decision is required (Smits et al., 1997). Finally, upon completion of the research, reflection is needed not only to plan for the next study, but also to pass on the experiences to others so that the ethical discussion can be expanded to the larger audience for consideration.

Cultural Diversity and Research Ethics

Respect for cultural diversity is mentioned several times in the CCA *Code of Ethics.* The CCA's commitment to respecting cultural differences is expressed in the preamble, Article B9 dealing with Counselling Relationships, and Article D10 dealing with evaluation and assessment. However, while "... development of ethical codes is desirable, it is important to note that such guidelines are the product of the culture that created them. The guidelines, though necessary, reflect the beliefs and values of that culture" (McCormick, 1998, p. 284).

Ethical codes may not reflect the beliefs and values of other cultures, and researchers must be constantly aware of Articles A9 and B9 (sensitivity to and respecting diversity). Researchers who pay attention to Articles A9 and B9 as well as E2 (the importance of protecting the welfare of the subject), will be in a better position to select the best research methodology to match both the research question and the individuals under study. (Scheurich & Young, 1998, p. 293).

How does a researcher from one culture interpret research data collected from another culture? That is, when a researcher extracts meaning from the stories of the informants from a culture different from their own, will the researcher's cultural background bias the interpretation? What measures must be taken to ensure that the researcher's cultural learning does not bias the interpretative process?

What I wish to suggest here is that ethnic modeling in qualitative research must in-

volve calling into serious question the vast warehouse of knowledge that researchers of European descent have been accumulating and legitimating as way of knowing and seeing. Until we engage in radical efforts to criticize and revise the paradigms underlying qualitative research strategies and, more important, to create and legitimate new ones, the more secondary traditions of critiquing racialized ethnic theories, methods, styles of data interpretation, and patterns of knowledge dissemination will remain grossly incomplete (Stanfield II, 1994, p. 183).

Misinterpretation not only means that the information published is inaccurate, but published, it can also do a great deal of damage to the culture under study when it leads to false generalization about an entire group of people (McCormick, 1998; Smith, 1999).

For the purposes of the following discussion, we have chosen to define "culture" from a broad perspective. From this perspective, culture would include not only the larger racial, ethnic, religious, or societal groups such as European, Canadian, Maori, Catholic, and Métis, but also the disabled culture, local community culture, school culture, and gender. While to discuss all of the issues related to culture and research is too complex to deal with adequately in a short article such as this one, we would like to stimulate researchers' sensitivity to issues of culture by discussing one area of concern.

McCormick (1998) and Smith (1999) wrote of the problems associated with comparing the behaviours of one culture with those of another. We are all products of our own culture, and as such, are incapable of making absolute correct interpretations about behaviours observed in another culture. When we interpret the observed behaviour of others, these interpretations are influenced by the lenses of our gender, age, religion, beliefs, lifestyle, attitudes, and value systems. An example provided by Smith was of white

European men comparing the behaviour of Maori women to that of European women. This type of comparison she writes:

> ....is a dangerous one in two respects: it reduces and decontextualizes Maori values and practices on one hand (in order to make the comparison), and, secondly, it poses unproblematically the normative "reality" of notions such as "women's place" and "domestic spheres" (1999, p. 171).

The point is not that it is impossible to carry-out research with people outside of the cultural experiences, rather the point is that counsellor-researchers must be sensitive to the differences that exist among cultures. Counsellor-researchers must be vigilant to ensure that they are not "seeing and interpreting" observed behaviour through lenses that have been tinted by their own cultural experiences. To help resist this tinting, we suggest two ways to help researchers avoid errors associated with cultural differences. First, we must ensure that the education of researchers includes the teaching of issues related to cultural differences and research methodologies. Second, we support McCormick's (1998) suggestion to involve research assistants and research advisory groups from the culture under study. Both authors have worked with graduate students in counselling programs that have successfully included Aboriginal people, and/or the wisdom of Aboriginal elders to help guide their research. Finally, adding members of the cultural community under study will not only help ensure that interpretations are correct, but it will also provide, "...the necessary role modelling and mentoring that will lead to increased numbers of minority researchers (McCormick, 1998, p. 293). Likewise, counsellor-researchers need to ask the members of the culture under study about how they might interpret the information collected. For example, in her counselling work with Aboriginal youth, the second author was ad-

vised by an elder that, "It is not our tradition to come and talk only about ourselves." This has huge implications for evaluating western European counselling strategies and research methodologies when working with Aboriginal peoples.

Informed Consent

Articles E2, E4 and E5 of the CCA *Code of Ethics* for counsellors states that counsellor-researchers are responsible for the welfare of their subjects, ensuring that participation in research is voluntary and informing the potential participant of the true purposes of the research study. The concept of informed consent means that the individual(s) under study not only completely understands what is expected of them, but also the possible consequences of having taken part in the study. For example, does the individual who agrees to take part in a qualitative study understand that the nature of qualitative studies is such that the researcher is always "on"? That is, does the individual realize that the comments she or he makes while having coffee, or at lunch, are considered by the qualitative researcher to be legitimate data, and that this information might be included in the final report? Furthermore, was it explained to the individual that in qualitative studies the researcher acts more like a friend then a researcher, and that this "friendship" type of relationship may result in the individual revealing secrets that they never intended to reveal, let alone find that they have been published for the world to see? A researcher who has good interpersonal skills can develop a client-counsellor relationship built and bonded by trust. This can result in far more intimate information being provided then the informant originally anticipated.

> In short, researchers can take advantage of a quasi-therapeutic relationship because of the attractiveness of one of our most treasured gifts to others—the gift of lending serious attention and a sympathetic ear

to what someone has to tell us (Eisner, 1991, p. 218).

When researchers request the involvement of non-researchers in a study, we cannot assume that the non-researchers will understand all the subtleties of their agreement to take part. A researcher who is also a counsellor has to be particularly cautious as she or he has specialized skills, which could be used to take advantage of a trusting volunteer. This issue can be further complicated when individuals from minority cultures are involved. That is, do the potential participants really understand the language or terms being used by the counsellor-researcher? Unfortunately, there are research projects that do not attempt to account for the subtleties found in the terminology common in the culture of the counsellor-researcher.

A second issue regarding the concept of informed consent concerns Article E6, which states that it is the responsibility of the counsellor-researcher to protect, "...unless otherwise authorized...," the identity of the individual who has agreed to participate in the research project (CCA 1999, p. 13-14). However, in qualitative research, the researcher pays close attention to the context in which the information was collected and therefore provides readers with a detailed description of the environment under study. Because of this detailed description, there is the real risk that someone will be able to recognize and identify the informant(s). Most researchers do not discuss this risk factor with their informants before signing them on as part of the study. This risk is especially high when a unique program, environment, or individual is under investigation. For example, the first author served as a member of a thesis committee for a student who conducted a qualitative study on a female badminton player who was ranked third in the world. While every effort was made to hide the identity of this individual (the year of the ranking was

kept secret as well as some other key factors), there was still a very strong possibility that someone would recognize her from the description provided in the study. In fact, while no one knew who this person was at the time, three years later when reading the sports section of the local newspaper, I came across an in-depth interview with a female badminton player and, from the information provided, was able to identify her as the informant of the thesis. While this may be an extreme case, it points to the importance of providing information about the possible risks of being identified once the material is made public.

A third issue concerns the interpretation of the events as recorded by the counsellor-researcher. Dockrell (1988) and Eisner (1991) suggested that the participants of a study be given the opportunity to read the material that has been written about them.

The purpose of doing this is twofold. First, it allows participants to review the material for misquotes and/or misinterpretations of the behavior under observation. However, the degree to which the researcher is willing to make changes to the material, if a participant objects to it, is open for debate. That is, if the researcher feels that she or he really heard or saw what was reported, then the text should not be altered just to please the participant. Altering accurate information might change the outcome of the study, and thus lead the researcher to make inaccurate conclusions. On the other hand, if a mistake has been made in recording the raw data, then it is the responsibility of the researcher to make the requested changes in order to prevent inaccurate conclusions. However, how does one tell the difference? There are no easy answers to this issue; it is a dilemma that must be addressed by the individual researcher based on the information and contextual factors on hand.

The second point concerns allowing the informants to be the first to read material that may place them in an unfavorable light.

It is much better for informants to have at least a warning that unfavorable information is about to be released about them. Lightfoot (1983) suggested that respondents go through several stages when they come face-to-face with written accounts of their actions. In the first stage, there is the terror associated with having been exposed for the world to judge. The second stage is characterized by the respondents alternating between recognizing themselves in the description, to denying that the individual being described has any resemblance to them. Finally, after a period of time, respondents are able to look at the description more dispassionately and view it as a means for reflection, self-criticism, and personal growth. Given this process, Lightfoot's stages suggest that it is much better if respondents are allowed to view material before it becomes public information.

A number of years ago, during the first author's tenure as a research consultant for a local school district, he was witness to a number of situations in which outside researchers reported information that did not show the district in a positive light. He found that when the district's administration and teachers had been given advanced copies of the material, the response, while not all love and warmth, was at least one of tolerance. They were able to prepare a response to the material, or to at least formulate and have ready a plan as to how they were going to alter the conditions that produced the unfavorable information. However, when the district read unflattering information in the media first, the reaction was always one of anger and total rejection of the information. In fact, in one extreme case when the district found out about negative information through phone calls from the media asking them to explain data they had never seen, the researchers involved were "unofficially" banned from carrying out further research within the district's schools. Furthermore, the

district totally rejected valuable information that might have assisted them in improving the quality of education. In short, the method used to inform the district of the results of the study resulted in an emotional reaction to the information. The main focus of this emotional reaction was based on the district's need to protect the system from outside attack.

The fourth and final issue to be discussed, concerning informed consent, deals with the "innocent bystanders." Innocent bystanders are individuals in a qualitative study, who come into contact with the individual under study, but who themselves are not the focus of the study. Here the question becomes: How far should informed consent be taken? If you are observing a particular informant, do you also need the consent of the individuals who might interact with your informant? In the example of the female badminton player presented earlier, should the researcher have obtained permission from her husband, children, parents, in-laws, friends and the players (who were under legal age of consent at the time) she coached? Some of our colleagues have made the case that obtaining the consent of these "innocent bystanders" is unnecessary because they are not the direct objective of the study. On the other hand, other colleagues have argued that the intrusive nature of qualitative research demands that informed consent applies to all contacts. In the case of the female badminton player, informed consent was obtained from the husband, but not from the other individuals. It was felt by the researcher and the thesis advisor that the privacy of the other individuals was not being invaded as their actions were not being recorded, only those of the badminton player. However, permission was obtained from the husband as the interactions between him and his wife were under direct study. That is, one of the research questions dealt with the interaction between the female athlete and her spouse. Was this a correct decision? We are not sure. This type of dilemma points to the importance of the researcher carefully weighing all the pros and cons of the situation before making a judgment.

Smits et al. (1997) in their paper on qualitative ethical dilemmas raised a second issue around "innocent bystanders." Briefly, they asked about the ethics concerning the publishing of opinions, complaints, and criticisms of one side of an issue while excluding a response by the other side? Going back to the example of the female badminton player: What if the researcher had collected and written-up information indicating that the husband had not been supportive of her, while not including the husband's side of the story? Given the importance qualitative research gives to providing the complete context in which an event takes, does the researcher have the right to publish a portrayal of the husband when he did not participate in the study? Plus, what is the responsibility of the researcher given that publishing this criticism from only one perspective might lead to personal conflicts between a wife and her husband?

Confidentiality

As was presented above, Article E6 states that it is the responsibility of the counsellor-researcher to protect, "...unless otherwise authorized...," the identity of the individual who has agreed to participate in the research project (CCA 1999, p. 13-14). The concept of confidentiality postulates that the individual(s) under study has a right to his or her privacy and thus the researcher has the responsibility to protect that identity (e.g. Bogdan & Biklen, 1997; McMillian & Schumacher, 1997; Palys, 1992; Shulman, 1990). The information collected in studies on sexual abuse or divorce may be information that respondents are willing to share with the researcher as long as their identity is not revealed to the general public. In fact, in some

cases the identification of the respondents may be very costly to them in terms of placing them in physical danger (e.g. a husband who physically abuses his wife to punish her for disclosing information) or may cost them their jobs (e.g. a teacher who provides negative information about a principal/superintendent). In both of these cases, the disclosure of the informant's identity can result in harm being done to him or her. If harm were done, then the number one ethical rule of "no harm to the subjects" would also be violated.

However, what if the respondent does not want to remain anonymous? Article E11 states that it is the responsibility of the counsellor-researcher to, "...give due credit through joint authorship, acknowledgment, footnote statements, or other appropriate means to those who have contributed significantly to the research and/or publication..." (CCA 1999, p. 14). Unlike quantitative methods, where research subjects simply respond to surveys, questionnaires, standardized tests or other procedures that require only a response, an individual(s) taking part in qualitative investigations contributes a great deal of his or her time, energy and personal thoughts to the researcher playing an active role in the research process. In fact, in a qualitative design, the individuals taking part in the investigation often play an important role in the formation of the research question(s) and interpretation of the data collected. Therefore, given this added involvement, these individuals are beginning to express the desire to be publicly recognized and given credit for their accomplishments and contributions to the research study.

Shulman (1990) was the first to point out that this desire for recognition has implications for how researchers deal with the ethical requirement of confidentiality. To simply identify all those who request to be identified avoids dealing with the rights of others. For example, if a counsellor requests to be identified, what are the effects of such identification on the institution that employs her or him? Furthermore, what are the possible effects on the rights of that counsellor's colleagues and clients? What if one of the participants wants to be identified, but the other participants do not? These are serious questions that cannot be ignored, because the identification of one individual may mean that the anonymity of the institution (e.g. school and/or school district, public service organization), other counsellors, and clients cannot be guaranteed. The dilemma arises in attempting to determine how the identification of one informant will affect other informants, and to what extent are we obligated to protect those who are on the periphery of our study (e.g. the institution or those who make use of the institution's services).

It would appear that one possible method of handling these dilemmas is to carry out multilevel negotiations that include all the affected stakeholders. This would ensure that all parties are given an opportunity for their opinions to be heard, and if a compromise cannot be reached, then those who feel threatened can be given the chance to withdraw from the study. It is the responsibility of the researcher to ensure that the rights of all parties are respected. However, we agree with Shulman when she stated:

> Some colleagues have urged me to propose a set of general principles or rules of thumb for dealing with such dilemmas in the future. I do not believe that general principles are of much use in these situations. These circumstances represent a serious tangle of competing ethical obligations complicated by political realities. They are best handled on a case-by-case basis, through negotiation and deliberation among all of the relevant stakeholders. (1990, p. 14-15)

Since research studies vary greatly with regards to the individuals studied, topics studied, research methods utilized, and pertinent political issues, the establishment of general principles would be of little value. Instead, what needs to happen is that all researchers must accept the obligation to carefully identify all parties who will be affected by the planned study, and then to make decisions that best fit the current situation.

A second issue, or dilemma, concerns the question of whether there are any circumstances in which a counsellor-researcher can ethically break the ethical requirement of confidentially. Clearly, there are such situations. For example, if a school-age student discloses that she or he has been, or is currently being sexually or physically abused, the researcher is required by law to file a report with the proper child protection agency or with the police. However, should the counsellor-researcher file a report with the proper professional organization if he or she observes a counsellor who is inept or who is using questionable counselling techniques? Or, in the interest of gathering information on counselling, which would be of benefit to the larger community of counsellors, should the counsellor-researcher ignore the behavior and protect the identity of the participant? Eisner (1991) pointed out the other side of the coin by asking: What if the researcher discovers someone who is doing great work, but whose work has gone unrecognized? "In other words, is the obligation, if it is an obligation, to commend as important as to give negative criticism?" (Eisner, 1991, p. 219). These are questions for which there are no easy answers, but which require the researcher's careful attention. Patton (1990) has stated that the researcher should develop a personal ethical framework for dealing with the possible occurrence of these events before beginning the research process. Waiting until an event or dilemma arises may place the counsellor-researcher in the difficult situation of trying to make a complex decision quickly without the luxury of having time to completely think out all the possible consequences of a particular option. Furthermore, by having a pre-established ethical framework, the researcher is more likely to have completely informed the participants of what their involvement in the research project might entail.

Finally, Douvanis and Brown (1995) point out that, "The concepts of confidentiality and privileged communication are frequently and incorrectly used interchangeably" (p. 27). The term privileged communication applies to information provided to lawyers, clergy, doctors, and psychologists, but not to researchers. "Confidentiality is an ethical principal in which one agrees that information given by one party will not be shared with others without consent. In general, confidentiality is controlled by custom with specific professions or organizations, or in written codes of ethics or agreement between researcher and the subject" (Douvanis & Brown, 1995, p. 27-28). Douvanis and Brown, and Patton (1990) warn researchers that they do not have the same legal protection that clergy and lawyers have, and therefore can be summoned to testify in court. Knowledge about activities such as the use and selling of illegal chemicals may be behaviours that local law enforcement agencies may request or demand. In these situations, the researcher is required to testify in court, regardless of a promise to keep such information confidential.

Participation as a Positive Experience

While taking part in a research study should be a positive experience for both the counsellor-researcher and the selected participants, there are many situations where this is not the case. A few years ago, the first author was working with two students who were doing thesis work in the area of sexual abuse. In the design stages of each of these research projects, we had to be aware of the likelihood that the process of interviewing female volunteers would touch on, not only very

personal and sensitive information, but also emotionally painful memories. Therefore, as part of the overall research designs in each of these projects, a debriefing session was added to the research process to deal with the possibility of the emergence of disclosure reactions. These debriefing sessions allowed the informants to make closure and provided them with a list of available counselling services. Furthermore, a process was developed that allowed for the termination of any interview session that was becoming too stressful for the informant. This later provision was, for the most part, a judgment call for the researchers to make. That is, what is too stressful for one individual might not be too stressful for another. It places the counsellor-researcher in the awkward situation of being part interviewer and part counsellor. This situation is awkward because the respondents are already in a counselling relationship, and thus, entering a second counselling situation could lead to a violation of ethical practice. While the information collected might help other victims of sexual abuse, we believed that is was not important enough to place the informant in an unreasonably stressful situation. How much stress was reasonable, and when did the interview stop being an interview and turn into a counselling session? This was a question that each of these two student-researchers had to ask, and answer, during every interview session. While we spent a great deal of time talking about this issue amongst ourselves and with other colleagues, the bottom line was that each student-researcher had to make this judgment for each informant. While, both student-researchers stated that the pre-data collection discussions helped them make the necessary decisions, it did not make the decisions easier.

Discussions were also held with the student-researchers to talk about how they would deal with questions they received. That is, what if one of the respondents asked for advice concerning reporting the sexual abuse to the police? Or, what if the respondent asked for advice concerning whether their current counsellor was providing them with quality treatment? It is very easy for the respondent to turn the interview around and make the researcher the interviewee. The problem of how to deal ethically with the questions of the respondent need to be worked out carefully before the first interview takes place. Once in the field, it is too late to say "time-out, while I go and get advice."

> The process of being taken through a directed, reflective process affects the persons being interviewed and leaves them knowing things about themselves that they didn't know — or at least were not aware of — before the interviews. Two hours or more of thoughtfully reflecting on an experience, a program, or one's life can be change inducing (Patton, 1990, p. 353-354).

This "change-inducing" process applies not only to the respondent, but also to the counsellor-researcher who is collecting the information and playing the role of empathic listener. In addition to the above procedure, which was developed for the respondents of the study, the design also included debriefing and support for the student-researchers to deal with issues of secondary, or, retraumatization. As was recommended by Patton (1990), a process was needed so that the student-researchers could deal with the things they heard. Given the atmosphere for negative information concerning the women they were listening to, the student-researchers in the above example needed to have a support network in place to deal with the pain and suffering they were hearing about.

In the example presented above, it is relatively easy to see the need for debriefing sessions, but there are other situations where the counsellor-researcher may not have predicted a need for such sessions, but for which they are needed, or should at least be planned for just in case. For example, a counsellor-researcher could be interviewing counsellors about their work experiences, and in the process of the interview, discover that some of them are suffering from "burnout" or from some other emotional problem. This disclosure can happen because of the intimate and trusting relationship that is desirable and fostered in interviewing situations. In order to obtain the most reliable and valid data, interviewers are trained in much the same way as counsellors are, in terms of questioning and listening techniques. Another situation can arise in which the interviewee asks the interviewer for advice. For example, in an evaluation study of a program for young children aged four- to-six years-old that the first author was conducting, the parents being interviewed would often ask interviewers for advice on discipline problems or problems concerning older children not included in the project. In short, it is difficult to predict what will happen in an interview situation, and, therefore, the researcher must always be prepared to handle the unexpected.

Handling Raw Data

In qualitative research, it is the written word that gives meaning to that which is heard and observed. Though the process of writing, the researcher selects, develops a theme, categorizes, and interprets what is seen and heard. The concern here is that the product of this process is a written description published in a journal, book or manuscript. While this process may establish meaning, has something been lost in the translation? That is, "It is a way of ordering the world, but also a way that carries the danger of reducing complexity and lived quality of that world into conceptual categories" (Smits et al., 1997, p. 201). Bringhurst (1999) made the analogy that the taking of oral or viewed behaviour and putting it into words on paper, is akin to attempting to understand the complexity of jazz from reading the written notes on a page of sheet music. In short, "something" is lost in the translation, and that "something" may be the essence of what is being studied. From an ethical perspective, the question that confronts the qualitative counsellor-researcher is, "Have I honestly and as completely as possible represented the stories I have seen or been told?" A negative reply to this question, not only means that "something" has been lost, it means that the readers may have been given misleading or incorrect information (McCormick, 1998; Smith, 1999). This question is of particular importance when the counsellor-researcher is studying a culture that is different from her or his own. The counsellor-researcher who studies people from a culture different from his or her own must keep in mind that the individuals under study are "...likely to have different ways of seeing the world" (McCormick, 1998, p. 284).

Dockrell (1988, p. 184) stated that "Research data are not private property. They are an individual's contribution to a common wealth of knowledge and understanding." A common research practice has been that researchers make their raw data available for at least five years after publication. This allows others to examine the original data set and to either re-analyse the data or to carry out further analyses.

When dealing with quantitative data, it is fairly easy to keep the original data that was used in the data-analysis process without fear of giving away the identity of the individual subjects. All the researcher has to do is to provide a code number for each individual in the data set. However, when using qualitative methods, it is much more difficult to hide the identities of the informants. The field notes and interviews will contain a great deal of specific information about individuals and their environment, which will make it all but impossible to keep the identities of

the participants confidential. Going through the material and removing all identifying information (e.g. names of individuals, places) is time consuming and may, in some cases, change the data. Therefore, the requirement by many university ethics committees is for researchers to destroy original documents containing subject names and other personal information once that information is no longer valid. Furthermore, the extent to which the researcher "blackens out" or replaces information with codes, abbreviations or letter designates, will be an individual one made according to the characteristics of each specific situation. Again, it comes down to the fact that it is the responsibility of the researcher to carefully review all the possible ethical dilemmas, and to make the best possible decisions based on the specific characteristics of the situation.

Conclusions

The purpose of this article is to review some of the ethical dilemmas associated with conducting qualitative research. Specifically, the purpose is to indicate that the codes of ethics, no matter how clearly stated, are unable to address all of the issues that may develop in the course of conducting a qualitative research study.

> Despite efforts to conduct qualitative educational research under strict ethical guidelines, in the course of conducting research and its reporting, there frequently emerges a surplus of ethical concerns. Such concerns are not necessarily anticipated by research protocols and guidelines. They happen despite conscientiously conducting research according to established norms (Smits et al., 1997, p. 193).

The basic conclusion that can be reached from the material presented here is that, in the long run, it is the responsibility of each counsellor-researcher to carefully review her or his research procedures to ensure those participants, subjects, and informants are not harmed either purposefully or accidentally. While all researchers agree to the importance of being guided by ethical principles, deciding what those principles should be for every situation can be a difficult, if not impossible task. In order to help maintain ethical standards, researchers should seek the advice of colleagues, ethics committees (e.g. at the university, professional organization, school district) and the potential participants, subjects, and informants themselves.

> But there are few right and wrong answers; the process is always one of weighing advantages and disadvantages. On the one hand, we have the contribution that a given piece of research might directly or indirectly make to knowledge and human welfare. On the other hand, there is the cost that doing this research entails to the human research participant. The general ethical question is thus always *whether there is a negative upon the dignity and welfare of the participants that the importance of research does not warrant.* Stated in other terms, any prospect of harm to research participants had better have a strong and explicit justification (emphasis in original, Palys, 1992, p. 96).

It is only though personal vigilance that each of us will avoid making ethical mistakes when we use qualitative research methods as part of our study of people, places and events. To avoid errors in judgement, we must view research as a "living practice" (Carson & Sumara, 1997), and not only reflect on what we are doing, but also continually discuss issues related to research ethics with our peers and participants.

References

Bogdan, R. C., & Biklen, S. K. (1997). *Qualitative research for education: An introduction to theory and methods* (3rd. ed.). Paramus: Prentice Hall.

Bringhurst, R. (1999). *A story as sharp as a knife: The classical Haida mythtellers and their world.* Vancouver: Douglas & Macintyre.

Canadian Counselling Association (1999). *Code of ethics.* Ottawa: Author.

Carson, T., and Sumara, D. (1997). *Action research as a living practice.* New York: Peter Lang.

Dockrell, W. B. (1988). Ethical considerations in research. In J. P. Keeves (Ed.), *Educational research methodology, and measurement: An international handbook* (pp. 180-185). Toronto: Pergamon Press.

Douvanis, G., and Brown, J. (1995). Privileged communication in educational research: The case for statutory protection. *Educational Researcher,* 24(5), 27-30.

Eisner, E. W. (1991). *The enlightened eye: Qualitative inquiry and the enhancement of educational practice.* Toronto: Collier Macmillan Canada, Inc.

Lightfoot, S. L. (1983). *The good high school: Portraits of character and culture.* New York: Basic Books.

McCormick, R. M. (1998). Ethical considerations in First Nations counselling and research. *Canadian Journal of Counselling,* 32(4), 284-297.

McIntosh, P. (1990). White privilege: Unpacking the invisible knapsack, *Independent School, Winter,* 31-36.

McMillian, J. H. & Schumacher, S. (1997). *Research in education: A conceptual introduction.* (4th ed.). Don Mills: Longman.

Palys, T. (1992). *Research decisions: Quantitative and qualitative perspectives.* Toronto: Harcourt Brace Jovanovich Canada Inc.

Patton, M. Q. (1990). *Qualitative evaluation and research methods* (2nd. ed.). Newbury Park: Sage Publications, Inc.

Scheurich, J. J., & Young, M. D.(1997). Coloring epistemologies: Are our research epistemologies racially biased? *Educational Researcher,* 26(4), 4-16.

Shulman, J. H. (1990). Now you see them, now you don't: Anonymity versus visibility in case studies of teachers. *Educational Researcher,* 19(6), 11-15.

Smith, L. T. (1999). *Decolonizing methodologies: Research and indigenous peoples.* New York: Zed Books Ltd.

Smits, H., Friesen, D., Hicks, N., and Leroy, C. (1997). Encountering obligation in qualitative educational research: A postmodern perspective. *The Alberta Journal of Educational Research, XLIII* (4), 192-206.

Stanfield II, J. H. (1994). Ethnic modeling in qualitative research. In N. Denzin & Y. Lincoln (Eds.), *Handbook of qualitative research* (pp. 175-188). Thousand Oaks: Sage Publications.

Chapter Seven

———— ❖ ————

Counsellor Education, Training and Supervision

———— ❖ ————

Counsellor-educators are in a unique position of not only teaching and discussing ethical guidelines, but also modelling ethical responsibilities. These ethical responsibilities are presented in the cases, discussions, questions and essays in this chapter

❖ ❖ ❖ ❖ ❖ ❖ ❖ ❖ ❖ ❖ ❖ ❖ ❖ ❖

ETHICAL ARTICLES ON COUNSELLOR EDUCATION, TRAINING AND SUPERVISION

F1 **General Responsibility**
Counsellors who are responsible for counsellor education, training, and supervision adhere to current CCA guidelines and standards with respect to such activities and conduct themselves in a manner consistent with the CCA *Code of Ethics* and Standards of Practice.

❖

F2 **Boundaries of Competence**
Counsellors who conduct counsellor education, training, and supervision have the necessary knowledge and skills to do so, and limit their involvement to such competencies.

❖

F3 **Ethical Orientation**
Counsellors who are responsible for counsellor education, training, and supervision have an obligation to make their students, trainees, and supervisees aware of their ethical responsibilities as expressed in the CCA *Code of Ethics*, and Standards of Practice.

❖

F4 **Clarification of Roles and Responsibilities**
Counsellors who engage in counselling supervision of students or trainees take responsibility for clarifying their respective roles and obligations.

❖

F5 **Welfare of Clients**
Counsellors who engage in counselling supervision of students or trainees take steps to ensure the welfare of clients during the supervised practice period, and intervene, when necessary, to ensure that this obligation is met.

F6 Program Orientation

Counsellors responsible for counsellor education programs and training activities take responsibility to orient perspective students and trainees to all core elements of such programs and activities, including to a clear policy with respect to all supervised practice components, both those simulated and real.

F7 Relational Boundaries

Counsellors who work as counsellor-educators, trainers, and supervisors establish relationships with their students, trainees, and supervisees such that appropriate relational boundaries are clarified and maintained, and dual relationships avoided.

F8 Obligation to Inform

Counsellors who work as counsellor-educators, trainers, and supervisors take steps to inform students, trainees, and supervisees, at the beginning of activities associated with these roles, of all reasonably foreseeable circumstances under which confidentiality may be breached during such activities.

F9 Self-Development and Self-Awareness

Counsellors who work as counsellor-educators, trainers, and supervisors, encourage and facilitate the self-development and self-awareness of students, trainees, and supervisees, so that they learn to integrate their professional practice and personal insight.

F10 Dealing With Personal Issues

Counsellors responsible for counsellor education, training, and supervision-recognize when such activities evoke significant personal issues for students, trainees, and supervisees and refer to other sources when necessary to avoid counselling those for whom they hold administrative or evaluative responsibility.

F11 Self-Growth Activities

Counsellors who work as counsellor-educators, trainors, and supervisors ensure that any professional experiences, which require self-disclosure and engagement in self-growth activities, are managed in a manner consistent with the principles of informed consent, confidentiality, and safeguarding against any harmful effects.

❖ ❖ ❖ ❖ ❖ ❖ ❖ ❖ ❖ ❖ ❖ ❖ ❖ ❖

CASE STUDIES IN COUNSELLOR EDUCATION, TRAINING AND SUPERVISION

| F1 | **GENERAL RESPONSIBILITY** Counsellors who are responsible for counsellor education, training, and supervision adhere to current CCA guidelines and standards with respect to such activities and conduct themselves in a manner consistent with the CCA *Code of Ethics* and Standards of Practice. |

CCA Position Paper (+)

A counsellor-educator phoned the CCA headquarters in Ottawa indicating that her department was reorganizing their counsellor-education program and they wanted to have the latest position of the CCA on training. The counsellor-educator was informed that the CCA *Position Paper for the Provision of Counselling Services in Canada* would be mailed to her. She was also told that Canadian Counsellor Certification requirements consisted of a graduate degree in counselling, a counselling theories course, a supervised counselling practicum and graduate course work in any six of the following areas: communication and relationship skills, group counselling, career development, assessment and testing, research and evaluation, consultation methods, learning and human development, psychological education, counselling intervention strategies, counselling girls and women, multi-cultural counselling and counselling in specialized settings.

CCA Accreditation (+)

At a meeting of the CCA board of directors, several counsellor-educators presented their proposal for accreditation of university counsellor-training programs.

These accreditation principles and guidelines were based on the CCA *Position Paper* on counsellor preparation. When asking for volunteers to pilot the accreditation procedures, four counsellor-educators from different Canadian universities offered to have their counsellor-education program go through the pilot accreditation process.

Counselling Practicum (-)

One university with a small number of counsellor-educators admits many graduate students to its counselling program. Nearly all the students are teachers or counsellors who plan to take all the courses during the summer months when they have vacation. Since a counselling field experience is not offered during the summer, these counsellors complete their program of studies without ever being supervised in an actual counselling situation.

Program Philosophy (-)

A school counsellor, interested in further graduate studies, phoned the department head of a counsellor-education program in a neighbouring province regarding the philosophy, admission requirements and other program specifics. The department head provided some information regarding admission and courses, but when asked whether their program followed the guidelines for training suggested by the CCA, the department head indicated he was not familiar with the CCA *Position Paper* or certification regulations.

COMMENTS AND QUESTIONS

The purpose of the CCA *Position Paper for the Provision of Counselling Services in Canada* is "to provide a statement of the basic needs of Canadians and the services which should be provided through CCA members in order to meet these needs..." Within a developmental perspective, Van Hestern and Pawlovich, the authors of the CCA *Position Paper*, identify human needs from infancy through middle childhood, adolescence, early adulthood, middle age and later maturity. They feel it is the challenge of all counsellors to become more developmentally focussed in their counselling orientation.

The CCA *Position Paper* also identifies people in Canadian society with particular needs. These groups include: female clients, single persons, exceptional clients and the handicapped, Aboriginals, prison inmates, unemployed people, apprentices, and immigrants.

Finally, Van Hestern and Pawlovich set a challenge for all counsellors: namely, to acquire "cultural awareness and to develop a critical consciousness of the social, economic, political, and technological factors and processes which either facilitate or impede optimal human development."

1. Should all university departments offering degree programs in counsellor education offer programs that reflect the course work and practica suggested in the CCA *Position Paper* and certification regulations?

2. What are your opinions regarding accreditation of counsellor-training programs in Canada?

3. Is the CCA *Position Paper* too general? Does it help clarify the position for specific groups of counsellors such as family and marriage counsellors, school counsellors or career counsellors?

4. Do you agree with the CCA certification requirements for counsellors: namely, a practicum, a counselling theories course and course work in six additional counselling-related areas?

5. What additional counselling courses would you add to the present CCA list?

F2 BOUNDARIES OF COMPETENCE
Counsellors who conduct counsellor education, training, and supervision have the necessary knowledge and skills to do so, and limit their involvement to such competencies.

Improved Teaching (+)
Because of complaints of poor teaching in this department of counselling psychology, the department head invited several professors from different departments (known to be excellent teachers), to offer a series of lectures and demonstrations on "effective college teaching."

Counselling Skills (+)
A professor had just been granted a year-long sabbatical leave. In applying for this leave, he had had some difficulty convincing the university administration that he wanted to devote time during this year not only to research and publication, but also to improving his skills as a counselling practitioner. He was convinced that if he improved his counselling skills by becoming involved in counselling others and receiving feedback on his counselling, he would be in a better position to help students in subsequent years when he taught the counselling-skills courses.

Outdated (-)
A professor in counsellor education regularly teaches an introductory course on the role, function and services of high school counsellors. Since this professor has seldom been in a high school since she left her high school counselling position 20 years ago, she continues to talk about the role and function of counsellors in the seventies and early eighties. All her examples are drawn from what she did in her high school many years ago.

Lack of Specialized Skills (-)
A counselling department has begun teaching courses and offering a supervised practicum in the area of family and marriage counselling. The backgrounds of the three counsellor-educators in the department are all in other areas such as career, school or crisis counselling. Nevertheless, the department head assigns one of the counsellor-educators to teach and supervise the practicum in family counselling.

COMMENTS AND QUESTIONS
In a 1991 study by Stuart Smith's Commission of Inquiry on Canadian University Education, Smith claimed that "the best teacher in the world given a poor or non-existent research record, has little or no chance of promotion at most of the research-intensive universities." On the other hand, Smith added, "a truly terrible teacher" with an excellent research record will be promoted. Many professors agreed with this report saying that there was no personal payoff to spend time on teaching well. In addition, several professors indicated that in spite of the fact that they had received only fair teaching evaluations, and their university had a service where they could receive help in improving their teaching, they would not take advantage of this service, feeling that the time was better spent on "writing another article." Nevertheless, it is of vital importance that counsellor-educators not only become competent teachers, but that they are successful practitioners who can demonstrate their counselling skills and can give personal examples of counselling effectiveness. Research/study leaves for counsellor-educators are readily available in most Canadian universities, but typically counsellor-educators decide, during their leaves, to do research rather than improve their teaching or practitioner skills.

1. In smaller counsellor-education departments, counsellor-educators through necessity may be required to teach outside their area of expertise. Is this acceptable?

2. What should universities do to encourage better teaching?

3. What recommendations would you make regarding the improvement of the practitioner skills of counsellor-educators?

4. Should counsellor-educators be required to be practitioners as well?

5. When hiring new counsellor-educators, what can the search committees do to ensure that they are getting skilled teachers and practitioners?

F3 ETHICAL ORIENTATION

Counsellors who are responsible for counsellor education, training, and supervision have an obligation to make their students, trainees, and supervisees aware of their ethical responsibilities as expressed in the CCA *Code of Ethics*, and Standards of Practice.

Course in Ethics (+)

This university has introduced a new course entitled "Legal and Ethical Issues in Counselling." The course is compulsory for all students in counselling. The course is taught by an acknowledged expert in the area of legal and ethical counselling issues.

Ethics Workshop (+)

One university provides all students with the CCA *Code of Ethics* during the first class of its compulsory introductory course in counselling. As well, a three-hour workshop is provided, which includes small group discussion on such issues as "confidentiality" and "danger" to self and others, an opportunity to discuss other articles in the CCA *Code of Ethics*, and a chance to examine ethical cases of interest to the students.

Ethics De-Emphasized (-)

The counselling program at one Canadian university does not have any course on ethical issues in counselling. Nor is the topic of ethics discussed or presented in any of the other counselling and related courses. Students are encouraged, however, to read the chapter on ethics in their introductory counselling course — "although," says the professor, "it will not be on your final test."

Practicum Experience (-)

A graduate student in a counselling practicum informs her practicum supervisor at the university of some of the practices of the counsellor she is working with in a high school. The male school counsellor at times gives female students back and neck massages in his office. The practicum supervisor does not discuss this with the graduate student and dismisses the issue by saying it is the school's business.

COMMENTS AND QUESTIONS

Stated in the preamble to the CCA *Code of Ethics* is the following:

> Members of CCA have a responsibility to ensure that they are familiar with this *Code of Ethics*, understand its application to their professional conduct, and strive to adhere to its principles and values. Counsellors should also be familiar with other sources of information which will assist them in making informed professional decisions. These include: the laws, regulations, and policies which are professionally relevant to their working environment.

Counsellor-educators have the further responsibility of teaching counselling students the issues around counselling ethics. Basic principles on which the CCA *Code of Ethics* is based, must be examined and understood. These principles are:

a) respect for the dignity of persons,

b) not willfully harming others,

c) integrity in relationships,

d) responsible caring,

e) responsibility to society, and

f) respect for self-determination.

1. Which ethical principles (just listed) would you want to change?

2. Should all counsellor-education programs offer a required course or courses in ethics?

3. What are the best ways of educating students regarding their ethical responsibilities and the standards of the counselling profession?

4. What values would you wish to maximize in any given situation?

5. Can we, or should we, prioritize values and principles in ethical decision making?

F4   CLARIFICATION OF ROLES AND RESPONSIBILITIES

Counsellors who engage in counselling supervision of students or trainees take responsibility for clarifying their respective roles and obligations.

Supervisor's Role (+)

Manny Lopez, a counsellor-educator in a Canadian university, was supervising his first group of counselling students in a practicum. He took to heart what he had recalled from his own training: namely, that as supervisor he was ultimately responsible for all the practicum trainees. Before the first practicum class, he contacted all the students and informed them of his expectations of them, and his own supervisory procedures. Among the things discussed were his training objectives, amount and type of feedback, assessment procedures, caseload requirements, classroom expectations and evaluation criteria.

Supervised Practicum (+)

One counsellor-educator feels it is extremely important for students to have a good understanding of counselling philosophy, counselling theory, psychological assessment and counselling techniques before students are placed in a supervised counselling practice situation. To make sure that he will have time to do intensive supervision of counselling practice, he arranges for all these aforementioned academic subjects to be scheduled in the first semester so that he can devote most of his time in the second semester for on-site supervision of students. He arranges weekly meetings for each student as well as a seminar for the whole practicum group, where students can discuss their philosophies and theories in light of the realities of their practice.

No Clarification of Supervisory Roles (-)

Evelyn Ducharme, a counsellor-educator, appeared to be much more interested in her research project than she was in meeting her obligations in supervising her students in the counselling practicum. She asked the six students in her practicum class to arrange their own supervision in the field, and do the type of counselling being done at the counselling centre that accepts them.

Counsellor or Supervisor (-)

Jill Field was a new collaborating counsellor for counsellor trainees from the major university in her city. She devoted much time in getting to know her counselling student, Samantha. As trust grew between the two, Samantha told Jill all about the many personal problems she was facing in her family and the many difficulties she was experiencing with the man whom she was living with at this time. Samantha was very upset when Jill, in her formative report to her university supervisor, wrote that "relationship problems with her family and boyfriend are getting in the way of Samantha being an effective counsellor."

COMMENTS AND QUESTIONS

The last case presented illustrates the difficulties that can arise when the roles of trainees, counsellor-educators, and collaborating counsellors in the field are not clearly stated. Close, trusting relationships should not get in the way of the responsibility that a supervisor has in evaluating trainees. On the other hand, using the personal problems that a trainee has as the reason for an inferior counselling report does a great disservice to the trainee. The roles and responsibilities of trainees, counsellor-educators and collaborating counsellors need to be clarified and understood by all before the practicum begins. Trainees need to know the amount of time or number of clients they must see. Clear

instructions on record keeping and taping must be provided. Evaluation criterion should be stated in measurable terms. Also, the amount and type of supervision by the co-operating counsellor and university supervisor must be specified clearly.

1. In the first case, "Supervisor's Role," the counsellor-educator says that he is "ultimately responsible for all the practicum trainees." What do you think?

2. The third case, "No Clarification of Supervisory Roles," happened at a Canadian university, only the name of the counsellor-educator has been changed. What would you do if you were the head of this counsellor-educator's department?

3. What are the professional obligations of counsellor trainees?

4. What would you have done if you were Jill in "Counsellor of Supervisor"?

5. What are the major obligations of supervisors of counsellor trainees?

F5	**WELFARE OF CLIENTS**

F5 **WELFARE OF CLIENTS** Counsellors who engage in counselling supervision of students or trainees take steps to ensure the welfare of clients during the supervised practice period, and intervene, when necessary, to ensure that this obligation is met.

Relationship Skills Lacking (+)

In a counselling practicum situation, co-taught and co-supervised by two counsellor-educators, one of the counsellors-in-training does not appear to relate very well to clients. Both counsellor-educators observe her in videotaped counselling situations and are not satisfied with her progress. Helpful suggestions are given to the trainee, but a month later her relationships with clients remain cool and distant. The counsellor-educators clearly tell the trainee that her skills in relating with clients must improve if she hopes to be a counsellor.

Pre-Practicum (+)

During the first semester of a counsellor-training program, all counselling students are required to take a pre-practicum laboratory course designed to help students develop their communication skills, but also to help staff determine whether or not a student should be recommended for the counselling practicum. At least two supervisors observe each student and write detailed evaluations of each student's communication and relationship skills. Students are informed that one of the main reasons for the pre-practicum is to make sure that their future clients will not experience negative results by being counselled by trainees.

Supervision Lacking (-)

The counselling practicum supervisor received a telephone message from a school counsellor that the practicum student, Joyce Smith, did not seem to be working out very

well. Several students that she had counselled had complained to the school counsellor that, "Miss Smith just doesn't seem to be very interested," and "She didn't even remember what I said earlier." The practicum supervisor phoned back and asked the school counsellor to be patient because he was sure that Joyce, given a little more time and experience, would be a fine counsellor.

No Guidelines for Collaborating Counsellors (-)

In one university counsellor-training program, full-time counselling students were placed in a community counselling program within two weeks of starting their one-year master's program. Although some of the collaborating counsellors in the field gradually introduced the counselling trainees into counselling, other counsellors immediately had the trainees begin one-on-one counselling with the clients. The university did not provide specific guidelines for the collaborating counsellors.

COMMENTS AND QUESTIONS

The first two cases presented demonstrate ethical behaviour on the part of the counsellor-educators. They are willing to evaluate the performance of counsellors-in-training, and are prepared to screen from the program the trainees who appear not to be suitable future counsellors. Counsellor-educators must at all times keep in mind that they are responsible for the actions of their counsellors-in-training, and the welfare of clients must be the main concern. Counsellor-educators are in a position to model, by professional supervision of trainees, ethical, legal and professional standards of counselling.

1. What would you have done in the case entitled "Supervision Lacking"?

2. In the last case, what guidelines should collaborating counsellors receive?

3. When counselling trainees are counselling their first few clients, should a collaborating counsellor be present during the counselling session? Discuss.

4. What criterion should be established to determine which trainees could be detrimental to clients?

5. What are the preferred methods of evaluation and appraisal for counsellors-in-training?

F6 PROGRAM ORIENTATION
Counsellors responsible for counsellor education programs and training activities take responsibility to orient perspective students and trainees to all core elements of such programs and activities, including to a clear policy with respect to all supervised practice components, both those simulated and real.

Student Information (+)
This department of counselling psychology sends a very detailed booklet to each graduate student applicant. Included in the booklet is material on admission requirements, programs of study, course expectations, student expectations and typical jobs received by graduates from this counselling psychology department.

Orientation (+)
Several weeks before class registration, the head of a department of counsellor education organizes an extensive orientation program. Various professors discuss the advantages and disadvantages of the thesis versus the practicum route; other professors give detailed outlines of the core courses in counselling as well as the elective courses; and former graduate students comment on their present jobs and field questions regarding their former programs of study at this university.

Professor Leaves (-)
At one small department of educational psychology (which included counsellor education), several good courses in consulting had been developed by a professor who specialized in the area of consultation. Several graduate students were attracted to this university and department because of their desire to learn a great deal about counselling and consulting. When registration for courses began, the graduate students learned that the pro-

fessor teaching the consulting courses had moved to another university and the consulting courses had been cancelled.

No Graduate Follow-Up (-)

Although the university department of counsellor education did spell out the basic program expectations, no attempt was made to link the counselling skills to specific courses or even the total program. At no time in the last 10 years had any efforts been made to follow-up graduates of the program in order to give prospective students some idea of the employment prospects.

COMMENTS AND QUESTIONS

This ethical article suggests that counsellor-education departments clearly delineate their program expectations, the basic counselling skills that must be developed and the supervisory practices of the department. This has not always been done, but in recent years more and more counselling departments are developing not only detailed brochures and other materials, but are offering extensive, in-person orientation programs to students prior to registration.

At a minimum, the orientation materials that prospective students receive should contain information on the following:

- Admission requirements, including not only minimum admission requirements, but the typical grades and other criteria that recently admitted students obtained;

- Complete descriptions of program and course expectations. This would include detailed course outlines for all courses. These outlines would indicate the nature of the course, teaching format, assignments and a grading system;

- The skills and attitudes that students are expected to develop; and

- The supervisory practices of the counsellor-educators.

1. What questions would you ask a department head if you were considering a graduate program in counselling in her or his department?

2. Is it realistic to expect counsellor-education departments to know and report on employment prospects of counselling graduates?

3. What would you include in an in-person orientation session prior to registration?

4. What would you include in the materials you would send to students who were interested in your counsellor education program?

5. Should students be screened before admission into a graduate counselling program?

F7 RELATIONAL BOUNDARIES
Counsellors who work as counsellor-educators, trainers, and supervisors establish relationships with their students, trainees, and supervisees such that appropriate relational boundaries are clarified and maintained, and dual relationships avoided.

Counselling Internship (+)
It is the practice of one university to offer several counselling internships to doctoral students in the university's counselling centre. A great deal of planning has gone into making this field placement a positive learning experience for the counselling interns. At the beginning of the year, a meeting is held with the interns, the counselling director and all the counsellors in the centre. All are made aware of the goals and expectations of the interns. As well, the counsellors are all encouraged to help provide clients for the interns and to arrange some discussion time with the interns. A schedule of supervision and evaluation procedures are also presented at this time.

Teamwork Supervision (+)
One counselling practicum supervisor sees the real need for co-operation among the students-in-training, the co-operating counsellors in the field, and the university counsellor-education department. The supervisor meets with all co-operating counsellors before the field placements are made. Not only does she determine their willingness to supervise student counsellors, but she develops a contract specifying the goals and objectives for the co-operating counsellor and the student-in-training.

Residence Hall Counsellors (-)
One practicum supervisor arranges for all the doctoral students in his practicum to spend one semester counselling undergraduate students in residence halls. The doctoral students are told to spend five hours a week at the residence hall and attempt to "drum-up some business." No suggestions are given as to how to get potential student clients involved in counselling and no guidelines are given as to interview structure or feedback. Furthermore, many of the doctoral students have friends and classmates in residence.

Professor and Group Facilitator (-)
In a small counsellor-education department, one professor is responsible for teaching most of the course work for counsellors-in-training as well as supervising practica. One of the major assignments for the group counselling course that the professor teaches is to be a participant in a "growth group" led by the professor teaching the course. The professor assigns a grade to each student based on their attendance, verbal participation, and openness during the group experience.

COMMENTS AND QUESTIONS
There is a need for counsellor-educators, trainers and supervisors to state clearly the expectations and roles of the counsellors-in-training. Clear instructions must be provided on the boundaries between co-operating counsellors in the field, counselling supervisors and course instructors. Dual relationships are a violation of ethical standards and can take many forms, including socializing, becoming emotionally or sexually involved, combining the role of counsellor-educator and counsellor and combining the role of supervisor and counsellor. These types of relationships can impair judgment and have the potential for conflicts of interest.

1. What are some situations where dual relationships among counsellor-educators, supervising counsellors in the field and counsellors-in-training could result in conflicts of interest?

2. What should be the role of counsellors?

3. Should collaborating counsellors assign grades to counsellors-in-training?

4. What should be stated in a field-placement policy guide?

5. What should be the supervisor's role in the field?

F8 OBLIGATION TO INFORM
Counsellors who work as counsellor-educators, trainers, and supervisors take steps to inform students, trainees, and supervisees, at the beginning of activities associated with these roles, of all reasonably foreseeable circumstances under which confidentiality may be breached during such activities.

"Duty to Warn" (+)

Tony Z., a counsellor trainee, had been counselling a high school student for several sessions when the student revealed to him that her uncle had on occasion touched her inappropriately. The student asked Tony what she should do to make her uncle stop his sexual advances. She did not want to tell her parents because she did not think that they would believe her, and, even if they did, it would "destroy the family." Tony remembered the informed consent form that his counsellor-educator had helped him prepare, and he pointed out to his client that he needed to break confidentiality because he felt that he had a "duty to warn" her parents and others of the actions of her uncle.

Ethics Course (+)

At this Canadian counsellor training program, no trainees are allowed to work with clients until they have completed a course on ethics in counselling; a course that includes students having to develop an appropriate "informed consent" form, which includes a statement on the limits of confidentiality and a duty inform others of dangers to the client or others.

Limitless Confidentiality (-)

A counsellor-in-training began her practicum at a local crisis centre soon after beginning her master's program in counselling. At the beginning of her counselling sessions she told clients a little about herself and assured them that everything they said would be kept strictly confidential. She had been told by her counselling practicum supervisor of the importance of confidentiality and telling clients about the confidentiality of everything said during counselling sessions.

Not Explaining Confidentiality (-)

Before sending trainees to their counselling sites, the practicum instructor told them "remember to keep things confidential unless your clients are in danger to themselves or others." No discussion was held regarding other limits of confidentiality such as court-ordered disclosures, fatal diseases, or client waivers.

COMMENTS AND QUESTIONS

Counsellor-educators, trainers and counselling supervisors have the responsibility to inform all the counsellors-in-training of exceptions to confidentiality. The ethical articles B2 and B3 are very clear about these exceptions:

• when disclosure is required to prevent clear and imminent danger to the client or others;

• when legal requirements demand that confidential material be revealed; and

• when a child is in need of protection.

Not only must trainees be aware of these ethical articles, but they must fully understand them. It is the responsibility of the trainers to assure that the limits of confidentiality are understood, by providing trainees with explanations and case studies that illustrate counsellor practice when exceptions to confidentiality are required.

1. What additional circumstances (see previous) would require counsellors to breach confidentiality?

2. What should the counsellor in "Limitless Confidentiality" do to rectify the dilemma she may get into?

3. What are the ways in which counsellor-educators can inform trainees of exceptions to confidentiality?

4. Should ethics courses be mandatory at Canadian universities that provide training for counsellors?

5. In the case "Duty to Warn," would you have done what Tony did?

| F9 | SELF-DEVELOPMENT AND
SELF-AWARENESS |

Counsellors who work as counsellor-educators, trainers, and supervisors, encourage and facilitate the self-development and self-awareness of students, trainees, and supervisees, so that they learn to integrate their professional practice and personal insight.

Performance Objectives (+)

Soon after two new members joined a small department of five counsellor-educators, the chairperson saw this as an opportune time to get all members involved in evaluating and modifying their counsellor education program. At the end, course objectives were written for all courses and performance standards for counsellors were presented in clear, measurable terms.

Group Leadership Skills (+)

In a group counselling course offered in a master's program in counselling, the course instructor requires all course members to lead a group to demonstrate interaction skills such as linking, process observing and limiting. At the end of the practice session, each student leader receives feedback on the specific leadership skills from the course instructor.

Research Emphases (-)

A potential graduate student sought information from six different Canadian universities regarding their master's programs in counsellor education. After studying the written materials from each of the universities, he applied and was accepted into one university program that seemed to promise training both in research and in counselling skills. Too late, the graduate student was disappointed to learn that the practicum was cancelled for that year, but he was allowed to substitute additional courses in research and statistics. He graduated with his master's degree without having taken a counselling practicum.

Practicum Supervision (-)

One professor is assigned to teach and supervise a counselling practicum for eight graduate students. This practicum course has been described in the university calendar as consisting of practice and supervision of counselling skills for participants. The professor assigns each practicum student to a school and his "supervision" consists of the occasional phone call to the school. No directions are given as to the counselling skills that are to be practised or supervised. At the end of the course, all eight practicum students are awarded grades of "A."

COMMENTS AND QUESTIONS

Opportunity must be provided for counselling students to not only relate their professional practice to relevant counselling theory, but also have time for personal development, insight and self-awareness as individuals in a helping profession. The revised counsellor certification regulations of CCA recognize this need by recommending graduate course work not only in specific areas like group work, career development and counselling theory, but also in more personal growth areas such as communication and relationships, learning and human development, and multicultural counselling. Specifically, the revised certification criteria indicate the following:

A. CCA Membership

All persons who are members in good standing of the Canadian Counselling Association are eligible for certification.

B. Graduate Training

A graduate degree, or equivalent, in counselling or related field from a CCA recognized higher education institution is required, showing evidence of GRADUATE work in:

1. **Counselling Theory**
   A study of basic counselling theories, models of counselling, principles and techniques of counselling.

2. **Supervised Counselling Practicum**
   A supervised counselling experience in an appropriate work setting of at least 120 hours should be spent in direct client contact.

   and GRADUATE course work in *six* of the following areas:

3. **Communication and Relationship Skills**
   A study of counsellor/client relationship skills.

4. **Group Counselling**
   A study of group leadership, types of groups, group practices, group methods and techniques, and group dynamics.

5. **Career Development**
   A study of areas such as career development theory, career choice and lifestyle, educational and career information, and decision making.

6. **Assessment and Testing**
   A study of individual and group assessment and testing, case-study approaches, individual differences, and methods of data collection and interpretation.

7. **Research and Evaluation**
   A study of research design, statistics, evaluation, and types of research.

8. **Consultation Methods**
   A study of consultation-theory research and practice. Topics include the process or stages of consultation, ethical issues, and approaches to consultation.

9. **Learning and Human Development**
   A study of the nature and needs of individuals at all developmental levels. Included would be topics such as learning theory, human behaviour, studies of change, and personality theory.

10. **Psychological Education**
    A study of topics in psychology such as personality, growth, development, attitude formation, and socialization.

11. **Counselling Intervention Strategies**
    Theory and practice in planning and implementing client-change interventions in counselling.

12. **Counselling Girls and Women**
    A study of sex role development, stereotyping and social roles, and corresponding counselling theories and counselling approaches.

13. **Multicultural Counselling**
    An examination of cross-cultural issues in counselling, influence of social and cultural contexts on client problems, and relevant counselling theories and counselling approaches.

14. **Counselling in Specialized Settings**
    A study of issues, applied theory, and relevant counselling approaches pertaining to a special client population or setting, e.g. families, rehabilitation, schools, disabled clients.

1. This particular ethical article suggests that academic study should be integrated with supervised practice. How can this best be done?

2. What areas of graduate course work would you add or delete from the list of 14 course areas for CCA certification?

3. Do you believe more of the areas should be compulsory? For example, should all counsellors have compulsory course work in group counselling, research and evaluation, and communication skills?

4. Is it realistic to require 120 hours of "direct client contact" during a counselling practicum?

5. What skills, knowledge, self-awareness and self-understanding activities, and practicum requirements would you include in a counsellor education program?

F10 DEALING WITH PERSONAL ISSUES

Counsellors responsible for counsellor education, training, and supervision, recognize when such activities evoke significant personal issues for students, trainees, and supervisees and refer to other sources when necessary to avoid counselling those for whom they hold administrative, or evaluative responsibility.

Avoiding a Dual Relationship I (+)

A counselling professor teaches counselling courses and supervises one section of the counselling practicum. He also has a small private practice in counselling. One of his practicum students phones him at his private counselling office to arrange for some personal counselling. The professor tells the student of the conflict with his supervisory duties and recommends several other counsellors to his student.

Avoiding a Dual Relationship II (+)

A counsellor in private practice agreed to supervise a trainee from the university counsellor-education program. Both the counsellor and trainee felt good about the supervisory relationship that was established between them during the first semester. During the second semester, however, the trainee began to ask for help in some of the things that were unresolved in her personal life. The counsellor pointed out that she would like to be helpful but was faced with the problem of being both her supervisor and counsellor. She explained to the trainee that a dual relationship between them might result in her being compromised in her first obligation, that of supervising the trainee's counselling.

Growth Group Revelations? (-)

One professor in a small counsellor education program teaches both the group counselling course and supervises four practicum students. Two of the practicum students are in his group counselling course. In this course students are required to be part of a personal growth group and are encouraged to talk freely about themselves, their counselling program and anything else that's important to them. The two students who are also being supervised by the professor are very reluctant to talk about their counselling practicum issues, in fear that it might influence the professor's evaluation of them. No alternative assignment to being part of the growth group is offered.

Relative Problem (-)

Mark H. is enrolled in a counselling practicum being taught and supervised by his father. Mark did not like the alternative: namely, to move out of his parent's home and take a counselling program in another university.

COMMENTS AND QUESTIONS

The issue of dual relationships raises many questions. What should the boundaries be between practicum supervisor and trainee? How can it be determined whether dual relationships will be harmful? Should a professor be friends with the students he supervises? If a student needs counselling, and no other counsellor is readily available, is it acceptable for a counsellor-educator to counsel the student? Some dual relationships fall in the "grey area" between ethical and unethical and will need careful examination. It is generally accepted that supervision and counselling have different purposes, and supervisors of counselling should leave the counselling for counsellors.

1. If you were a colleague of the professor in "Relative Problem," what would you advise him to do?

2. How can the situation in "Growth Group Revelations?" be resolved?

3. Was the counselling supervisor in "Avoiding a Dual Relationship II" being too careful? Could she not have tried to be helpful with some of the trainee's personal issues?

4. What are the boundaries between counsellor-educators and counselling students with regards to social relationships?

5. What other situations can you think of that might compromise a counselling supervisor's role as a supervisor?

F11 SELF-GROWTH ACTIVITIES
Counsellors who work as counsellor-educators, trainors, and supervisors ensure that any professional experiences, which require self-disclosure and engagement in self-growth activities, are managed in a manner consistent with the principles of informed consent, confidentiality, and safeguarding against any harmful effects.

Dealing With Group Pressure (+)

In a counselling practicum class, all the students are required to practice their counselling skills for one day per week at a school or agency. In addition, the students in this class meet for three-hours weekly with their practicum instructor to discuss counselling issues, their counselling experiences and their own personal development as counsellors. During one class, seven of the eight students in the class had shared some of their personal development as counsellors. There was a silence as the class members waited for the last member to say something. The practicum instructor, sensing the reluctance of this last person to say something at this time, interjected and pointed out that all disclosures were completely voluntary and she did not want anyone to feel any pressure to say something simply because everyone else had. The instructor then introduced a new topic for discussion.

Informing Graduate Student Applicants (+)

At a university in western Canada, all graduate students, before admission, are provided with detailed brochures and statements from the counsellor education department regarding the expectations and challenges that are part of the training program. These materials contain comments on ethical standards, non-sexist language, involvement in personal growth group experience, and personal counselling expectations.

Group Counselling (-)
Prior to students beginning an advanced group counselling course, they were unaware of the fact that they would be required to become part of a growth group where they would be under both group-leader and group-member pressure to reveal personal aspects of their lives. Furthermore, they were given a grade for this "growth group assignment" portion of the course.

Personal Counselling (-)
During their first counselling practicum seminar, students learn for the first time that one requirement of their practicum is for each of them to receive counselling by one of the counsellors at the university counselling centre. No substitute for this "assignment" is allowed.

COMMENTS AND QUESTIONS
It has been my experience that many Canadian universities pay some attention to this article, but may not be going far enough. Most universities ask professors for detailed course outlines including teaching approaches, assignments and student expectations. In group counselling courses and practica, students are informed that they will be expected to role-play clients, they will be asked to disclose personal information, and that they will be part of a personal growth group.

In most Canadian universities, students are not informed of these types of expectations prior to admission, although many, probably most, graduate students welcome the opportunity to be involved in personal counselling and be part of a growth group experience.

1. What should counsellor-educators do when students become highly emotional during a practicum or group counselling course?

2. Are students given enough information if they are informed of the need for personal disclosures at the beginning of the course?

3. How legitimate are the personal disclosure activities as part of counsellor training?

4. Will counsellor-educators allow personal growth activities to be voluntary?

5. Should all personal growth activities be voluntary?

❖ ❖ ❖ ❖ ❖ ❖ ❖ ❖ ❖ ❖ ❖ ❖ ❖

ESSAYS ON COUNSELLOR EDUCATION, TRAINING AND SUPERVISION

Ethical Reasoning and Ethics Instruction

Beth E. Haverkamp

Kathleen A. Irvine

Teaching Ethics

When a counselling student encounters an ethical dilemma, supervisors will often refer him or her to a set of ethical standards. The student, however, often returns with the lament "But it doesn't tell me what to DO!" Paradoxically, that frustrating realization is the beginning of ethical awareness because learning about ethics means learning how to deal with ambiguity, how to discern underlying principles in a complex situation. Experienced practitioners know that even well-intentioned efforts to follow ethical codes do not ensure ethical consequences, and that actions, which benefit one client, can introduce the risk of harm to others.

The goal of ethics instruction is to help trainees develop an ethical stance toward counselling that they will carry into their professional lives. Kitchener's (1986) listing of the goals of ethics training captures the expectations we have for ourselves and our students: to create sensitivity to ethical issues and to the implications of our actions; to acquire the ability to reason about ethical dilemmas; to promote moral responsibility and an innate determination to act in an ethical manner; and to acquire a tolerance for the ambiguity inherent in ethical reasoning.

The developers of the Canadian Counselling Association (CCA) *Code of Ethics* have recognized this complexity and have provided a useful tool to guide counsellors in recognizing and handling ethical dilemmas. The section of the Code on "The CCA Process of Ethical Decision Making" is a valuable resource for both beginners and experienced professionals. Its practical guidelines for decision making can effectively promote the awareness and reasoning ability that Kitchener (1986) has identified as important. The purpose of the present chapter is to offer additional suggestions for the counsellor-educator who is engaged in the teaching of ethics.

It is our belief that the preparation of ethical counsellors requires specific coursework or seminars on this subject. Zibert et al. (1998) report that only 47 per cent of counsellors in one of the largest U.S. state counselling organizations had taken a formal course in ethics. The Council for the Accreditation of Counseling and Related Education Programs (CACREP), the accreditation agency for most counselling programs in the U.S. and some in Canada, requires that ethics instruction be included in counselling programs. At present, this can be through either a formal, separate course in ethics, or informally within clinical courses and experiences. While the latter approach has the advantage of demonstrating real-life applications of the issues, it can result in incomplete or cursory coverage of the subject. The practice of incorporating ethics instruction within clinical supervision often means that ethical issues are discussed as they occur for a particular counselling case. However, the supervisor has little control over which issues present themselves for discussion; one group may work with a suicidal client, and have an opportunity to discuss the ethics related to preventing harm, while another group may never face these concerns but will encounter dilemmas related to confidentiality in family counselling. The supervisor needs to incorporate a structured outline to ensure that a broad range of ethical issues are addressed, rather than relying on discussion of the particular issues that arise during the course of supervision.

The following article provides a range of suggestions for teaching ethics, including several ideas for experiential learning. While we recommend formal instruction, the coverage of content areas could also be adapted for use within clinic supervision. Just as the skill of establishing rapport requires that the trainee both acquire knowledge about the dynamics of a counselling relationship and then have opportunities to practice applying this knowledge, ethical conduct has both knowledge and application components. Each program will undoubtedly need to tailor a curriculum that meets the needs of its students and the settings in which they are most likely to practice, but it is hoped that these suggestions will provide a starting point for your own creative approaches to teaching in this important area.

Foundations of Ethical Decision Making

An essential but often neglected component of ethics instruction is some discussion of the source of our ethics codes. If asked, "Where do ethics codes come from?" most would answer "from my professional association," an answer that reflects little awareness of our code's philosophical roots.

Viewing one's professional association as the source of a code carries the risk that the ethical standards will be viewed as a set of rules, imposed by an external authority. Such a posture increases the likelihood that the "rules" will be viewed as something that one may agree or disagree with, similar to speed limits on a highway. Attention to the philosophical underpinnings of a code gives students the opportunity to consider the logic underlying specific principles; this reflection increases the chance that the principles will be incorporated into one's thinking, increasing the sophistication of ethical reasoning.

The need for sophistication is reflected in a common misperception with regard to ethical practice. Many students (and professionals) new to the literature on ethics make the assumption that "well-intentioned practice" is equivalent to "ethical practice." This is not the case. A well-intentioned counsellor might contact a client's employer to argue that poor work performance is due to a family crisis and that the client should not be dismissed. However, if the counsellor has not obtained permission for this release of information, such actions are unethical in constituting a violation of confidentiality. All counsellors are familiar with the requirement to maintain confidentiality; however, there are many counsellors who are not familiar with the subtleties of managing confidentiality in couples counselling, in work with private sector Employee Assistance Programs (EAPs), or in cases involving both custodial and non-custodial parents. A counsellor facing this range of cases may act in a well-intentioned manner, but may not act in an ethical manner.

Given that an ethics instructor wants to incorporate information on the philosophical base of the CCA *Code of Ethics*, where can one begin? Fine and Ulrich (1995) have identified four levels of ethical decision making; their model provides a guide for understanding the relationship between philosophy, ethics codes, and "well-intentioned" decisions.

The level of intuitive judgments (Kitchener, 1984) is most familiar to counsellors. This is the province of our well-intentioned acts, and represents the culmination of our personal understanding of what is right and wrong. Because our individual sense of right and wrong has developed over a lifetime, we are not always aware of the beliefs or attitudes that inform our position. The goal of ethics instruction is to acquaint students with the remaining three levels of ethical analysis; by gaining familiarity with the underlying levels, the student increases the body of knowledge that he or she can draw upon in resolving ethical dilemmas.

The second level of decision making is that of ethical "rules," which is the domain of standards that comprise the ethics codes. Students must become familiar with these standards; but, as noted above, facility in ethical decision making requires that one become familiar with the reasoning underlying the standards.

The third level of ethical reasoning is that of ethical principles. Principles are more general statements that underlie the specific standards and provide students with an expanded understanding of "where the code comes from." The CCA *Code of Ethics* incorporates six fundamental principles: respect for the dignity of persons, not willfully harming others, integrity in relationships, responsible caring, responsibility to society, and respect for self-determination.

The fourth level represents the foundational frameworks upon which the general principles are based. These frameworks are drawn from philosophy and reflect the fact that ethics, as a discipline, is part of the larger field of philosophy. The frameworks most commonly cited as foundations for contemporary ethics codes are those of utilitarianism and deontology; taken together, they represent western culture's answer to the question of what is right, what is good. Providing students with an opportunity to examine the relationship between standards, principles and these philosophical frameworks will enhance their ability to deal with the complexity and ambiguity of specific ethical dilemmas. To assist in guiding such student exploration, a brief description of these philosophical positions is offered below.

Utilitarianism is based on the philosophy of John Stuart Mill and Jeremy Bentham, who stated that an action should be considered ethically appropriate when it provides the greatest good or the least harm for the greatest number of people. Deontology, grounded in Immanuel Kant's philosophy, is based on the categorical imperative, which states that every person must be treated as an end and never as a means only and that actions are moral-based on their intrinsic rightness, rather than on the consequences.

Even superficial consideration of these two positions illustrates the ways that they may come into conflict in a given counselling case. How does maintaining confidentiality about a university student's report of criminal behaviour, such as selling cocaine, serve the "greatest good?" How does one make choices between two courses of action when both appear to be "intrinsically right," such as the choice between protecting society and honouring a promise (confidentiality)?

Writers in the area of ethics (e.g. Fine & Ulrich, 1995; Kitchener, 1986; Meara, Schmidt, & Day, 1996) are unanimous in asserting that discussion of difficult, ambiguous issues will enhance students' sophistication in handling ethical dilemmas. Consideration of the philosophical frameworks expands the number of questions that the counsellor will ask himself or herself when faced with ethical choices, which can lead to better decisions.

As an example of how to apply the philosophical frameworks, consider the example of "honesty." Honesty is a virtue that all counsellors recognize as important but, in a situation of ethical uncertainty that involves questions of honesty, the two foundational frameworks may suggest different courses of action. Deontology might point toward being honest because it is the right thing to do, while utilitarianism would call for consideration of who might be harmed if one is honest in a particular situation. A counselling case that presents questions about honesty becomes an ethical dilemma when there is no clear answer, no single course of action that will be problem free. The philosophical frameworks will not provide an answer as to what is always right or avoids all harm; their value is in raising questions that are worth considering, so that the resulting decision can be as ethical as possible, under the circumstances.

Dimensions of Ethical Decision Making

In order to fully appreciate ethical codes and their application, it is helpful for trainees to have some knowledge of the factors that in-

fluence how counsellors live out these standards. There are three domains that influence, or form a context for, all ethical decision making: the person of the counsellor, the diversity among clients and practice settings, and the federal and provincial laws that pertain to counselling practice. While information related to each of these areas will arise in classroom discussion of particular areas of decision making (e.g. informed consent, child-abuse reporting, test use with ethnic groups), we have found it useful to discuss each area as a prelude to coverage of the code itself. The following sections note the relevance of each area to ethical decision making.

The Person of the Counsellor
Most counselling theories recognize the centrality of the person of the counsellor in making the counselling relationship a therapeutic process (Egan, 1998). In particular, counsellors are encouraged to examine the role of their personal values, where values can be understood to include assumptions, beliefs, and attitudes. Counsellors' self-awareness is essential in recognizing and accepting differences between their own and client values and to provide for clients "an ethical experience where growth and change can occur within one's own value framework" (Bergin, Payne, & Richards, 1996, p. 297). Since clients can be greatly influenced by therapist values, it is sometimes necessary to make these values explicit, so that client informed choice and autonomy are maintained (Bergin et al., 1996). Students can be continually encouraged to identify and articulate their own values and to consider how these impact their ethical decision making.

Diversity Among Clients and Practice Settings
The CCA principles of respect for the dignity of persons and respect for self-determination focus our attention on the rich diversity in our client populations. While specific

CCA articles (A9, B8, and D10) mandate a recognition of client diversity, North American ethics codes have been charged with a lack of sensitivity to client cultural and gender differences (Casas, Ponterotto, & Gutierrez, 1986; Payton, 1994).

McCormick (1998) reminds counsellors that ethical codes are culturally bound, reflecting the values and beliefs of the defining culture, and these may be inappropriate standards to apply to therapeutic experiences with clients from differing cultures. He uses the example of dual relationships, which are defined as problematic and potentially harmful by most ethics codes (CCA *Code of Ethics*, B7). However, in counselling First Nations communities, the counsellor may have kinship relations with many people in the community; McCormick suggests that this fact may enhance the acceptability of counselling and the counsellor for these clients.

We have seen a growing awareness that both our formulation and interpretation of ethical codes take into consideration the rights and well-being of women. Both the Canadian and American Psychological Associations have written guidelines on conducting therapy with women (American Psychological Association, 1978; Canadian Psychological Association, 1996). Research on the psychology of women (Jordan, Kaplan, Miller, Stiver, & Surrey, 1991). suggests that relationship is a central consideration in normal growth and development. In accord with this, the ethical principle of individual autonomy has been critiqued as being overemphasized at the expense of community (Meara, Schmidt, & Day, 1996).

Religion and spirituality are areas in which counsellors must be sensitive and respectful of difference. Although attention to spirituality in counselling has grown tremendously in the past few years, and spirituality has been shown to be integral to mental health for many clients, its inclusion in counselling presents some major challenges and ethical concerns (Bergin et al., 1996; Kelly, 1995). Counsellors must be aware of their own values about religion and spirituality before they can be comfortable inviting clients to engage in such discussion. At present there is little training in counsellor education programs about how to address spirituality effectively and in an ethical manner (Kelly, 1995).

At the most essential level, an appreciation of "diversity" requires attention to the unique needs and context of individual clients. Our goal of sensitizing counsellors to diversity can be expanded to include attention to the specific challenges posed by different practice settings. Clinics situated in schools, in medical settings, in rural areas, or on the streets in urban centres, all require attention to context. Counsellors working in school settings often face difficult decisions regarding confidentiality and disclosure. For instance, a school administrator might regard counselling records as school property and not subject to the standards of confidentiality that most counsellors find acceptable. Counsellors in rural settings often face unavoidable multiple relationships and pressures to practice outside the boundaries of competence (see Schank, 1998, for a practical discussion of some of the ethical quandaries that rural practitioners often encounter). Each setting can present its own set of unique ethical dilemmas. The challenge is to apply the ethics code in a manner that is respectful of the particular setting, and of counsellor, client, and community values, yet does not violate the code's requirements or underlying principles. The metaethical principle of "do no harm" becomes a central reference point for counsellors facing this challenge.

Legal Issues in Counselling Practice

In order to uphold the profession's standards of practice and commitment to the wider society, counsellors must be knowledgeable about federal, provincial, and territorial laws that relate to their area of practice. Most counsellors are familiar with the legal requirement to report suspected child abuse and with the designation of the age when an adolescent is considered an adult. Some counsellors, however, do not realize that such laws differ from province to province. The ethics instructor should acquaint the counsellor with relevant laws and statutes governing the province or territory in which he or she resides and practices.

Legal proceedings are becoming a more common aspect of professional life for many counsellors, particularly those involved with children or adult survivors of sexual abuse (McEvoy & Reid, 1996). Consequently, students in an ethics course should be alerted to their responsibilities to both clients and courts when subpoenas are issued. At a minimum, we recommend that ethics courses include information on legal requirements related to record keeping and disclosure, mandated reporting of child abuse, responsibilities relating to parental custody and permission for treatment, and duty to warn with regard to clients who may present either suicidal or homicidal risk. The annotated bibliography contains several useful resources of coverage in this area.

Structured Learning Experiences

As noted above, an understanding of ethics rests on both a knowledge base that has been assembled by professionals in the field and on experiential learning, which provides opportunities to debate and reflect upon the subtleties of ethical decision making. A useful exercise is to have students interview professionals who practice in different settings about the ethical issues that they encounter most frequently. Other activities, which have proved useful in generating discussion and self reflection among counselling trainees, are described below.

Discussion of Ethical Vignettes

Vignettes describing actual or hypothetical situations that present ethical dilemmas can provide vivid, memorable examples of the guidelines. Feedback from students indicates that discussion of case vignettes can be an effective way to teach decision making skills (Corey, Corey & Callahan, 1988). Hypothetical situations may be most useful with beginning students, as they can be written to provide clear illustrations of a single guideline, whereas actual situations (with names and other identifying information altered or deleted) can stimulate discussion of the complexity that exists in many ethical decisions.

Client Rights and Responsibilities

An effective way of helping a class understand the ethical issues that surround informed consent and confidentiality is to assign the development of a handout on Client Rights and Responsibilities. The idea is that the class, or small groups, will produce a document that a practitioner could hand to all clients who enter for counselling.

A variation on this assignment that will accomplish many of the same objectives would be to ask students to compile a list of questions that clients have a right to ask counsellors. This assignment is based on Handelsman and Galvin's (1988) client handout, "Information you have a right to know," a comprehensive series of questions that clients might want to ask their counsellors (e.g. "What should I do if I feel therapy isn't working?" "Do I need to pay for missed sessions?"). While the Handelsman and Galvin (1988) model would be useful for the instructor to consult, the primary value of the exercise for students derives from identifying, debating and writing the questions themselves.

Self-Monitoring of One's Ethical Practice

The task of becoming familiar with the ethical standards is most readily accomplished within the curriculum of formal ethics coursework. At the same time, knowledge gained in classroom settings must be transferred to real-life settings in order to be consolidated. Stoll (1999), in a qualitative study of self-reflective counsellors who reported familiarity with formal ethics codes, found that these counsellors did engage in a daily practice of self-monitoring. For many, the self-monitoring process consisted of two elements: a combination of a background awareness of those ethical issues likely to emerge in a given case, and use of formal procedures (e.g. written consent forms, regular peer-supervision group meetings) to guard against ethical infractions. To help students incorporate ethical practices in their day-to-day work, we recommend that ethics courses include discussion of how to monitor one's professional conduct.

Pettifor's (1996) recommendations for maintenance of professional conduct range from forming peer-consultation networks to creating agency resource libraries of ethics materials. In addition, she describes a self-evaluation checklist that the Alberta Psychological Association has developed. Using a question format (e.g. "Do I keep records up to date?" "Do I regularly alert clients to the limits of confidentiality?"), counsellors are able to assess areas where their practice is consistent with professional standards and to identify areas where greater attention to the ethical guidelines may be warranted. Class discussion can be used to generate alternatives for those areas where students are uncertain as to how to proceed.

Court Room Role-Plays

In order to more fully appreciate the legal implications of counselling practice, trainees can become involved in role plays that depict situations that counsellors periodically face, such as records being subpoenaed, or testifying in court (see Colby & Long, 1994, for information on organizing a mock trial). These role plays will be more effective and meaningful for trainees if a legal professional (e.g. crown prosecutor, judge, lawyer) is invited to participate in the classroom experience. This person can provide guidance about legal issues and perhaps some "real-life" scenarios for the role-plays. He or she may also be able to arrange for some actual courtroom experience by having the class attend a legal proceeding involving a counsellor's testimony, or by reserving a courtroom to be used as the setting for the role plays. Counsellors often feel intimidated and fearful when they are compelled to become involved in the legal process. Exposure and preparation, as described above, can help to "desensitize" counsellors and increase their knowledge and confidence in handling situations that are becoming increasingly commonplace.

Conclusion

As Mark Twain once said, "To be good is noble, but to teach others to be good is nobler–and less trouble." While Twain's humor will bring a smile to many faces, the counsellor familiar with social learning theory will also recall that modelling is one of the most potent forms of learning. It seems appropriate, therefore, to end our discussion of teaching ethics with a reminder that as educators, our most potent form of instruction is the model that we, our programs and curricula provide for our students. Ethical dilemmas abound as soon as one moves away from the textbook and into relationships with others, whether as client, supervisee or colleague. Allowing our students to see how we grapple with these issues, and to learn from each other as we resolve them, will surely contribute to the trust our clients have in our profession.

References

American Psychological Association. (1978). *Task force on sex bias and sex-role stereotyping in psychotherapeutic practice*. Washington, DC: American Psychological Association.

Bergin, A. E., Payne, I. R., & Richards, P. S. (1996). Values in psychotherapy. In E. P. Shafranske (Ed.), *Religion and the clinical practice of psychology* (pp. 297-325). Washington, DC: American Psychological Association.

Canadian Counselling Association. (1999). *Code of ethics*. Ottawa, Ontario: Canadian Counselling Association.

Canadian Psychological Association. (1996). *Guidelines for therapy and counselling with women*. Ottawa, Ontario: Canadian Psychological Association.

Casas, J. M., Ponterotto, J. G., & Gutierrez, J. M. (1986). An ethical indictment of counselling research and training: The cross-cultural perspective. *Journal of Counseling & Development, 64*, 347-349.

Colby, C. R., & Long, L.L. (1994). The use of a mock trial as an instructional method in counselor preparation. *Counseling Education and Supervision, 34*(1), pp. 58-67.

Corey, G., Corey, M. S., & Callahan, P. (1988). *Issues and ethics in the helping professions (3rd ed.)*. Pacific Grove, CA: Brooks-Cole.

Egan, G. (1998). *The skilled helper: a problem-management approach to helping* (6th ed.). Pacific Grove, CA: Brooks-Cole.

Fine, M. A., & Ulrich, L. P. (1995). Integrating psychology and philosophy in teaching a graduate course in ethics. In D. N. Bersoff (Ed.), *Ethical conflicts in psychology*. Washington, DC: American Psychological Association, 116-117.

Handelsman, M. M., & Galvin, M. D. (1988). Facilitating informed consent for outpatient psychotherapy: A suggested written format. *Professional Psychology: Research and Practice, 19*, 223-225.

Jordan, J. V., Kaplan, A. G., Miller, J. B., Stiver, I. P., & Surrey, J. L. (1991). *Women's growth in connection: Writings from the Stone Center*. New York: The Guilford Press.

Kelly, E. W. J. (1995). *Spirituality and religion in counseling and psychotherapy: Diversity in theory and practice*. Alexandria, VA: American Counseling Association.

Kitchener, K. S. (1984). Intuition, critical evaluation and ethical principles: The foundation for ethical decisions in counseling psychology. *The Counseling Psychologist, 12*, 43-55.

Kitchener, K. S. (1986). Teaching applied ethics in counselor education: An integration of psychological processes and philosophical analysis. *Journal of Counseling and Development, 64*, 306-310.

McCormick, R. M. (1998). Ethical considerations in First Nations counselling and research. *Canadian Journal of Counselling, 32*(4), 284-297.

McEvoy, M., & Reid, G. (1996). *Balancing conflicting interests: A counsellor's guide to the legal process*. New Westminster, BC: Justice Institute of BC.

Meara, N. M., Schmidt, L. D., & Day, J. D. (1996). Principles and virtues: A foundation for ethical decisions, policies, and character. *The Counseling Psychologist, 24*(1), 4-77.

Payton, C. R. (1994). Implications of the 1992 ethics code for diverse groups. *Professional Psychology: Research and Practice, 25*, 317-320.

Pettifor, J. L. (1996). Maintaining professional conduct in daily practice. In Bass, L. J., et al. (Eds.). *Professional conduct and discipline in psychology*. Washington, DC: American Psychological Association and Association of State and Provincial Psychology Boards, pp 91-100.

Schank, J. A. (1998). Ethical issues in rural counselling practice. *Canadian Journal of Counselling, 32*(4), 270-283.

Stoll, T. (1999). *Counsellor's self-monitoring of day-to-day ethical practice*. Unpublished masters thesis, University of British Columbia, Vancouver, British Columbia, Canada.

Zibert, J., Engels, D. W., Kern, C. W., & Durodoye, B.A. (1998). Ethical knowledge of counselors. *Counseling and Values, 43*(1), 34-48.

Resources for Teaching Ethics:
An Annotated Bibliography

American Counseling Association website: <www.counseling.org>.

ACA has a host of resources; some are available directly on the website, others can be ordered.

Bass, L.J., et al. (Eds.). *Professional conduct and discipline in psychology*. Washington, DC: American Psychological Association and Association of State and Provincial Psychology Boards.

While this book is written from a psychological perspective, it is one of the few ethics resources that covers material from both a Canadian and American perspective. Chapters on "common problems" and "maintaining professional conduct" are useful resources for counsellors. Appendix 1 (pp 277 - 293) contains a self-evaluation form for ethical practice designed by the Alberta Psychological Association.

Bersoff, D. N. (1999). *Ethical conflicts in psychology (2nd ed.)*. Washington, DC: American Psychological Association.

This updated book provides a comprehensive examination of conflicts in areas such as psychotherapy, assessment, forensics, academia, and more.

Brabeck, M. M. (2000). *Practicing feminist ethics in psychology*. Washington, DC: American Psychological Association.

This book provides a comprehensive examination of how feminist values and principles illuminate ethical dilemmas commonly faced by therapists.

Corey, G., Corey, M. S., & Callahan, P. (1997). *Issues and ethics in the helping professions (5th ed.)*. Pacific Grove, CA: Brooks-Cole.

The 5th edition of this accessible volume could be used as a text in an ethics course. Many instructors have found the discussion questions and exercises useful in course planning.

Haverkamp, B. E. (Guest Ed.). (1998). Ethical and legal issues in counselling [Special issue]. *Canadian Journal of Counselling, 32*(4).

This special issue of the journal is devoted to ethical and legal issues in counselling. Topics such as counselling First Nations clients and counselling in rural areas are discussed.

Marsh, D. J., & McGee, R. D. (Eds.). (1997). *Ethical and legal issues in professional practice with families*. Toronto: Wiley.

Given the unique ethical dilemmas that arise in family and marital counselling, this edited volume provides practical and well-researched guidance for a difficult area.

Meara, N. M., Schmidt, L. D., & Day, J. D. (1996) Principles and values: A foundation for ethical decisions, policies and character [Major contribution]. *The Counseling Psychologist, 24*, 4-77.

This substantive article is followed by three reaction papers, and a response by the authors. Because it includes attention to some of the philosophical underpinnings of current ethics codes, it would be a useful adjunct to the philosophy segment of an ethics course.

McEvoy, M., & Reid, G. (1996). *Balancing conflicting interests: A counsellor's guide to the legal process*. New Westminster, BC: Justice Institute of BC.

This manual explores the clinical and ethical dilemmas counsellors face in their increasing involvement with the legal system, and suggests ideas for resolving them. The content is most specific for the British Columbia legal system, however much can be applied to any province or territory. It can be ordered from the Justice Institute of BC, 715 McBride Boulevard, New Westminster, BC, V3L 5T4.

Pope, K. S., & Vasquez, M. J. T. (1998). *Ethics in psychotherapy and counseling: A practical guide for behavioral and healthcare professionals (2nd ed.)*. San Francisco, CA: Jossey-Bass

Designed as a general instructional reference for ethics in counselling practice, this text provides numerous case vignettes and linkages to practice. In addition, models of informed consent forms and a "client's bill of rights" are included as appendices.

Sieber, J. E. (1992). *Planning ethically responsible research: A guide for students and institutional review boards*. Applied Social Science Research Methods Series, Vol. 31. Newbury Park: Sage.

This handbook includes major sections on research ethics, the institutional review process; risk/benefit assessment; and discussion of vulnerable populations. It would serve as a useful resource for teaching ethics or as a supplement to a graduate course on research methodology.

Teaching Professional Issues for Counselling Practice in the New Millennium

Max R. Uhlemann

John C. Gawthrop

In response to concerns from within the psychology profession and pressures from consumers of psychological services, there has been increased attention to ethics education in graduate programs. (Newmark & Hutchins, 1981; Pettifor & Pitcher, 1982; Eberlein, 1993). The issue has shifted from whether to include ethics education in applied programs to how best to teach ethics (Corey, Corey, & Callanan, 1998; Pettifor & Pitcher, 1982; Welfel & Kitchener, 1992).[1]

However, the literature on the effect of current ethics education (Haas, Malouf, & Mayerson, 1985, 1986, 1988; Shertzer & Morris, 1972; Tymchuk, 1982) indicates wide variability among counsellors and psychologists on how to deal with hypothetical ethical dilemmas. Consensus on how to respond to ethical vignettes varies across studies (all other demographic variables being equal) as a function of whether the ethical issues encountered are of a high- or low-profile nature (Haas, et al., 1985, 1986; Tymchuk, 1982). Even practitioners who agree on how to respond still vary widely in their reasons for choosing their responses (Haas, et al., 1988). A survey of the ethicality and frequency of using 40 forms of technology in the independent practice of psychologists found wide variability in what was considered ethical on 60 per cent of the practices (McMinn, Buchanan, Ellens, & Ryan, 1999).[2] These data are less than reassuring for those seeking psychological services. It appears that the unsystematic nature of much of ethics education is matched only by the unsys-

tematic ethical decision-making processes used by practitioners.

The increased emphasis placed on ethics education of counsellors and psychologists, concern expressed in the literature about lack of rigor in ethics education that still exists, and professionals' apparent weakness in demonstrating consistent ethical decision-making abilities have implications for all counsellors and counsellor-educators, including those who belong to the Canadian Counselling Association (CCA). The revised CCA *Code of Ethics* (1999) includes a section on counsellor preparation standards which includes the following statement: "Counsellors who are responsible for counsellor education, training, and supervision have an obligation to make their students, trainees, and supervisors aware of their ethical responsibilities as expressed in the CCA *Code of Ethics*, (p. 16). This mandate makes it clear that counsellor-educators have a strong obligation to educate students about ethical responsibilities in all aspects of professional conduct.

The purpose of this paper is to provide counsellor-educators and counsellors in the field with a summary of the professional literature dealing with research on ethics education and reports describing models used for teaching ethics. Also, a description is presented of two ethics education courses, one for graduate students in counselling psychology and a second for undergraduate students specializing in addictions.

Impact of Formal Ethics Education

The research undertaken on the impact of formal ethics education attempts to deal with the lack of clarity on how to educate students in ethics and ethical decision making. Only a handful of studies in the literature assess the effects of a formal learning experience with an ethics component. These studies are examined below.

Utilizing a post-test only, control group design, Paradise (1976) found that master's level counselling students who participated in a small group discussion of general moral dilemmas (experimental condition) scored higher on a test measuring ethical judgment than other counselling students who did not receive the exposure (control condition). The results supported the hypothesis that ethical judgment could be influenced by academic training. The test instrument, the Ethical Judgment Scale (Van Hoose & Paradise, 1979), has since been the focus of considerable debate over validity and reliability (Doromal, 1987; Post, 1989; Welfel & Lipsitz, 1984). Regardless, the Paradise study made a significant contribution to the literature, since it was the first to examine counsellor performance on an ethics-related task based on previous exposure to ethics-related discussion.

Granum and Erickson (1976) presented master's- and doctoral-level counselling students with a self-paced, seven-hour, independent learning module on confidentiality. A paper-and-pencil test containing 36 case vignettes measured students' retention of confidential information presented in each vignette. Pre- and post-test change scores on the test showed that, compared with a no-treatment control group, subjects studying alone or in pairs became significantly less willing to compromise confidential information. This study contributed to the literature by demonstrating that ethical decision making can be affected by pertinent instruction.

Morrison and Teta (1979) studied graduate students in nursing, education, and social service work who were enrolled in a course in humanistic psychology. A significant component of the course was discussion of ethical conflicts in the clinical field. One of the self-report instruments used in the study was a questionnaire that presented 20 situations that involve ethical conflict for clinicians. Participants were to indicate the degree of conflict they experienced along a seven-point rating scale. Pre-test, post-test,

and three-month-follow-up scores on this instrument indicated a significant increase in ethical conflict scores among students. Students had therefore become more aware of ethical issues during the course, and were more sensitive to situations that would present an ethical dilemma.

A survey by Baldick (1980) focussed on the efficacy of previous formal education in ethics. Clinical psychology interns were sent the Ethical Discrimination Inventory (EDI), an instrument consisting of 12 hypothetical clinical situations containing a variety of hidden ethical issues. Respondents were asked to determine and list, in a two- to five-word phrase, as many ethical issues present in the situations as possible. The results indicated that subjects who had either received a formal ethics course during their training or at least five hours of ethics discussion (details of which were not provided) were able to discriminate ethical issues better on the EDI, and thus scored significantly higher than subjects who had received less or no ethics instruction during training. Exposure to ethics at the graduate level apparently resulted in a greater ability to discriminate ethical problems in given situations.

In a pilot study involving a treatment group only, Elliot (1991) reported the pretest to post-test effects of an ethics education module of a course for masters' students in educational psychology on actions in ethical-dilemma resolution and level of ethical orientation. Thirty-seven graduate students participated in a three-week module that included 15 1/2 hours of class time devoted to increasing awareness of ethical problems and to teaching problem-solving skills to deal with ethical dilemmas. The course focussed on a case study and problem-solving approach to ethical, legal, and professional issues described by Eberlein (1987; 1993). Scores on the Haas Ethical Dilemma Questionnaire (Haas, et al., 1986;

1988) across the two administrations indicated that in four of the 10 dilemmas the students' awareness of alternate options and actions appeared to increase. Scores on the Ethical Orientation Checklist, an application of Van Hoose and Paradise's (1979) five-stage model of assessing ethical reasoning, indicated that student level of ethical orientation increased significantly on two of the 10 ethical dilemmas. These results suggested that the ethics learning component did have an effect on some aspects of the students' ethical orientation.

Gawthrop and Uhlemann (1992) examined the effects of a workshop on ethical decision making using a case study and problem-solving approach (Canadian Psychological Association, 1986; Eberlein, 1987, 1988a; Tymchuk, 1986) to ethics education. The study included three participant conditions composed of undergraduate students randomly assigned from child and youth care, social work, and counselling psychology courses. The treatment group received a three-hour ethical decision-making workshop involving the discussion of prepared and self-generated case vignettes of ethical dilemmas. This group of participants were presented with the content of two sections (Section A - General and Section B - Individual and Group Counselling Relationships) of the Canadian Guidance and Counselling Association (CGCA) *Code of Ethics* (1981) and a copy of the decision-making model for resolving ethical dilemmas from the *Canadian Code of Ethics for Psychologists* (1986) developed by the Canadian Psychological Association (CPA). The informed control group worked on the standardized case vignette with the aid of the two sections from the CGCA *Code of Ethics* and the CPA ethical decision-making model. The uninformed control group completed the case vignette unaided by the CGCA *Code* sections and the CPA ethical decision-making model, and were given brief written instructions to indicate in writing what they would

do if they were the counsellor in the vignette and why. Written responses were scored for decision-making quality on the Tymchuk Rating Scale (Tymchuk, Ouslander, Rahber, & Fitten, 1988; Ouslander, Tymchuk, & Rahbar, 1989). The treatment group scored significantly higher than did either of the control groups on decision-making quality. There were no significant differences between the scores of the two control groups. These findings suggest that even when it is not possible to devote a full course to ethics education, counsellors can learn content and decision-making skills for improving their response to ethical dilemmas, especially when a well-defined teaching model is used.

Another group of researchers (Fisher, Rollins, Rubin, & McGinn, 1993) conducted a large study of the Ethical Case Management Practices Training Program (Rubin, Millard, & Wong, 1990), a five-unit training program designed for rehabilitation counsellors. The five instructional units dealt with the following four topics: 1) increasing understanding of ethical principles; 2) increasing understanding of articles in codes of ethics; 3) practicing identification and analysis of ethical dilemmas; 4) and learning an ethical decision-making model for solving ethical dilemmas. In a treatment group-only design, the 10- to 16-hour program, was administered to nine groups of rehabilitation counsellors. To provide a behavioural measure of the effect of the program to enhance ethical decision-making ability, participants wrote pre- and post-test justifications to resolve an ethical dilemma. Post-test ratings on this behavioral measure were significantly higher than pre-test ratings. Self-report feedback also indicated that participants believed they had a greater ability to recognize and resolve ethical dilemmas. Though the research of this program is promising, more rigorous research is required before the impact of this program is clearly demonstrated.

Fisher and Kuther (1997) studied the impact of integrating six case studies on research ethics into the introductory psychology curricula at two universities. One-half of the students received the ethics education based on the study of classic empirical studies cited in most introductory psychology textbooks and half did not. No information is given about the time devoted to this education, but students received guidance through a workbook containing abstracts of each study, detailed description of each study, and homework assignments that included four study questions for each case. The findings from the pre-test to post-test design of the study revealed that the students receiving the ethics education exhibited increased awareness of procedures used to protect subjects' rights and welfare. To a lesser extent those same students increased their sensitivity to experimental issues and subject welfare when making ethical decisions. This study is unique in studying ethics education related to research issues, and provides a model for others in this domain of study.

In a study of ethics education with upper-level undergraduates in psychology, La Cour and Lewis (1998) compared a group of students receiving a course in ethics with a second group of students who did not receive the course. The ethics course covered the following six content areas: 1) confidentiality; 2) malpractice; 3) informed consent; 4) dual relationships; 5) duty to warn and protect; and 6) working with culturally diverse populations. In a post-test only design it was found that those students taking the ethics course obtained a significantly higher mean score on a test of actual knowledge than those students who did not receive the course. The findings clearly showed the benefit of ethics education with these students. To the dismay of the researchers, however, it was also found that both groups believed they knew more about ethics than they actually knew. This raised concerns for the investigators

about bachelor-level practitioners failing to consult supervisors for advice when they are faced with ethical decisions in practice.

In summary, relatively few studies assessing the effects of ethics education are reported in the professional literature. The more recent studies generally used stronger methodological conditions, so a clearer interpretation of the research findings are possible. Still there is a need for stronger experimental designs, more standardization in evaluation methods, and a more extensive description of the treatment procedures and content used in teaching ethics. Regardless, this small group of studies that consistently suggested positive effects from ethics education with undergraduate and graduate students will help programs and practitioners. The findings from these studies provide a base for future research and practice in ethics education.

Models for Teaching Moral Reasoning and Ethics

An early example of an ethics teaching model was a 10-week graduate seminar designed and taught by Abeles (1980). Students were presented with ethical dilemmas and selected readings. During class discussions the students were challenged on their values and beliefs in the process of dealing with the dilemmas. Lack of formal evaluation was a drawback of this course, but there was some movement beyond sole reliance on ethical codes as course content.

An unusual approach was introduced by McMinn (1988), who designed a generic case-study simulation program for use with computers. When integrated into McMinn's ethics course, this tool provided students with the opportunity to select from dichotomous responses in each of two case studies, to be presented with results based on their choices, and to repeat the process through a series of text screens toward one of 16 possible case outcomes per case study. After each decision was made, the program requested the reason for the decision. Student responses were accessed afterwards for analysis in class. Following the case outcome, the program evaluated the student's decisions based on ethical guidelines that were written into the software. This software was used as a springboard for discussion on moral issues and ethical decision making (McMinn, 1988). This contribution to ethics education has so far not been evaluated elsewhere in the literature.

A course designed by McGovern (1988) provided a semester-long examination of numerous issues such as moral behaviour, competence, professional relationships, critical thinking, case studies, and values. All topics were structured around the American Psychological Association's ethical principles (APA, 1981). The process of the course moved from early attention to information and content, toward, and then to, analysis and philosophical understanding of ethics in order to foster increasing complexity in student thinking.

A strength of this course resides in its use of evaluation (McGovern, 1988). Students were subject to pre- and post-course testing and self-evaluation. They were given three essay examinations during the course, and produced five position papers on case studies for critique by instructor and peers. Finally, the students provided post-course evaluation of the instructor. A weakness of the course lay in the failure to provide an ethical decision-making model to help students reconcile conflicts between their own values, current ethical guidelines, and societal norms.

Kitchener's (1986) proposed curriculum for ethics education is based on the following four goals: a) sensitizing students to ethical issues in the profession; b) improving ethical reasoning; c) developing moral responsibility and the ego strength to act ethically; and d) teaching tolerance of ambiguity in ethical decision making. Suggestions for

achieving these goals in ethics courses included the following: a) reading and discussing ethical codes and case vignettes; b) student generation of ethical cases from experience; c) the study of Kitchener's (1984) model for levels of ethical decision making and ways it can be applied in specific cases; d) generating and justifying ethical decisions about specific cases; e) role playing; and f) utilizing professional resource people in seminars. Although Kitchener's model is theory-based and shows much attention to content and process, no suggestions for evaluation were included.

Eberlein (1987; 1988a) described another teaching approach that evolved out of work on the new CPA *Code of Ethics* (CPA, 1986). This code contains a decision-making model based on work by Tymchuk (1981, 1986). Ethics teaching that used this approach involved the study of ethical guidelines but included a consideration of personal values and consultation around case vignettes. In addition, a decision-making model is used to assist in the weighing of alternatives and to foster a move away from simplistic conceptualizations of ethical dilemmas. The decision-making model used in the problem-solving approach (CPA, 1986, 1988; Eberlein, 1987; Tymchuk, 1986) included a final step, calling upon the practitioner to remain accountable during the consequences of a decision.

Eberlein (1987) has used this model in the ethics component of the regular graduate clinical and counselling course at the University of Alberta. Course content and process include the following: a) written statements outlining students' policies with clients on the issues of confidentiality, competence and informed consent; b) preparation and discussion of case dilemmas with use of the CPA *Code* and its ethical decision-making model; and c) a final exam that tests knowledge of the code and its ethical decision-making model. The exam is graded on "the appropriateness of a student's choice of ethical principles and on the quality and completeness of the rationale for the decision chosen" (p. 357). Throughout the course, critical-evaluative moral reasoning (Kitchener, 1984) is fostered.

Another feature of Eberlein's (1987) examination of the current nature of ethics education was noteworthy. Eberlein distinguished between two approaches that seemed to describe most teaching models: the "Correct-Answer" approach and the "Problem-Solving" approach. The former was characterized by reliance on codified ethical principles and guidelines as providing solutions to ethical problems. The latter also used ethical principles but added consideration of personal values, consultation, the weighing of alternatives and the use of decision-making models in the search for solutions to ethical problems.

More recently, Eberlein (1993) provided the reader with an excellent update and elaboration of his experience in the education of psychologists in ethics and professional conduct. He proposed that ethics education courses consider the following "issues and goals": a) students must become sensitive to the existance of an ethical problem; b) they need to learn to "cope with the anxiety associated with moral ambiguity and uncertainty" in ethical dilemmas (p. 2), where more than one acceptable alternative exists or where no alternative seems desirable; c) they should realize that "values and moral principles" vary among the codes of ethics of different professional associations, rules of the law, and policies of institutions and agencies; d) it is important for students to develop a decision-making procedure that leads to "moral judgment" and to a "moral responsibility to act" (p. 3); e) students need to learn about "professional norms" that are included in ethical decision making and that address the professional and business aspects of the profession; and f) the professional needs "to

be aware at all times that consultation is important when making decisions that can have serious legal or ethical consequences" (p. 3). As well, a listing of professional issues to be covered in a graduate course on professional issues is presented for consideration. Counsellor-educators are encouraged to read this comprehensive and thought-provoking examination of the issues in ethics education.

Fine and Ulrich (1988) reported a 15-week formal course in ethics, which integrated the perspectives of psychology and philosophy. The course was offered in small-group format to graduate clinical-psychology students, and was team taught by two instructors with academic and professional backgrounds in philosophy, counselling and clinical psychology. Based on the ideas of Kitchener (1984), Eberlein (1987), Keith-Spiegel and Koocher (1985), and others, the course included didactic instruction, case presentations, discussion and student presentation of cases. Course evaluation included a mid-term exam, a written case presentation to the class by each student, and a thorough written case analysis from each student's own clinical experience. A three-month follow-up was conducted with former students who were working in clinical settings. Returned questionnaires showed that students still perceived the course as having had a strong impact on them. The authors recommended clinical supervision in practicum settings as a future part of an ethics course, as well as more attention to process in ethical decision making.

In summary, the courses and curricula presented in this section indicate that the formalization of ethics education has increased in recent years. They show that the underlying rationale for content and process of ethics instruction has been considered, articulated and incorporated into classroom instruction. There has also been progress made in the area of formal evaluation, in keeping with the assumption that ethics is an academic subject requiring normal evaluation procedures like other subjects.

A Course on Professional Issues in Counselling Psychology

For a number of years, the first author has had the opportunity to teach professional issues courses to master's- and doctoral-level students in counselling psychology. This author's thinking on the teaching of professional issues has been particularly influenced by the work of three writers. The first writer is Alexander Tymchuk (1981; 1982; 1986), who was among the earliest to discuss ethical decision making in values' issues. He suggested that the original impetus for our increasing concern about ethical practice and research comes from our awareness of Nazi atrocities and the resulting Nuremberg Code to protect human rights in research or treatment.

Also, the work of Larry Eberlein (1987, 1988a, 1988b, 1993), who enunciated the importance of ethics education in values and moral reasoning, and stressed the importance of teaching students how to deal effectively with ethical dilemmas in professional practice. Eberlein (1993) proposed, "When clients present problems involving human relationships, these will almost always involve some conflict among the values, rights and responsibilities of the psychologist, the client, related persons, one or more agencies, other professionals, and the community at large" (p. 98).

More recently, this author has been influenced by Naomi Meara and her colleagues (Jordan & Meara, 1990; Meara, Schmidt, & Day, 1996), who brought a new perspective to ethics education when they proposed the need for professionals to add virtue ethics to the traditional principle-ethics approach to solving ethical dilemmas. Principle ethics emphasize the use of a relatively narrow set of ethical concepts to find a rational, objective, and universal solution to a definable dilemma. Jordan and Meara suggested this approach involves a focus on acts and choices (p. 108) that leads to answering the question, "What should I do?" (p. 108) when facing a tough decision. Such an approach is acceptable although not sufficient for Meara and her colleagues, who suggested adding virtue ethics to this process that places emphasis "on agents or actors" (p. 109). This focus involves development of the "internal qualities, traits, or mature habits" (p. 109) of the counsellor and answering the question "Who shall I be?" (p. 108) in this situation. This broader ethical approach means asking the traditional principle-ethics question, "Is this situation unethical?" (Corey, et al., 1998, p. 10) in addition to the virtue-ethics question of, "Am I doing what is best for my client?" (Corey, et al., 1998, p. 10). It is suggested that stronger ethical decisions are made when both aspects are addressed.

The content of the graduate course taught by the first author includes an examination of professional, ethical, and legal issues relevant to counselling psychology (see Table 1). This author proposes that a trained counsellor must be: well-versed with the many issues involved in working with clients in a helping interaction; be a member of an agency or larger institution; and be capable of responding to societal and professional organizations. As well, helping professionals must be aware of their personal beliefs, values, biases, and moral structure when in the helping role. Emphasis is given to learning through the use of case studies and the adaptation of Eberlein's (1987) problem-solving approach to decision making.

This outline of course content is presented only as one example for others to expand upon and develop to meet their own needs. The number and range of professional issues to be covered in such a course are extensive and variable depending on the interests of the instructor, the training program, and the students. As well, these content areas can be

Table 1

Content Areas for a Course on Professional Issues in Counselling Psychology

Class 1
History of ethics education; What a code of ethics is and its key components; The need for a decision-making model; Client rights.

Class 2
Conditions that lead to ethical dilemmas; Ideal conditions for decision making; Violating ethical sanctions; Preventive actions for making ethical decisions under pressure.

Class 3
Malpractice; Negligence law; Civil and criminal issues; Reasonable standard of care.

Class 4
Counsellor's role as a person and professional; Self-awareness, transference, counter transference; Stress and burnout.

Class 5
Values and value conflicts in lifestyle and philosophy.

Class 6
Informed consent; Record-keeping practices; other client rights.

Class 7
Issues of confidentiality, privilege, privacy; Duty to warn and protect.

Class 8
Issues of boundaries and multiple relationships.

Class 9
Issues of professional competence and training.

Class 10
Multicultural and diversity issues.

Class 11
Ethical issues in group or family counselling (Determined with student input).

adapted for use in alternative formats, such as a designated segment of a larger course, or as a series of professional-development sessions in applied field settings.

The format of the course is a series of 13-weekly, three-hour seminars. The instructor conducts the first four seminars to build a basis of knowledge and process to be used by students throughout the course. Teams of two or three students then take responsibility for a portion of subsequent class sessions. The student teams are to study widely those topic areas to be covered during the class of their responsibility, select additional readings for the class to study, and conduct a 45-minute workshop that educates the class through planned didactic, experiential and discussion activities in the areas of focus for the seminar. The remaining class time is devoted to the presentation of additional material by the instructor and student problem solving of a client case study related to the topic for the week. Evaluation in the course is based on the quality of workshops presented by student groups, and the quality of student performance on a take-home project in which students analyse client case studies using the decision-making process learned in the course.

A Course on Professional Issues in the Addictions Field

When the teaching of professional ethics in counselling is delivered to an audience with specialized interests in practice, the educational impact can be enhanced by dealing with those content areas that may be of particular relevance to that audience. One such area is addictions. The second author, whose background includes addictions counselling, has designed and conducted a course on professional ethics for addictions workers as part of the Addiction Studies Certificate program at Camosun College in Victoria, B.C. Students are comprised of addictions counsellors, nurses, youth workers, social workers, and other professionals and para-professionals who deal with addictions issues in their work.

Two challenges exist in presenting a 36-hour ethics course focussed on addictions. First, it is difficult to provide an in-depth treatment of issues needing coverage. A second, related challenge is specializing the curriculum without giving up the components essential to teaching a solid base in general professional ethics. Though these challenges exist, a strong course can be developed. Table 2 presents the current content of the course taught by the second author.

In addition to the use of lecture, small-group discussion and case vignettes, the second author includes role-playing as a learning activity in this course. Based on an ethics committee simulation model developed by Johnson and Corser (1998), the present course includes two class role-plays involving an ethics tribunal hearing, one halfway through the course and one near the end of the course. After the class is carefully oriented to the purpose and potential impact of the role-play exercise, a tribunal is chosen from the students at random, with an additional student randomly chosen to take the role of the "respondent," an addictions worker who is accused of an ethics violation. While the rest of the class observes, a mock hearing is conducted, wherein a formal "complaint" is read and the respondent is interviewed and defends his or her "position" (based on a scripted role not explained to the class until later) on the complaint. The respondent is then excused from the room while the tribunal deliberates. The respondent is then brought back into class for either another round of questions or for the decision of the tribunal. When the exercise is over, the class debriefs the experience, with emphasis on the ethical issues arising from the case as well as on the process of the tribunal. Students participating in this process, and those observing frequently, report an almost visceral

Table 2

Content Areas for a Course on Professional Issues in Addictions

Class 1
Philosophical foundations of professional ethics; Principles, codes and standards vs. virtues; Decision-making models.

Class 2
Autonomy vs. paternalism; Competence — Personal recovery, negligence, burnout; Professional peer issues; Relationships with co-workers; Relationships with professional peers.

Class 3
Informed consent/informed refusal — What are clients consenting to? Can children and adolescents seek or refuse treatment?

Class 4
Confidentiality, limits to confidentiality; Service notes and reports, fax transmissions, file security and disposition

Class 5
Misconduct complaints — Life cycle/prevention of complaints; Ethics tribunal simulation #1 setup.

Class 6
Ethics tribunal-hearing simulation #1 and debriefing; The treatment industry — Who is the client?; Exploitation of clients and families, fundraising, use of resources; Boundary issues — Physical touch/verbal intimacy, dual relationships, small and rural community issues.

Class 7
Organizational Issues — Agency politics/use of resources; Ethics tribunal simulation #2 setup.

Class 8
Ethics tribunal-hearing simulation #2 & debriefing. Termination & referral — When/when not to terminate, refusal of treatment, ethical issues in referrals; Course issues integration — Review & future trends, written assignment/course evaluation.

understanding of the tensions and hard choices faced by colleagues in real-life complaint situations.

This course is presented as only one of many possible ways of satisfying the minimum requirements for education in professional ethics for a specialized-target student group. As can be seen from the content areas of both courses presented in this article, differences in course length, focus, and structure are not as great as the similarities they share. Both courses are representative of how the teaching of professional ethics is developing in professional programs with widely varying student populations.

Resources for Teaching Professional Issues in Counselling Psychology and Addictions

Only 15 years ago, the number of resources available for teaching courses on professional issues in helping programs was relatively small compared to today. In recent years an increasing number of texts, journal articles, and other resources have become available to inform students and practicing professionals about the range of professional issues they face in their daily contacts with clients. Presented in Table 3 is a core list of resource material that the authors use in conducting their courses. However, the range of quality

---

Table 3

Resources on Ethics and Legal Issues in Counselling Psychology and Addictions

Canadian Code of Ethics for Psychologists: Companion Manual (Rev. Ed.), Canadian Psychological Association, 1992.

Ethics for Addictions Professionals by L. Bissell & J. Royce, Hazelden, 1994.

Ethics in the Practice of Psychology by M. A. Carroll, H. Schneider, & G. Wesley, PrenticeHall, 1985.

Issues and Ethics in the Helping Professions (Fifth Ed.) by G. Corey, M. Corey, & P. Callanan, Brooks/Cole, 1998.

ACA Ethical Standards Casebook (Fifth Ed.) by B. Herlihy & G. Corey, Association Counseling Association, 1996.

The Law, Standards of Practice, and Ethics in the Practice of Psychology by D. Evans, Edmond Montgomery, 1997.

Boundary Issues in Counseling: Multiple Roles and Responsibilities by B. Herlihy & G. Corey, American Counseling Association, 1997.

Children, Ethics and the Law by G. Koocher & P. Keith-Spiegel, University of Nebraska Press, 1990.

Ethics in Psychology: Professional Standards and Cases (Sec. Ed.) by G. Koocher & P. Keith-Spiegel Random House, 1998.

Alcohol and Drug Problems: A Practical Guide for Counsellors (Sec. Ed.) by S. Harrison & V. Carver (Eds.), Addiction Research Foundation of Ontario, 1997.

Balancing Conflicting Interests: A Counselling Guide to the Legal Process, by M. McEvoy & G. Reid, Justice Institute of British Columbia, 1997.

Sexual Feelings in Psychotherapy by K. Pope, J. Sonne, & J. Holroyd, American Psychological Association, 1993.

Ethics in Psychotherapy and Counseling: A Practical Guide for Psychologists by K. Pope & M. Vasquez, Jossey-Bass, 1991.

Counselling Ethics Casebook (Sec. Ed.), by W. Schulz, Canadian Counselling Association, 2000.

A Legal Handbook for the Helping Professional (Sec. Ed.) by M. Uhlemann & D. Turner, Sedgewick Society for Consumer and Public Education, 1998.

Critical Incidents: Ethical Issues in Substance Abuse Prevention and Treatment by W. White, Lighthouse, 1993

resource material is more extensive than that listed. Readers are encouraged to go beyond this list in their search for resource material.

Conclusion

Expectations mount from within the counselling profession and from the public through increased consumer advocacy for professional accountability in counselling practice. One of the most important actions, which the counsellor-educators and counsellors in the field can take, is to be proactive in responding to these demands through increased knowledge and skill in dealing with the daily ethical dilemmas encountered. The time for learning ethical decision making only through incidental discussions in courses or practice, or by "osmosis" as Handlesman (1986) expresses it, is a part of the past. The literature provides the counsellor-educator and the counsellor in the field with the mandate, rationale, teaching models, and content material for developing sensitive and informed decision-making abilities for the complex world of professional issues in counselling practice. It is hoped that the content and resources listed in this article will assist all counsellors to further their abilities in ethical decision making and to encourage them to further refine academic and professional development curricula in the area.

Endnotes

[1] Portion from Effects of the Problem-Solving Approach in Ethics Training by J. C. Gawthrop and M. R. Uhlemann, 1992, Professional Psychology: Research and Practice, 23, 38-42.

[2] Portion from Effects of the Problem-Solving Approach in Ethics Training by J. C. Gawthrop and M. R. Uhlemann, 1992, Professional Psychology: Research and Practice, 23, 38-42.

References

Abeles, N. (1980). Teaching ethical principles by means of value confrontations. *Psychotherapy: Theory, Research and Practice*, 17(4), 384-391.

American Psychological Association (1981). Ethical principles of psychologists. *American Psychologist*, 36, 633-638.

Baldick, T. (1980). Ethical discrimination ability of intern psychologists: A function of training in ethics. *Professional Psychology*, 11, 276-282.

Bissell, L., & Royce, J. (1994). *Ethics for addiction professionals*. Center City, MN: Hazelden.

Canadian Guidance and Counselling Association, (1981). *Guidelines for ethical behaviour*. Ottawa, Ontario: Author.

Canadian Counselling Association, (1999). *Code of ethics*. Ottawa, Ontario: Author.

Canadian Psychological Association, Committee on Ethics. (1986). *Code of Ethics. Highlights*, 8(1), 6E-12E.

Canadian Psychological Association, Committee on Ethics (1988). *Canadian code of ethics for psychologists: Companion manual*. Old Chelsea, Quebec: Author.

Corey, G., Corey, M. S., & Callanan, P. (1979). *Issues and ethics in the helping professions*. Pacific Grove, Calif: Brooks/Cole.

Corey, G., Corey, M., & Callanan, P. (1998). *Issues and ethics in the helping professions* (Fifth Edition). Pacific Grove, CA: Brooks/Cole.

Doromal, Q. S. (1987). An evaluation of selected psychometric characteristics of the Ethical Judgement Scale (Doctoral dissertation, Virginia Polytechnic Institute and State University, 1986). *Dissertation Abstracts Intenational*, 47(7), 2456A.

Eberlein, L. (1987). Introducing ethics to beginning psychologists: A problem solving approach. *Professional Psychology: Research and Practice*, 18(4), 353-359.

Eberlein, L. (1988a). The new CPA code of ethics for Canadian psychologists: An education and training perspective. *Canadian Psychology*, 29(2), 206-212.

Eberlein, L. (1988b). The use of the Ethical Judgement Scale for ethics education. *Canadian Journal of Counselling*, 22, 242-245.

Eberlein, L. (1993). The eduction of psychologists in ethical and professional conduct. In K. S. Dobson & D. J. Dobson (Eds.), *The practice of psychology in Canada*. Toronto: Hogrefe & Huber.

Elliot, M. M. (1991). *Ethical decision making and judgements of psychologists: An exploratory study.* Unpublished doctoral dissertation, University of Alberta, Edmonton.

Fine, M., & Ulrich, L. (1988). Integrating psychology and philosophy in teaching a graduate course in ethics. *Professional Psychology: Research and Practice*, 19(5), 542-546.

Fisher, C. B., & Kuther, T. L. (1997). Integrating research ethics into the introductory psychology course curriculum. *Teaching Psychology*, 24(3), 172-175.

Fisher, M. F., Rollins, C. W., Rubin, S. E., & McGinn, F. (1993). The ethical case management practices training program: An evaluation. *Rehabilitation Education*, 7, 7-16.

Gawthrop, J., & Uhlemann, M. (1992). Effects of the problem-solving approach in ethics training. *Professional Psychology: Research and Practice.* 23, (1), 38-42.

Granum, R., & Erickson, R. (1976). How a learning module can affect confidential decision making. *Counselor Education and Supervision*, 15(4), 276-284.

Haas, L., Malouf, J., & Mayerson, N. (1985, August). *Ethics training and professional characteristics of practicing psychologists: Are they related to ethical decision making?* Paper presented at the annual convention of the American Psychological Association, Los Angeles, CA.

Haas, L., Malouf, J., & Mayerson, N. (1986). Ethical dilemmas in psychological practice: Results of a national survey. *Professional Psychology: Research and Practice*, 17(4), 316-321.

Haas, L., Malouf, J., & Mayerson, N. (1988). Personal and professional characteristics as factors in psychologists' ethical decision making. *Professional Psychology: Research and Practice*, 19(1), 35-42.

Handelsman, M. (1986). Problems with ethics training by "osmosis". *Professional Psychology: Research and Practice*, 17(4), 371-372.

Harrison, S., & Carver, V. (Eds.) (1997). *Alcohol and drug problems: A practical guide for counsellors* (2nd Edition). Toronto: Addiction Research Foundation.

Johnson, W., & Corser, R. (1998). Learning ethics the hard way: Facing the ethics committee. *Teaching of Psychology*, 25(1), 26-28.

Jordan, A., & Meara, N. (1990). Ethics and the professional practice of psychologists: The role of virtues and principles. *Professional Psychology: Research and Practice*, 21(2), 107-114.

Keith-Spiegel, P., & Koocher, G. P. (1985). *Ethics in psychology: Professional standards and cases.* New York: Random House.

Kitchener, K. (1984). Intuition, critical evaluation and ethical principles: The foundation for ethical decisions in counseling psychology. *Counseling Psychologist*, 12(3), 43-55.

Kitchener, K. (1986). Teaching applied ethics in counselor education: An integration of psychological processes and philosophical analysis. *Journal of Counseling and Development*, 64(5), 306-310.

LaCour, J., & Lewis, D. (1998). Effects of a course on self-rated and actual knowledge of undergraduate psychology majors. *Psychological Reports*, 82, 499-504.

Meara, N. M., Schmidt, L. D., & Day, J. D. (1996). A foundation for ethical decision, policies, and character. *The Counseling Psychologist*, 24(1), 4-77.

McGovern, T. (1988). Teaching the ethical principles of psychology. *Teaching of Psychology*, 15(1), 22-26.

McMinn, M. (1988). Ethics case-study simulation: A generic tool for psychology teachers. *Teaching of Psychology*, 15(2), 100-101.

McMinn, M., Buchannan, T., Ellens, B., & Ryan, M. (1999). Technology, professional practice, and ethics: Survey findings and implications. *Professional Psychology: Research and Practice*, 30(2), 165-172.

Morrison, J., & Teta, D. (1979). Impact of a humanistic approach on students' attitudes, attributions, and ethical conflicts. *Psychological Reports*, 45, 863-866.

Newark, C., & Hutchins, T. (1981). Survey of professional education in ethics in clinical psychology internship programs. *Journal of Clinical Psychology.* 37(3), 681-683.

Ouslander, J., Tymchuk, A., & Rahbar, B. (1989). Health care decisions among elderly long-term care residents and their potential proxies. *Archives of Internal Medicine*, 149 (June), 1367-1372.

Paradise, L. (1976). Towards a theory on the ethical behavior of counselors. (Doctoral dissertation, University of Virginia). *Dissertation Abstracts International,* 1977, 37, 4140A-4141A. (University Microfilms No. 77- 204)

Pettifor, J., & Pitcher, S. (1982). Ethics training in Canadian graduate schools of psychology. *Canadian Psychology,* 23(4), 235-242.

Post, P. (1989). The use of the Ethical Judgement Scale in counselor education. *Counselor Education and Supervision,* 28(3), 229-233.

Rubin, S. E., Millard, R., & Wong, H. (1990). *Ethical case management practices: A training package for dealing with ethical dilemmas encountered by rehabilitation counselors in the case management process.* (2nd ed.). Carbondale, IL.: Southern Illinois University, Rehabilitation Institute.

Shertzer, B., & Morris, K. (1972). APGA members' ethical discriminatory ability. *Counselor Education and Supervision,* 11(3), 200-206.

Tymchuk, A. (1981). Ethical decision making and psychological treatment. *Journal of Psychiatric Treatment and Evaluation,* 3, 507-513.

Tymchuk, A. (1982). Strategies for resolving value dilemmas. *American Behavioral Scientist,* 26(2), 159-175.

Tymchuk, A. (1986). Guidelines for ethical decision making. *Canadian Psychology,* 27(1), 36-43.

Tymchuk, A., Ouslander, J., Rahbar, B., & Fitten, J. (1988). Medical decision making among elderly people in long term care. *The Gerontologist,* 28 (Suppl.), 59-63.

Van Hoose, W., & Paradise, L. (1979). *Ethics in counseling and psychotherapy.* Cranston, R. I.: Carroll Press.

Welfel, E., & Lipsitz, N. (1984). The ethical behavior of psychologists: A critical analysis of the research. *The Counseling Psychologist,* 12(3), 31-42.

Welfel, E. R., & Kitchener, K. S. (1992). Introduction to special section: Ethics education - An agenda for the '90s. *Professional Psychology: Research and Practice,* 23(3), 179-181.

White, W. (1993). *Critical incidents: Ethical issues in substance abuse prevention and treatment.* Bloomington, IL: Lighthouse.

Appendices

APPENDIX A

Code of Ethics and Standards of Practice of the American Counseling Association

As Approved by Governing Council
April 1997
Effective July 1, 1997

PREAMBLE

The American Counseling Association is an educational, scientific and professional organization whose members are dedicated to the enhancement of human development throughout the life span. Association members recognize diversity in our society and embrace a cross-cultural approach in support of the worth, dignity, potential, and uniqueness of each individual.

The specification of a code of ethics enables the association to clarify to current and future members, and to those served by members, the nature of the ethical responsibilities held in common by its members. As the code of ethics of the association, this document establishes principles that define the ethical behavior of association members. All members of the American Counseling Association are required to adhere to the Code of Ethics and the Standards of Practice. The Code of Ethics will serve as the basis for processing ethical complaints initiated against members of the association.

SECTION A:
THE COUNSELING RELATIONSHIP

A.1. Client Welfare

a. *Primary Responsibility*
The primary responsibility of counselors is to respect the dignity and to promote the welfare of clients.

b. *Positive Growth and Development*
Counselors encourage client growth and development in ways that foster the clients' interest and welfare; counselors avoid fostering dependent counseling relationships.

c. *Counseling Plans*
Counselors and their clients work jointly in devising integrated, individual counseling plans that offer reasonable promise of success and are consistent with abilities and circumstances of clients. Counselors and clients regularly review counseling plans to ensure their continued viability and effectiveness respecting clients' freedom of choice. (See A.3.b.)

d. *Family Involvement*
Counselors recognize that families are usually important in clients' lives and strive to enlist family understanding and involvement as a positive resource when appropriate.

e. *Career and Employment Needs*
Counselors work with their clients in considering employment in jobs and circumstances that are consistent with the clients' overall abilities, vocational limitations, physical restrictions, general temperament, interest and aptitude patterns, social skills, education, general qualifications, and other relevant characteristics and needs. Counselors neither place nor participate in placing clients in positions that will result in damaging the interest and the welfare of clients, employers, or the public.

A.2. Respecting Diversity

a. *Nondiscrimination*
Counselors do not condone or engage in discrimination based on age, color, culture, disability, ethnic group, gender, race, religion, sexual orientation, marital status, or socioeconomic status. (See C.5.a., C.5.b., and D.1.i.)

b. *Respecting Differences*
Counselors will actively attempt to understand the diverse cultural backgrounds of the clients with whom they work. This includes, but is not limited to, learning how the counselor's own cultural/ethnic/racial identity impacts her/his values and beliefs about the counseling process. (See E.8. and F.2.i.)

A.3. Client Rights

a. *Disclosure to Clients*
When counseling is initiated, and throughout the counseling process as necessary, counselors inform clients of the purposes, goals, techniques, procedures, limitations, potential risks and benefits of services to be performed, and other pertinent information. Counselors take steps to ensure that clients understand the implications of diagnosis, the intended use of tests and reports, fees, and billing arrangements. Clients have the right to expect confidentiality and to be provided with an explanation of its limitations, including supervision and/or treatment team professionals; to obtain clear information about their case records; to participate in the ongoing counseling plans; and to refuse any recommended services and be advised of the consequences of such refusal. (See E.5.a. and G.2.)

b. *Freedom of Choice*
Counselors offer clients the freedom to choose whether to enter into a counseling relationship and to determine which pro-

fessional(s) will provide counseling. Restrictions that limit choices of clients are fully explained. (See A.1.c.)

c. *Inability to Give Consent*

When counseling minors or persons unable to give voluntary informed consent, counselors act in these clients' best interests. (See B.3.)

A.4. Clients Served by Others

If a client is receiving services from another mental health professional, counselors, with client consent, inform the professional persons already involved and develop clear agreements to avoid confusion and conflict for the client. (See C.6.c.)

A.5. Personal Needs and Values

a. *Personal Needs*

In the counseling relationship, counselors are aware of the intimacy and responsibilities inherent in the counseling relationship, maintain respect for clients, and avoid actions that seek to meet their personal needs at the expense of the clients.

b. *Personal Values*

Counselors are aware of their own values, attitudes, beliefs, and behaviors and how these apply in a diverse society and avoid imposing their values on clients. (See C.5.a.)

A.6. Dual Relationships

a. *Avoid When Possible*

Counselors are aware of their influential positions with respect to clients, and they avoid exploiting the trust and dependency of clients. Counselors make every effort to avoid dual relationships with clients that could impair professional judgment or increase the risk of harm to clients. (Examples of such relationships include, but are not limited to, familial, social, financial, business, or close personal relationships

with clients.) When a dual relationship cannot be avoided, counselors take appropriate professional precautions, such as informed consent, consultation, supervision, and documentation, to ensure that judgment is not impaired and no exploitation occurs. (See F.1.b.)

b. *Superior/Subordinate Relationships*

Counselors do not accept as clients superiors or subordinates with whom they have administrative, supervisory, or evaluative relationships.

A.7. Sexual Intimacies With Clients

a. *Current Clients*

Counselors do not have any type of sexual intimacies with clients and do not counsel persons with whom they have had a sexual relationship.

b. *Former Clients*

Counselors do not engage in sexual intimacies with former clients within a minimum of two years after terminating the counseling relationship. Counselors who engage in such relationship after two years following termination have the responsibility to thoroughly examine and document that such relations did not have an exploitative nature, based on factors, such as duration of counseling, amount of time since counseling, termination circumstances, client's personal history and mental status, adverse impact on the client, and actions by the counselor suggesting a plan to initiate a sexual relationship with the client after termination.

A.8. Multiple Clients

When counselors agree to provide counseling services to two or more persons who have a relationship (such as husband and wife, or parents and children), counselors clarify at the outset which person or persons are clients and the nature of the relationships they will have with each involved person. If it becomes apparent that counselors may be called upon to perform potentially conflicting roles, they clarify, adjust, or withdraw from roles appropriately. (See B.2. and B.4.d.)

A.9. Group Work

a. *Screening*
Counselors screen prospective group counseling/therapy participants. To the extent possible, counselors select members whose needs and goals are compatible with goals of the group, who will not impede the group process, and whose well-being will not be jeopardized by the group experience.

b. *Protecting Clients*
In a group setting, counselors take reasonable precautions to protect clients from physical or psychological trauma.

A.10. Fees and Bartering

(See D.3.a. and D.3.b.)

a. *Advance Understanding*
Counselors clearly explain to clients, prior to entering the counseling relationship, all financial arrangements related to professional services including the use of collection agencies or legal measures for nonpayment. (A.11.c.)

b. *Establishing Fees*
In establishing fees for professional counseling services, counselors consider the financial status of clients and locality. In the event that the established fee structure is inappropriate for a client, assistance is provided in attempting to find comparable services of acceptable cost. (See A.10.d., D.3.a., and D.3.b.)

c. *Bartering Discouraged*
Counselors ordinarily refrain from accepting goods or services from clients in return for counseling services because such arrangements create inherent potential for conflicts, exploitation, and distortion of the professional relationship. Counselors may participate in bartering only if the relationship is not exploitive, if the client requests it, if a clear written contract is established, and if such arrangements are an accepted practice among professionals in the community. (See A.6.a.)

d. *Pro Bono Service*
Counselors contribute to society by devoting a portion of their professional activity to services for which there is little or no financial return (pro bono).

A.11. Termination and Referral

a. *Abandonment Prohibited*
Counselors do not abandon or neglect clients in counseling. Counselors assist in making appropriate arrangements for the continuation of treatment, when necessary, during interruptions, such as vacations, and following termination.

b. *Inability to Assist Clients*
If counselors determine an inability to be of professional assistance to clients, they avoid entering or immediately terminate a counseling relationship. Counselors are knowledgeable about referral resources and suggest appropriate alternatives. If clients decline the suggested referral, counselors should discontinue the relationship.

c. *Appropriate Termination*
Counselors terminate a counseling relationship, securing client agreement when possible, when it is reasonably clear that the client is no longer benefiting, when services are no longer required, when counseling no longer serves the client's needs or interests, when clients do not pay fees charged, or when agency or institution limits do not allow provision of fur-

ther counseling services. (See A.10.b. and C.2.g.)

A.12. Computer Technology

a. *Use of Computers*

When computer applications are used in counseling services, counselors ensure that (1) the client is intellectually, emotionally, and physically capable of using the computer application; (2) the computer application is appropriate for the needs of the client; (3) the client understands the purpose and operation of the computer applications; and (4) a follow-up of client use of a computer application is provided to correct possible misconceptions, discover inappropriate use, and assess subsequent needs.

b. *Explanation of Limitations*

Counselors ensure that clients are provided information as a part of the counseling relationship that adequately explains the limitations of computer technology.

c. *Access to Computer Applications*

Counselors provide for equal access to computer applications in counseling services. (See A.2.a.)

SECTION B: CONFIDENTIALITY

B.1. Right to Privacy

a. *Respect for Privacy*

Counselors respect their clients' right to privacy and avoid illegal and unwarranted disclosures of confidential information. (See A.3.a. and B.6.a.)

b. *Client Waiver*

The right to privacy may be waived by the client or their legally recognized representative.

c. *Exceptions*

The general requirement that counselors keep information confidential does not ap-

ply when disclosure is required to prevent clear and imminent danger to the client or others or when legal requirements demand that confidential information be revealed. Counselors consult with other professionals when in doubt as to the validity of an exception.

d. *Contagious, Fatal Diseases*

A counselor who receives information confirming that a client has a disease commonly known to be both communicable and fatal is justified in disclosing information to an identifiable third party, who by his or her relationship with the client is at a high risk of contracting the disease. Prior to making a disclosure the counselor should ascertain that the client has not already informed the third party about his or her disease and that the client is not intending to inform the third party in the immediate future. (See B.1.c. and B.1.f.)

e. *Court Ordered Disclosure*

When court ordered to release confidential information without a client's permission, counselors request to the court that the disclosure not be required due to potential harm to the client or counseling relationship. (See B.1.c.)

f. *Minimal Disclosure*

When circumstances require the disclosure of confidential information, only essential information is revealed. To the extent possible, clients are informed before confidential information is disclosed.

g. *Explanation of Limitations*

When counseling is initiated and throughout the counseling process as necessary, counselors inform clients of the limitations of confidentiality and identify foreseeable situations in which confidentiality must be breached. (See G.2.a.)

h. *Subordinates*

Counselors make every effort to ensure that privacy and confidentiality of clients are maintained by subordinates including employees, supervisees, clerical assistants, and volunteers. (See B.1.a.)

i. *Treatment Teams*

If client treatment will involve a continued review by a treatment team, the client will be informed of the team's existence and composition.

B.2. Groups and Families

a. *Group Work*

In group work, counselors clearly define confidentiality and the parameters for the specific group being entered, explain its importance, and discuss the difficulties related to confidentiality involved in group work. The fact that confidentiality cannot be guaranteed is clearly communicated to group members.

b. *Family Counseling*

In family counseling, information about one family member cannot be disclosed to another member without permission. Counselors protect the privacy rights of each family member. (See A.8., B.3., and B.4.d.)

B.3. Minor or Incompetent Clients

When counseling clients who are minors or individuals who are unable to give voluntary, informed consent, parents or guardians may be included in the counseling process as appropriate. Counselors act in the best interests of clients and take measures to safeguard confidentiality. (See A.3.c.)

B.4. Records

a. *Requirement of Records*

Counselors maintain records necessary for rendering professional services to their clients and as required by laws, regulations, or agency or institution procedures.

b. *Confidentiality of Records*

Counselors are responsible for securing the safety and confidentiality of any counseling records they create, maintain, transfer, or destroy whether the records are written, taped, computerized, or stored in any other medium. (See B.1.a.)

c. *Permission to Record or Observe*

Counselors obtain permission from clients prior to electronically recording or observing sessions. (See A.3.a.)

d. *Client Access*

Counselors recognize that counseling records are kept for the benefit of clients and, therefore, provide access to records and copies of records when requested by competent clients unless the records contain information that may be misleading and detrimental to the client. In situations involving multiple clients, access to records is limited to those parts of records that do not include confidential information related to another client. (See A.8., B.1.a., and B.2.b.)

e. *Disclosure or Transfer*

Counselors obtain written permission from clients to disclose or transfer records to legitimate third parties unless exceptions to confidentiality exist as listed in Section B.1. Steps are taken to ensure that receivers of counseling records are sensitive to their confidential nature.

B.5. Research and Training

a. *Data Disguise Required*

Use of data derived from counseling relationships for purposes of training, research, or publication is confined to content that is disguised to ensure the anonymity of the individuals involved. (See B.1.g. and G.3.d.)

b. *Agreement for Identification*

Identification of a client in a presentation or publication is permissible only when the client has reviewed the material and has agreed to its presentation or publication. (See G.3.d.)

B.6. Consultation

a. *Respect for Privacy*

Information obtained in a consulting relationship is discussed for professional purposes only with persons clearly concerned with the case. Written and oral reports present data germane to the purposes of the consultation, and every effort is made to protect client identity and avoid undue invasion of privacy.

b. *Cooperating Agencies*

Before sharing information, counselors make efforts to ensure that there are defined policies in other agencies serving the counselor's clients that effectively protect the confidentiality of information.

SECTION C: PROFESSIONAL RESPONSIBILITY

C.1. Standards Knowledge

Counselors have a responsibility to read, understand, and follow the Code of Ethics and the Standards of Practice.

C.2. Professional Competence

a. *Boundaries of Competence*

Counselors practice only within the boundaries of their competence, based on their education, training, supervised experience, state and national professional credentials, and appropriate professional experience. Counselors will demonstrate a commitment to gain knowledge, personal awareness, sensitivity, and skills pertinent to working with a diverse client population.

b. *New Specialty Areas of Practice*

Counselors practice in specialty areas new to them only after appropriate education, training, and supervised experience. While developing skills in new specialty areas, counselors take steps to ensure the competence of their work and to protect others from possible harm.

c. *Qualified for Employment*

Counselors accept employment only for positions for which they are qualified by education, training, supervised experience, state and national professional credentials, and appropriate professional experience. Counselors hire for professional counseling positions only individuals who are qualified and competent.

d. *Monitor Effectiveness*

Counselors continually monitor their effectiveness as professionals and take steps to improve when necessary. Counselors in private practice take reasonable steps to seek out peer supervision to evaluate their efficacy as counselors.

e. *Ethical Issues Consultation*

Counselors take reasonable steps to consult with other counselors or related professionals when they have questions regarding their ethical obligations or professional practice. (See H.1.)

f. *Continuing Education*

Counselors recognize the need for continuing education to maintain a reasonable level of awareness of current scientific and professional information in their fields of activity. They take steps to maintain competence in the skills they use, are open to new procedures, and keep current with the diverse and/or special populations with whom they work.

g. *Impairment*

Counselors refrain from offering or accepting professional services when their physical, mental or emotional problems are likely to harm a client or others. They are alert to the signs of impairment, seek assistance for problems, and, if necessary, limit, suspend, or terminate their professional responsibilities. (See A.11.c.)

C.3. Advertising and Soliciting Clients

a. *Accurate Advertising*

There are no restrictions on advertising by counselors except those that can be specifically justified to protect the public from deceptive practices. Counselors advertise or represent their services to the public by identifying their credentials in an accurate manner that is not false, misleading, deceptive, or fraudulent. Counselors may only advertise the highest degree earned which is in counseling or a closely related field from a college or university that was accredited when the degree was awarded by one of the regional accrediting bodies recognized by the Council on Postsecondary Accreditation.

b. *Testimonials*

Counselors who use testimonials do not solicit them from clients or other persons who, because of their particular circumstances, may be vulnerable to undue influence.

c. *Statements by Others*

Counselors make reasonable efforts to ensure that statements made by others about them or the profession of counseling are accurate.

d. *Recruiting Through Employment*

Counselors do not use their places of employment or institutional affiliation to recruit or gain clients, supervisees, or consultees for their private practices. (See C.5.e.)

e. *Products and Training Advertisements*

Counselors who develop products related to their profession or conduct workshops or training events ensure that the advertisements concerning these products or events are accurate and disclose adequate information for consumers to make informed choices.

f. *Promoting to Those Served*

Counselors do not use counseling, teaching, training, or supervisory relationships to promote their products or training events in a manner that is deceptive or would exert undue influence on individuals who may be vulnerable. Counselors may adopt textbooks they have authored for instruction purposes.

g. *Professional Association Involvement*

Counselors actively participate in local, state, and national associations that foster the development and improvement of counseling.

C.4. Credentials

a. *Credentials Claimed*

Counselors claim or imply only professional credentials possessed and are responsible for correcting any known misrepresentations of their credentials by others. Professional credentials include graduate degrees in counseling or closely related mental health fields, accreditation of graduate programs, national voluntary certifications, government-issued certifications or licenses, ACA professional membership, or any other credential that might indicate to the public specialized knowledge or expertise in counseling.

b. *ACA Professional Membership*

ACA professional members may announce to the public their membership status. Regular members may not announce their

ACA membership in a manner that might imply they are credentialed counselors.

c. *Credential Guidelines*
Counselors follow the guidelines for use of credentials that have been established by the entities that issue the credentials.

d. *Misrepresentation of Credentials*
Counselors do not attribute more to their credentials than the credentials represent and do not imply that other counselors are not qualified because they do not possess certain credentials.

e. *Doctoral Degrees From Other Fields*
Counselors who hold a master's degree in counseling or a closely related mental health field but hold a doctoral degree from other than counseling or a closely related field do not use the title, "Dr.," in their practices and do not announce to the public in relation to their practice or status as a counselor that they hold a doctorate.

C.5. Public Responsibility

a. *Nondiscrimination*
Counselors do not discriminate against clients, students, or supervisees in a manner that has a negative impact based on their age, color, culture, disability, ethnic group, gender, race, religion, sexual orientation, or socioeconomic status, or for any other reason. (See A.2.a.)

b. *Sexual Harassment*
Counselors do not engage in sexual harassment. Sexual harassment is defined as sexual solicitation, physical advances, or verbal or nonverbal conduct that is sexual in nature, that occurs in connection with professional activities or roles, and that either (1) is unwelcome, is offensive, or creates a hostile workplace environment, and counselors know or are told this; or (2) is sufficiently severe or intense to be perceived as harassment to a reasonable person in the context. Sexual harassment can consist of a single intense or severe act or multiple persistent or pervasive acts.

c. *Reports to Third Parties*
Counselors are accurate, honest, and unbiased in reporting their professional activities and judgments to appropriate third parties including courts, health insurance companies, those who are the recipients of evaluation reports, and others. (See B.1.g.)

d. *Media Presentations*
When counselors provide advice or comment by means of public lectures, demonstrations, radio or television programs, prerecorded tapes, printed articles, mailed material, or other media, they take reasonable precautions to ensure that (1) the statements are based on appropriate professional counseling literature and practice; (2) the statements are otherwise consistent with the Code of Ethics and the Standards of Practice; and (3) the recipients of the information are not encouraged to infer that a professional counseling relationship has been established. (See C.6.b.)

e. *Unjustified Gains*
Counselors do not use their professional positions to seek or receive unjustified personal gains, sexual favors, unfair advantage, or unearned goods or services. (See C.3.d.)

C.6. Responsibility to Other Professionals

a. *Different Approaches*
Counselors are respectful of approaches to professional counseling that differ from their own. Counselors know and take into account the traditions and practices of other professional groups with which they work.

b. *Personal Public Statements*

When making personal statements in a public context, counselors clarify that they are speaking from their personal perspectives and that they are not speaking on behalf of all counselors or the profession. (See C.5.d.)

c. *Clients Served by Others*

When counselors learn that their clients are in a professional relationship with another mental health professional, they request release from clients to inform the other professionals and strive to establish positive and collaborative professional relationships. (See A.4.)

SECTION D: RELATIONSHIPS WITH OTHER PROFESSIONALS

D.1. Relationships With Employers and Employees

a. *Role Definition*

Counselors define and describe for their employers and employees the parameters and levels of their professional roles.

b. *Agreements*

Counselors establish working agreements with supervisors, colleagues, and subordinates regarding counseling or clinical relationships, confidentiality, adherence to professional standards, distinction between public and private material, maintenance and dissemination of recorded information, workload, and accountability. Working agreements in each instance are specified and made known to those concerned.

c. *Negative Conditions*

Counselors alert their employers to conditions that may be potentially disruptive or damaging to the counselor's professional responsibilities or that may limit their effectiveness.

d. *Evaluation*

Counselors submit regularly to professional review and evaluation by their supervisor or the appropriate representative of the employer.

e. *In-Service*

Counselors are responsible for in-service development of self and staff.

f. *Goals*

Counselors inform their staff of goals and programs.

g. *Practices*

Counselors provide personnel and agency practices that respect and enhance the rights and welfare of each employee and recipient of agency services. Counselors strive to maintain the highest levels of professional services.

h. *Personnel Selection and Assignment*

Counselors select competent staff and assign responsibilities compatible with their skills and experiences.

i. *Discrimination*

Counselors, as either employers or employees, do not engage in or condone practices that are inhumane, illegal, or unjustifiable (such as considerations based on age, color, culture, disability, ethnic group, gender, race, religion, sexual orientation, or socioeconomic status) in hiring, promotion, or training. (See A.2.a. and C.5.b.)

j. *Professional Conduct*

Counselors have a responsibility both to clients and to the agency or institution within which services are performed to maintain high standards of professional conduct.

k. *Exploitive Relationships*

Counselors do not engage in exploitive relationships with individuals over whom they have supervisory, evaluative, or instructional control or authority.

l. *Employer Policies*

The acceptance of employment in an agency or institution implies that counselors are in agreement with its general policies and principles. Counselors strive to reach agreement with employers as to acceptable standards of conduct that allow for changes in institutional policy conducive to the growth and development of clients.

D.2. Consultation (See B.6.)

a. *Consultation as an Option*

Counselors may choose to consult with any other professionally competent persons about their clients. In choosing consultants, counselors avoid placing the consultant in a conflict of interest situation that would preclude the consultant being a proper party to the counselor's efforts to help the client. Should counselors be engaged in a work setting that compromises this consultation standard, they consult with other professionals whenever possible to consider justifiable alternatives.

b. *Consultant Competency*

Counselors are reasonably certain that they have or the organization represented has the necessary competencies and resources for giving the kind of consulting services needed and that appropriate referral resources are available.

c. *Understanding with Clients*

When providing consultation, counselors attempt to develop with their clients a clear understanding of problem definition, goals for change, and predicted consequences of interventions selected.

d. *Consultant Goals*

The consulting relationship is one in which client adaptability and growth toward self-direction are consistently encouraged and cultivated. (See A.1.b.)

D.3. Fees for Referral

a. *Accepting Fees from Agency Clients*

Counselors refuse a private fee or other remuneration for rendering services to persons who are entitled to such services through the counselor's employing agency or institution. The policies of a particular agency may make explicit provisions for agency clients to receive counseling services from members of its staff in private practice. In such instances, the clients must be informed of other options open to them should they seek private counseling services. (See A.10.a., A.11.b., and C.3.d.)

b. *Referral Fees*

Counselors do not accept a referral fee from other professionals.

D.4. Subcontractor Arrangements

When counselors work as subcontractors for counseling services for a third party, they have a duty to inform clients of the limitations of confidentiality that the organization may place on counselors in providing counseling services to clients. The limits of such confidentiality ordinarily are discussed as part of the intake session. (See B.1.e. and B.1.f.)

SECTION E: EVALUATION, ASSESSMENT, AND INTERPRETATION

E.1. General

a. *Appraisal Techniques*

The primary purpose of educational and psychological assessment is to provide measures that are objective and interpretable in either comparative or absolute terms. Counselors recognize the need to interpret the statements in this section as applying to the whole range of appraisal techniques including test and nontest data.

b. *Client Welfare*

Counselors promote the welfare and best interests of the client in the development, publication, and utilization of educational and psychological assessment techniques. They do not misuse assessment results and interpretations and take reasonable steps to prevent others from misusing the information these techniques provide. They respect the client's right to know the results, the interpretations made, and the basis for their conclusions and recommendations.

E.2. Competence to Use and Interpret Tests

a. *Limits of Competence*

Counselors recognize the limits of their competence and perform only those testing and assessment services for which they have been trained. They are familiar with reliability, validity, related standardization, error of measurement, and proper application of any technique utilized. Counselors using computer-based test interpretations are trained in the construct being measured and the specific instrument being used prior to using this type of computer application. Counselors take reasonable measures to ensure the proper use of psychological assessment techniques by persons under their supervision.

b. *Appropriate Use*

Counselors are responsible for the appropriate application, scoring, interpretation, and use of assessment instruments whether they score and interpret such tests themselves or use computerized or other services.

c. *Decisions Based on Results*

Counselors responsible for decisions involving individuals or policies that are based on assessment results have a thorough understanding of educational and psychological measurement including validation criteria, test research, and guidelines for test development and use.

d. *Accurate Information*

Counselors provide accurate information and avoid false claims or misconceptions when making statements about assessment instruments or techniques. Special efforts are made to avoid unwarranted connotations of such terms as IQ and grade equivalent scores. (See C.5.c.)

E.3. Informed Consent

a. *Explanation to Clients*

Prior to assessment, counselors explain the nature and purposes of assessment and the specific use of results in language the client (or other legally authorized person on behalf of the client) can understand unless an explicit exception to this right has been agreed upon in advance. Regardless of whether scoring and interpretation are completed by counselors, by assistants, or by computer or other outside services, counselors take reasonable steps to ensure that appropriate explanations are given to the client.

b. *Recipients of Results*

The examinee's welfare, explicit understanding, and prior agreement determine the recipients of test results. Counselors include accurate and appropriate interpretations with any release of individual or group test results. (See B.1.a. and C.5.c.)

E.4. Release of Information to Competent Professionals

a. *Misuse of Results*

Counselors do not misuse assessment results, including test results, and interpretations and take reasonable steps to prevent the misuse of such by others. (See C.5.c.)

b. *Release of Raw Data*

Counselors ordinarily release data (e.g. protocols, counseling or interview notes, or questionnaires) in which the client is identified only with the consent of the client or the client's legal representative. Such data are usually released only to persons recognized by counselors as competent to interpret the data. (See B.1.a.)

E.5. Proper Diagnosis of Mental Disorders

a. *Proper Diagnosis*
Counselors take special care to provide proper diagnosis of mental disorders. Assessment techniques (including personal interview) used to determine client care (e.g. locus of treatment, type of treatment, or recommended follow-up) are carefully selected and appropriately used. (See A.3.a. and C.5.c.)

b. *Cultural Sensitivity*
Counselors recognize that culture effects the manner in which clients' problems are defined. Clients' socioeconomic and cultural experience is considered when diagnosing mental disorders.

E.6. Test Selection

a. *Appropriateness of Instruments*
Counselors carefully consider the validity, reliability, psychometric limitations, and appropriateness of instruments when selecting tests for use in a given situation or with a particular client.

b. *Culturally Diverse Populations*
Counselors are cautious when selecting tests for culturally diverse populations to avoid inappropriateness of testing that may be outside of socialized behavioral or cognitive patterns.

E.7. Conditions of Test Administration

a. *Administration Conditions*
Counselors administer tests under the same conditions that were established in their standardization. When tests are not administered under standard conditions or when unusual behavior or irregularities

occur during the testing session, those conditions are noted in interpretation, and the results may be designated as invalid or of questionable validity.

b. *Computer Administration*
Counselors are responsible for ensuring that administration programs function properly to provide clients with accurate results when a computer or other electronic methods are used for test administration. (See A.12.b.)

c. *Unsupervised Test-Taking*
Counselors do not permit unsupervised or inadequately supervised use of tests or assessments unless the tests or assessments are designed, intended, and validated for self-administration and/or scoring.

d. *Disclosure of Favorable Conditions*
Prior to test administration, conditions that produce most favorable test results are made known to the examinee.

E.8. Diversity in Testing

Counselors are cautious in using assessment techniques, making evaluations, and interpreting the performance of populations not represented in the norm group on which an instrument was standardized. They recognize the effects of age, color, culture, disability, ethnic group, gender, race, religion, sexual orientation, and socioeconomic status on test administration and interpretation and place test results in proper perspective with other relevant factors. (See A.2.a.)

E.9. Test Scoring and Interpretation

a. *Reporting Reservations*
In reporting assessment results, counselors indicate any reservations that exist regarding validity or reliability because of the circumstances of the assessment or the inappropriateness of the norms for the person tested.

b. *Research Instruments*
Counselors exercise caution when interpreting the results of research instruments possessing insufficient technical data to support respondent results. The specific purposes for the use of such instruments are stated explicitly to the examinee.

c. *Testing Services*
Counselors who provide test scoring and test interpretation services to support the assessment process confirm the validity of such interpretations. They accurately describe the purpose, norms, validity, reliability, and applications of the procedures and any special qualifications applicable to their use. The public offering of an automated test interpretations service is considered a professional-to-professional consultation. The formal responsibility of the consultant is to the consultee, but the ultimate and overriding responsibility is to the client.

E.10. Test Security

Counselors maintain the integrity and security of tests and other assessment techniques consistent with legal and contractual obligations. Counselors do not appropriate, reproduce, or modify published tests or parts thereof without acknowledgment and permission from the publisher.

E.11. Obsolete Tests and Outdated Test Results

Counselors do not use data or test results that are obsolete or outdated for the current purpose. Counselors make every effort to prevent the misuse of obsolete measures and test data by others.

E.12. Test Construction

Counselors use established scientific procedures, relevant standards, and current professional knowledge for test design in the development, publication, and utilization of educational and psychological assessment techniques.

SECTION F: TEACHING, TRAINING, AND SUPERVISION

F.1. Counselor Educators and Trainers

a. *Educators as Teachers and Practitioners*
Counselors who are responsible for developing, implementing, and supervising educational programs are skilled as teachers and practitioners. They are knowledgeable regarding the ethical, legal, and regulatory aspects of the profession, are skilled in applying that knowledge, and make students and supervisees aware of their responsibilities. Counselors conduct counselor education and training programs in an ethical manner and serve as role models for professional behavior. Counselor educators should make an effort to infuse material related to human diversity into all courses and/or workshops that are designed to promote the development of professional counselors.

b. *Relationship Boundaries with Students and Supervisees*
Counselors clearly define and maintain ethical, professional, and social relationship boundaries with their students and supervisees. They are aware of the differential in power that exists and the student's or supervisee's possible incomprehension of that power differential. Counselors explain to students and supervisees the potential for the relationship to become exploitive.

c. *Sexual Relationships*
Counselors do not engage in sexual relationships with students or supervisees and do not subject them to sexual harassment. (See A.6. and C.5.b.)

d. *Contributions to Research*
Counselors give credit to students or supervisees for their contributions to research and scholarly projects. Credit is given through coauthorship, acknowledgment, footnote statement, or other appropriate means in accordance with such contributions. (See G.4.b. and G.4.c.)

e. *Close Relatives*
Counselors do not accept close relatives as students or supervisees.

f. *Supervision Preparation*
Counselors who offer clinical supervision services are adequately prepared in supervision methods and techniques. Counselors who are doctoral students serving as practicum or internship supervisors to master's level students are adequately prepared and supervised by the training program.

g. *Responsibility for Services to Clients*
Counselors who supervise the counseling services of others take reasonable measures to ensure that counseling services provided to clients are professional.

h. *Endorsement*
Counselors do not endorse students or supervisees for certification, licensure, employment, or completion of an academic or training program if they believe students or supervisees are not qualified for the endorsement. Counselors take reasonable steps to assist students or supervisees who are not qualified for endorsement to become qualified.

F.2. Counselor Education and Training Programs

a. *Orientation*
Prior to admission, counselors orient prospective students to the counselor education or training program's expectations including but not limited to the following: (1) the type and level of skill acquisition required for successful completion of the training, (2) subject matter to be covered, (3) basis for evaluation, (4) training components that encourage self-growth or self-disclosure as part of the training process, (5) the type of supervision settings and requirements of the sites for required clinical field experiences, (6) student and supervisee evaluation and dismissal policies and procedures, and (7) up-to-date employment prospects for graduates.

b. *Integration of Study and Practice*
Counselors establish counselor education and training programs that integrate academic study and supervised practice.

c. *Evaluation*
Counselors clearly state to students and supervisees, in advance of training, the levels of competency expected, appraisal methods, and timing of evaluations for both didactic and experiential components. Counselors provide students and supervisees with periodic performance appraisal and evaluation feedback throughout the training program.

d. *Teaching Ethics*
Counselors make students and supervisees aware of the ethical responsibilities and standards of the profession and the students' and supervisees' ethical responsibilities to the profession. (See C.1. and F.3.e.)

e. *Peer Relationships*
When students or supervisees are assigned to lead counseling groups or provide clinical supervision for their peers, counselors take steps to ensure that students and supervisees placed in these roles do not have personal or adverse relationships with peers and that they understand they have the same ethical obligations as counselor educators, trainers, and supervisors. Coun-

selors make every effort to ensure that the rights of peers are not compromised when students or supervisees are assigned to lead counseling groups or provide clinical supervision.

f. *Varied Theoretical Positions*

Counselors present varied theoretical positions so that students and supervisees may make comparisons and have opportunities to develop their own positions. Counselors provide information concerning the scientific basis of professional practice. (See C.6.a.)

g. *Field Placements*

Counselors develop clear policies within their training program regarding field placement and other clinical experiences. Counselors provide clearly stated roles and responsibilities for the student or supervisee, the site supervisor, and the program supervisor. They confirm that site supervisors are qualified to provide supervision and are informed of their professional and ethical responsibilities in this role.

h. *Dual Relationships as Supervisors*

Counselors avoid dual relationships, such as performing the role of site supervisor and training program supervisor in the student's or supervisee's training program. Counselors do not accept any form of professional services, fees, commissions, reimbursement, or remuneration from a site for student or supervisee placement.

i. *Diversity in Programs*

Counselors are responsible to their institution's and program's recruitment and retention needs for training program administrators, faculty, and students with diverse backgrounds and special needs. (See A.2.a.)

F.3. Students and Supervisees

a. *Limitations*

Counselors, through ongoing evaluation and appraisal, are aware of the academic and personal limitations of students and supervisees that might impede performance. Counselors assist students and supervisees in securing remedial assistance when needed and dismiss from the training program supervisees who are unable to provide competent service due to academic or personal limitations. Counselors seek professional consultation and document their decision to dismiss or refer students or supervisees for assistance. Counselors assure that students and supervisees have recourse to address decisions made, to require them to seek assistance, or to dismiss them.

b. *Self-Growth Experiences*

Counselors use professional judgment when designing training experiences conducted by the counselors themselves that require student and supervisee self-growth or self-disclosure. Safeguards are provided so that students and supervisees are aware of the ramifications their self-disclosure may have on counselors whose primary role as teacher, trainer, or supervisor requires acting on ethical obligations to the profession. Evaluative components of experiential training experiences explicitly delineate predetermined academic standards that are separate and not dependent on the student's level of self-disclosure. (See A.6.)

c. *Counseling for Students and Supervisees*

If students or supervisees request counseling, supervisors or counselor educators provide them with acceptable referrals. Supervisors or counselor educators do not serve as counselor to students or supervisees over whom they hold administrative, teaching, or evaluative roles unless this is a brief role associated with a training experience. (See A.6.b.)

d. *Clients of Students and Supervisees*
Counselors make every effort to ensure that the clients at field placements are aware of the services rendered and the qualifications of the students and supervisees rendering those services. Clients receive professional disclosure information and are informed of the limits of confidentiality. Client permission is obtained in order for the students and supervisees to use any information concerning the counseling relationship in the training process. (See B.1.e.)

e. *Standards for Students and Supervisees*
Students and supervisees preparing to become counselors adhere to the Code of Ethics and the Standards of Practice. Students and supervisees have the same obligations to clients as those required of counselors. (See H.1.)

SECTION G: RESEARCH AND PUBLICATION

G.1. Research Responsibilities

a. *Use of Human Subjects*
Counselors plan, design, conduct, and report research in a manner consistent with pertinent ethical principles, federal and state laws, host institutional regulations, and scientific standards governing research with human subjects. Counselors design and conduct research that reflects cultural sensitivity appropriateness.

b. *Deviation from Standard Practices*
Counselors seek consultation and observe stringent safeguards to protect the rights of research participants when a research problem suggests a deviation from standard acceptable practices. (See B.6.)

c. *Precautions to Void Injury*
Counselors who conduct research with human subjects are responsible for the subjects' welfare throughout the experiment and take reasonable precautions to avoid causing injurious psychological, physical, or social effects to their subjects.

d. *Principal Researcher Responsibility*
The ultimate responsibility for ethical research practice lies with the principal researcher. All others involved in the research activities share ethical obligations and full responsibility for their own actions.

e. *Minimal Interference*
Counselors take reasonable precautions to avoid causing disruptions in subjects' lives due to participation in research.

f. *Diversity*
Counselors are sensitive to diversity and research issues with special populations. They seek consultation when appropriate. (See A.2.a. and B.6.)

G.2. Informed Consent

a. *Topics Disclosed*
In obtaining informed consent for research, counselors use language that is understandable to research participants and that (1) accurately explains the purpose and procedures to be followed; (2) identifies any procedures that are experimental or relatively untried; (3) describes the attendant discomforts and risks; (4) describes the benefits or changes in individuals or organizations that might be reasonably expected; (5) discloses appropriate alternative procedures that would be advantageous for subjects; (6) offers to answer any inquiries concerning the procedures; (7) describes any limitations on confidentiality; and (8) instructs that subjects are free to withdraw their consent and to discontinue participation in the project at any time. (See B.1.f.)

b. *Deception*

Counselors do not conduct research involving deception unless alternative procedures are not feasible and the prospective value of the research justifies the deception. When the methodological requirements of a study necessitate concealment or deception, the investigator is required to explain clearly the reasons for this action as soon as possible.

c. *Voluntary Participation*

Participation in research is typically voluntary and without any penalty for refusal to participate. Involuntary participation is appropriate only when it can be demonstrated that participation will have no harmful effects on subjects and is essential to the investigation.

d. *Confidentiality of Information*

Information obtained about research participants during the course of an investigation is confidential. When the possibility exists that others may obtain access to such information, ethical research practice requires that the possibility, together with the plans for protecting confidentiality, be explained to participants as a part of the procedure for obtaining informed consent. (See B.1.e.)

e. *Persons Incapable of Giving Informed Consent*

When a person is incapable of giving informed consent, counselors provide an appropriate explanation, obtain agreement for participation and obtain appropriate consent from a legally authorized person.

f. *Commitments to Participants*

Counselors take reasonable measures to honor all commitments to research participants.

g. *Explanations After Data Collection*

After data are collected, counselors provide participants with full clarification of the nature of the study to remove any misconceptions. Where scientific or human values justify delaying or withholding information, counselors take reasonable measures to avoid causing harm.

h. *Agreements to Cooperate*

Counselors who agree to cooperate with another individual in research or publication incur an obligation to cooperate as promised in terms of punctuality of performance and with regard to the completeness and accuracy of the information required.

i. *Informed Consent for Sponsors*

In the pursuit of research, counselors give sponsors, institutions, and publication channels the same respect and opportunity for giving informed consent that they accord to individual research participants. Counselors are aware of their obligation to future research workers and ensure that host institutions are given feedback information and proper acknowledgment.

G.3. Reporting Results

a. *Information Affecting Outcome*

When reporting research results, counselors explicitly mention all variables and conditions known to the investigator that may have affected the outcome of the study or the interpretation of data.

b. *Accurate Results*

Counselors plan, conduct, and report research accurately and in a manner that minimizes the possibility that results will be misleading. They provide thorough discussions of the limitations of their data and alternative hypothesis. Counselors do not engage in fraudulent research, distort data, misrepresent data, or deliberately bias their results.

c. *Obligation to Report Unfavorable Results*
Counselors communicate to other counselors the results of any research judged to be of professional value. Results that reflect unfavorably on institutions, programs, services, prevailing opinions, or vested interests are not withheld.

d. *Identity of Subjects*
Counselors who supply data, aid in the research of another person, report research results, or make original data available take due care to disguise the identity of respective subjects in the absence of specific authorization from the subjects to do otherwise. (See B.1.g. and B.5.a.)

e. *Replication Studies*
Counselors are obligated to make available sufficient original research data to qualified professionals who may wish to replicate the study.

G.4. Publication

a. *Recognition of Others*
When conducting and reporting research, counselors are familiar with and give recognition to previous work on the topic, observe copyright laws, and give full credit to those to whom credit is due. (See F.1.d. and G.4.c.)

b. *Contributors*
Counselors give credit through joint authorship, acknowledgment, footnote statements, or other appropriate means to those who have contributed significantly to research or concept development in accordance with such contributions. The principal contributor is listed first and minor technical or professional contributions are acknowledged in notes or introductory statements.

c. *Student Research*
For an article that is substantially based on a student's dissertation or thesis, the student is listed as the principal author. (See F.1.d. and G.4.a.)

d. *Duplicate Submission*
Counselors submit manuscripts for consideration to only one journal at a time. Manuscripts that are published in whole or in substantial part in another journal or published work are not submitted for publication without acknowledgment and permission from the previous publication.

e. *Professional Review*
Counselors who review material submitted for publication, research, or other scholarly purposes respect the confidentiality and proprietary rights of those who submitted it.

SECTION H: RESOLVING ETHICAL ISSUES

H.1. Knowledge of Standards
Counselors are familiar with the Code of Ethics and the Standards of Practice and other applicable ethics codes from other professional organizations of which they are member or from certification and licensure bodies. Lack of knowledge or misunderstanding of an ethical responsibility is not a defense against a charge of unethical conduct. (See F.3.e.)

H.2. Suspected Violations

a. *Ethical Behavior Expected*
Counselors expect professional associates to adhere to Code of Ethics. When counselors possess reasonable cause that raises doubts as to whether a counselor is acting in an ethical manner, they take appropriate action. (See H.2.d. and H.2.e.)

b. *Consultation*

When uncertain as to whether a particular situation or course of action may be in violation of Code of Ethics, counselors consult with other counselors who are knowledgeable about ethics, with colleagues, or with appropriate authorities.

c. *Organization Conflicts*

If the demands of an organization with which counselors are affiliated pose a conflict with Code of Ethics, counselors specify the nature of such conflicts and express to their supervisors or other responsible officials their commitment to Code of Ethics. When possible, counselors work toward change within the organization to allow full adherence to Code of Ethics.

d. *Informed Resolution*

When counselors have reasonable cause to believe that another counselor is violating an ethical standard, they attempt to first resolve the issue informally with the other counselor if feasible providing that such action does not violate confidentiality rights that may be involved.

e. *Reporting Suspected Violations*

When an informal resolution is not appropriate or feasible, counselors, upon reasonable cause, take action, such as reporting the suspected ethical violation to state or national ethics committees, unless this action conflicts with confidentiality rights that cannot be resolved.

f. *Unwarranted Complaints*

Counselors do not initiate, participate in, or encourage the filing of ethics complaints that are unwarranted or intend to harm a counselor rather than to protect clients or the public.

H.3. Cooperation With Ethics Committees

Counselors assist in the process of enforcing Code of Ethics. Counselors cooperate with investigations, proceedings, and requirements of the ACA Ethics Committee or ethics committees of other duly constituted associations or boards having jurisdiction over those charged with a violation. Counselors are familiar with the ACA Policies and Procedures and use it as a reference in assisting the enforcement of the Code of Ethics.

APPENDIX B

Best Practice Guidelines of the Association for Specialists in Group Work

Approved by the Executive Board, March 29, 1998

Prepared by Lynn S. Rapin and Linda Keel, ASGW Ethics Committee Co-Chairs

PREAMBLE

The Association for Specialists in Group Work (ASGW) is a division of the American Counseling Association whose members are interested in and specialize in group work. We value the creation of community; service to our members, clients, and the profession; and value leadership as a process to facilitate the growth and development of individuals and groups.

The Association for Specialists in Group Work recognizes the commitment of its members to the Code of Ethics and Standards of Practice (as revised in 1995) of its parent organization, the American Counseling Association, and nothing in this document shall be construed to supplant that code. These Best Practice Guidelines are intended to clarify the application of the ACA Code of Ethics and Standards of Practice to the field of group work by defining Group Workers' responsibility and scope of practice involving those activities, strategies and interventions that are consistent and current with effective and appropriate professional ethical and community standards. ASGW views ethical process as being integral to group work and views Group Workers as ethical agents. Group Workers, by their very nature in being responsible and responsive to their group members, necessarily embrace a certain potential for ethical vulnerability. It is incumbent upon Group Workers to give considerable attention to the intent and context of their actions because the attempts of Group Workers to influence human behavior through group work always have ethical implications. These Best Practice Guidelines address Group Workers' responsibilities in planning, performing and processing groups.

SECTION A: BEST PRACTICE IN PLANNING

A.1. Professional Context and Regulatory Requirements

Group Workers actively know, understand and apply the ACA Code of Ethics and Standards of Best Practice, the ASGW Professional Standards for the Training of Group Workers, these ASGW Best Practice Guidelines, the ASGW diversity competencies, the ACA Multicultural Guidelines, relevant state laws, accreditation requirements, relevant National Board for Certified Counselors Codes and Standards, their organization's standards, and insurance requirements impacting the practice of group work.

A.2. Scope of Practice and Conceptual Framework

Group Workers define the scope of practice related to the core and specialization competencies defined in the ASGW Training Standards. Group Workers are aware of personal strengths and weaknesses in leading groups. Group Workers develop and are able to articulate a general conceptual framework to guide practice and a rationale for use of techniques that are to be used. Group Workers limit their practice to those areas for which they meet the training criteria established by the ASGW Training Standards.

A.3. Assessment

a. *Assessment of self.* Group Workers actively assess their knowledge and skills related to the specific group(s) offered. Group Workers assess their values, beliefs and theoretical orientation and how these im-

pact upon the group, particularly when working with a diverse and multicultural population.

b. *Ecological assessment.* Group Workers assess community needs, agency or organization resources, sponsoring organization mission, staff competency, attitudes regarding group work, professional training levels of potential group leaders regarding group work; client attitudes regarding group work, and multicultural and diversity considerations. Group Workers use this information as the basis for making decisions related to their group practice, or to the implementation of groups for which they have supervisory, evaluation, or oversight responsibilities.

A.4. Program Development and Evaluation

a. *Group Workers identify the type(s) of group(s) to be offered and how they relate to community needs.*

b. *Group Workers concisely state in writing the purpose and goals of the group.* Group Workers also identify the role of the group members in influencing or determining the group goals.

c. *Group Workers set fees consistent with the organization's fee schedule, taking into consideration the financial status and locality of prospective group members.*

d. *Group Workers choose techniques and a leadership style appropriate to the type(s) of group(s) being offered.*

e. *Group Workers have an evaluation plan consistent with regulatory, organization and insurance requirements, where appropriate.*

f. *Group Workers take into consideration current professional guidelines when using technology, including but not limited to Internet communication.*

A.5. Resources

Group Workers coordinate resources related to the kind of group(s) and group activities to be provided, such as: adequate funding; the appropriateness and availability of a trained co-leader; space and privacy requirements for the type(s) of group(s) being offered; marketing and recruiting; and appropriate collaboration with other community agencies and organizations.

A.6. Professional Disclosure Statement

Group Workers have a professional disclosure statement which includes information on confidentiality and exceptions to confidentiality, theoretical orientation, information on the nature, purpose(s) and goals of the group, the group services that can be provided, the role and responsibility of group members and leaders, Group Workers' qualifications to conduct the specific group(s), specific licenses, certifications and professional affiliations, and address of licensing/credentialing body.

A.7. Group and Member Preparation

a. *Group Workers screen prospective group members if appropriate to the type of group being offered.* When selection of group members is appropriate, Group Workers identify group members whose needs and goals are compatible with the goals of the group.

b. *Group Workers facilitate informed consent.* Group Workers provide in oral and written form to prospective members (when appropriate to group type): the professional disclosure statement; group purpose and goals; group participation expectations including voluntary and involuntary membership; role expectations of members and leader(s); policies related to entering and exiting the group; policies governing substance use; policies and pro-

cedures governing mandated groups (where relevant); documentation requirements; disclosure of information to others; implications of out-of-group contact or involvement among members; procedures for consultation between group leader(s) and group member(s); fees and time parameters; and potential impacts of group participation.

c. *Group Workers obtain the appropriate consent forms for work with minors and other dependent group members.*

d. *Group Workers define confidentiality and its limits (for example, legal and ethical exceptions and expectations; waivers implicit with treatment plans, documentation and insurance usage).* Group Workers have the responsibility to inform all group participants of the need for confidentiality, potential consequences of breaching confidentiality and that legal privilege does not apply to group discussions (unless provided by state statute).

A.8. Professional Development

Group Workers recognize that professional growth is a continuous, ongoing, developmental process throughout their career.

a. *Group Workers remain current and increase knowledge and skill competencies through activities such as continuing education, professional supervision, and participation in personal and professional development activities.*

b. *Group Workers seek consultation and/or supervision regarding ethical concerns that interfere with effective functioning as a group leader.* Supervisors have the responsibility to keep abreast of consultation, group theory, process, and adhere to related ethical guidelines.

c. *Group Workers seek appropriate professional assistance for their own personal problems or conflicts that are likely to impair their professional judgment or work performance.*

d. *Group Workers seek consultation and supervision to ensure appropriate practice whenever working with a group for which all knowledge and skill competencies have not been achieved.*

e. *Group Workers keep abreast of group research and development.*

A.9. Trends and Technological Changes
Group Workers are aware of and responsive to technological changes as they affect society and the profession. These include but are not limited to changes in mental health delivery systems; legislative and insurance industry reforms; shifting population demographics and client needs; and technological advances in Internet and other communication and delivery systems. Group Workers adhere to ethical guidelines related to the use of developing technologies.

SECTION B: BEST PRACTICE IN PERFORMING
B.1. Self Knowledge
Group Workers are aware of and monitor their strengths and weaknesses and the effects these have on group members.

B.2. Group Competencies
Group Workers have a basic knowledge of groups and the principles of group dynamics, and are able to perform the core group competencies, as described in the ASGW Professional Standards for the Training of Group Workers. Additionally, Group Workers have adequate understanding and skill in any group speciality area chosen for practice (psychotherapy, counseling, task, psychoeducation, as described in the ASGW Training Standards).

B.3. Group Plan Adaptation
a. *Group Workers apply and modify knowledge, skills and techniques appropriate to group type and stage, and to the unique needs of various cultural and ethnic groups.*

b. *Group Workers monitor the group's progress toward the group goals and plan.*

c. *Group Workers clearly define and maintain ethical, professional, and social relationship boundaries with group members as appropriate to their role in the organization and the type of group being offered.*

B.4. Therapeutic Conditions and Dynamics
Group Workers understand and are able to implement appropriate models of group development, process observation and therapeutic conditions.

B.5. Meaning
Group Workers assist members in generating meaning from the group experience.

B.6. Collaboration
Group Workers assist members in developing individual goals and respect group members as co-equal partners in the group experience.

B.7. Evaluation
Group Workers include evaluation (both formal and informal) between sessions and at the conclusion of the group.

B.8. Diversity
Group Workers practice with broad sensitivity to client differences including but not limited to ethnic, gender, religious, sexual, psychological maturity, economic class, family history, physical characteristics or limitations, and geographic location. Group Workers continuously seek information regarding the cultural issues of the diverse population with whom they are working both by inter-

action with participants and from using outside resources.

D.9. Ethical Surveillance

Group Workers employ an appropriate ethical decision making model in responding to ethical challenges and issues and in determining courses of action and behavior for self and group members. In addition, Group Workers employ applicable standards as promulgated by ACA, ASGW, or other appropriate professional organizations.

SECTION C: BEST PRACTICE IN GROUP PROCESSING

C.1. Processing Schedule

Group Workers process the workings of the group with themselves, group members, supervisors or other colleagues, as appropriate. This may include assessing progress on group and member goals, leader behaviors and techniques, group dynamics and interventions; developing understanding and acceptance of meaning. Processing may occur both within sessions and before and after each session, at time of termination, and later follow-up, as appropriate.

C.2. Reflective Practice

Group Workers attend to opportunities to synthesize theory and practice and to incorporate learning outcomes into ongoing groups. Group Workers attend to session dynamics of members and their interactions and also attend to the relationship between session dynamics and leader values, cognition and affect.

C.3. Evaluation and Follow-Up

a. *Group Workers evaluate process and outcomes.* Results are used for ongoing program planning, improvement and revisions of current group and/or to contribute to professional research literature. Group Workers follow all applicable policies and standards in using group material for research and reports.

b. *Group Workers conduct follow-up contact with group members, as appropriate, to assess outcomes or when requested by a group member(s).*

C.4. Consultation and Training With Other Organizations

Group Workers provide consultation and training to organizations in and out of their setting, when appropriate. Group Workers seek out consultation as needed with competent professional persons knowledgeable about group work.

APPENDIX C

Code of Ethics (1990) of the Ontario School Counsellors' Association

PREAMBLE

The Ontario School Counsellors' Association is a professional organization of school counsellors actively engaged in guidance in Ontario schools, in the training of guidance personnel, or in duties related to the supervision of guidance programs.

As set out in the constitution of the Association, members are required to have an acceptable level of professional training and experience. One obligation of membership is that members support the aims and objectives of the Association. To this end, it is incumbent upon each member to maintain professional standards and to seek opportunities for continued professional growth.

Adherence to the O.S.C.A. Code of Ethics is a condition of membership in the Association. In addition to adhering to the O.S.C.A. Code of Ethics all counsellors must adhere to the legal requirements of those acts and regulations which govern teachers and counsellors. Some of these are referenced in the section titled "Legal Matters."

SECTION A: PROFESSIONAL COMPETENCE AND CONDUCT

1. Counsellors are expected to seek opportunities to continue their own professional growth and to work towards the improvement of their profession.

2. Counsellors expect ethical behaviour from their professional associates; counsellors will attempt to rectify unethical behaviour on the part of their associates and will assist colleagues to observe ethical practices related to the work of the counsellor.

3. Counsellors shall not indicate that they
have professional qualifications beyond
those they possess and should attempt to
correct misrepresentation or misunderstanding of their qualifications by others.

4. Counsellors, as employees of a school or
other institution, accept policies and principles of the institution as a condition of
employment, unless they conflict with
professional standards and ethics. If there
are policies and principles which conflict,
and counsellors are unable to effect desirable changes in these, they should seek employment elsewhere.

5. Counsellors shall offer professional services only through the context of a professional relationship. Except through the
medium of a recognized agency, it would
be unethical practice to offer the services
of counselling or testing through the mail,
newspaper or magazine or other remote
means of communication such as telephone, radio or television.

SECTION B: COUNSELLOR-COUNSELLEE RELATIONSHIP

1. Counsellors are obliged to respect the integrity and promote the welfare of the
counsellees with whom they are working.

2. In group situations, particularly those
oriented to self-understanding or growth,
the counsellor is obligated to make clear
to the group members the purposes,
goals, techniques, rules of procedures and
limitations that may affect the continu-
ance of the relationship. The counsellor
will attempt to protect individuals from
physical and/or psychological traumas
which might result from group interaction.

3. In providing orientation to prospective
group participants, especially when the

emphasis is on self-understanding and
growth through self-disclosure, the counsellor is responsible for ensuring that the
purposes of the group situation are appropriate to the needs of the counsellee.

4. Counsellors, when they become aware of
information which indicates that there
is imminent physical and/or emotional
danger to the counsellee or others, are
obligated to report the fact to the appropriate authorities and/or take such other
emergency measures as the situation demands. If at all feasible, the counsellee
should be informed of this obligation by
the counsellor.

5. Counsellors take into account and show
prudential regard for the social codes and
moral expectations of the communities
within which they work.

6. Records of the counselling relationship,
including interview notes, test data, correspondence, tape recordings and other
documents retained by the counsellor,
are to be considered professional information for use in counselling, research
and teaching of counsellors, but always
with the full protection of the counsellees. These records shall be available
to the counsellee upon request, and the
counsellor shall assist the counsellee to
interpret them. Tape recordings or film-
ing of an interview shall not be done
without the knowledge and consent of
the counsellee.

7. Counsellors are obligated to respect the
confidentiality of information gained in
the counselling relationship. Counsellees
should be informed, at or before the time
counselling begins, of conditions (e.g.
conditions imposed by school policy) under which they may receive counselling.
In a group counselling setting, the counsellor is expected to set a norm of con-

fidentiality regarding all group participants' disclosure.

8. Counsellors, where they feel that it would
be in the best interests of the counsellee
to do so, will relate confidential information to parents, guardians, teachers or
school administrators only with the
knowledge and consent of the counsellee.

9. Counsellors, when reporting research results and supporting data will not reveal
the identity of the persons used as subjects without their express permission.

10. Counsellors shall carefully consider requests by prospective employers, private
investigating agencies, or other persons,
for confidential information about
counsellees. Such information will only
be provided upon written consent of the
counsellees, and their parents where the
counsellees are minors. Even when consent has been given, counsellors shall use
professional discretion in complying with
such a request.

11. Counsellors reserve the right to consult
in confidence with any other professionally competent person about their
counsellees. In choosing professional
consultants, counsellors must avoid placing the consultant in a conflict of interest situation.

12. Counsellors, upon reaching their own
limitations in a counselling relationship,
should:

   a) seek consultation from other professional persons, or

   b) refer the counsellee to a known professional person, or

   c) terminate the counselling relationship, with appropriate explanation to
   the counsellee.

SECTION C: MEASUREMENT AND EVALUATION

1. Counsellors have a responsibility to ensure that evaluative information about
counsellees shall be shared only with those
persons who will use such information for
professional purposes.

2. In general, test results provide only one
factor of a variety of pertinent data for
counselling purposes. It is the responsibility of the counsellor to supply adequate
orientation and information to the counsellee so that the results of testing may be
placed in proper perspective with other
relevant factors. In so doing, the counsellor must recognize the effects that socio-
economic, ethnic and cultural factors may
have on test scores.

3. Counsellors, when using standardized tests
for the assessment of counsellees, will consider only appropriate tests of recognized
validity and reliability. They will use only
tests which they are competent to administer.

4. Counsellors are obligated to administer
standardized tests in strict accordance with
the published directions and will ensure
that examinees have adequate orientation
to test procedures. They are obligated to
maintain test security and will avoid coaching in preparing examinees for testing.

5. Counsellors have an obligation to interpret test results to counsellees in the light
of all other evaluation data, but will do so
only within their level of competency to
make interpretations.

6. Counsellors, when making statements to
the public, counsellees or associates about
tests and testing, will take care to give accurate information and proper interpretation in order to avoid false claims and
misconceptions.

APPENDIX D

Ethical Standards for Internet Online Counseling

These guidelines establish appropriate standards for the use of electronic communications over the Internet to provide online counseling services, and should be used only in conjunction with the latest ACA Code of Ethics & Standards of Practice.

CONFIDENTIALITY

A. Privacy information

Professional counselors ensure that clients are provided sufficient information to adequately address and explain the limitations of (i) computer technology in the counseling process in general and (ii) the difficulties of ensuring complete client confidentiality of information transmitted through electronic communications over the Internet through online counseling. (See A.12.a., B.1.a., B.1.g.)

1. **Secured Sites:** To mitigate the risk of potential breaches of confidentiality, professional counselors will provide one-on-one online counseling only through "secure" websites or e-mail communications applications which use appropriate encryption technology designed to protect the transmission of confidential information from access by unauthorized third parties.

2. **Non-secured sites:** To mitigate the risk of potential breaches of confidentiality, professional counselors provide only general information from "nonsecure" websites or e-mail communications applications.

3. **General information:** Professional counselors may provide general information from either "secure" or "nonsecure" websites, or through e-mail communications. General information includes nonclient-specific, topical information on matters of general interest to the professional

counselor's clients as a whole, third-party resource and referral information, addresses and phone numbers, and the like. Additionally, professional counselors using either "secure" or "nonsecure" websites may provide "hot links" to third-party websites such as licensure boards, certification bodies, and other resource information providers. Professional counselors investigate and continually update the content, accuracy and appropriateness for the client of material contained in any "hot links" to third-party websites.

4. **Limits of confidentiality:** Professional counselors inform clients of the limitations of confidentiality and identify foreseeable situations in which confidentiality must be breached in light of the law in both the state in which the client is located and the state in which the professional counselor is licensed.

B. Informational Notices

1. **Security of professional counselor's site:** Professional counselors provide a readily visible notice that

(i) information transmitted over a website or e-mail server may not be secure;

(ii) whether or not the professional counselor's site is secure;

(iii) whether the information transmitted between the professional counselor and the client during online counseling will be encrypted; and

(iv) whether the client will need special software to access and transmit confidential information and, if so, whether the professional counselor provides the software as part of the online counseling services. The notice should be viewable from all website and e-mail locations from

which the client may send information. (See B.1.g.)

2. **Professional counselor identification:** Professional counselors provide a readily visible notice advising clients of the identities of all professional counselor(s) who will have access to the information transmitted by the client and, in the event that more than one professional counselor has access to the website or e-mail system, the manner, if any, in which the client may direct information to a particular professional counselor. Professional counselors inform clients if any or all of the sessions are supervised. Clients are also informed if and how the supervisor preserves session transcripts. Professional counselors provide background information on all professional counselor(s) and supervisor(s) with access to the online communications, including education, licensing and certification, and practice area information. (See B.1.g.)

3. **Client identification:** Professional counselors identify clients, verify identities of clients, and obtain alternative methods of contacting clients in emergency situations.

C. Client Waiver

Professional counselors require clients to execute client waiver agreements stating that the client

(i) acknowledges the limitations inherent in ensuring client confidentiality of information transmitted through online counseling and

(ii) agrees to waive the client's privilege of confidentiality with respect to any confidential information transmitted through online counseling that may be accessed by any third party without authorization of the client and despite the reasonable efforts of the professional counselor to arrange a secure online environment. Professional counselors refer clients to more traditional methods of counseling and do not provide online counseling services if the client is unable or unwilling to consent to the client waiver. (See B.1.b.)

D. Records of Electronic Communications

Professional counselors maintain appropriate procedures for ensuring the safety and confidentiality of client information acquired through electronic communications, including but not limited to encryption software; proprietary onsite file servers with fire walls, saving online or e-mail communications to the hard drive or file server computer systems; creating regular tape or diskette back-up copies; creating hard copies of all electronic communications, and the like. Clients are informed about the length of time for, and method of, preserving session transcripts. Professional counselors warn clients of the possibility or frequency of technology failures and time delays in transmitting and receiving information. (See B.4.a., B.4.b.)

E. Electronic Transfer of Client Information

Professional counselors electronically transfer client confidential information to authorized third-party recipients only when

(i) both the professional counselor and the authorized recipient have "secure" transfer and acceptance communication capabilities,

(ii) the recipient is able to effectively protect the confidentiality of the client confidential information to be transferred, and

(iii) the informed written consent of the client, acknowledging the limits of confidentiality, has been obtained. (See A.3.a., B.6.a., B.6.b.)

ESTABLISHING THE ONLINE COUNSELING RELATIONSHIP

A. The Appropriateness of Online Counseling

Professional counselors develop an appropriate in-take procedure for potential clients to determine whether online counseling is appropriate for the needs of the client. Professional counselors warn potential clients that online counseling services may not be appropriate in certain situations and, to the extent possible, informs the client of specific limitations, potential risks, and/or potential benefits relevant to the client's anticipated use of online counseling services. Professional counselors ensure that clients are intellectually, emotionally, and physically capable of using the online counseling services, and of understanding the potential risks and/or limitations of such services. (See A.3.a., A.3.b.)

B. Counseling Plans

Professional counselors develop individual online counseling plans that are consistent with both the client's individual circumstances and the limitations of online counseling. Professional counselors shall specifically take into account the limitations, if any, on the use of any or all of the following in online counseling: initial client appraisal, diagnosis, and assessment methods employed by the professional counselor. Professional counselors who determine that online counseling is inappropriate for the client should avoid entering into or immediately terminate the online counseling relationship and encourage the client to continue the counseling relationship through an appropriate alternative method of counseling. (See A.11.b., A.11.c.)

C. Continuing Coverage

Professional counselors provide clients with a schedule of times during which the online counseling services will be available, including reasonable anticipated response times, and provide clients with an alternate means of contacting the professional counselor at other times, including in the event of emergencies. Professional counselors obtain from, and provide clients with, alternative means of communication, such as telephone numbers or pager numbers, for back-up purposes in the event the online counseling service is unavailable for any reason. Professional counselors provide clients with the name of at least one other professional counselor who will be able to respond to the client in the event the professional counselor is unable to do so for any extended period of time. (See A.11.a)

D. Boundaries of Competence

Professional counselors provide online counseling services only in practice areas within their expertise and do not provide online counseling services to clients located in states in which professional counselors are not licensed. (See C.2.a., C.2.b.)

E. Minor or Incompetent Clients

Professional counselors must verify that clients are above the age of minority, are competent to enter into the counseling relationship with a professional counselor, and are able to give informed consent. In the event clients are minor children, incompetent, or incapable of giving informed consent, professional counselors must obtain the written consent of the legal guardian or other authorized legal representative of the client prior to commencing online counseling services to the client.

LEGAL CONSIDERATIONS

Professional counselors confirm that their liability insurance provides coverage for online counseling services, and that the provision of such services is not prohibited by or otherwise violate any applicable

(i) state or local statutes, rules, regulations, or ordinances;

(ii) codes of professional membership organizations and certifying boards; and/or

(iii) codes of state licensing boards.

Professional counselors seek appropriate legal and technical assistance in the development and implementation of their online counseling services.